CW00621158

Love and Liberty

For Professor Tom Sutherland
who, during 2354 days as a hostage in Beirut,
drew strength from Burns. Each testifies to the
human spirit at its finest

Love and Liberty

Robert Burns: A Bicentenary Celebration

edited by Kenneth Simpson

TUCKWELL PRESS

ENTERPRISE AYRSHIRE

developing companies, skills and places

The publishers thank Enterprise Ayrshire
for a generous subvention towards
publication of this volume.

First published in 1997 in Great Britain by
Tuckwell Press Ltd
The Mill House
Phantassie
East Linton East Lothian EH40 3DG

ISBN 1 898410 89 5

British Library Cataloguing-in-Publication Data
A catalogue record for this book is available
on request from the British Library

Typeset by Carnegie Publishing, 18 Maynard St, Preston
Printed and bound by
Cromwell Press, Broughton Gifford, Melksham, Wiltshire

Contents

Acknowledgements

THE INTERNATIONAL BICENTENARY BURNS CONFERENCE, 11–13 January
1996, formed part of the bicentenary celebration of the founding of the
University of Strathclyde as Anderson's Institution. A grant from the Univer-
sity's Bicentenary Task Force, convened by Deputy Principal Tom Bone, is
acknowledged with gratitude. Further support came from *The Herald*, the
Scottish Arts Council, John Smith and Son, United Distillers, J. & B. (Scotland),
Whyte & Mackay, and United Biscuits. Archie Fleming, Colin MacFarlane,
and G. Ross Roy advised during the preparatory stages. The success of the
Conference was owing to the efforts of its administrator, Cath Wales, and her
assistants, Pat Clark and Valerie Lynn.

This volume would not have appeared without the generous support of
Enterprise Ayrshire. The task of editing was facilitated by research leave funded
jointly by the Humanities Research Board of the British Academy and the
Research and Development Fund of the University of Strathclyde. Teaching-
cover provided by the editor's colleagues is gratefully acknowledged. In the
gathering of material and its preparation for publication Cath Wales was char-
acteristically generous with her help. Gerard Carruthers advised throughout
and compiled the index with speed and expertise. Val and John Tuckwell have
been all that an editor could wish for in a publisher.

Edwin Morgan's poem, 'The Five-Pointed Star', first appeared in *The Dark
Horse*, no. 3 (1996).

Notes on Contributors

VALENTINA BOLD is a Research Fellow at Aberdeen University. She is completing her doctoral thesis on Scottish autodidacts and has published articles on poets including James Hogg and James Young Geddes.

GERARD CARRUTHERS has held posts at the Universities of Aberdeen, Glasgow and Strathclyde. He has published on eighteenth- and twentiety-century Scottish literature and is completing a study of the Scottish Enlightenment.

TED COWAN, Professor of Scottish History, University of Glasgow, taught for twelve years at Edinburgh University and for fourteen years at the University of Guelph, Ontario. His publications include *Montrose for Covenant and King* and *The People's Past*.

THOMAS CRAWFORD, author of *Burns: A study of the Poems and Songs* (1960) and *Society and the Lyric* (1977), is currently editing two volumes of Correspondence for the Yale Boswell Edition.

DAVID DAICHES regards himself as 'the last of the non-specialists'. His many books include works on Scottish literature and cultural history and on many other topics from Milton to Scotch whisky.

SHEILA DOUGLAS, a graduate of the Universities of Glasgow and Stirling, is a writer, editor, singer, songwriter, storyteller, broadcaster, and lecturer. Co-founder of Merlin Press, and member of the Greig-Duncan editorial team and International Ballad Conference.

ROGER FECHNER is Professor of History at Adrian College, Michigan. His research focuses on the intellectual relationships between Scotland and America in the eighteenth century. He has published essays on Adam Smith and John Witherspoon.

RICHARD J. FINLAY is Lecturer in History at the University of Strathclyde. He is author of *Independent and Free: Scottish Politics and the Origins of the S.N.P.*

HENRY L. FULTON, Professor of English at Central Michigan University, has completed a biography of Dr. John Moore and is at work on Admiral Graham Moore's maternal grandfather, John Simpson, Professor of Divinity at Glasgow University, prosecuted twice by his church for unsound teaching.

DAVID HUTCHISON is a Senior Lecturer in Communication Studies at Glasgow Caledonian University. His published work has been concerned principally with media policy and the history of the modern Scottish theatre.

R. D. S. JACK is Professor of Scottish and Mediaeval Literature at the University of Edinburgh. His major publications are on Renaissance Scottish literature, comparative literature, and J. M. Barrie. He is at work on a major anthology of early Scottish literature.

MAURICE LINDSAY, Glasgow poet, born 1918, has published *Collected Poems 1940–1990*, *On the Face of It*, *News of the World*, and, forthcoming, *Speaking Likenesses*;

also *Thank You For Having Me* (autobiography), *The Burns Enclyclopedia*, and *The Castle of Scotland*.

DONALD LOW is Professor of English Studies at Stirling University. His books on Burns include the first edition, with music, of all *The Songs of Robert Burns* (Routledge, 1993) and *Robert Burns: Poems in Scots and English* (Everyman Paperbacks, 1996).

EMILY LYLE is a Lecturer at the School of Scottish Studies, University of Edinburgh, and is general editor of *The Greig-Duncan Folk Song Collection*.

J. DERRICK MCCLURE is Senior Lecturer in English at Aberdeen University and author of *Why Scots Matters* and numerous articles on Scots linguistic topics, and of *Scotland o Gael and Lawlander*, a collection of translations from modern Gaelic poetry.

MARGERY PALMER MCCULLOCH is the author of *Edwin Muir: Poet, Critic and Novelist* and *The Novels of Neil M. Gunn*. She teaches Scottish Literature at the University of Glasgow.

RODERICK MACDONALD's main contribution to Burnsian literature is his translation of the complete poetical works of the Bard into Scottish Gaelic using the same material and rhyming patterns as in the original – a 'world first' in any language?

CARL MACDOUGALL is a Glasgow writer whose third novel, *The Casanova Papers*, is published by Secker & Warburg. *The Lights Below* and *Stone Over Water* are Minerva paperbacks. *The Devil and The Giro* is available from Canongate Classics.

CAROL MCGUIRK is Professor of English at Florida Atlantic University. Author of *Robert Burns and the Sentimental Era*, she is editor of the Penguin edition of the Poems and Songs of Burns. She is also editing a collection of Burns criticism.

LIAM MCILVANNEY is completing a doctoral thesis, on Burns and Presbyterianism, at Christ Church, Oxford. He has presented papers on eighteenth-century Scottish literature at various conferences and is a regular reviewer of contemporary fiction.

STEVEN R. MCKENNA is Associate Professor of English at Columbia College, Missouri. He is the author of *Robert Henryson's Tragic Vision* and numerous articles on Middle Scots literature.

DOUGLAS S. MACK is Reader in the Department of English Studies at Stirling University, and General Editor of the Stirling/South Carolina Edition of James Hogg, published by Edinburgh University Press.

EDWIN MORGAN's *Collected Poems* appeared in 1990 from Carcanet (paperback, 1996). A further volume of poems, *Sweeping Out the Dark*, came out in 1994. *Collected Translations* was published in November 1996.

MURRAY G. H. PITTOCK is Professor in Literature at the University of Strathclyde and the author of books on Jacobitism, Scottish literature and national identity, including *Poetry and Jacobite Politics in Eighteenth-Century Britain and Ireland* (1994).

THOMAS R. PRESTON is Professor of English at the University of North Texas, where for ten years he was Dean of the College of Arts and Sciences. He is the author of a book on eighteenth-century satire and sentiment, *Not in Timon's Manner*, and, most recently, the *Humphry Clinker* volume for the University of Georgia's Critical Edition of Smollett's *Works*.

RICHARD PRICE's books include *The Fabulous Matter of Fact: the Poetics of Neil*

M. Gunn, and *Sense and a Minor Fever, Tube Shelter Perspective*, and *Marks and Sparks* (poetry).

JOHN PURSER: musicologist, playwright, poet, composer, and broadcaster, Purser has won prestigious awards in all these categories, including the 1992 *McVitie Scottish Writer of the Year* award for his ground-breaking *Scotland's Music*.

IAN S. ROSS is Emeritus Professor of English, University of British Columbia, who came to love Burns's art as a schoolboy in Dundee. He has written extensively on Scottish literature and thought, his most recent book being *The Life of Adam Smith* (OUP, 1995).

G. ROSS ROY, Founding Editor of *Studies in Scottish Literature*, is particularly interested in eighteenth-century Scottish poetry, and Anglo-French literary relations. He has edited Burns's Letters, and written on and edited various Scottish poets.

PAUL H. SCOTT was born and educated in Edinburgh and spent many years abroad as a diplomat. Writer, editor, and broadcaster, he is active in many Scottish causes. His most recent book is *Defoe in Edinburgh*.

KENNETH SIMPSON is Director of the Centre for Scottish Cultural Studies, University of Strathclyde, and organiser of the Burns Conferences held annually since 1990. He is author of *The Protean Scot, Robert Burns* (Scotnotes), and editor of *Burns Now*.

CHRISTOPHER A. WHATLEY, Reader in Scottish History, University of Dundee, contributed to *Burns Now* (1994). He has numerous publications in social and economic history and recently completed *The Industrial Revolution in Scotland* (CUP, 1997).

Introduction

QUEUES FORM DAILY outside a Boston bar, 'The Bull and Finch'. The inspiration for the long-running series, 'Cheers', it attracts from all corners of the globe people determined at least once to be part of the place 'where everybody knows your name'. Despite the more limited circulation of the printed word, Burns's Cottage became a place of pilgrimage soon after the poet's death. It fulfilled, and continues to fulfil, a comparable function. For an octogenarian American lady a recent first visit marked the fruition of a life-long ambition; when she needed to be assured that she was part of the human family it was always to Burns that she turned, she told me. At the Burns centenary celebrations in Boston in 1859 Ralph Waldo Emerson observed that 'the people who care nothing for literature and poetry care for Burns'.[1] The reasons for this breadth of appeal are to be found in Burns's essential qualities – his humanity, his celebration of the individual in all his aspects, his recognition of the dignity and worth of ordinary human beings. No poet combines lyric tenderness and satiric vigour in such measures. Burns both entertains and arouses a range of feelings – pity, outrage, laughter, wonder – and he does so with an expressive verve which is remarkable. The emotional flux of many of his poems and songs rings true to life and elicits a complex response. In short, his is, as Maurice Lindsay here suggests, 'People Poetry'.

People came – and in numbers (a daily average of 250) – to the International Bicentenary Burns conference, held 11–13 January 1996 as part of the University of Strathclyde's own bicentenary programme. Speakers and delegates from all over the world and from diverse walks of life testified to Burns's universality of appeal, and twelve distinguished Scottish writers paid tribute with readings from their own work. In essence, the conference was a three-day celebration of the poet's life and works. Some academics, for whom this was the first encounter with such a broadly based gathering of enthusiasts, acknowledged that it was a salutary experience to put their ideas to the test of a public forum. It was widely agreed that the lively and always-convivial cut-and-thrust of debate drew inspiration from the example of Burns himself. As Edwin Morgan's poem written for the occasion, 'The Five-Pointed Star', so wittily and movingly demonstrates, everyone has a handle on Burns. Something of the diversity of approach which he engenders is reflected in the range of the essays included here.

That Burns is multi-faceted is one of the sources of his accessibility. Several contributors deem such accessibility a mixed blessing. For Carl MacDougall, Scots have found in Burns a compensation for the loss of nationhood; in appropriating his work as public property, 'we have robbed ourselves of its diversity and uniqueness, not to mention its integrity and subtlety'. It is questionable if any writer has ever been so exploited, be it commercially (witness the 'Aphrodisiac Haggis' which David Hutchison adduces), politically, or intellectually. The tendency is neatly summed up by Maurice Lindsay: 'some people like to assume that he would have supported this or that cause which happens to involve their own interest'. Richard Finlay shows how in the nineteenth and twentieth centuries 'perceptions of Burns have been shaped and reshaped to give credence and authority to particular ideologies in Scotland'. Selective vision enables both Socialists and Nationalists to enlist Burns in support of their respective causes; political versatility is the key feature of the 'lad o' pairts' myth. Thus, paradoxically, the status as icon of the obligingly chameleon Burns is assured. As Finlay points out, 'So long as the man and his work can be appropriated by lots of political factions and none has exclusive ideological ownership his centrality as a Scottish cultural icon is guaranteed'. Corroboration comes in the finding of David Hutchison's survey of media coverage of Burns Night: Burns is cited by newspapers in accordance with their political allegiance. Designating Burns 'the elastic symbol', Hutchison notes that, by virtue of the 'robust survival and universality of his work', he bucks the national trend to defeatism in the choice of symbolic figures and events – Mary, Queen of Scots, Flodden, Bonnie Prince Charlie – and also scores over the more heroic Scottish figureheads, such as Wallace and Bruce, by reason of his enduring appeal to the emotions. As Hutchison indicates, it will be 'fascinating to watch how the political and cultural aspects of Burns the symbol are reconstructed by the media' both during and after such constitutional change as Scotland may experience.

One of the aims of the Strathclyde conference was to penetrate the iconic dimensions of Burns – be they those of Scotia's Bard, Rhinestone Ploughboy, Jock Tamson's Bairn, or whatever – and identify the man and the poet. By their very nature icons simplify, reduce, stabilise. While the statue may be physically larger than life, it can never convey the essence, far less the totality, of its subject. The staticity of the enshrined Burns is totally at odds with both what Carl MacDougall terms the poet's 'almost demonic' energy and his 'ability to move ideas', his 'gift of fluidity'. Experience of the entire corpus – poems, songs, and letters – produces a Burns who is, socially, a charismatic chameleon (as contemporaries, and most notably Maria Riddell, testify);[2] as an individual, psychologically complex; and, as a writer, a virtuoso in terms of both language and forms.

How, then, did the mythopoeic process originate and how did it gather such momentum? As G. Ross Roy intimates, Currie's edition of 1800 gave rise to misconceptions about the poet – including the alleged alcoholism – which have been corrected only recently. So vivid was the image of Burns the libertine that only seven years after his death Mrs Ann Grant, in her 'Remarks on the

Character of Burns', could exclaim, 'I do not know whether most to pity or admire Burns. Why were such people made?'. If further proof were wanted of Burns's elasticity as symbol one need only note, as Valentina Bold does, that in the course of the nineteenth century Burns's life was 'imbued with Christ-like quality' by such as Henry Shanks.

In respect of one aspect of the myth-making Burns himself is far from blameless. Here is part of his self-characterisation in the preface to his Commonplace Book: 'As he was but little indebted to scholastic education, and bred at a plough-tail, his performances must be strongly tinctured with his unpolished, rustic way of life'.[3] In formal, polished, Augustan English Burns claims he is uneducated. Why? The answer lies in the way in which, mainly by virtue of a historical coincidence, Scotland came to play a major role in the shift in values and tastes in the second half of the eighteenth century. Integral to European Enlightenment thought was the belief that if man trusted his rational powers the inevitable result would be an improvement in the human condition. By the middle of the century the process of industrialisation was under way, but to some it seemed that it represented anything but an improvement. Here is the response of Burns on visiting Carron ironworks:

> We cam' na here to view your warks,
>   In hopes to be mair wise,
> But only, lest we gang to hell,
>   It may be nae surprise:
> But whan we tirl'd at your door,
>   Your porter dought na bear us;
> Sae may, shou'd we to hell's yetts come,
>   Your billy Satan sair us!
> ('Verses written on a window of the Inn at Carron')

The new world, created by Reason, is an industrial hell; it prepares us for Hell itself. Reason has failed man by creating this nightmare world. Where can he turn? 'Back to Nature!' was the cry sounded by Rousseau in the middle of the eighteenth century. Rousseau contended that rationalist civilisation corrupted; we must put our faith in our feelings, rather than our reason. Our remote ancestors had been naturally and openly emotional; they trusted, and showed, their feelings. Furthermore, the capacity to feel was proof of one's moral sense (an idea which appears variously in the work of Hutcheson and Hume but, above all, in Adam Smith's *The Theory of Moral Sentiments* (1759)). The search began to find the people who most closely resembled our ancestor, the Noble Savage. Prime candidates were the American Indian and the Scottish Highlander (the latter because the fate of the Jacobite rebellion seemed to represent the destruction of an ancient and noble order by the forces of the new commercialism). Now at the same time, Scots were in search of their identity: were they, since the Union of 1707, North Britons, Caledonians, or what? Courtesy of this historical coincidence they found the solution to their identity crisis: they were the descendants of the Noble Savage, and thus the prime exponents of feeling and the moral dimension to feeling. Enter the Noble Savage as poet: Burns. Here we have the background to Burns's masquerading as uneducated peasant. Here we have, too, part of the reason for his writing poems to a mouse and to a mountain daisy whose stem he has severed: in so doing he shows his capacity for feeling and his moral sense.

Burns undoubtedly believed in the virtues of the feeling heart which he advocates so vigorously in such poems as 'Epistle to J. Lapraik, An Old Scotch Bard' and 'Epistle to Davie, a Brother Poet'. However, there is a sense – certainly in some of the letters and several of the poems – in which, true to the concept of the 'self-approving joy', he relishes the spectacle of himself manifesting his finer feelings. This was the Burns who would read passages of *The Man of Feeling* to Edinburgh ladies and join them in communal displays of sensibility, the Burns who took satisfaction in recording that *Lounger* No. 61 'has cost me more honest tears than any thing I have read of a long time'.[4] With the telling metaphor of the tightrope-walker, David Daiches, in his keynote address, depicts Burns accomplishing a balancing-act between extremes of culture, language, and social class; and, perhaps most remarkably, but in a way that was to take its toll of the psychological equilibrium of the performer, he contrived to maintain a balance between illusion and reality.

Part of the reality was that Burns was relatively well educated, read avidly through adolescence and manhood, and had phenomenal powers of absorption and recall. Little that he read failed to make its mark. Literary borrowings invariably returned a profit: witness the debt (noted by Thomas Crawford)[5] of Burns's lines, 'The best laid schemes o' Mice an' Men,/Gang aft agley' to Robert Blair's 'The best-concerted schemes men lay for fame/Die fast away' (*The Grave*, ll. 185–6), but it is – and deservedly – Burns lines that are remembered. Carol McGuirk cites a fine example of the way in which Burns brings his reading to bear on his representation of historical events: identifying the relationship between 'Strathallan's Lament' and the conclusion of *Paradise Lost*, McGuirk comments, 'the forlorn hero of Burns's stanzas speaks of and for the end, not the beginning, of historical process'.

Burns's literary roots are in two traditions. His formal education, at the hands of Murdoch, was in English literature derived mainly from Arthur Masson's anthology. The lasting legacy of the emphasis Murdoch placed on rhetoric is recognised by R. D. S. Jack, and Ian S. Ross discerns in Murdoch's further choice of text in Fénelon's novel, *Les Aventures de Télémache*, an antecedent to the hostility to luxury and empire-building which Burns was later to encounter in Rousseau. As for Scottish literature, however, Burns had, as David Daiches records, no formal education whatsoever. Via his mother and her kinswoman, Betty Davidson, he had access to the native oral tradition. In the course of his own reading he was to find Hamilton of Gilbertfield's recension of Blind Harry's *Wallace* and, later, the poetry of Fergusson; that of Ramsay ('the famous Ramsay of jingling memory')[6] came later still. Features of the native vernacular tradition figure prominently in Burns' poetry: the rendering of communal life typified in a poem such as 'The Holy Fair' can be traced back via Fergusson and Ramsay to Dunbar; the flyting mode is used for a variety of effects in, among other, 'The Brigs of Ayr', 'To a Haggis', and 'To a Louse'; 'The Twa Dogs' and 'The Death and Dying Words of Poor Mailie' maintain the tradition of the talking-animal poem; while the self-revealing and self-ironising monologue is brought to perfection in 'Holy Willie's Prayer'. His schooling had familiarised Burns with the techniques of the social satirist as exemplified by Pope. In the Makars, Ramsay, and Fergusson was proof of the additional effectiveness as a reductive mode of the juxtaposition of vernacular Scots and standard English. 'Auld Scotland has a raucle tongue': so Burns informs us in 'The Author's Earnest Cry and Prayer'. For Liam McIlvanney, 'the familiar, irreverent style which Burns employs was identified by contemporaries as characteristic of Presbyterianism and its "levelling" doctrines'.

Various contributors allude to Burns's formal, stylistic, and linguistic range. J. Derrick McClure refers to the 'exuberant variety in mood and style' (which even Japanese, the 'most unpromising medium', has accommodated in translation), and Ian S. Ross finds evidence of 'both the mocking laughter of Voltaire and the tears of Rousseau'. The literary range, of both influence and achievement, as reflected in the poems and letters, and the personal complexity of the poet, manifested principally in the prose writings, combine to thwart monist approaches and absolutist conclusions. A salutary warning comes from Liam McIlvanney: 'to attempt to abstract a rigorously coherent political philosophy from Burns's work would be a futile project. As well as contradictions in the poetry there are tensions between the poetry and the biography to which the student of Burns's politics must attend'. Thomas Crawford observed (and is cited here by Steven McKenna), 'Most of [Burns's] poems are made out of a highly inconsistent man's battle with the world'.[7] The situation was further compounded by Burns's acknowledged inability to 'resist an impulse of any thing like Wit',[8] which led to the adoption of a wide range of *personae*, while the needs of his personality induced the projection of a series of self-images.[9]

Thus, a common feature of many of these essays is a recognition of the constant need for qualification when dealing with Burns. In a welcome antidote to the trend of the generalist Scottish critical tradition, Gerard Carruthers argues that its problems in coming to terms satisfactorily with Burns bespeak the limitations, not of the poet, but of the tradition itself. For Carruthers, to impose holist criteria of cultural and linguistic identity on Scottish literature is to convert the manifest strength of its linguistic and formal range into an alleged weakness. There has been regular condemnation of Burns's standard English poems as artificial, a view sometimes influenced, one suspects, by patriotic motives (and if, as Christopher A. Whatley reminds us, 'what is good patriotism is not necessarily good history', it is, equally, not good literary criticism). For R. D. S. Jack, for whom Burns 'contains multitudes', the linguistic range is a strength: 'For Dunbar, James VI, and Montgomerie, as for Ramsay, Fergusson, and Burns, our very advantage lay in NOT being delimited to English alone'.

Such a conclusion is totally at odds with the Anglicising bias of the Scottish literary establishment of Burns's day. Here is the view of Lord Buchan (cited by Thomas R. Preston): 'Burns appeared to me a real *Makar* a *Creator* a *Poet* & I wished him to assume the language as well as the character of a Briton & to throw off the masquerade garb of Allan Ramsay, whom, he so greatly surpassed'.[10] As Tom Preston indicates, 'the point of Burns's poetic project, however, was precisely that to be properly British the Scots needed to be properly Scottish, and this presupposed for Burns a vigorous Scottish language' (and the same might be said of Ramsay seventy years earlier; witness such poems as 'Richy and Sandy on the Death of Mr. Addison' and the various mock-elegies). In a sophisticated application of Bakhtin's dialogic approach, Preston designates Burns's poetry 'a project founded ... on a Scottish cultural nationalism engaged in dialogue with English and other cultures'. Preston identifies clearly the nexus between Burns's cultural nationalism and his egalitarianism: 'In contrast to the literati's interest in the past as a way of wrapping an anglicised future in a nostalgic Scottish patriotism, Burns's song-work offers the basis for a continuing renewal of Scottish identity within a palpable, lived, Scottish culture that unites all social ranks'.

Several contributors meet the need, first expressed by Thomas Crawford, to locate Burns in a European context. Hearing in the 'But pleasures are like poppies spread' section of 'Tam o' Shanter' qualification of Tam's experiences by a modern, sceptical voice, Gerard Carruthers warns, 'This should not be taken merely as an index of fissures in specifically Scottish experience: it is the response of the European Enlightenment to traditional folklore in general'; and he considers 'The Vision' in terms of a problem which is European, rather than specifically Scottish – 'the bankruptcy of older myths of cultural unity within the context of the nation which is applicable across Europe'. Thus Burns, whose true strengths are as 'a poet of social and cultural tension', is 'in receipt of the Scottish and European Enlightenments' embryonic awareness of cultural relativism'. For Edward J. Cowan, it is the 'tension at the very heart of the Enlightenment' that is epitomised in these words of Burns to Dr Moore (which follow his account of hearing in childhood the folk-tales of Betty Davidson):

> This cultivated the latent seeds of Poesy; but had so strong an effect on my imagination, that to this hour, in my nocturnal rambles, I sometimes keep a sharp look-out in suspicious places; and though nobody can be more sceptical in these matters than I, yet it often takes an effort of Philosophy to shake off these idle terrors.[11]

Justifiably Cowan suggests Burns might be regarded as a 'superstitious sceptic'.

In the realms of music, too, there is ambivalence: John Purser comments, 'Burns, like Oswald, saw Scottish music as worthy of Apollonian status, though what he describes is decidedly Dionysiac. The dichotomy remains unresolved to this day'.

The ambivalence that characterises so many aspects of Burns informs both his relations with his local community and the poems which spring from the experience of rural life. Burns wrote to Moore, 'My first ambition was, and still my strongest wish is, to please my Compeers, the rustic Inmates of the Hamlet'.[12] The aim is to entertain the peasantry, with whom he wishes to identify, but the very language of the claim indicates the distance between them, or at least the remoteness from them of this *persona*. Consequently, many of the poems function on more than one level. 'The Death and Dying Words of Poor Mailie' offers a rural commonplace – a sheep fallen over on its back – but courtesy of the transfigurative power of the imagination Burns is able to engage with major issues in the thinking of Rousseau and Smith and the 'self-approving joy' of the age of sensibility. Likewise in 'The Twa Dogs' retriever and collie enable the poet to raise questions of social and class division, their shared vernacular underlining the contrast with the hierarchical human society which is their subject. In 'To a Louse' an amusing, trivial incident forms the bedrock of a subtly comprehensive satire on the vanity of aspirations. Habitually the life of the parish becomes part of the world of the imagination. The Presbytery of Ayr's rejection of William Fisher's charges against Gavin Hamilton made local news. By his creation of the *persona* of Holy Willie, Burns makes of the circumstances the most powerful indictment in world literature of bigotry and hypocrisy, and it is all the more effective because the speaker unwittingly condemns himself from his own mouth. Nowhere is Burns's mastery of irony used to greater effect.

Such poetical ability distinguishes its possessor. To have the expressive powers of Burns was to be marked out in the community, and in a small community the effect was heightened. David Sillar commented, 'His social disposition easily procured him acquaintance; but a certain satirical seasoning, with which he and all poetical geniuses are in some degree influenced, while it set the rustic circle in a roar, was not unaccompanied by its kindred attendant – suspicious fear'.[13] The 'sorcery' with words, to which Maria Riddell testified, proved ambivalent in its effect: the poet was both entertainer and threat.

Burns may sometimes be a participant in the activities he depicts; certainly, he is always the observer; and, increasingly, he is aware of the ambivalent nature of his status as such. 'Hallowe'en' renders the superstitious practices of the rural community, but the voice of the preface is that, not of participant, but of cultural tour-guide:

> The passion of prying into futurity makes a striking part of the history of human
> nature in its rude state, in all ages and nations; and it may be some entertainment

to a philosophic mind, if any such should honour the author with a perusal, to see the remains of it, among the more unenlightened in our own.[14]

Even in the material of informal letters there is evidence of his awareness of his role as spectator. A letter from Ellisland to Thomas Sloan includes both his favourite quotation from Edward Young's *Night Thoughts* – 'On Reason build RESOLVE!/That Column of true majesty in Man' ('Night' I, ll. 30–1) – and this account of market-day celebrations:

> ... such a scene of drunkenness was hardly ever seen in this country. After the roup was over, about thirty people engaged in a battle ... and fought it out for three hours. Nor was the scene much better in the house. No fighting, indeed, but folks lieing drunk on the floor, and decanting, untill both my dogs got so drunk by attending them, that they could not stand. You will easily guess how I enjoyed the scene as I was no farther over than you used to see me.[15]

Here there is the characteristic discernment of the comic detail in the exuberant communal life, but it is from the eye of the man who has stepped back to observe.

Burns's celebrity in Edinburgh, where he masqueraded as Noble Savage as Poet, had the effect of accentuating both the role-playing and the distancing from his native community. In letters there is an increasing tendency to write of rural life in mock-heroic terms.[16] Writing to George Thomson he appears at times as the collector of not just songs but an entire lifestyle: 'I have not painted Miss Mc____ in the rank which she holds in life, but in the dress and character of a Cottager; consequently the utmost simplicity of thought and ex- pression was necessary'; and (of 'Geordie's Byre') 'the sprinkling of Scotch in it gives it an air of rustic naivete'.[17] Increasingly there are signs both of uncer- tainty as to personal and cultural identity and of alienation. As early as 1787 are two letters to William Nicol in Edinburgh which say much of Burns's uncertainty as to his identity. One, at the end of his Borders tour with Ainslie, is entirely in vernacular Scots.[18] The next, a fortnight later, begins, 'I am now arrived safe in my native country after a very agreable [*sic*] jaunt', and includes this outburst: 'I never, My friend, thought mankind very capable of any thing generous; but the stateliness of the Patricians in Edin[r], and the damn'd servility of my plebeian brethren, who perhaps formerly eyed me askance, since I returned home, have nearly put me out of conceit altogether with my species'.[19] Burns was not the first or the last Scot to experience the distinctive Scottish attitude to fame.

With this question David Daiches encapsulates Burns's problem: 'An unsuccessful tenant farmer who became a junior excise officer and a much acclaimed poet to boot – where in the stratified life of late eighteenth-century Scotland did he stand?'. Certainly the theatricality of Edinburgh life during the Scottish experience of the vogue of sensibility exacerbated Burns's inherent tendency to role-playing. But there is also a sense in which his condition is symptomatic, in perhaps extreme form, of both the Scottish Enlightenment focus on the individual in his social context and the proto-Romantic recognition of not just the worth of individual experience but the need for self-identification in an increasingly relativist world – the essential Romantic paradox, in effect, in that the individual is free to assert his individuality in a world which lacks the guidance of an absolutist order, a paradox compounded if the individual happens also to be an artist and public figure. A fascinating article on George Washington by Richard Brookhiser [20] (adduced by Roger Fechner) includes the following observation, which has a relevance far beyond its immediate subject: 'Character was seen in Washington's time as a role one played until one became it; character also meant how one's role was judged by others. It was both the performance and the review'. Herein is an aspect of one of the most tantalising of paradoxes in that most paradoxical of centuries: libertarianism, Romantic idealism and individualism go hand in hand with increased self-consciousness and a tendency, an obligation even, to play roles. The erosion of the old hierarchical social order allowed for individual aspirations and ideals but also fostered self-consciousness; roles could now be shaped, rather than being given. Rightly Fechner claims that 'in the two centuries since his death, Burns has become the world's foremost poet of democratic aspirations'. Yes, but at some personal cost. 'Character was a role one played until one became it': for the personally chameleon Burns the outcome was the perplexing question – which of the self-created roles was he?

In this context the work of Mikhail Bakhtin – cited by various contributors – is acutely relevant. In *Rabelais and His World*, in which he identifies the nature and function of carnival in classical, medieval, and modern times, Bakhtin describes 'the complex nature of carnival laughter' as follows:

> It is a festive laughter ... it is universal in scope; it is directed at all and everyone, including the carnival's participants ... [it is] ambivalent: it is gay, triumphant, and at the same time mocking, deriding. It asserts and denies, it buries and revives.[21]

Bakhtin draws a clear distinction between the laughter of carnival and that of satire:

> Let us enlarge upon the second important trait of the people's festive laughter: that it is also directed at those who laugh. The people do not exclude themselves from the wholeness of the world. They, too, are incomplete, they also die and are revived and renewed. This is one of the essential differences of the people's festive laughter from the pure satire of modern times. The satirist whose laughter is negative places himself above the object of his mockery, he is opposed to it. The wholeness of the world's comic aspect is destroyed, and that which appears comic becomes a private reaction. The

people's ambivalent laughter, on the other hand, expresses the point of view of the whole world; he who is laughing also belongs to it.[22]

It might be suggested that in his poems celebrating communal life Burns the satirist is seeking to re-identify himself in terms of the wholeness of the community in its carnival, cherishing the restorative effect of its inclusiveness: 'he who is laughing also belongs to it'.

Bakhtin's account of the development of what he terms 'grotesque realism' also has relevance to Burns. Discerning a process, starting in the seventeenth century, of 'gradual narrowing down of the ritual, spectacle, and carnival forms of folk culture', Bakhtin finds that, 'having lost its living tie with folk culture and having become a literary genre, the grotesque underwent certain changes'. Foremost was 'a formalization of carnival-grotesque images, which permitted them to be used in many different ways and for many different purposes'.[23] By way of exemplification, Bakhtin cites the *commedia dell' arte*, Molière, Voltaire, Diderot, and Swift, and he then offers this summation, which might have been written with Burns (and above all 'Tam o' Shanter') in mind:

> In all these writings, in spite of their differences in character and tendency, the carnival-grotesque form exercises the same function: to consecrate inventive freedom, to permit the combination of a variety of different elements and their rapprochement, to liberate from the prevailing point of view of the world, from conventions and established truths, from clichés, from all that is humdrum and universally accepted. This carnival spirit offers the chance to have a new outlook on the world, to realize the relative nature of all that exists, and to enter a completely new order of things.[24]

This represents exactly the Burns who prided himself on being one of 'the harum-scarum Sons of Imagination and Whim',[25] Rab the Rebel-Writer. Realising 'the relative nature of all that exists', the creative imagination relishes its 'inventive freedom'. It is revealing that it is Sterne's *Tristram Shandy*, beloved of Burns, influential upon his prose style, and the source of two of his favourite self-images – the victim of providence and the whimsical spirit – that is designated by Bakhtin 'the first important example of the new subjective grotesque ... a peculiar transposition of Rabelais' and Cervantes' world concept into the subjective language of the new age'. In the hands of Sterne the Romantic (subjective) grotesque became 'an individual carnival, marked by a vivid sense of isolation'.[26] The multiplicity of voices of Burns's poems and letters comprise his 'individual carnival'. The suggestions – more than suggestions – of morbidity, depression, and alienation which appear in letters from 1787 onwards testify to his own 'vivid sense of isolation'.

Citing Rilke's 'That's what longing is: to dwell in a state of flux/And to have no homeland in the World of Time', Margery Palmer McCulloch argues that 'this motif of longing, of desire for the unattainable, links Burns with the Romantics'. The crucial role of the imagination for Burns has again to be stressed here, particularly to those who persist in seeing the poet simply holding a mirror to rural life (a trend, established in Currie's judgement, 'If fiction be, as some suppose, the soul of poetry, no one had ever less pretensions to the name of poet than Burns',[27] which survived despite Burns's own testimony to the contrary, '*Fiction* is the soul of many a song that's nobly great').[28] In a letter to James Dalrymple, Burns associates poets with the Devil.[29] Several essayists here allude to his various representations of Satan (who emerges as almost as much of a chameleon as Burns himself). Carol McGuirk contends that 'Milton's Satan is invoked (as he so often is by Blake) to characterize the transgressive spirit of poetry itself'. For Burns, poetry and Satan are equally liberated and liberating. But, at the same time, McGuirk shows that Satan also serves for Burns as a basis of cultural synthesis: 'Satan in Burns's mind is not only Milton's unrepentant rebel but also an umbrella signifier for multiple realms of discourse from the so-called "high" (the Bible, or the stories God has told us about Satan) to the so-called "low" (folklore, or the stories our grannies may have told us about Satan)'. The Devil's prominence in Burns's poems and letters implies that he fulfilled not just a culturally but a psychologically synthetic function for the poet: he is the constantly chameleon, fallen, but free, spirit. Burns's fallen condition is a given; it is courtesy of his imaginative power that he becomes kin to the Devil as free chameleon.

In the case of Burns, the poetic imagination liberates, but it also facilitates the quest for identity by providing means of externalising the self. In 'Death and Doctor Hornbook' the convivial peasant lends a sympathetic ear to Death, a pathetic figure, down on his luck; 'Tam o' Shanter' finds the Devil providing the music for the witches' night out; 'Address to the Deil' has the Devil addressed affectionately as a familiar, in effect the neighbourhood pest, and, integrating the Scottish philosophers' doctrine of sympathy with the redemptive tendency at the heart of Romanticism, Burns has his *persona* express the hope that the Devil, for his own sake, may yet mend his ways since even he does not warrant the permanent torments of 'yon den', his 'black pit': these are not simply the last manifestations of a folk tradition; rather, Burns is finding in his cultural heritage means of externalising, and hopefully identifying, the self. What Carol McGuirk terms Burns's 'ambidextrous capacity to give equal weight to the so-called high and so-called low – to folk-collected bawdry and to English epic' has a cultural significance, it may well have a political significance, but it most definitely does have a psychological significance. In the expressive range of the poet is the attempt to render the complex totality of the man. Bakhtin states, 'Romanticism made its own important discovery – that of the interior, subjective man with his depth, complexity, and inexhaustible resources'.[30] In the formal, linguistic, and emotional range of Burns's poems, songs, and letters there is much more than a hint of what Bakhtin terms 'the interior infinite'.

It is hoped that these essays may be helpful in suggesting possible directions for Burns study. Above all, however, it is hoped that they may encourage readers to discover (in Carl MacDougall's words) 'how good Robert Burns actually is'.

NOTES

1. *Centenary Edition of the Complete Works of Ralph Waldo Emerson*, edited by E. W. Emerson (Boston and New York, 1911), XI, 441.
2. Donald A. Low (ed.), *Burns: The Critical Heritage* (London and Boston, 1974), p. 102.
3. *Robert Burns's Commonplace Book 1783–1785*, introduced by David Daiches (London, 1965), p. 1.
4. J. De Lancey Ferguson (ed.), *The Letters of Robert Burns*; 2nd edn, ed. G. Ross Roy (Oxford, 1985), II, 25.
5. Thomas Crawford, *Burns: A Study of the Poems and Songs* (2nd edn, reprinted Edinburgh, 1978), p. 167 n. 45.
6. *Letters*, I, 30.
7. *Burns: A Study*, xii.
8. *Letters*, I, 392.
9. See further Kenneth Simpson, *The Protean Scot* (Aberdeen, 1988), chs 7 and 8.
10. Letter to James Currie, 14 September 1797, Cowie Collection, Mitchell Library, Glasgow; cited Carol McGuirk, *Robert Burns and the Sentimental Era* (Athens, Georgia, 1985), p. 72.
11. *Letters*, I, 135.
12. *Letters*, I, 88.
13. Robert Chambers (ed.), *The Life and Works of Robert Burns*, rev. William Wallace, 4 vols (Edinburgh and London, 1896), I, 68–9.
14. James Kinsley (ed.), *The Poems and Songs of Robert Burns*, 3 vols (Oxford, 1968), I, 152.
15. *Letters*, II, 104.
16. See, for instance, letters to Alexander Cunningham. *Letters*, II, 145–8; II, 284–5.
17. *Letters*, II, 228; II, 246
18. *Letters*, I, 120–1.
19. *Letters*, I, 122–3.
20. 'A Man on Horseback', *Atlantic Monthly*, vol. 277, no. 1 (Jan. 1996), 50–64.
21. Mikhail Bakhtin, *Rabelais and His World*, translated by Hélène Iswolsky (Bloomington, 1984), pp. 11–12.
22. *Ibid.*, p. 12
23. *Ibid.*, pp. 33–4.
24. *Ibid.*, p. 34.
25. *Letters*, I, 109.
26. *Op. cit.*, p. 37.
27. *The Works of Robert Burns, with an Account of his Life* (Liverpool, 1800), I, 267.
28. *Letters*, I, 326.
29. *Letters*, I, 93.
30. *Op. cit.*, p. 44.

The Five-Pointed Star

Catherine the Great

He sounds like just the man. I'll have him here.
His genius deserves a wider sphere.
I wrote to Voltaire, why not try for Burns?
He'll serve me, yes he will, he'll serve my turns!
What could he miss? He'll be at home with us.
Cold blasts? An unmistakable plus.
Strong drink? We'll toast him under the table.
Superstitions? We've reams of myth and fable.
They say he's rather hard on royalty.
Well well, but that was France, we'll see, we'll see.
In any case, I want to pick his brains
On profitable subjects, crops and drains,
To take steps to improve the steppes (I must
Stop this word-play) which are more *thrang* with dust
Than waving stalks (yes, I've been reading Scotch),
Scotch stalks, ha ha, I really ought to watch
This tongue of mine, it must be the new year
Or the full moon or getting into gear
To send a letter to Caledonia.
I don't need either onions or ammonia
To get my eyes to glisten when I think
Of Rob – I know he isn't Rabbie – and clink
My bracelets and my ambers and twitch my gown
And scratch an impatient pen and throw it down
And pick it up again and make myself proper
To write a dignified yet piquant offer.

(What I did not say was how we'd take a sleigh,
The two of us, one tingling frosty day,
With trusty driver, trusty horse, and skim
The wolfish forest paths, I'd sing to him,
He'd sing to me, we'd both be wrapped in sable,
Wishing the swishing tracks interminable.
And if his hand should creep into my muff,
That would be nice, that would be nice enough.
I did not say that there are joys and joys.)

You get so tired of raw-boned stable-boys,
A jump, a thrust, a grunt, and *do svidaniya*.
I'd rather sleep with Anna or with Tanya!
I'm only joking. But a clean and witty farmer
Might be my last and unresisted charmer.
All this I did not write, but he can read
Between the lines, for his need is my need.)

James Macfarlan

'A man's a man for a' that' – how does *he* know?
Traipsing with his plough, the rural hero,
Swaggering down the lea-rigs, talking to mice,
Sweating his sickly verses to entice
Lassies he'd never see again, strutting
Through the salons in his best breeches, rutting
In a cloud of claret, buttonholing
Lord This, sweet-talking Doctor That, bowling
His wit down levees, bosoms, siller quaichs –
D'ye think he's ever heard the groans and skraighs
Of city gutters, or marked the shapes that wrap
Fog and smoke about them as if they could hap
Homelessness or keep hunger at bay? What,
Not heard or seen, but has he even thought
How some, and many, and more than many, survive,
Or don't survive, on factory floors, or thrive
Or fail to thrive by foundry fires, or try
To find the words – sparks scatter and bolts fly –
That's feeble – to show the new age its dark face?
The Carron Ironworks – he laughed at the place,
Made a joke of our misery, passed on
To window-scratch his diamond trivia, and swan
Through country-house and customs-post, servile
To the very gods from which he ought to resile!
'Liberty's a glorious feast', you said.
Is that right? Wouldn't the poor rather have bread?
Burns man, I'm hard on you, I'm sorry for it.
Your flame dazzled, folk gave you glory for it.
I think such glory is dangerous, that's all.
Poetry must pierce the filthy wall
With cries that die on country ways. The glow
Of bonhomie will not let the future grow.

Sir James Murray

'I pick a daimen icker from the thrave
And chew it thoughtfully. I must be brave
And fight for this. My English colleagues frown
But words come skelpin rank and file, and down
They go, the kittle kimmers, they're well caught
And I won't give them up. Who would have thought
A gleg and gangrel Scot like me should barge,
Or rather breenge, like a kelpie at large
In the Cherwell, upon the very palladium
Of anglophilia? My sleekit radium
Is smuggled through the fluttering slips. My shed,
My outhouse with its thousand-plus well-fed
Pigeon-holes, has a northern exposure. Doon
Gaed stumpie in the ink all afternoon,
As Burns and I refreshed the dictionar
With cantrips from his dancing Carrick star!
O lovely words and lovely man! We'll caw
Before us yowes tae knowes; we'll shaw the braw
Auld baudrons by the ingle; we'll comb
Quotations to bring the wild whaup safely home.
Origin obscure? Origin uncertain? Origin unknown?
I love those eldritch pliskies that are thrown
At us from a too playful past, a store
Of splore we should never be blate to semaphore!
Oxford! here is a silent collieshangie
To spike your index-cards and keep them tangy.
Some, though not I, will jib at houghmagandy:
We'll maybe not get that past Mrs Grundy.
But evening comes. To work, to work! to words!
The bats are turning into bauckie-birds.
The light in my scriptorium flickers gamely.
Pioneers must never labour tamely.
We steam along, we crawl, we pause, we hurtle,
And stir this English porridge with a spurtle.

Franz Kafka

Poetry, I think, is but a minor art.
In this dark life of ours the hardest part
's to make ends meet and not go mad. He knows
Better than most, this Burns, this exciseman, he chose
The business, he fed his family, he manipulated
The system with some success, some panic. He rated

A 'does pretty well for a poet' in the records,
Was due promotion when they dropped the cords
On his early coffin. What was the cost of this?
Patrons rise behind patrons, you hit, you miss,
You try again, grovelling's a groove of the time.
As for rivals, watch them watch you climb.
Who's a pretty boy republican?
Not me, I'm royal blue, I'll kiss the crown.
How well I know his guilt and fear! I see him
Riding eight hours a day, nothing can free him
From the dismal well-paid search of auld wives' barrels
To find among a wheen stowed cheese or farls
The beer, the brandy, the baccy, even the tea
He has to impound for half the goods and a fee.
He warned them sometimes, let them off. Was that good?
What is a good exciseman? How can he brood
Over the shillings in his ledger – the king's
Shilling! – when heads are rolling and rings
Are cut from the half-dead on battlefields?
Battlefields? Nearer home nothing yields
To pity. My last client lost his arm
On the shop floor. Everyone knows the harm
Was 'accidental', management was clean.
No one's going to subpoena a machine.
How could I stretch the wretched compensation?
His empty sleeve mocked my deliberation.
We're both bookkeepers, Burns, so what adds up?
Who kicks the bucket and who wins the cup?
Did you do your best after all? Did I?
You were a fighter with a melting eye,
And what more can be honoured? You had reach –
'I am going to smash that shite Creech!' –
But the blue devils could penetrate your shell
And dance the black exciseman off to hell
If you let them. You didn't. I don't. I think I don't.
How can we live with only use and wont?

An Anonymous Singer of the 21st Century

It's all on CD-ROM. Look under Song.
It's hyperpackaged and you can't go wrong.
It's under Scotland too, and Education.
Burns holds up his umbrella for the nation.
Possess this sangschaw and you'll think no book
Need burden you shelves. Click, listen, look.

The text of every song is there, the notes
Of every setting, sounds from the blended throats
Of the best singers made electronically one.
Every place referred to is flashed or run:
Here you have Afton Water, Ailsa Craig,
The Pier o Leith, Largo, and Stirling Brig.
See Auchterairder! See Parnassus Hill!
Abraham's Bosom! take a pill, make a will.
And press the translation service, do not miss:
Drive the ewes to the hillocks. One affectionate kiss
And then we separate. Of all the directions the wind
Can come from. O what happiness I gained
Fixing new teeth in a comb for dividing flax.
– But what of the man himself, you ask? What tracks
In the snow, what drawing-rooms, horses, shebeens?
No actors melodramatize those screens.
Digitized Burns is mixed from every portrait,
Strides like life across the fields, goes straight
To his chair, frowns, hums, fidgets, sings.
Remember his 'rich, deep' voice? It rings
Through the room, his eye smoulders the wallpaper.
Is this, you think, at last, the mover and shaper,
The makar and not the Mandelbrot? It's not.
Its strange perfection disinherits thought.
Switch on a hundred times, you'll learn no more
Than what was doled out at the cold blank door.

The real songs linger at a fugitive table,
Amazing, changing, bold, supreme, able
To get the hardest eye to glisten, heart
To throb, vessels of a profuse art.
I sing to please myself now, or for friends.
Great songs may have uncovenanted ends.
The stream of love, hope, memory, incitation
's too naked for this packaged generation.
But hear me if you will, and then you'll take
A joyful draught with me for that man's sake.

NOTE

James Macfarlan, Glasgow working-class poet (1832–1862).
Sir James Murray, born Roxburghshire, editor of the *New English Dictionary*
(now the *Oxford English Dictionary*) (1837–1915).

Robert Burns: The Tightrope Walker

IN APRIL 1783, when he was just over 24 years old and was working on the farm of Lochlie with his father, Robert Burns commenced a Commonplace Book. He was at that time quite unknown, except in his immediate circle in Ayrshire where he was regarded as a rude rhymester who could turn out satirical verses about local characters he disliked, write witty verse-letters to his friends, and produce elegant prose love-letters to help his rustic contemporaries in their affairs of the heart. He was considered a bit of a rebel, too, because of his passionate egalitarian views and his preference for character over social position.

He was well educated, having been tutored from the age of six by a genteel young man, John Murdoch, just twelve years older than himself, who gave him a thorough grounding in English grammar and in English literature (especially the poets) from Shakespeare to Shenstone. His literary text-book was an anthology of English literature compiled by Arthur Masson, a Scottish dominie: it included extracts from Milton, Dryden, Pope, Gray, Thomson (the only Scottish poet, but one who lived in England and wrote in English) and prose extracts from Addison and others. Burns also learned to read French, and he acquired a smattering of Latin. He went on to read for himself whatever he could lay his hands on – poetry, fiction, history, philosophy. He had no formal education whatever in Scottish literature. He had discovered for himself, probably as a chapbook, at an early age, Hamilton of Gilbertfield's modernisation of Blind Harry's fifteenth-century poem on the life and exploits of Sir William Wallace, which, as he told Dr. Moore in his famous autobiographical letter, 'poured a Scottish prejudice in my veins which will boil along till the flood-gates of life shut in eternal rest'. And he grew up with Scottish folk-lore – traditional tales of ghosts and goblins and the remnants of Scottish folk-song that lingered in the countryside. Later – we don't know exactly when, but well after his study of Masson's anthology with Murdoch – he encountered Fergusson's Scots poems which made him realise that there was a lively tradition of poetry in Scots still available from which he could – and did – draw inspiration.

When he began his Commonplace Book Burns was thus a young man well read in English literature from Shakespeare to his own day, able to express himself in elegant Addisonian English. He was also the hard-working son of a struggling tenant farmer and, after his father's death in February 1784, a tenant farmer himself, struggling to make a success of the farm of Mossgiel.

This young Ayrshire peasant, educated in English literature (all formal education in Scotland was now English-orientated) and still deeply involved in the daily struggle to wrest a living from indifferent and ill-drained land, starts his Commonplace Book with a flourish:

> Observations, Hints, Songs, Scraps of Poetry &c. by Robt Burness; a man who had little art in making money and still less in keeping it; but was, however, a man of some sense, a great deal of honesty, and unbounded good-will to every creature rational or irrational – As he was but little indebted to scholastic education, and bred at a plough-tail, his performances must be strongly tinctured with his unpolished, rustic way of life; but as I believe, they are really his own, it may be some entertainment to a curious observer of human-nature to see how a plough-man thinks, and feels, under the pressure of Love, Ambition, Anxiety, Grief with the like cares and passions, which, however diversified by the Modes, and Manners of life, operate pretty much alike I believe, in all the Species.

This is an extraordinary performance. Young Burns is holding himself up as a rustic character to be studied by those students of human nature, led by Adam Smith and David Hume, whose curiosity about what they called the 'passions' was such a characteristic of the Scottish Enlightenment. Who is he addressing? The assumption is clearly that someone will some day read what he has written. When it *is* read, the reader will be expected to note the poised (and posed) stance of the writer, as he proceeds to quote Shenstone:

> Pleasing when youth is long expired to trace
> The forms our pencil or our pen design'd!
> 'Such was our youthful air and shape and face!
> Such the soft image of our youthful mind –'

In September 1783 Burns writes in his Commonplace Book:

> I intirely agree with that judicious philosopher Mr. Smith in his excellent Theory of Moral Sentiments, that remorse is the most powerful sentiment that can embitter the human bosom.

So this young farmer thinks that Adam Smith is a judicious philosopher and his *Theory of Moral Sentiments* is excellent. Earlier in the same year he enters in the Commonplace Book a youthful poem of his, 'the first of my performances and done at an early period of life, when my heart glowed with honest warm simplicity, unacquainted and uncorrupted with the ways of a wicked world'. It is his first poem, and a love poem, a song indeed, written to an existing tune. It begins:

> O once I lov'd a bonny lass
> Ay and I love her still
> And whilst that virtue warms my breast
> I'll love my handsome Nell.

What is he doing here? The opening line is in the pure folk tradition: the second line adds an essential touch; but the third line – !

> And whilst that virtue warms my breast.

Ayrshire peasants did not normally talk about virtue warming their breasts. Or rather, they did if they were Robert Burns. This line comes straight out of the sophisticated sentimental-rhetorical tradition so conspicuous in the eighteenth century. Here, in his very first poem, Burns is trying to balance two very different traditions, the folk and the sophisticated genteel.

In March 1784 this young Ayrshire peasant is writing:

> I have often observed in the course of my experience of human life that every man, even the worst, have something good about them, though very often nothing else than a happy temperament of constitution inclining to this or that virtue; on this likewise, depend a great many, no man can say how many of our vices; for this reason no man can say in what degree any other person besides himself can be, with strict justice called wicked.

This characteristic of the optimism about human nature was shared by all the writers of the Scottish Enlightenment. Here is David Hume:

> All mankind so far resemble the good principle, that, where interest or revenge or envy perverts not our disposition, we are always inclined, from our natural philanthropy, to give the preference to the happiness of society, and consequently to virtue above its opposite. Absolute, unprovoked, disinterested malice has never perhaps place in any human breast.

To return to Burns's Commonplace Book. In April 1784 he writes:

> As I am, what men of the world, if they knew of such a man, call a whimsical Mortal, I have various sources of pleasure & enjoyment which are, in a manner, peculiar to myself; or some here & there such other out-of-the-way person.

And he goes on in a fit of Sterne-like rambling about his own character to conclude with a sad song about the gloomy winter scene matching his mood. There is a touch of Macpherson's Ossian too – a work Burns greatly admired and read with enthusiasm. But just after this comes the rollicking rhapsody, set to a known tune:

> My father was a farmer upon the Carrick Border – O
> And carefully he bred me in decency and order – O
> He bade me act a manly part, though I had ne'er a farthing – O
> For without an honest manly heart no man is worth regarding – O.

In August we see the mixture again. First the abandoned song, 'Green grow the rashes O':

> Green grow the rashes – O
> Green grow the rashes – O
> The sweetest hours that ere I spend
> Are spent amang the lasses – O.

This is immediately followed by:

> As the grand aim of human life is to cultivate an intercourse with that Being,
> to whom we owe life, with ev'ry enjoyment that renders life delightful; and
> to maintain an integritive conduct towards our fellow creatures; that so by
> forming Piety & Virtue into habit, we may be fit members for that society
> of the Pious, and the Good, which reason and revelation teach us to expect
> beyond the grave – I do not see that the turn of mind, and pursuits of such
> a one as the above verses describe – one who spends the hours & thoughts
> which the vocations of the day can spare with Ossian, Shakespeare, Thomson,
> Shenstone, Sterne & or as the maggot takes him, A gun, a fiddle, or a Song
> to make, or mend; and at all times some hearts-dear bonny lass in view-I
> say that I do not see that the turn of mind & pursuits of such a one are in
> the least more inimical to the sacred interests of Piety & Virtue, than the,
> even lawful, bustling & straining after the worlds riches & honors: and I do
> not see but he may gain Heaven as well, which by the bye is no mean
> consideration, who steals thro the Vale of Life, amusing himself with every
> little flower that fortune throws in his way; as he, who straining strait
> forward, & perhaps spattering all about him, gains some of Life's little
> eminences which, after all, he can only see & be seen a little more conspicu-
> ously, than, what in the pride of his heart, he is apt to term the poor, indolent
> devil he has left behind him.

The last entry in Burns's First Commonplace Book is dated October 1785:

> If ever any young man, on the vestibule of the world, chance to throw his
> eye over these pages, let him pay a warm attention to the following obser-
> vations; as I assure him they are the fruit of a poor devil's dear bought
> Experience. – I have literally like that great Poet and great Gallant, and by
> consequence that great Fool Solomon, – 'turned my eyes to behold Madness
> and Folly.' – Nay, I have, with all the ardor of a lively, fanciful and whimsical
> imagination, accompanied with a warm, feeling, Poetic heart – shaken hands
> with their intoxicating friendship.
>
> In the first place, let my Pupil, as he tenders his own peace, keep up a
> regular, warm intercourse with the Deity.

The movement between sententiousness and sheer abandonment to the relish
of experience ('I seek nae mair o' Heav'n to share/Than sic a moment's pleasure,
O!') is clearly indicated in this extraordinary collection of jottings in which
young Burns, not yet a published poet, acts out his role as somebody whom
posterity would want to study and profit from. This movement reflects the

two worlds in which Burns lived – that of the Scottish folk tradition and the revived art tradition of Scots poetry in Ramsay and more especially Fergusson on the one hand and the gentility, sentimentality and moral sententiousness of many writers of the Scottish Enlightenment on the other. Burns adored Henry Mackenzie's novel *The Man of Feeling*, he relished Macpherson's *Ossian*, he believed with Hugh Blair that benevolence was more important than theological orthodoxy, he was adept at sententious moral attitudinising; he was also bawdy, passionate, wickedly ironic, cruelly satirical, jovially celebratory, tenderly protective. And all his life he walked a tightrope between the world of urban Scottish gentility and the world – in W. E. Henley's phrase – of 'humanity caught in the act'.

Let us listen to Burns again, this time in a letter to his father written in December 1781 from Irvine where he was studying (or supposed to be studying) flax-dressing. 'I am quite transported,' he writes, 'at the thought that ere long, perhaps very soon, I shall bid an eternal adieu to all the pains and uneasiness and disquietudes of this weary life; for I assure you I am heartily tired of it, and, if I do not very much deceive myself, I could contentedly and gladly resign it.

> The Soul uneasy & confin'd from home,
> Rests & expatiates in a life to come.
>   Pope.

... As for this world, I despair of ever making a figure in it. – I am not formed for the bustle of the busy nor the flutter of the Gay ...' (This last sentence is an unacknowledged quotation from Mackenzie's *The Man of Feeling*.) It is interesting that Burns has absorbed the Mackenzie quotation into his own style, so he does not identify it, but the Pope he proudly identifies, as a couplet could not be assumed to be part of the writer's own prose.

It is worth remembering that Burns knew much of Pope by heart; he quotes him, paraphrases him, and refers to him innumerable times. And Pope's presence can be identified both in his poems and in his letters more than that of any other poet. Even that proudly anarchic cantata 'Love and Liberty' (often known as 'The Jolly Beggars') takes its title from a line in Pope's 'Eloisa to Abelard' – a line Burns actually quotes in one of his earliest letters, that extraordinary piece of exhibitionist posturing that he wrote as a love-letter, probably to Alison Begbie, as a very young man:

> I do not remember in the course of your acquaintance and mine, ever to have heard your opinion on the ordinary way of falling in love, amongst people in our station of life. I do not mean the persons who proceed in the way of bargain, but those whose attraction is really placed on the person.

The letter continues in this strain for a page and a half. No wonder the girl rejected him. He did not approach Jean Armour in this way, nor was this the way in which he described his amours to his male friends:

> A' ceremony laid aside
> I fairly found her cuntie-O.

In a letter to his old tutor John Murdoch he shows off as might be expected:

> I seem to be one sent into the world, to see and observe; and I very easily
> compound with the knave who tricks me of my money, if there be anything
> original about him which shews me human nature in a different light from
> any thing I have seen before. In short, the joy of my heart is to 'Study men,
> their manners, and their ways'. (Another quotation from Pope)

Later in the same letter he writes:

> My favourite authors are of the sentiml. kind, such as Shenstone, particularly
> his Elegies, Thomson, Man of feeling, a book I prize next to the Bible, Man
> of the World, Sterne, especially his Sentimental journey, Mcpherson's Ossian,
> &c. these are the glorious models after which I endeavour to form my
> conduct, and 'tis incongruous, 'tis absurd to suppose that the man whose
> mind glows with sentiments lighted up at their sacred flame – the man whose
> heart distends with benevolence to all the human race – he 'who can Soar
> above this little scene of things' [a quotation from Thomson's *Autumn*] –
> can he descend to mind the paultry concerns about which the terrae-filial
> race fret, and fume, and vex themselves?

In this correspondence Burns, long before he had any poems published,
assumed the role of the Poet with a self-conscious bow to contemporary
aesthetic jargon: 'Poets, Madam, of all Mankind, feel most forcibly the power
of BEAUTY; as, if they are really Poets of Nature's making, their feelings must
be finer, and their taste more delicate than most of the world'. 'Poets of Nature's
Making.' This phrase points the way to the most blatant example of Burns's
adopting contemporary theory to pose as the untutored Peasant Poet, the
Natural Man.

I refer of course to his Preface to the Kilmarnock edition, in which he
presented himself as an untutored rustic 'unacquainted with the necessary
requisites for commencing Poet by rule', singing 'the sentiments and manners
he felt and saw in himself and his rustic compeers around him, in his and their
native language'. We all know the *literati* of Edinburgh took the bait, with
Henry Mackenzie hailing him as 'this Heaven-taught ploughman'. What has
been insufficiently examined, however, is how this strategy of Burns trapped
him in a dilemma that he spent most of his life trying to solve. Was he a rustic
phenomenon or a poet not only of natural genius but of refined taste and
cultivated mind? How should he conduct himself when he was trotted round
the drawing-rooms of the Edinburgh gentry? There are many tributes to Burns's
genius as a conversationalist. 'Nothing is more remarkable,' wrote Dugald
Stewart, 'among his various attainments, than the fluency, and precision, and
originality of his language.' Maria Riddell, in the memoir of the poet that she

wrote for the *Dumfries Journal*, maintained that Burns was more brilliant as a conversationalist than as a poet. None outshone him, she maintained, 'in the charms – the sorcery I would almost call it, of fascinating conversation; the spontaneous eloquence of social argument, or the unstudied poignancy of brilliant repartee'. Burns was aware of his predicament. He accepted with good humour his role as the peasant of genius while at the same time asserting his right to talk with the literati as an equal. 'If there had been a little more of gentleness and accommodation in his temper,' wrote Dugald Stewart, 'he would, I think, have been still more interesting.' Stewart recognised and resented Burns's assertion of his intellectual equality with his Edinburgh hosts and his often only thinly disguised egalitarianism. At the same time, Burns retained a sense of humour about his ambivalent position in Edinburgh society. 'I am in a fair way of becoming as eminent as Thomas à Kempis or John Bunyan: And you may expect henceforth to see my birthday inserted among the wonderful events, in the Poor Robin's and Aberdeen Almanacks, along with the black Monday & the battle of Bothwell bridge.'

The social problem was a bit more tricky than the intellectual. The bounds set for flirtation by a Heaven-taught ploughman were not at first easy for him to understand. He wrote innumerable poems of compliment and often something more to girls and ladies of high – or relatively high – social station, but if he tried to go further he was rebuffed in very positive terms. It was different with the country girls he was used to. Social relationships with pretty ladies were a minefield. The extraordinary story of his affair with Mrs. M'Lehose (Clarinda) illustrates in a fascinating way the complexities of Burns's social and indeed moral situation in Edinburgh and in the homes of the gentry generally.

My interest, however, is less in the biographical aspect than in the consequences all this had for Burns's use of language, both in his poetry and in his letters. It has often been noticed that Burns's letters, with one single exception, are written in an elegant, often somewhat formal, English. The single exception is the racy letter in Scots written to William Nicol on 1st June 1787. Burns had learned his letter-writing style from Elizabeth Rowe's *Letters Moral and Entertaining* and, although in writing to close friends he often lightened the formality of his prose with lively colloquialisms and in moments of emotion could alter the somewhat stately rhythms of his normal epistolary style to something more vivid and personal, for the most part the Burns of the letters is far from the Burns of 'Tam o' Shanter' or 'Holy Willie's Prayer'.

There is a rhetorical ring in many of the letters that shows a skill in ordering and modulating the run of his feelings. 'You will very probably think, my honoured friend, that a hint about the mischievous nature of intoxicated vanity may not be unseasonable.' (He is writing to Robert Aiken from Edinburgh in December 1786.) 'But alas! you are wide of the mark. – Various concurring circumstances have raised my fame as a Poet to a height which I am absolutely certain I have not merits to support; and I look down on the future as I would into the bottomless pit.' The cadence of this reminds me of Dr. Johnson: 'Is not a patron, my lord, one who looks with unconcern on a man struggling in the water, and when he has reached land encumbers him with help?'

There is an ordered eloquence in many of Burns's letters that shows him as an accomplished practitioner of neo-classic English prose. There is also a wit and an intelligent playfulness that make for attractive reading. There are also blatant posturings and rhetorical extravagances that are an embarrassment to read. 'O Love and Sensibility, Ye have conspired against my Peace!! I love to madness, and I feel to torture! Clarinda, how can I forgive myself, that I ever touched a single chord in your bosom with pain!' Of course the letters to Clarinda are in a class by themselves. The very names Clarinda and Sylvander testify to the extraordinary hot-house atmosphere in which this relationship was conducted. 'I like the idea of Arcadian names in a commerce of this kind,' Burns write to Clarinda in January 1788. 'Commerce of this kind' is an odd expression, but very indicative of what was going on in Burns's mind at this time.

A revealing example of Burns walking the tightrope between modesty and self-esteem, between deference and independence, can be seen in his letter to Hugh Blair of 4 May 1787:

I often felt the embarrassment of my very singular situation; drawn forth from the veriest shades of life to the glare of remark; and honored by the notice of those illustrious Names of my country, whose Works, while they are applauded to the end of time, will ever instruct and mend the heart. However the meteor-like novelty of my appearance in the world may attract notice, and honor me with the acquaintance of the permanent lights of genius and literature, those who are truly Benefactors of the immortal nature of Man, I knew very well that my utmost merit was far unequal to the task of preserving that character, when once that novelty was over; and have made up my mind that abuse or almost even neglect will not surprise me in my quarters.

Does this represent a deliberate strategy in Burns's relationship with the *literati*? Only a few weeks before, he had written to Mrs. Dunlop: 'I have the advice of some very judicious friends among the Literati here, but with them I sometimes find it necessary to claim the privilege of thinking for myself'.

How to preserve the balance between self-esteem and proper recognition of established men of letters? This is in some degree a problem with any writer, but it is a special problem for a self-proclaimed child of Nature who is in fact nothing of the sort.

Who did he measure himself against? He was clearly in earnest when he described Fergusson as 'by far my elder brother in the Muse'. Is he equally in earnest when he writes to Dr. Moore in February 1787: '... in a language where Pope and Churchill have raised the laugh, and Shenstone and Gray drawn the tear; where Thomson and Beattie have painted the landskip, and Littleton and Collins described the heart, I am not vain enough to hope for distinguished Poetic fame'?

This is a remarkably diverse collection of names of poets, where Pope and Churchill are equated and the forgotten Littleton is paired with Collins. Is Burns here performing a balancing act? Did he really mean what he said? It is difficult to say. Burns from his first entry into the world as a poet had been a role-taker. He played many parts. Sometimes I think his professed literary opinions were part of his role-playing. He certainly had confidence in his own merits as a poet and was well able to defend himself on any issue that a critic might raise. And in the matter of song-writing he was an assured expert, as his correspondence with George Thomson makes clear. At the same time his literary taste was uncertain: he *did* inordinately admire Shenstone and Henry Mackenzie and Macpherson's *Ossian*. Of course, he was far from unique in this: these writers were hugely popular in their day and were praised by the most esteemed critics.

But Burns the Heaven-taught ploughman, the inspired peasant poet, had to play the part he had chosen for himself. It could land him in social disasters like the notorious incident of the rape of the Sabine women at Friar's Carse. It could trap him in a relationship with Mrs. M'Lehose that he could not sustain: the story of his relations with Jean after his protestations to Clarinda is only the most conspicuous example of Burns on the tightrope. An unsuccessful tenant farmer who became a junior excise officer and a much acclaimed poet to boot – where, in the stratified life of late eighteenth-century Scotland did he really stand? He wrote Jacobite and anti-Jacobite poems. He supported the French Revolution and professed admiration for the British constitution. He twisted and turned to get himself out of political trouble as an exciseman. He had a military funeral when he died, as a member of the Dumfries Volunteers.

In a sense it was his discovery of his vocation as a re-creator of Scottish song that saved him, that gave him wholeness. Here he was in a field where he was quite unchallenged: he knew exactly what he was doing and exactly how to do it.

But let me return first to the letters and then to the poetry. I have talked of the formality of Burns's epistolary style. But this falls away when he writes to his intimates like John Richmond or Bob Ainslie. 'Writing sense is so damn'd, dry, hide-bound a business I am determined never more to have anything to do with it. – I have such an Aversion to right line and method, that when I don't get over the hedges which bound the highway, I zig-zag across the road just to keep my hand in.' This is a different style altogether from that of his letters to Hugh Blair or Dr. Moore or Mrs. Dunlop. His correspondence with Mrs. Dunlop is of special interest. His style grows less and less formal as he gets to know her and sends her songs and poems, until finally he forgets that he is still on a tightrope and makes an ill-advised jocular remark approving the execution of the French King and Queen, and he falls off the tightrope. Mrs. Dunlop withdraws her friendship, leaving him puzzled and upset. It was the epistolary equivalent of the rape of the Sabines incident.

There is however a quite different kind of letter that Burns was able to write, an epistolary form based on a known Scottish tradition that he developed in his own way with a high degree of skill. This was the verse letter, a form which Burns developed early in his career. The first, to John Lapraik, is entered in his Commonplace Book on April 1st 1785. The combination of an intricately patterned verse form with a note of chatty informality required a technical mastery that Burns developed quickly and easily. His verse letters are among the most splendid and original of his poems. They are for the most part beautifully structured, beginning with setting the scene, himself writing in the farmhouse at a particular moment in the farming year, then steadily moving out to a larger context until he reaches the centre of the poem where some generalisation about life or love or society or moral behaviour easily emerges, after which the context contracts again until at the end we are back with the poet in the farmhouse to see him sign off gracefully and often wittily. In this kind of writing there is no adjustment of language and attitude to the needs of a Heaven-taught ploughman addressing a genteel audience, there is no sense at all of the poet's walking a tightrope or of his forcing language to an artificially high pitch. He is at ease with himself and his correspondent.

He could not of course write this kind of letter to the ladies and gentlemen whose society he enjoyed (if that is the word) in Edinburgh and in Scottish country houses. His prose letters to such people were posed efforts in which he assumed the *persona* he thought would be most agreeable to the recipient. And, as we have seen, even in writing to his father and his former tutor he could assume a *persona*. But in writing to his Ayrshire friends in verse forms he developed as vehicles for genuine communication, self-expression and friendly display, he showed how the counterpointing of informality of tone and formality of structure could result in poems where artful speech is made to sound spontaneous. There is much more to be said about Burns's letters – an analysis of his letters to George Thomson alone would be immensely fruitful – but I must content myself with only one more point. This concerns Burns's eventual acquisition of a certain ease in combining what could be called a high social tone with confident teasing. This is a balancing act indeed, especially to a man of Burns's background. How well he eventually learned to perform it is illustrated in a letter to Maria Riddell of April 1793 about French gloves. It begins:

I remember, Madam, to have heard you lately inveigh against this unfortunate country, that is so barren of comforts, the very necessaries of life were not to be found in it. – In particular, you told me, you could not *exist* without FRENCH GLOVES. Had Fate put it in my power any way to have added one comfort to your existence, it could not perhaps have done anything which would have gratified me more; yet, poor as I am in every thing, except

Inclination, I have been fortunate enough to obviate the business of FRENCH GLOVES. – In order that you may have the higher idea of my merits in this MOMENTOUS affair, I must tell you that all the Haberdashers here are on the alarm, as to the necessary article of French Gloves. – You must know that FRENCH GLOVES are contraband goods, & expressly prohibited by the laws of this wise-governed Realm of ours. – A Satirist would say, that this is one reason why the ladies are so fond of them; but I, who have not one grain of GALL in my composition, shall alledge that it is the PATRIOTISM of the dear Goddesses of men's idolatry, that makes them so fond of dress from the LAND OF LIBERTY & EQUALITY.

I cannot resist a final quotation from Burns's letters to provide a complete contrast. This is his short last letter to his wife Jean written shortly before his death. He was, on the lunatic advice of his doctor, bathing in the Solway Firth as a cure for his rheumatic heart disease. 'My dearest Love,' it begins, 'I delayed writing until I could tell you what effect sea-bathing was likely to produce. It would be injustice to deny that it has eased my pains ... but my appetite is still extremely bad.' It concludes: 'I will see you on Sunday. Your affectionate husband, R. B.' No tightrope walking here.

Except for his verse letters, I have said little so far about Burns as a poet. If he had not been a great poet we should not be discussing him here today. I have written elsewhere at length about Burns's poetry, and all I want to point out here is that the conflicting forces working on Burns are reflected in his poetry even more clearly than they are in his letters. From his very earliest attempts, Burns moved between a rhetorical English verse tradition and a variety of Scots traditions. I have noted the mixture in 'Handsome Nell'. One sees it, beautifully integrated, in what is perhaps his first wholly successful poem, the song 'Mary Morison'. It opens in pure English:

> O Mary at thy window be,
> It is the wish'd the trysted hour;
> Those smiles and glances let me see,
> That make the miser's treasure poor.

But *is* this pure English? Should not 'hour' be pronounced as Scots 'oor', to rhyme with 'poor'? Yet these lines *sound* English, and we are aware of a shift to Scots when the stanza continues

> How blithely wad I bide the stour,
> A weary slave frae sun to sun.

yet the next two lines –

> Could I the rich reward secure
> The lovely Mary Morison –

– are English again.

The fact is that in all his songs Burns moved easily between English and Scots, using an English tipped with Scots or a Scots tipped with English as the spirit moved him. 'My luve is like a red, red rose' begins in English then modulates easily into Scots. This is true of dozens of songs.

Is Burns at his freeest and truest when he writes in Scots? I do not think that one can say this, although it is true that poems in Scots throughout, such as the 'Second Epistle to J. Lapraik' or 'Holy Willie's Prayer' have a special magnificence. 'Tam o' Shanter' has a few lines in English ('But pleasures are like poppies spread ...') to indicate a mock-moralising tone intruding on the vernacular raciness of the narrative. Should we, as some have maintained, pronounce 'pleasures' as 'pleesures'? There is a case for this, but I am not sure. To do so would spoil the contrast in tone that Burns was clearly aiming at. While Burns must have spoken Ayrshire Scots to his friends and family at home, he spoke English in Edinburgh with fluency, precision and originality according to Dugald Stewart, who added that he 'avoided more successfully than most Scotsmen, the peculiarities of Scottish phraseology'. Dr. Currie, Burns's first biographer, said that Burns spoke with a less pronounced Scottish accent than David Hume. Nevertheless this was an acquired speech, and in undress, as it were, he must have spoken Scots. And even if 'pleasure' in the passage from 'Tam o' Shanter' is to be pronounced in the English manner, certainly in the lines

> O Tam! hadst thou but been sae wise
> As taen thy ain wife Kate's advice

'wise' is to be pronounced as the Scots 'wice'.

The successful move from Scots to English can be seen in the 'Epistle to Davie', which begins splendidly –

> While winds frae aff Ben-Lomond blaw,
> And bar the doors wi' drivin' snaw,

using a complex old Scots stanza, and moves effortlessly into English in Stanza 4: 'What tho', like commoners of air, We wander out, we know not where,' skipping into Scots again – 'But either house or ha'' – then back into English:

> Yet Nature's charms, the hills and woods,
> The sweeping vales and foaming floods,
> Are free alike to all.

Then into Scots again:

> On braes when we please then
>   We'll sit and sowth a tune;
> Syne rhyme till't, we'll time till't,
>   And sing't when we hae done.

The fact is that Scots poets from the Middle Scots period on always had the option of turning to English; they had the resources of this closely related language open to them if they wished to draw on them, and to this extent had a richer vocabulary than the English poets, who had only their own language. Burns's immediate predecessor Fergusson could pronounce the same word now as Scots and now as English, as the rhyme required. So Burns's movement between Scots and English is no necessary part of his tightrope walking.

While some of his best songs are largely in English, his best narrative and satirical verse is in Scots – 'Tam o' Shanter', 'The Holy Fair', 'Holy Willie's Prayer' – as are such poems as 'To a Mouse', 'To a Louse', 'Address to the Deil', 'Death and Dr. Hornbrook' (with its masterly opening), 'The Auld Farmer's New-year-morning Salutation to his Auld Mare, Maggie', 'The Twa Dogs' and of course the 'Address to a Haggis'. ('Auld Scotland wants nae skinking ware that jaups in luggies' is far more pungently expressed than 'Old Scotland needs no soup-like stuff that jumps up and down in soup tureens with ear-shaped handles'.)

Burns could write poetry in English with ease and effectiveness, as we see in so many of his songs. We rarely find evidence of tightrope walking there. It is in his rhetorical-sentimental poems in English, where he seems to be making claims to be considered a Scottish Shenstone, that we find a deliberate posturing, or in that awful duty poem to Edinburgh beginning with what I think is the worst line he ever wrote, 'Edina! Scotia's darling seat'. We can sometimes see the rhetorical poseur taking over from the genuine poet. At least, that is how I read 'The Vision', where the opening is in marvellous descriptive Scots:

> The sun had clos'd the winter day,
> The curlers quat their roaring play,
> And hunger'd maukin taen her way
>   To kail-yards green,
> While faithless snaws ilk step betray
>   Whare she has been.

When the poem moves into English, however, it seems to me a posed piece of hollow rhetoric:

> With musing-deep astonished stare
> I view'd the heavenly-seeming Fair; ...

'The heavenly-seeming Fair' indeed!

Yet Burns could use neo-classic English to excellent effect. Indeed, he could write extremely competently in Popeian couplets, as in the 'Epistle to Robert Graham, Esq., of Fintry', which begins with an actual echo of Pope:

> When Nature her great Masterpiece designed,
> And framed her last, best Work, The Human Mind,

> Her eye intent on all the mazy Plan,
> She forms of various stuff the various Man.

This is competent enough, but sounds like many another eighteenth-century poet. Compare it with how Burns turns Pope's lines:

> Heav'n, when it strives to polish all it can,
> Its last, best work, but forms a softer man.

Here is Burns's version:

> Auld Nature swears the lovely Dears
> Her noblest work she classes, O.
> Her prentice han' she tried on man,
> An' then she made the lasses, O.

He is on no tightrope here, but safely on *terra firma*.

Rabbietising Reality

ROBERT BURNS was my mother's favourite poet, and the only poet I remember being quoted outside the classroom during the whole of my childhood – by family, relations, friends' parents, adults in general.

My mother had four books of poetry. Palgrave's *Golden Treasury*, an edition of William Wordsworth's *Selected Poems*, the works of Adam Lindsay Gordon and an edition of the poems of Robert Burns.

I have three of these books, all bought between 1922 and 1926 when she was aged between 17 and 21. The Adam Lindsay Gordon edition is dated April, 1926, bought when she was in service at 1 Randolph Place, Edinburgh.

My mother told me the housekeeper took her aside, showed her round the house and went over her duties – taking hot water to the bedrooms, cleaning the grates, sweeping stairs, that sort of thing. She told my mother that if she was forced to use the main stairway, to do so when no member of the family was present, and if, by accident, she met one of the family on the stairs or in the corridors she should turn her face to the wall until they were past. For my mother this was a simple working condition. For me it was a source of anger.

She had Wednesday afternoons off, and for two hours on Sunday morning was expected to accompany the household to church. She bought the books from barrows parked along the High Street, near the area where, she told me, Robert Burns had lived.

Adam Lindsay Gordon's work is not well known. He has gone out of fashion. He wrote energetic poems of military conquest and sporting achievement, mostly using rhyming couplets, the sort of poems that can date an attitude, an ideal and a period precisely and far more quickly than anything else; quicker than music, photographs, a newspaper extract, Hansard or any other written form:

> One line of swart profiles, and bearded lips dressing,
> One ridge of bright helmets, one crest of fair plumes,
> One streak of blue sword-blades all bared for the fleshing,
> One row of red nostrils that scent battle fumes.[1]

Having got the subject and rhythm, the sense is subordinate, and the poem can go on in that vein for as long as it likes. It is a poem which is compiled rather than written.

For my mother, these poems were a memory of childhood. Her teacher, who was always referred to as Teeny Ann, read an extract from one of the military pieces to the children at the end of every schoolday in Muir of Ord primary school during the First World War. My mother was not taught Robert Burns during this time. He was considered a reprobate.

She had been sent to Muir of Ord from Glasgow with her two sisters, because their father, Carl Kaufman, had been born in Baden Baden and was interned in Knockaloof on the Isle of Man for the whole of the war. My grandmother stayed in Glasgow with the younger children.

In spite of never being introduced to Burns's poetry in childhood and not being able to remember where she first heard it or what it was about the work that initially attracted her, my mother rarely recited anything but Burns. Her own edition of his poems was given to my father when he left for the Second World War. It was lost the first time his ship was torpedoed, though his edition was replaced by a wee book which was a gift from the Lord Provost and City of Glasgow, given to all servicemen at a concert held in the St Andrews Halls and which he dated 26 12 43.

I am trying to indicate, from personal and limited experience, the great love and respect felt for Burns by the working people of Scotland, and I haven't even mentioned the uncle who on everything from etiquette to personal conduct or morality consulted Burns before the Bible. There is something to be said for Lord Birsay's assertion that we celebrate Burns because he is uniquely ordinary, or Edwin Morgan's observation that there is no one quite like him;[2] but such statements in this context account for his accessibility, and Burns has always suffered by being too accessible.

At the ASLS Schools Conference [3] a couple of years ago, Ken Simpson quoted the question Allan Cunningham heard on the streets of Dumfries after Burns's death, 'Who will be our poet now?' [4] – a question which suggests that Robert Burns to some extent compensated for the loss of nationhood.

I find that particularly poignant, maybe even tragic; most obviously because it puts Burns in an impossible position; but also because it is evidence of our second hand attitude towards ourselves, our lack of self-worth as a nation. We need a writer, not a body of literature, not writers plural, but a single writer in whom we invest our national identity. What I find even more pathetic is that two hundred years later this position has, if anything, been intensified. Burns is still seen as a national icon, and as such he suffers. His work is quoted and misquoted, appropriated as public property, yet in so doing we have robbed ourselves of its diversity and uniqueness, not to mention its integrity and subtlety.

While considering Burns as an icon of national identity, we must ask whose interests this image serves. To do that, we must firstly look at what the image does, both to us and to the icon.

This point has been made many times before, but I think it cannot be made too often. For all that Burns is probably quoted more than any other poet, for all that many of his lines and phrases are now part of everyday speech and often are reduced to clichés, there is danger in familiarity. The effect, especially when coupled with continuous mythologising, is to encourage acceptance rather than stimulate study or even challenge.

Burns, of course, was mythologised in his own lifetime, a role he both encouraged and despised with his usual mixture of foxy quiddity. Recently, a diverse and growing body of literary and historical scholarship has placed the poet in his time, suggesting he became a focus for our national pride as a compensation for the loss of nationhood. One way or another, we have invested a fair amount in Robert Burns, not only making his image an icon, but turning his friends and acquaintances into a catalogue of lesser saints, raising his birth-place and the house where he died in the Mill Vennel, Dumfries, renamed Burns Street, into shrines.

Early Rabbietisers desecrated his last resting-place, dug him up and removed his bones nearer to the entrance of the St. Michael kirkyard, entirely for their own convenience. Above these bones they raised the ugliest piece of official sculpture outside the now-defunct Soviet Union.

What has happened in Dumfries is bad enough, but Alloway beggars belief. The thing I find appalling is that the changes are recent; someone thought it was a good idea. At no time in this progress towards banality did they stop to consider what they were doing or why, much less see it as anything other than improvement. It's embarrassing, but not unusual. For Robert Burns has been successfully manipulated into an icon which upholds the very values he detested:

> A' they've to say was aften said afore
> A lad was born in Kyle to blaw aboot.
> What unco fate mak's him the dumpin'-grun'
> For a' the sloppy rubbish they jaw oot?[5]

The surrounding dozen or so verses encapsulate the phenomenon as clearly as Richard Finlay describes the two-way traffic towards apotheosis, how aspects of our own identity have shaped our view of Burns,[6] something which continues to the present day.

It is tempting to suggest today's attitude is healthier, insofar as the 20–20 vision of hindsight and the manic conceit of MacDiarmid have made us per-sistently aware of the problem, and however much we may scorn the Rabbietisers, to do so without responding to them is to deny their pervasive sweep, their potency, or even their existence. We may even think help is at hand. After all, by recycling their dross, they get more than they deserve, which is where Iain Crichton Smith's brilliant satire comes into its own.

Is there here not a lesson for us all?
What indeed may 'a bickerin brattle' not signify? May it not call us to be human beings? And what indeed is 'an icker in a thrave'? All of us can afford one. We are not so poor that we cannot afford 'an icker.' We may of course

be so armoured in the luxuries of the world that we feel we cannot do so, but if we think for a moment we find we can.[7]

Murdo is Iain Smith's finest creation, and though the *Thoughts of Murdo* volume suffers from the character being removed from his context, it does provide a wonderful springboard for a broad range of farcical lampoons at targets which are not always as visible as the Rabbietisers.

To understand the cosmeticised Rabbie phenomenon, we must firstly recognise that we inhabit a dream kingdom, a place which has little or no basis in reality and where the mythology is so powerful that we have been given a series of symbols to validate our identity. Burns was being transformed as the Highlands were being tartanised, cleared and mythologised. But Burns is particularly interesting because he bestrides more than one camp and has generated more than a single mythology.

As he was being iconographied in one direction, he was almost simultaneously being mutated into another form, as a symbol of progressive Scottish causes. He was placed alongside William Wallace as a nationalist, anti-aristocratic statuette of Scottish ideas and values.[8]

Symbolic representation has a high degree of wastage. It is a visual equivalent of the sound bite, and we need only look at the number of road signs there are and how often they are repeated to see what little effect a symbol can have on its own. The messages need to be reinforced, so one image borrows another. Scotland has a multiplicity of images which singly or collectively tell the same story: stags and heather, dogs and thistles, even the landscape which is usually dark, dour and romantic with ruined castles and, very importantly, no people. Reality would include the towns and cities of the Central Lowlands, where four fifths of the population live.

As an image, Robert Burns embraces more than his country. Just as his work is used to justify and peddle both his likes and dislikes, so representations of the Nasmyth or Skirving portraits sell a variety of products with which his name can be vaguely associated, beer and whisky, Scotch Drink being the more obvious. And alongside his image are placed the artifacts of his existence.[9]

In this context, and viewed from the perspective of the wee and couthy, Alloway is very important. It spawned the whole nonsense: an object, a place, rather than a series of words and ideas, a symbol which embraces the poet and whatever family, relative or class values one may wish to sell. The place would have been demolished long ago were it not for the fact that Robert Burns was born there. But since he was born there and since it still exists, the cottage fits perfectly into that most treasured of all our national myths, the parish, the village, the small community, birthplace of self-reliance and the best education system in the world. No other icon in the whole Burns panoply so clearly detaches the writer from his work. There must be few writers who have been subjected to such intense mythologising, turning Burns into a sort of Scottish Forrest Gump.

I am going to resist the temptation to ponder the kind of society, nation even, which turns a person who said sensible things well into a banal travesty, where his work is his least important aspect. It is the same nation which systematically obliterated their way of life in favour of a system where children were read jingoistic rubbish during the bloodiest conflict of the century.

It now seems obvious and as a corollary to Carol McGuirk's investigations into the nostalgic consequences of Burns's life, work and background,[10] that the nineteenth century's cosmeticisation laid the foundations of the road to the Kailyard, a movement which nourished all that was mawkishly escapist and unremittingly sentimental in Scottish writing. It gave rise to a glut of short fiction which amply displayed what J. H. Miller in the *New Review* in 1895 called 'a diseased craving for the pathetic.' It was a movement through which the huge populations concentrated in Scotland's cities could enjoy a version of country life which was familiar enough to be funny and foreign enough to be patronised. The charm is often beguiling, but the attitude effectively wrote the rural poor out of existence or used them as set-dressing for moralising romps disguised as country life viewed from the manse window.

I think there is something interesting in the fact that I, a Scottish writer, living and working in Scotland and an unashamed Burns enthusiast, am trying to pick my way through the Burns and concomitant mythologies. Carol McGuirk has remarked that Scott, Stevenson and MacDiarmid all had to repudiate Burns in order to replace his mythic Scotland with one of their own imagining.[11] And Ken Simpson further suggests the Scotlands these and other writers have imagined are not without their own mythic qualities.[12]

That a single recognisable place can spawn so many and diverse interpretations is scarcely a phenomenon, especially when we look at what a similar mythological surfeit has done and is currently doing to Ireland.

I have already said Burns suffers from accessibility. I believe this is because he is a very direct poet, a writer almost without artifice. This is especially true of his songs, where it seems as though he speaks directly to us, inviting a response. But that is not the only sense in which he is direct. He rarely uses poetic tricks or devices. Here I can do nothing but acknowledge Donald Low's wonderful phrase: in his essay on Burns's song he says Burns is a writer who does nothing by halves.[13]

Burns is accessible because he makes poetry look easy, and this accounts for him being the most imitated poet. The reason every Scottish writer has to take him on is because the first thing a writer does is establish a voice. It is a badge of individual and national identity. It has to do with rhythm and with speech, with class, dialect and position. It is one of the few devices open to a writer which fulfils more than one function simultaneously. When writing, the first decision a writer continually makes is what voice to use; it then becomes a means of identity, a style of writing which the reader could recognise without referring to the name at the top of the page.

Interestingly, this is often not a conscious decision. Subjects often suggest a voice to the writer, so that the subject can become part of the voice, a necessary component insofar as deliberately choosing a subject is an act of sympathy. It is inconceivable for any writer to choose a subject which does not suit their voice.

Burns in his work and in his life was a fascinating contradiction. He was what he claimed to be, a man of independent mind who managed to cross classes, countries and abilities. I can think of no other writer with such a varied range of voices. Nor can I think of a body of poetry where the voice is used to such effect.

But what of Allan Cunningham's reported question and what has happened in two hundred years to render it meaningless?

Nothing.

If anything, the position is worse; at best, the same. We still see the writer as a spokesperson, speaking on our country's behalf. MacDiarmid deliberately courted such a position and there are currently a few pretenders to the throne, folk who would love to be asked to their own coronation. This is especially sad since it is now more than evident that the MacDiarmid cult obscured other voices which were not poetic and undervalued those that were. I am thinking especially of the work of novelists and short-story writers such as Edward Gaitens, George Friel, Naomi Mitchison and Lewis Grassic Gibbon.

Maybe every country does it, perhaps it is part of the writer's job-description, but I think we still look to the writer with the big voice, the big idea, or, increasingly, the big reputation. It is a virus. And we need to find an antidote or a cure; at least we need to vaccinate ourselves and our idea of consciousness, because so long as we refuse to take the medicine we undervalue ourselves, the chosen and their work. If there are, and I believe there must be, contenders for the crown of national bard, they should look at what has happened to the one we have. And if we still see Burns as our national bard, whose interests does it serve, his or ours?

I believe it comes as a profound shock to any Scottish writer when he or she realises how good Robert Burns actually is; not because we necessarily feel a need to emulate him, but because there is so much in Scottish life and history that is second-rate and to come across something of a real, international achievement in one's own field can be disturbing.

After reading 'Tam o'Shanter', Sir Walter Scott said of Burns: 'No poet, with the exception of Shakespeare, ever possessed the power of exciting the most varied and discordant emotions with such rapid transition.'[14] This, to my mind, is Burns's greatest gift as a writer. It is a gift which, I think, many writers would cherish, and recognise almost immediately. It incorporates a willingness, and ability, to take extraordinary risks, an ability to effect sudden change, to alter tack immediately or to set entirely disparate, opposing or unrelated ideas together and not only fuse them, but to do so in an entirely natural way. This often occurs in a way which we only notice when we take a second or third look at the text, when we take things apart and ask ourselves, What is going on here? How does this work?

For the most important aspect of all is that Burns always carries his readers with him. That is an essential part of his appeal and a reason for the excesses of the Burns cult. This ability to move ideas, to move from one concept and in the space of a few lines to embrace another, totally separate, unheralded concept, is in places breathtaking; all the more so because this is writing of the very highest quality, so good it is capable of being taken for granted, ignored or misunderstood. A casual reader might think he could do it. Burns makes poetry look easy, which is why he is one of the most widely imitated poets.

Overall, I think this gift of fluidity works best in the songs. We all know Burns was sleekit, but to use music to disguise his methods is spectacularly crafty. I have for some time now, certainly since the publication of *The Devil and The Giro*,[15] been arguing that readers of Scottish stories have been blinded by narrative. Here, I think those who listen to Burns's songs are, to some degree, blinded by a similar misfortune.

At last we seem to be moving from the entrenched position of insisting that the lyrics of Burns's songs be separated from the music, in much the same way, I imagine, as one would consider buying a car without turning over the engine. For all that there has been some movement in the right direction, I think the nature of Burns's songs remains widely misunderstood. Even allowing for the missionary work done by such as David Daiches, Donald Low and Tom Crawford, Burns's songs until recently lacked proper critical assessment as integrated works of art. The assumption stills appears to be that the music is a minor factor, something we have to accept, but which is endorsed reluctantly. This is especially sad since most of the songs I can think of would never have existed were it not for the tunes. It is therefore absurd to see them as poetry, to be read or spoken aloud. That was certainly not the way Burns saw them.

Cedric Thorpe Davie says that a fifth of Burns's 323 songs can be classified as 'outstanding successes, as integrated and unified products' where words and tune match each other perfectly. This, he says, puts Burns on a level with most great creative artists. Schubert in his 600 songs did not achieve such a proportion. 'A disinterested assessment of the lyric output of any of the great poets or composers would usually lead to a similar conclusion,' he says.[16]

To illustrate Scott's 'rapid transition', I have chosen something which shouldn't work at all. It's an early song, taken from the Kilmarnock edition: *Song, Composed in August*, it says on Page 224. I have chosen it for no reason other than the fact that it is something of a personal favourite. Written when Burns was 16, it is, to my mind, a miracle of compressed writing.

> Now westlin winds, and slaught'ring guns
> Bring Autumn's pleasant weather;
> The moorcock springs, on whirring wings,

Amang the blooming heather:
Now waving grain, wide o'er the plain,
Delights the weary Farmer;
The moon shines bright, as I rove at night
To muse upon my Charmer.

This stanza is packed with details. The rhythm of the first two lines relies on heavily accented adjectives. The winds and guns are almost casually contrasted with the farmer, as day is contrasted with night. This astonishing ability comes from no untutored rustic; he uses internal rhyme, places figures in a landscape in four lines, then uses the landscape to launch an entirely separate, unheralded idea. And he does it again, following a couple of almost pedestrian stanzas:

The Pairtrick lo'es the fruitfu' fells;
The Plover lo'es the mountains;
The Woodcock haunts the lanely dells;
The soaring Hern the fountains:
Thro' lofty groves, the Cushat roves,
The path o' man to shun it;
The hazel bush o'erhangs the Thrush,
The spreading thorn the Linnet.

Wildlife is placed in a natural landscape, which, in the third stanza is threatened with the 'slaught'ring guns' of the first line. The detail of 'the flutt'ring, gory pinion' is to my mind very distinguished:

Thus ev'ry kind their pleasure find,
The savage and the tender;
Some social join, and leagues combine;
Some solitary wander:
Avaunt, away! the cruel sway,
Tyrannic man's dominion;
The Sportsman's joy, the murd'ring cry,
The flutt'ring, gory pinion!

Then come the last two verses, where the last line of the first stanza reaches to fruition, where the poet, Peggy Thomson and all are seen as part of a landscape where human beings are placed in a natural union with nature, which leads the poet to imply natural unions of another variety. The 'rapid transition' from 'the flutt'ring gory pinion' to 'Peggy dear' is a remarkable touch of genius, which not only signals the writer he would later become, but also needs to be heard for its impact to be fully appreciated:

But Peggy dear, the ev'ning's clear,
Thick flies the skimming Swallow;
The sky is blue, the fields in view

All fading-green and yellow:
Come let us stray our gladsome way
And view the charms o' Nature;
The rustling corn, the fruited thorn,
And ilka happy creature.

We'll gently walk, and sweetly talk,
While the silent moon shines clearly;
I'll clasp thy waist, and fondly prest
Swear how I lo'e thee dearly:
Not vernal show'rs to budding flow'rs,
Not Autumn to the Farmer,
So dear can be, as thou to me,
My fair, my lovely Charmer.

It was in the Kilmarnock edition that Burns asked his readers – 'particularly the Learned and the Polite, who may honour him with perusal, that they will make every allowance for Education and the Circumstances of Life.' And so the myth of the ploughman poet was born. The learned and polite took him at his word; successive generations of the ignorant and the impolite have followed their example.

Burns, of course, was being more than slightly disingenuous. Others have pointed out his learning, his reading, his subtle understanding of society, nature, human nature, words and music, folk tales and the accepted literary forms of his time. It is possible, I suppose, to persist with the fiction and all it implies, that part of the reason for his popularity is the fact that folk feel he was one of them, something again which the accessibility of his work has helped perpetuate.

It also, I suggest, gives a new slant to the national bard ideal. Rather than asking who will be our poet, are we not actually asking, Who will be us? Who will explain this country, its history, perspectives and positions in a way we can understand, in a way with which we can identify, and recognise and use as a benchmark for our thinking? Would that Burns were indeed a benchmark for contemporary thinking.

Which brings me to the place where Burns breaks free from this fiction, free from the unstated, maybe even unrecognised shackles we place on him by perpetuating the myth:

I don't know if you have a just idea of my character, but I wish you to see me as I am. – I am, as most people of my trade are, a strange will o'wisp being; the victim too frequently of much imprudence and many follies. – My great constituent elements are Pride and Passion: the first I have endeavoured to humanise into integrity and honour; the last makes me a Devotee to the warmest degree of enthusiasm, in Love, Religion, or Friendship; either of them or altogether as I happen to be inspired. – I think 'tis true I never saw you but once; but how much acquaintance did I form with you in that once! Don't think I flatter you, or think I have a design upon you.[17]

The letters are also where we find the working Burns, where he speaks to us directly. Here he emerges as many things, but I think especially as a man fully conscious of his learning, conscious of his considerable gifts, yet aware of the limitations his environment and station have placed upon him and upon the development and, more importantly, on the means of developing these powers.

We rarely see a clean copy. This is where he changes and amends his texts, can't stop himself from scoring out certain phrases, from balancing a sentence, from looking for the right word; where, more than is usual with any artist, we feel we come to know the man and what he thought; there are places where I feel we can even catch a glimpse of what his conversation might have been like.

These letters are, to my mind, comparable with the letters of Vincent van Gogh and Mozart in their directness and intensity, as well as for the insight they give into the way a great mind works. In his letters, Burns is thinking aloud.

It is certainly true that more than one Robert Burns emerges from the 700-odd published letters. But that is equally true of any such collection. Burns was obviously tied by the restraints of his time. As Tom Crawford has pointed out,[18] Burns was brought up to suit his style to the needs and personalities of his correspondents. Yet James De Lancey Ferguson's assertion is also correct, that the biographers of few modern authors are so dependent on their subjects' letters for knowledge and details of their lives as are those of Robert Burns.[19]

He knew how to approach those from whom he needed favours, especially the gentry. He was mindful that some of his letters would be kept – in fact, a surprising number were kept, and others have been subsequently lost – and indeed he showed the famous autobiographical letter, which he eventually sent to Dr. John Moore, to Mrs Frances Dunlop for her consideration. This is where Burns uses a highly polished prose to claim he is unpolished.

The letters are where Burns's industry becomes most evident. At times his energy seems almost demonic. And for what? To become a nation's favourite writer? To become a nation's misunderstood writer? Both, or a compromise: the writer to whom we look for our national identity.

Surely it is time for us to free him from his own and our impositions. It's the least we can do. He has given us so much.

It's time to set him free. We owe him his dignity.

NOTES

1. Adam Lindsay Gordon, *Poems* (London, 1894).
2. Edwin Morgan, 'A Poet's Response To Burns', *Burns Now*, edited by Kenneth Simpson (Edinburgh, 1994), p. 12.

3. Kenneth Simpson, *Why Read Burns?* Lecture to the Association for Scottish Literary Studies Schools Conference, October, 1993.

4. Allan Cunningham, *Life of Burns* (1834).

5. Hugh MacDiarmid, *A Drunk Man Looks at the Thistle*, annotated edition, edited by Kenneth Buthlay (Edinburgh, 1987).

6. Richard J. Finlay, 'The Burns Cult and Scottish Identity in the Nineteenth and Twentieth Centuries', *Love and Liberty* (East Linton, 1997), pp. 69–78.

7. Iain Crichton Smith, *Thoughts of Murdo* (Nairn, 1993).

8. Finlay, *ibid.*

9. For a diverse and comprehensive survey, with illustrations, see *Burnsiana*, James A. Mackay (Ayr, 1988).

10. Carol McGuirk, 'Burns and Nostalgia', *Burns Now*, pp. 31–69.

11. *Ibid.*

12. Kenneth Simpson, 'Robert Burns: "Heaven-taught ploughman?"', *Burns Now*, p. xviii.

13. Donald A. Low. '"My Tocher's the Jewel": Love and Money in the Songs of Burns', *Burns Now*, p. 127.

14. Sir Walter Scott, *Quarterly Review*, February, 1809, and almost annually thereafter.

15. Carl MacDougall (ed.), *The Devil and The Giro* (Edinburgh, 1989 and 1995).

16. Cedric Thorpe Davie, 'Robert Burns, Writer of Songs', *Critical Essays on Robert Burns*, edited by Donald A. Low (London, 1975).

17. J. De Lancey Ferguson and G. Ross Roy, *The Letters of Robert Burns*, 2 vols (Oxford, 1985).

18. Thomas Crawford, *Burns: A Study of the Poems and Songs* (Edinburgh, 1960 and 1994).

19. J. De Lancey Ferguson, *Selected Letters of Robert Burns* (Oxford, 1953).

Inmate of the Hamlet: Burns as Peasant Poet

M Y TITLE, 'Inmate of the Hamlet', is taken from a letter Burns wrote to Dr Moore in 1787. There, the poet declares his lasting allegiance to those considered his cultural peer-group:

> my first ambition was, and still my strongest wish is, to please my Compeers, the rustic Inmates of the Hamlet, while ever-changing language and manners will allow me to be relished and understood.[1]

By exploring the notion of Burns as an 'inmate of the hamlet' I hope to identify the precise ways in which his peasant affiliations affected the poet. In addition, I will consider the lasting influence the 'heaven-taught ploughman' image exerted on Burns's compeers and their poetic descendants.

Scotland has enjoyed a long and noble tradition of working-class writing. The 'hamlet' provided a rich vein of traditional material for Burns to work, from songs to narratives, customs, beliefs and subjects for satire. However, as the word 'inmate' suggests, there was a repressive side to being considered as a 'rustic' phenomenon. The term 'heaven-taught ploughman', invented by Henry Mackenzie in *The Lounger* of 1786 (with a nod to Beattie's 'heaven-taught' Minstrel), is deeply ambiguous. Despite the obvious compliment, the term neglects important aspects of the poet's creativity. Not least, it minimises Burns's knowledge of literary traditions. The 'heaven-taught ploughman' label, drawing on prototypes like Ramsay's 'gentle shepherd' and Macpherson's Ossian, precariously typecast Burns and his self-taught successors. The 'peasant' poet, from a humble background with minimal formal education, would be perceived as a curiosity: inherently inferior and unsophisticated.[2]

Mackenzie's critique typifies a set of aesthetic assumptions applied to the self-taught. The 'divinity of genius' he saw in Burns was accorded to autodidacts thereafter: double-edged praise implying a lack of conscious artistry. In a similar way, the *Monthly Review* of 1786 admired Burns's 'artless simplicity'. Drawing attention to the writer's 'humble and unlettered station' Mackenzie stated Burns should be patronised: 'to call forth genius ... and place it where it may profit or delight the world; these are exertions which give to wealth an enviable superiority'. The argument Burns deserved charity, even if well meant, did no real favours. Disliking the poems in Scots (read 'even in Scotland' with difficulty), Mackenzie preferred 'almost English' pieces like 'The Vision' and

'To a Mountain Daisy'. These, presumably, showed God's hand on Burns as opposed to those in mundane 'provincial dialect'.[3]

Burns did, of course, collaborate in creating his myth. Robert Anderson, in 1799, noted the ploughman's consummate role-playing:

> It was ... a part of the machinery, as he called it, of his poetical character to pass for an illiterate ploughman ... in company he did not suffer his pretensions to pure inspiration to be challenged, and it was seldom done where it might be supposed to affect the success of the subscription for his *Poems*.[4]

No doubt economic, and even more complex, motivations, affected Burns's presentation for public and semi-public consumption. The self-styled 'Professor of the Belles [*sic*] Lettres de la Nature' (*Letters* i, 73) offered a volatile mix of learned ingenuity.

Burn's correspondence, moreover, suggests what would become a characteristic peasant-poet blend. A resistance to debasing himself, for the benefit of patrons, is combined with an understandable desire to please. Preparing to depart for Jamaica in 1786, Burns complained to Mrs Stewart of Stair about social expectations: 'The obscure Bard, when any of the Great condescend to take notice of him, should heap the altar with the incense of flattery'. If only 'those in exalted stations' realised how their 'condescension & affability' pleased 'their Inferiours' they would treat Burns as well as Mrs Stewart (*Letters* i, 53). At times like this the ploughman-poet role let Burns endear himself, as an unthreatening rustic, to lofty ladies. In a similar way, refining the peasant-poet position as neo-classical Sylvander, Burns claimed spiritual kinship with Mrs McLehose. Together, they were: 'a Poet and Poetess of Nature's making' (*Letters* i, 211).

It was necessary to maintain a finely-drawn balance, when dealing with those who thought themselves socially elevated, to avoid giving offence. In May 1787, recognising the 'benevolence' of his patron Glencairn with the required blend of worth and humility, Burns attributed his success to 'Your good family', avowing 'not selfish design' but his 'devotion' (*Letters* i, 113). After Glencairn's death in 1791, Burns gave a similar assurance to John, the new Earl (*Letters* ii, 191). More openly, to John Gillespie, excise officer, Burns regretted the difficulties he now faced in gaining promotion. While there are no grounds for believing the admiration for Glencairn insincere, Burns's mourning had a poignant twist: 'Among the many wise adages which have been treasured up by our Scotish Ancestors, this is one of the best – "Better be the head o' the Commonality, as the tail o' the Gentry"' (*Letters* ii, 74).

The correspondence with Mrs Dunlop of Dunlop is even more intriguing, revealing Burns's irritation with suspicious patrons (Mrs Dunlop's critical advice surely rankled). He becomes highly defensive at her claim that he will 'grow intoxicated with [his] prosperity as a poet'. On the contrary, Burns asserted, 'to be dragged forth to the full glare of learned and polite observation, with all my imperfections of awkward rusticity and crude unpolished ideas ... I tremble for the consequences'. Drawing attention to 'the novelty of a poet in my obscure situation', Burns feared the 'tide of public notice', unsupported by 'advantages' would 'recede' (*Letters* i, 85).[5] The letter, blending independence and melancholic passivity, convinced Mrs Dunlop (temporarily) of Burns's integrity.

Wooing the *literati*, and their acolytes, meant treading a fine line between subservience and friendliness. Burns expressed his predicament succinctly to Mrs Dunlop in 1789. It is tempting to speculate this is a frank confession but there may be a little posturing on the part of the offended innocent:

> God help a poor man! for if he take a pecuniary favor from a friend with that acquiescence which is natural to Poverty ... the poor devil is in the greatest danger of falling into an abjectness of soul equally incompatible with the independence of Man and the dignity of Friendship; on the other hand, should he bristle up his feelings [like (*deleted*)] in irritated Manhood, he runs every chance of degrading his [heart (*deleted*)] magnaminity into an exceptious pride. (*Letters* i, 451)

I do not mean to deny that Burns faced real obstacles to creativity due to his poverty and manner of employment. Certainly, he expressed great anxiety relating to semi-professional poetic status. Deploring his treatment of Jean Armour in 1786, Burns termed himself a 'worthless, rhyming reprobate' (*Letters* i, 9)' 'a rhyming, mason-making, raking, aimless, idle fellow' to James Smith in 1787 (*Letters* i, 126). There is manifest, heart-rending evidence of the effects of financial crises, like the letter to George Thomson of 1796, pleading for five pounds to pay the 'scoundrel of a Haberdasher' and avoid jail (*Letters* ii 389). Sending three guineas to the bookseller Peter Hill in 1791, Burns wrote with despair, and some prickliness (characteristic of later peasant poets):

> Poverty! Thou half-sister of Death, thou cousin-german of Hell ... – By thee the Man of Genius whose ill-starred ambition plants him at the tables of the Fashionable & Polite, must see in suffering silence his remark neglected & his person despised, while shallow Greatness in his idiot attempts at wit shall meet with countenance & applause. (*Letters* i, 65).

The 'simple plough-boy' (*Letters*, i, 343A), while playing up to the heaven-taught ploughman image, hugely resented it. At times, he overstepped the bounds of what was considered to be suitable behaviour for a peasant. Abject apologies followed, as in the letter 'from the regions of Hell' to Mrs Robert Riddell. Damned for 'the impropriety of my conduct yesternight under your roof', Burns offers 'humblest contrition'. He adds, 'my errors, though great, were involuntary – an intoxicated man is the vilest of beasts ... to be rude to a woman, when in my senses, was impossible with me' (*Letters* ii, 272). This anticipates Lockhart's account of Hogg's impropriety, when 'hauf-seas-over', in addressing Scott as 'Wattie' and Mrs Scott as 'Charlotte' though Burns, perhaps, offended more blatantly.[6]

Seen in this context, Burns's work is a potent mixture of accepting and rejecting the peasant-poet image. On the one hand, he excelled in scenes of rural life from 'Halloween' to 'Tam o' Shanter' (*Poems*, 73, 321). The Muse of 'The Vision' (*Poems*, 62), with her 'wildly-witty, rustic grace' proved a successful type for working-class writers. Hogg's comic Muse in *The Spy* (1810) is very similar to this.[7] 'The Cotter's Saturday Night' (*Poems*, 72) became a peasant-poet anthem, offering a prototype scene of 'hamlet' life:

> To you I sing, in simple Scottish lays,
>   The *lowly train* in life's seqester'd scene;
> The native feelings strong, the guileless ways,
>   What A**** in a *Cottage* would have been;
> Ah! tho' his worth unknown, far happier there I ween!

The 'toil-worn COTTER', a pious father surrounded by bairns, including a nubile daughter, supping on '*Porritch*', was a powerful model for peasant representations of their world. Few autodidacts escaped its influence, even educated autodidacts like John Leyden and David Gray (university-taught yet considered peasant poets on the grounds of rustic origins).

There are strong hints the poet of 'Scots Wha Hae' (*Poems*, 425) and 'For a' that and a' that' (*Poems*, 482) parallelled his belief, 'The rank is but the guinea's stamp', with his predicament as a peasant poet. In 'The Twa Dogs' (*Poems*, 71) dependant cotters are: 'huff'd, an' cuff'd, an' disrespeket!' by the gentry (paralleling the peasant poet's precarious state). As Caesar says: 'But *human-bodies* are sic fools,/For a' their Colledges an' Schools'. Perhaps 'A Fragment – On Glenriddel's Fox breaking his chain' (*Poem*, 527), too, is allegorical of Burns's position as heaven-taught ploughman. The theme is 'Liberty'; the situation: 'a fox,/ ... caught among his native rocks,/ ... to a dirty kennel chain'd'. This Northern (like the Burnesses) fox canvassed for 'The Rights of Men, the Powers of Women', recalling both Paine and 'The Rights of Women' (*Poems*, 390). By listening, the fox learnt about politics and 'Nature's Magna charta'. It 'Suck'd in a mighty store of knowledge./As much as some folks at a college' and won freedom from its enforced patronage.

'On the death of Echo, a Lap-Dog' (*Poems*, 416) and the pithy tribute, probably by Burns, 'On a dog of Lord Eglintons' (*Poems*, 622), equally sum up the 'heaven-taught ploughman' role, with biting irony:

> I NEVER barked when out of season,
>   I never bit without a reason;
>   . . . .
> We brutes are placed a rank below;
>   Happy for man could he say so.

It is in this light an anecdote from Joseph Train's notes of 1829–30 should be read. Burns, feted in Edinburgh, was encouraged to join a certain company: 'he, at last, observed, "On one condition I shall come. [*sic*] It is that you secure the Learned Pig also to be of the Party." – The Learned Pig was exhibiting in Edinr. at that time'.[8] (Coincidentally, Hogg would be depicted as the 'boar' of Ettrick).

However ridiculous it is to consider Burns solely as a 'heaven-taught ploughman', the dogma was increasingly held. Currie's biography established stereotypical elements in Burns which conformed to national attributes. The 'Scottish Peasantry', apparently, possessed 'intelligence' without equal:

> In the very humblest condition of the Scottish peasants, every one can read, and most persons are more or less, skilled in writing and arithmetic; and, under the disguise of their uncouth appearance, and of their peculiar manner and dialect, a stranger will discover that they possess a curiosity, and have obtained a degree of information, corresponding to these acquirements.

This palatable picture had crucial effects on the image of the peasant poet. Currie asserted the national Muse's attraction to love. The identification of the oral and, by extension, peasant tradition with a lyric tendency would become a commonplace of 'peasant poet' theory. Burns, in this context, was the archetypal Scottish peasant: raised by a religious father and tradition-bearer mother; devoted family-man. While the biographer was right to stress such formative influences, the composite is part fact, part 'Cotter's Saturday Night'.[9]

Currie offers evidence of urbane qualities in Burns (from Dugald Stewart, for instance) but the lasting impression is of the peasant poet who, despite changed circumstances, 'might ... still be seen in the spring, directing his plough, a labour in which he excelled'. For Currie, Burns's peasant affiliations led to 'rudeness' in rhyme, 'strange and uncouth' language and 'repulsive' first impressions mitigated by underlying 'sentiment'. Currie wonders how far Burns might have approached Ariosto, Shakespeare or Voltaire, 'by proper culture, with lengthened years, and under happier auspices'; simultaneously refuting and affirming peasant-poet theory. This codified the process begun by Mackenzie.[10]

Swiftly two aspects of the heaven-taught ploughman appeared. First there was the inspired poet of nature. He moved fully formed from Mackenzie and Currie into R. H. Cromek's *Reliques of Robert Burns* (1808). Cromek appreciated 'the wild-flowers of his muse' unabashedly. The *Eclectic Review* of 1809 likened Burns to a 'poetical Franklin', who 'caught his lightnings from the cloud while it passed over his head and ... communicated them, too, by a touch, with electrical swiftness and effect'. Burns had fortunately only experienced 'partial education': 'higher cultivation would unquestionably have called forth richer and fairer harvests, but it would have so softened away the wild and magnificent diversity'.[11]

Then there was the emphasis on 'Rantin, rovin Robin', drawing Currie's 'dissipated' strand into a view which offended the 'Unco Guid'. Jeffrey, reviewing Cromek's *Reliques* in the *Edinburgh Review* of 1809, raged: 'it is a vile prostitution of language to talk of that man's generosity or goodness of heart, who sits raving about friendship and philanthropy in a tavern, while his wife's heart is breaking'. The only excuse was in 'the original lowness of his situation'. Scott, in *The Quarterly Review* of 1809, was indulgently superior: as 'the child of impulse and feeling', Burns was incapable of sustaining 'the steady principle which cleaves to that which is good'. Burns's soul was 'plebeian' and he lacked the 'chivalry' Scott prized because of 'the lowness of his birth'.[12]

There were, of course, attempts to reject such wilful misrepresentations. Alexander Peterkin's *Review of the Life of Robert Burns* (1815) did not see the poet as 'immaculate and perfect' but decried, in Currie, 'pedantry ... which induces persons of circumscribed habits to regard all beyond the little circle of their own movement ... as low'. Peterkin disliked 'assumptions and errors in reference to "the Scottish rustic"', particularly the presentation of Burns as one of a band of peasant poets: 'a poetical prodigy, on a level with Stephen Duck, and Thomas Dermody; men, the glimmering of whose genius are extinct'. Peterkin raged at the applied epithet 'plebeian poet', given 'the high soul, the manly, sublime, and truly British spirit of Robert Burns'. Among the evidence Peterkin cites is a letter from David Gray, drawing attention to Burns's 'singularly hard' fate. Certain critics, according to Gray, contributed to the poet's demise, by 'caricature' portraits.[13] Gray was not only Burns's friend but Hogg's brother-in-law, possibly offering the persona, and its inherent grievances, first-hand to the Ettrick Shepherd.

Lockhart, whose *Peter's Letters to his Kinsfolk* (1819) contributed to the creation of the Ettrick Shepherd myth, exhibited some sense in *The Life of Robert Burns* (1828). Burns is presented as a wholly romanticised peasant poet through a reading dedicated to his supposed acolytes, Hogg and Allan Cunningham. Astutely, Lockhart notes Burns's self-awareness: 'how soon even really Bucolic Bards learn the tricks of their trade'. There is justification, too, to the inspirational picture Lockhart produces of Burns, in relation to his peasant compatriots. 'The Cotter's Saturday Night', especially, is admired by Lockhart, for fostering among '"the first-born of Egypt" ... feelings which would never have been developed within their being, had there been no Burns'.[14]

Allan Cunningham, the Nithsdale Mason, was among those 'inmates of the hamlet' who drew inspiration from Burns. Cunningham exhibits a great deal of sensitivity in *The Works of Robert Burns* (1834). He decries Jeffrey's implication Burns was coarse: 'I see the reluctance of an accomplished scholar to admit the merits of a rustic poet who not only claimed, but took, the best station on the Caledonian Parnassus'. Man and poet are almost identical for Cunningham; sustaining this idea a later, illustrated version of his edition has plates with the poet 'in situ'. Burns is portrayed as a living character in 'Green Grow the Rashes O' and 'A Man's a Man for a' that'.[15]

James Hogg on Burns seemed an obvious project, given the supposed affinity between peasant poets but, although Hogg visited Jean Armour for first-hand research, his main sources were Lockhart and Cunningham. The posthumous *Memoir* (1836) of Burns is, perhaps, more of interest for the light it sheds on the Ettrick Shepherd's notion of the peasant poet, than on Burns. By-now-standard biographical details had profound influences on Hogg's self-presentation as a man with six weeks' schooling, writing on the hillside as he tended his sheep. Hogg discerned scholarly 'jealousy' as interfering with the appreciation of his own work. Hogg dismissed moralistic judgements on the poet, drawing attention, like Scott, to the 'strong passions' which informed Burn's nature and made him 'the splendid meteor of our imagination'. There are implicit parallels, too, between peasant-poet identities and that of the Good shepherd.[16]

During the nineteenth century Burns's life was often imbued with a Christ-like quality. Henry Shanks, in his seminal *The Peasant Poets of Scotland* (1881), has Burns born in 'a humble clay biggin' without 'public rejoicing', as 'Nature's great high priest'. Scots should, 'remember his teaching ... and with their hearts attuned to praise evince their love to God, to man, and to the world, in singing by turns the psalms of David and the songs of Burns'. Such images were sustained and reinforced through iconography: the prints of Burns at the plough, for instance, divine inspiration descending on his head; sanctified and sublime, in direct contact with the Muse. The Nasmyth portrait was adapted and sentimentalised into statues throughout Scotland's major cities. Take, for instance, the 1891 statue in Union Terrace, Aberdeen. There, Burns holds a 'mountain daisy' in his left hand, a large bonnet in his right, and stands simpering, his hair side-parted as in Nasmyth. Such a latter-day noble savage provided an attractive image at home and abroad.[17]

The prototype of a heaven-taught ploughman did offer real encouragement to Scottish poets of a like background. Contemporary 'compeers' of Burns, like 'Daintie' David Sillar, purloined the image for themselves. Sillar stressed that he was a true peasant poet, in his 'Epistle to the Critics':

> I n'er depended for my knowledge
> On school, academy, nor college,
> I gat my learning' at the flail,
> An' some I catch'd at the plough-tail.

Despite the Epistles to Sillar, J. Lapraik and Simson, written before his rise to fame, Burns was less than wholly encouraging to those who tried to jump on his bandwagon. He ignored, for instance, two pedestrian 'Epistles' from the tailor Thomas Walker. Nor was the heaven-taught ploughman particularly helpful to Janet Little 'The Scotch Milkmaid', a protégée of his own patron,

Mrs Dunlop.[18] Such examples question how far the popular poet supported fellow autodidacts.

Nevertheless, the image of 'heaven-taught ploughman', as well as inspiring a host of the poet's 'rhyming friends', was hugely influential on later working-class poets. Hogg claimed to be Burns's natural successor, on more than one occasion. Others agreed. Paralleling 'Burns and the Ettrick Shepherd' in *Blackwood's Magazine* (1819), Wilson thought Scotland the greatest nation in the world for 'peasant poets'. Hogg's strength (and limitations) lay in peasant traditions, relating to 'nature': 'in the imitation of the ancient ballad – and in that wild poetry which deals with imaginary beings'. Scott, and Shanks, considered Hogg to be educationally disadvantaged beyond Burns. For Shanks, Hogg was: 'the only known eminent Shepherd-poet since the days of the sweet singer of Israel', a comparison Hogg made himself. 'The Ettrick Shepherd' would act as a transmission model for later autodidacts.[19]

The product of Burns's image as 'inmate of the hamlet' was what might cynically be termed a 'cottage industry', with workshops of 'weaver poets' in Galloway, 'shepherd poets' in the Borders, and the 'artisan poets' of central Scotland. Even a railway 'Surfaceman' like Alexander Anderson (later chief librarian of Edinburgh University Library) adapted elements of Burns's image into his poetic persona, posing for photographs with pick (rather than plough) in hand. A parallel tradition developed in England, with poets like Ann Yearsley and John Jones, many documented in Robert Southey's *The Lives and Works of the Uneducated Poets* (1831). John Clare was fascinated by Burns's work and life and composed several poems, in Scots, after Burns. Intriguingly, *Blackwood's Magazine* considered Clare as part of a peasant-poet quorum whose other members were Burns, Hogg and Cunningham.[20]

Autodidacts contributed to their own mythologising. From Hogg's 'Memoir' to Janet Hamilton on 'Self-Education' to John Younger's *Autobiography* (1881) a standard tale is told. Grim, hard working-lives are portrayed, replete with struggles and persistence in writing. Without minimising genuine hardships, it seems that such an emphasis was designed to construct near-hagiographical accounts derived from Burns's life. Financial failure was inevitable because of devotion to the Muses. Despite the odd sexual indiscretion (among men at least) peasant poets were expected to be family stalwarts in the tradition of 'The Cotter's Saturday Night'. Periods of ill health were stressed and, paradoxically, early death in the manner of Burns, experienced by Leyden and Gray, ensured some critical attention. This all contributed to the 'lad o' pairts' myth popularised by the kailyard school.[21]

Burns's treatment as the first, great, 'inmate of the hamlet', had dual implications. The *literati*'s patronising attitude, on one hand, meant self-taught poets were encouraged into marginalising 'rustic' styles. MacDiarmid thought the idea of 'Burns as a "ploughman poet" has been fatal', and dismissed Scottish autodidactic poetry as 'crambo-clink'. Tom Leonard, in *Radical Renfrew*, has demonstrated the persistent, negative influence of academic condescension on autodidactic poets. Modern critics, though, from Mary Ellen Brown to Kenneth Simpson, are attuned to the capacity for role-playing which affected Burns and, to a lesser extent, his 'compeers'. On a positive note, too, the idea of the 'inmate of the hamlet', if not strictly applicable to Burns, allowed a rise in poetic confidence among the genuinely self-taught. Writers, from the Scotch Milkmaid Janet Little to the Liberal Baillie James Young Geddes, drew creative energy from the achievements of their fellow 'inmate'. Encouraged by the example of Burns, poets like Ellen Johnson, 'The Factory Girl', and the gardener's daughter, Elizabeth Hartley, expressed themselves in locally-focused, innovative verse.[22] While, then, the 'inmate of the hamlet' notion interfered with the appreciation of Burns and his compeers, the 'heaven-taught ploughman' facilitated a new crop of writing, ripe for reassessment.

NOTES

1. J. De Lancey Ferguson and G. Ross Roy (eds), *The Letters of Robert Burns*, 2 vols (Oxford, 1985), i, 88. Hereafter references to Burns's *Letters* are given within the text in parentheses.
2. *The Lounger*, 97 (9 Dec. 1786), reprinted by Donald A. Low (ed.), *Robert Burns, The Critical Heritage* (London, 1974), p. 4.
3. Mackenzie, repr. Low, p. 4.; Introduction, pp. 16–17. James Kinsley (ed.), *The Poems and Songs of Robert Burns*, 3 vols (Oxford, 1968), Nos 62, 92. Hereafter references to Burns's *Poems* are given within the text in parenthesis. Anderson, reprinted Low, p. 5.
4. Anderson, quoted in Low, pp. 8–9.
5. See William Wallace (ed.), *Robert Burns and Mrs Dunlop* (London, 1898).
6. J. G. Lockhart, *The Life of Sir Walter Scott, Bart* (1837–8; reprinted Edinburgh, 1900), vol. 1, pp. 357–58.
7. See James Hogg, 'Mr Shuffleton's Allegorical Survey of the Scottish Poets of the Present Day', *The Spy*, 8 Sept. 1810, 29 Sept. 1810, 2 Nov. 1810.
8. Train Ms, in Robert H. Fitzhugh (ed.), *Robert Burns. His Associates and Contemporaries* (Chapel Hill, North Carolina, 1943), p. 59.
9. James Currie, *The Works of Robert Burns* (1800); reprinted in 2 vols (Montrose, 1816), i p. 3, p. 13.
10. Currie, pp. 158–59, pp. 214–15, p. 268.
11. R. H. Cromek, *Reliques of Robert Burns*, 4th edn (1817), p. iv; James Montgomery, *Eclectic Review*, reprinted Low, p. 42.
12. Francis Jeffrey, reprinted Low, p. 39; Walter Scott, reprinted Low, p. 40.
13. Alexander Peterkin, *A Review of the Life of Robert Burns* (Edinburgh, 1815), p. xiv, p. li, p. lvii, p. lxviii–lxix. Gray quoted in Peterkin, pp. lxxxiii–xci.
14. See John Gibson Lockhart, *The Life of Robert Burns* (1828); reprinted by William Scott Douglas (ed.), 2 vols (Liverpool, 1914), i, p. 92, p. 106; ii, pp. 202–3.
15. See Allan Cunningham (ed.), *The Works of Robert Burns; with his Life*, 8 vols (London, 1834), i, pp. 365–78. See Allan Cunningham (ed.), *The Complete Works of Burns Illustrated* (London, n.d.).

16. The Ettrick Shepherd and William Motherwell (eds), *The Works of Robert Burns*, 5 vols (Glasgow, 1834–1836), v, especially pp. 1–11, p. 44, p. 63. See James Hogg, 'Memoir of the Life of James Hogg', prefacing *The Mountain Bard* (Edinburgh and London, 1807; revised Edinburgh and London, 1821).

17. Henry Shanks, *The Peasant Poets of Scotland* (Bathgate, 1881), p. 4, p. 31. See illustrations in Carol McGuirk, 'Burns and Nostalgia', Kenneth Simpson (ed.), *Burns Now* (Edinburgh, 1994), Chapter 3.

18. See John D. Ross, *Robert Burns and his Rhyming Friends* (Stirling, 1928), [James Paterson], *The Contemporaries of Burns* (Edinburgh, 1840), p. 38. See Valentina Bold, 'Janet Little "The Scotch Milkmaid" and "Peasant Poetry"', *Scottish Literary Journal*, vol. 20 (Nov. 1993), pp. 21–30.

19. John Wilson, repr. Low, p. 59. Scott, repr. Low, p. 50. Shanks, p. 94; See Hogg's 1821 'Memoir', p. lxviii.

20. Robert Southey, *the Lives and Works of the Uneducated Poets* 1831, reprinted by J. S. Childers (ed.) (London, 1925). See, for instance, Clare's 'Coy Maidens o' Drysail', *The Later Poems of John Clare*, edited by Eric Robinson and David Powell, 2 vols (Oxford, 1984), ii, 843; and Valentina Bold, 'James Hogg and the Scottish Self-Taught Tradition', John Goodridge (ed.), *The Independent Spirit, John Clare and the self-taught tradition* (Helpston, 1994), pp. 69–86. See John Wilson, *Noctes Ambrosianae*, 4 vols (Edinburgh, 1863), i, p. 218.

21. See John Younger, *The Autobiography of John Younger, Shoemaker, St Boswell's* (Kelso, 1881); Janet Hamilton, *Poems, Sketches and Essays* (Glasgow, 1885), pp. 435–47.

22. See Hugh MacDiarmid, *Scottish Eccentrics* (1936; reprinted London, 1972), p. 64; *The Scotsman* (25th Nov. 1959), quoted in Alan Bold (ed.), *The Letters of Hugh MacDiarmid* (London, 1984), p. 80; Tom Leonard, *Radical Renfrew* (Edinburgh, 1990); Mary Ellen Brown, *Burns and Tradition* (London, 1984), Kenneth Simpson. *The Protean Scot* (Aberdeen, 1988).

'The Mair They Talk, I'm Kend the Better': Poems About Robert Burns to 1859

ANY STUDENT of Robert Burns will know that the writing about the poet seems to be without end: scholarly books and articles, entries in magazines, guidebooks to the poet's haunts, newspaper accounts, novels, plays, radio and television scripts, movies—and of course poems. They all bear witness to the enduring fame of the Bard. I have chosen to discuss some of the poems which have been written to honor him. Not all of them are good, few are memorable, but they all bear witness to the fact that Burns is a poet who has attracted other poets' attention.

Even before his death there were poems about Burns; in a fashion the rhyming epistles which he received from Thomas Blacklock, Janet Little, David Sillar and others are poems about him. Some of these we know were actually sent to the poet, probably they all were. During his lifetime, too, there were poems about Burns in chapbooks. James Maxwell's *Animadversions on Some Poets and Poetasters of the Present Age Especially R—t B—s, and J—n L—k* (for John Lapraik) which was published in Paisley in 1788, with a poem entitled 'On the Ayrshire Ploughman Poet, or Poetaster, R. B.' as well as Alexander Tait's *Poems and Songs* of 1790, with three scurrilous poems about Burns, are instances of early chapbook literature about him—all four of these poems, one may note, are unfavorable to Burns. He ignored most of these attacks, but his fame was such that poems attributed to him began to appear. He complained about these bogus works in a letter to John Francis Erskine in 1793 and also to an unnamed correspondent in 1795 concerning the Patrick Heron election campaign.

Selections from Burns's poetry appeared in one of the most successful collections, *Poetry; Original and Selected*, published by the Glasgow firm Brash & Reid. One of the earliest of these chapbooks was devoted to 'Tam o' Shanter', published in 1795. The next number contained 'The Soldier's Return' which was a perennial favorite during and shortly after the Napoleonic Wars. By the time the series was into its second volume (there were 24 chapbooks per volume) Burns had died. The first seven chapbooks of Volume II are devoted in whole or in part to eulogies in prose or verse to Burns, and to selections of his poems and songs. As I have examined this material elsewhere, I shall not repeat it here.[1] The whole question of Burns and chapbook literature would certainly repay attention, but would be far too lengthy for a paper such as this one.

The next event which requires our notice was the publication in 1800 of James Currie's four-volume *Works of Robert Burns; With an Account of his Life*, an edition of such importance that every one since it owes a major debt to Currie's efforts. With the good there also came some bad, for in his enthusiasm to promote the edition for the benefit of Jean Armour Burns and her children, Currie suppressed and altered documents, giving rise to misconceptions about Burns's life which were not corrected until this century. What is important for this paper is that a minor writer of historical works and children's literature, William Roscoe, had his poem 'On the Death of Burns' appear in Currie. Also included in subsequent editions of Currie, the poem was later reprinted in dozens of editions of the poet; I would venture that Roscoe's elegy is the most frequently published poem about Burns, so often that I do not intend to spend time on it here. There are other poets whom I shall exclude because their work is too well known to require attention in a paper such as this one. Among them are Thomas Campbell, Wordsworth, Coleridge, James Montgomery, James Hogg, Longfellow, and several others.

To show how far afield such poems can go, the University of South Carolina has in its library an untitled 39-line poem addressed to James Currie, congratulating him upon the publication of his edition of Burns, signed Willie Pender Porcupine (probably William Shepherd, 1768–1847). Equally idiosyncratic is a MS poem in my collection entitled 'Australia's Memorial to Robert Burns' with the dedication 'To the Canberra Burns Memorial Fund ... for the erection at the Federal Capital of a worthy memorial to the Poet.'

I shall concentrate in this paper on early nineteenth-century poems about Burns because these, like early criticism of the poet, give us an instructive insight into what early authors thought were Burns's strengths and weaknesses, what events in his life were important. These writers set the tone for what was to come.

The year 1801 saw the appearance in print of several poems about Burns, quite possibly a spin-off of James Currie's 1800 edition of the poet's works. One of these was the re-appearance of Elizabeth Scot's 1787 poem to Burns and his answer, which had, in fact, first appeared in Currie. The two poems were re-published in Scot's *Alonzo and Cora* where there was joined to them a third rhyming epistle by Thomas Blacklock, who had died in 1791. Oddly Blacklock addressed Scot as though she had been critical of Burns, although her epistle to him had been most cordial. Blacklock's poem opens:

> Dear Madam, hear a suppliant's pray'r,
> And on our bard your censure spare,
> Whase bluntness slights ilk trivial care
>   Of mock decorum:[2]

The epistle must have been written between February 1787, when Scot sent her epistle to Burns, and 1789, when she died; the poem was first published in *Alonzo and Cora*. It is interesting to find a reference during this time frame to a perceived decline in Burns's poetic abilities. Blacklock writes: 'This by-past time, as fame reports, / The author's Muse was out of sorts' (p. 162). On 24 August 1789 Blacklock, in a rhyming epistle to Burns, hints at this problem when he mentions that he would '... wish to know ... Whether the Muse persists to smile, / And all thy anxious cares beguile?'[3] In his rhymed reply written two months later, Burns did admit to being 'scant o' verse and scant o' time' (I, 491) and indeed Kinsley ascribes only 33 poems and songs to that year.

Currie's edition of 1800 with its 2,000 copies, and reprints in each of the three successive years (in addition to an American edition in 1801), meant that the poet's work was very well known throughout Great Britain and America at the beginning of the nineteenth century. We are not, therefore, surprised to find a poem entitled 'Addressed to Mrs. Dunlop of Dunlop: On Reading Burns's Letters to that Lady' in a book of Mrs. Ann Grant's poems published in 1803. Mrs. Dunlop is, of course, the friend and confidante of Burns, and Currie had been given access to both portions of their numerous correspondence while preparing his edition. True to the tone of the letters, in which Mrs. Dunlop frequently received confessions from the poet, and answered as would a mother to her erring son, Mrs. Grant's poem stresses this quality in the correspondence. Whenever Burns needed it, Frances Dunlop:

> Consol'd him with the name of *Friend*:
>
> That name, his best and dearest boast,
>   Whene'er his erring steps would stray,
> Rever'd, belov'd, and honour'd most,
>   Recall'd him back to wisdom's way.
>
> And when the wounds of Anguish bled,
>   Thy kindness dropt the healing balm;
> And when the storm of Passion fled,
>   Thy counsel breath'd the sacred calm.[4]

Mrs. Grant devotes more than half of the 84-line poem to singing the praises of the Dunlop family, with its connections to Wallace, Mrs. Dunlop's maiden name. It will be recalled that Burns named his second son (1789–1803) Francis Wallace in honor of Frances Dunlop:

> And while, through all her winding vales
>   Sad SCOTIA for her poet mourns,
> And far as Britain's conquering sails
>   Extends the deathless name of BURNS:
>
>   (Grant, p. 270)

A further poem, 'On the Death of Burns,' is to be found in the collection. The author nods to the poets Collins and Shenstone, but not Pope, as influences on Burns, but she astutely recognizes where the major influence lies:

> And RAMSAY, once the HORACE of the North,
> Who charm'd with varied strains the listening *Forth*,
> Bequeath'd to him the shrewd peculiar art
> To Satire nameless graces to impart,
> To wield her weapons with such sportive ease,
> That, while they wound, they dazzle and they please:
>
> (pp. 262–3)

The poetess perceives Burns's later life as one of licentiousness and debauchery, with the result that

> The blushing Muse indignant scorns his lays,
> And fortune frowns, and honest fame decays,
> Till low on earth he lays his sorrowing head,
> And sinks untimely 'midst the vulgar dead!
>
> (p. 264)

Jean is mentioned first as victim of the poet's folly and then the poem ends with the plea to

> ... let the stream of bounty flow for JEAN!
> The mourning matron and her infant train,
> Will own you did not love the Muse in vain,
> While Sympathy with liberal hand appears,
> To aid the Orphan's wants, and dry the Widow's tears!
>
> (p. 265)

In addition to these two poems, Mrs. Grant included five pages of 'Remarks on the Character of Burns' which may be summed up in her words: 'I do not know whether most to pity or admire BURNS. Why were such people made?' (p. 259)

A year before Mrs. Grant's poems appeared, John Gerrond produced a small volume entitled *Poems on Several Occasions* with the subtitle, yet again, *Chiefly in the Scottish Dialect*. Born in 1765, the author was a blacksmith in Leith, but he had obviously travelled because his epistle 'to Robert Burns' bears a note that it was 'written in the State of Pennsylvania, in ... 1797'.[5] According to Gerrond, inhabitants were amazed that such a one as Burns could have written the poetry ascribed to him: 'They asked me whiles if it was true,/That you were bred up to the plough' (p. 49). The author vouches for the fact:

> But I maintain'd 'twas true ye said,
> In youth ye were to ploughing bred,
> An' now ye've taen the gaging trade,
> Altho' sae bitter   (p. 49)

even though Burns does not enjoy the employment according to Gerrond. The poem is addressed to Burns as though he were alive and the author admits, 'Your footsteps here, you see, I trace' (p. 48). He mentions that Burns's poems are well known in America, but complains:

> Yet some forget their mother tongue,
> Can read it but unco hum-drum,
> But when ever I alang-side come,
>   I rattle't o'er   (p. 49).

According to Gerrond, he is particularly suited to such recitation because he hails from the town where the poet lives—Dumfries, we may assume. The poem ends with the author's fondest wish—to be acknowledged 'A brither Poet' by Burns.

James Thomson, a weaver in Kenleith, published in 1801 a poem in the Habbie Simson stanza which shows the author's familiarity with Ramsay as well as Burns:

> Come, hing your heads, ye poets a',
> An' let the tears in plenty fa',
> Since death has ta'en Rob Burns awa,
>   That canty callan;
> O! sic a loss we never saw,
>   Sin we lost Allan.[6]

Born in 1763, Thomson grew up knowing the works of Ramsay over whose songs he would 'pour with delight ... and on his Gentle Shepherd (... most of which he ... could repeat from memory) he would dwell with rapture ...' (p. iv). Although Thomson does not mention Fergusson in the introduction to his *Poems in the Scottish Dialect*, he includes a poem on meeting a gentleman at the gravestone of the poet. It is an irony, of which Thomson was probably unaware, that it was Burns who had ordered and eventually paid for the stone.

D[avid?] Bruce in that same year also borrowed the title of his book from Burns for a volume issued in Washington, Pennsylvania. A native of Caithness, Bruce included some interesting poems on that still largely unsettled part of the state as well as satires on its few inhabitants. The collection contains two poems on Burns: the first, 'Verses to the Memory of Robert Burns', can be passed over. The second, 'Verses on Reading the Poems of Robert Burns,' in broad Scots, humorously catalogues what the poet would find in Bruce's corner of America, while at the same time making references to Burns's own works. Three lines are devoted to Jean:

> Just like your ain bra' bonny *Jean*,
> Sae gracefu', simple, tight and clean,
>   Clad in her ilk-day claiths.[7]

Given the broad humor of many of his poems, it is perhaps not a coincidence that Bruce's two poems on Burns immediately follow three poems devoted to whisky.

The Selector; Consisting of Pieces Moral, Literary, and Humorous, Extracted from Publications of Merit; Together with Original Essays and Poems appeared in four volumes published in Glasgow during 1805 and 1806. Not surprisingly the collection contains several poems on Burns. There are also to be found poems by Burns, prose accounts of the poet and the text of a letter from Burns to Peter Hill in Edinburgh, of March 1791, presenting him with a cheese and listing those friends he would have Hill invite to share it. The letter is a nice example of Burns's sly wit, but as it had already appeared in Currie in 1800, one wonders why the Editor of *The Selector* bothered to reprint it.[8]

The first volume contains a summons to attend a meeting of the Burns's Anniversary Society, set up along the lines of Burns's own 'Libel Summons' and signed by the clerk of the society with the pseudonym Modestus (I, 196). Unfortunately we do not know where the society met. A very interesting poem is entitled 'Ode: Written for, and Read at the Celebration of the Birth of Burns, in Paisley, 29th January, 1805'. Although not incorporated into the Burns Federation until 1891, the Paisley Burns Club is credited by the Federation as having been founded at that meeting. The plot of the poem is that Caledonia appears before Jove to 'grant my country one true Patriot Bard' (II, 56). The request is approved and Burns is named:

> His merit's proven, Fame her blast hath blown,
> Now Scotia's Bard o'er all the world is known—
>
> . . . .
> Yet, while revolving Time this day returns,
> Let Scotsmen glory in the name of Burns (II, 57).

The poem was first published there under the initials R. T., which stand for Robert Tannahill who became quite well known before taking his life in 1810 at thirty-five.

A further 'Ode' was written by Tannahill for a similar event two years later. The production consists of a recitative, a song, another recitative and a further song. The second recitative ends:

> Our country's melodies shall perish never,
> For, Burns, thy songs shall live for ever.[9]

Tannahill's 'Ode' had a patriotic theme to it, which brings to mind Burns's own song 'Does Haughty Gaul Invasion Threat?' The final song in Tannahill's 'Ode' would appear to have been based on Burns's song. One stanza of the younger poet's work begins: 'Haughty Gallia threats our coast' and it continues that Britons boast 'The Patriot, and the Patriot Bard', and the stanza ends:

> But chiefly, Burns, above the rest,
>   We dedicate this night to thee;
> Engraved in every Scotchman's breast,
>   Thy name, thy worth shall ever be! (p. 81)

A year later the society met again, and again a poem was forthcoming. The opening lines are not unpromising:

> Again we mark the changeful year
> Ride forth upon the stormy gale,
> While musing Fancy starts to hear
> Wild Echo's wild and weary wail
> (*The Selector*, IV, 185).

Unfortunately there follow seven pages containing a sorry mixture of complaints about the political and moral decay abroad, with a good lacing of temperance indoctrination. Predictably it ends:

> Let Reason spread the frugal feast,
> And Friendship give the flow of soul;
> Benevolence warm every breast,
> And healthful Temperance mix the bowl!
> (IV, 190)

J. Y. of Glasgow also read a poem that day in Paisley. The poet evokes the shade of Burns and moves on 'To kindle up old Scotia's Bards sublime, / Still to survive the ravages of Time' (IV, 193), invoking Freedom through the shades of Douglas, Wallace, and Bruce. But, the poet continues, it will be Burns who, 'sailing down the stream of Time', will 'dare the man of blood to place / Slavery's grim ensign o'er ... [Scotia's] warlike race' (IV, 194). There were other poems, too, including a clever acrostic on the name Robert Burns.

An attractive, but poorly printed, volume of poems by Thomas Donaldson, a weaver of Glanton, was produced at Alnwick in 1809 by William Davison, re-using some of the Thomas Bewick woodcuts which had appeared in the 1808 edition of Burns's poems. Donaldson's poem entitled 'On Reading Burns' Works' may have been inspired by a reading of the Alnwick edition. The poem contains but twelve lines praising Burns with such hackneyed phrases as 'Thy work abounds with sentiment, / There manly beauties shine', or again 'Thy genius glows in ev'ry page'. [10]

The anonymous author of *Tranquility; A Poem, To which are added, Other Original Poems ...* was not very giving of praise in the title of a poem which we find in the volume: 'On Reading Some Trifling Verses, By a Scottish Poet, "To the Memory of Robert Burns"'. Oddly the author adds as a note to the 72-line poem a quotation from Burns's Preface to the 1787 Edinburgh edition of his poems, where he says that 'poetic genius ... bade me sing the loves, the joys, the rural scenes and rural pleasures of my natal soil, in my native tongue'. [11]

The author assures us that 'long to Nature he was true' while he sang 'the joys of guileless love' (p. 61) and faithfully traced 'wonder-working Nature' (p. 62) recording the cotter's evening 'Where all is love and joy serene' (p. 62) all of which Burns does 'With charms beyond the reach of art' (p. 62). Even when the poet was 'Debased, amid the inglorious throng' he was able to 'cheer Misfortune's darkening day' and to charm us 'In plaintive air or mirthful sound' (p. 63). Thus the author of *Tranquility* drew from the few words that he had quoted from Burns almost the entire subject of his/her poem—an interesting, though by no means a great, achievement.

In a poem entitled 'On a Black Marble Bowl that Belonged to Burns' there appears once more the possibility of using the poet's life as a vehicle for preaching temperance. Although the author, identified only as Braine, never mentions the name Burns except in the title of the poem, we are led through the mixing of alcoholic punch in the bowl to the voice of 'A sainted maid serene' who calls upon the revellers to abjure strong drink, offering in its stead health, peace and happiness. The poem ends on her note of warning:

> Abstain—for deep beneath,
> Though Joys upon the surface swim,
> And laughing Loves sport round the brim,
> Lurk dire disease and death.[12]

Peter Forbes of Dalkeith sent an invitation in Standard Habbie to friends to join him at his home on January 25th 1811 to 'crack an' joke, / O'er Scot's kail brose',[13] as well, we are told, as haggis and other country fare. What is interesting about this poem is that it points out that it had by this time become a custom for admirers of Burns to forgather in houses in what appear to have been almost spontaneous celebrations which were later to become Caledonian Societies, St. Andrew's Societies and Burns Clubs.

Forbes opens his collection with another poem on the poet: 'To the Friends of Burns, on Reading the Contents of Burns' Poems'. It is a clever poem which works a number of Burns's subjects, and even titles, into the text. For instance one stanza reads:

> Your holy fair when on't I look,
> It gars me cour in till a nook,
> But death and doctor Hornbook,
>   Gars me ay stare;
> I leave them baith, an' turns the stook
>   Tae briggs o' Ayr (p. 5).

Another interesting poem is 'The Library'. Forbes certainly was a well-educated man if he had read all the authors he mentions as available in the library; he also assumes that his readers will be able to follow. For example, we get two sides of a story in as many lines with 'There's Voltaire, Volney, but beside, /

There's Fuller, wha does trim their hide' (p. 14). There is a work 'that does ilk parish tell, / By Sir John Sinclair' (p. 15), and of course there are the Scottish poets:

> Rob Fergusson, auld reikie's ranter,
> And Jamie Alves's sweet saunter;
> Then next comes up, at a roun canter,
> Blyth Robin Burns   (p. 13).

Oddly enough, Forbes nowhere mentions Allan Ramsay.

Another developing custom is noted in Forbes' volume: a pilgrimage to the birthplace of the poet—in this case his 'Lament for Burns, from the Place of his Birth', which forlornly sings of Scotland's loss. 'Caledonia may sigh,' the Doon dash over its rocks, but the poet asks the river to 'Move murmuring slow thro' the auld brig o' Doon' (p. 72).

C. Buchanan, about whom little is known, included two poems on Burns in *A Walk from the Town of Lanark to the Falls of Clyde, on a Summer Afternoon* of 1816. One is undated, entitled 'Written for the Anniversary of Robert Burns'; a good deal of the poem is about Jean. What is intriguing is that the author accepts the attribution of Lady Nairne's 'Land of the Leal' to the pen of Robert Burns. As early as *c.* 1810 it was about in printed form with the opening line altered to 'I'm wearin awa, Jean', a line which Buchanan incorporates into his poem. Another poem to Burns is dated 1812. In it the author celebrates Scotland's poets past with due respect to Burns, whose mantle the poet says has been picked up by Scott and Campbell.

I noted earlier the developing custom for people to travel to Alloway to visit the home in which Burns was born—a mark of the fame which was expanding around the poet's life. Wordsworth travelled there and produced a poem, and so did Keats. Amédée Pichot wrote an account of his 'Historical and Literary' travels, devoting nearly thirty pages to Burns.[14] Another visitor was Richard Gall, of Dunbar (1776–1801), whose poems were not published until 1819. The anonymous author of the 'Memoir of Richard Gall' notes that the poet developed 'an almost idolatrous admiration of Burns'.[15] We are not surprised, then, to find three 'Burnsian' poems in the volume. One bears the note, 'Written on visiting the house in which the celebrated Robert Burns was born, and the surrounding scenery, in autumn 1799' (p. 58). Into the poem Gall worked a direct quote from 'The Banks o' Doon':

> O Doon! aft wad he [Burns] tent thy stream,
> Whan roaming near the flowery thorn,
> And sweetly sing 'departed joys,
> Departed, never to return!'   (p. 59)

Unfortunately our poet got a little carried away, and ended the poem: 'While Nature lilts a waefu' sang, / An' o'er her Shakespeare Scotia mourns' (p. 60).

Another of Gall's poems is entitled 'On the Death of Burns'. The first stanza (of five) celebrates Ramsay's *The Gentle Shepherd*, even mentioning Patie, Peggy and Bauldy by name. The musical reed is then passed to Burns who becomes 'Nature's Minstrel ... o' deathless name' (p. 83). The unidentified person to whom Gall's poem is addressed, B——r, is to take over: 'Anither Burns kythes on the landwart mead' (p. 84) the poet wrote with more than a bit of exaggeration.

Gall rounded out his trio of poems with 'Epistle: Addressed to Robert Burns' in which he writes that Burns took over after Fergusson's death when Mirth hung her pipe 'In Fingal's ha'' (p. 47). Like several other authors who addressed poems to Burns, Gall wishes that he could please him with his own songs:

> Yet could I think my sangs to thee
>   Wad pleasure bring,
> Gosh, man! I'd gladly sit the lee–
>   Lang day, an' sing (p. 50).

We cannot know if Gall's songs would have pleased Burns, but they apparently pleased others because two of them were published as Burns's own. The first, entitled, perhaps by the editor, 'Song', opens with a Burnsian ring:

> Now bank an' brae are clad in green,
>   An' scattered cowslips sweetly spring;
> By Girvan's fairy-haunted stream
>   The birdies flit on wanton wing; (p. 120)

This song first appeared in R. H. Cromek's *Reliques of Robert Burns* in 1808.

The story about the other song is a little more involved. Entitled 'Farewell to Ayrshire', the work does not have the quality and power which we associate with the productions of Burns: 'Bowers, adieu! whare love decoying,/ First enthralled this heart o' mine' (p. 146). According to the note in Gall's volume (pp. 167–8) it was the poet himself who sent the song to James Johnson as the work of Burns and it was published as such in *The Scots Musical Museum* and was from there picked up by Currie for inclusion in his collection.

Born in 1792, Hew Ainslie was an Ayrshireman who attended Ayr Academy and later worked on the estate of Sir Hew Dalrymple, where he must have grown up hearing stories about Burns, so we are not surprised that in 1820 he led friends from Edinburgh to visit the Burns country. From the experience came a book entitled *A Pilgrimage to the Land of Burns; Containing Anecdotes of the Bard, and of the Characters he Immortalized, with Numerous Pieces of Poetry, Original and Collected*, which Ainslie published in 1822, the same year that he emigrated to America. The book opens with twelve lines obviously in imitation of Burns's 'John Barleycorn'. Ainslie's poem begins:

> There was three carles in the east,
>   Three carles of credit fair,
> And they ha'e vowed a solemn vow,
>   To see the shire of Ayr.[16]

As the title suggests, there are references to characters from the Burns story sprinkled throughout the book. Ainslie printed, for example, what he called a 'modern Scotch composition ... supposed by some to refer to Burn's [*sic*] unfortunate amour with his dear Highland Mary' (p. 80). He then devotes a page to 'Mary, A Sang', a competent composition which Ainslie probably wrote himself. The poets who wrote earlier about Burns had little to say about Mary; perhaps we hear in Ainslie's poem the beginnings of the Mary Campbell myth which was to engross readers for a century.

The poet's 'Address to Alloway Kirk' also supposed that readers knew their Burns, whose real-life experience with the cutty stool is transferred to the ruined church, or, as Ainslie puts it, 'The bit whare fornicators sat ... is now forgotten', but there is also borrowed from 'Tam o' Shanter' a reference to 'Whare Satan blew his bag' (p. 110). The assumed familiarity with Burns extended to events in the poet's life, friends and the topography of Ayrshire, and snippets quoted from Burns without reference to where they appear, as when he quotes without further comment, 'French ragout, / Or olio that wou'd sta' a sow' (p. 181), confident that the reader will recognize these few words as borrowed from 'Address to a Haggis'. When the travellers were enjoying themselves of an evening they passed the time by singing or reciting poems. One five-stanza song, entitled 'Landlady Count your Lawin'', has a stanza which is an obvious parody of Burns:

> Then lady count your lawin',
> The cock is near the crawin',
> The day is near the dawin'
>   An' bring us ben mair beer (p. 116).

Although the group left Edinburgh on 23rd June 1820 (p. 5), Ainslie works in a poem, 'On Burns' Anniversary', which ends:

> What heart hath ever match'd his flame?
>   What spirit match'd his fire?
> Peace, to the prince of Scottish song!
>   Lord of the Bosom's Lyre! (p. 256)

If imitation is the sincerest flattery, then George Beattie must be accounted one of the greatest admirers of Burns. Beattie (*c.* 1786–1823) was a native of Montrose and contributed 'John o' Arnha'' to *The Montrose Review*, originally nearly half of it in prose. In the Preface to the book version Beattie immediately admits his debt to Burns:

It will be pretty evident that, in writing this Tale, 'Tam o' Shanter' was kept in view ... It ran so much in my head, however, that I was more cramped in avoiding palpable imitation, and involuntary plagiarism, than I was benefited in any other respect, by attempting to adopt it as a model ...[17]

Beattie alerts the reader to a scene in the poem when John is led to Logie Kirk, where there is a graveyard scene, without the comic relief of Burns's tale:

> Nae 'winsome wench' was there, I ween,
> Like *Cutty Sark*, to cheer the scene;
> But blackest horror reign'd profound,
> And threw its veil o'er all around (p. 36).

There follow three 'fatal sisters' brewing up a fiendish mixture which owes a good deal more to *Macbeth* than to 'Tam o' Shanter'. The poem then takes off in another direction, mocking Scott, and especially Southey for accepting the Poet Laureateship. But can Britain's 'best of kings,' Beattie asks,

> ... mak' an Honest Man?—
> Ah! sorrow fa' me if he can!
> So sang the Bard, now dead and gone—
> Poor Burns! Apollo's dearest son! (pp. 48–9).

The ironic jibes which Beattie made at his contemporaries no longer make their points, but 'John o' Arnha'' (republished in 1883) retains its freshness most where it was most inspired by Burns's tale of diablerie.

We can move forward now to the celebrations of 1859. To say that there was a deluge of verse produced for the event is to be very conservative indeed. For a celebration at the Crystal Palace a competition was organized to judge the best poem submitted; the only requirement was that the poem be in *English* [18] and between 100 and 200 lines in length. A selection of the 621 poems submitted was published along with other prize poems from other competitions in *The Burns Centenary Poems*, edited by George Anderson and John Finlay. The editors do not rank the poems which they include; in fact the order of appearance does not appear to follow any particular plan of arrangement. One of the poems which received quite a bit of attention was, as we should expect, 'The Cotter's Saturday Night.' For example, it was the first of the sumptuously illustrated folios published by the Royal Association for the Promotion of the Fine Arts in Scotland, in 1855. Frederic W. H. Myers contributed an untitled poem with the line 'O noblest poem, "Let us worship God!"' (p. 3), while an anonymous contributor supplied 'The Birth-Day of Burns' in which the penultimate stanza refers to the 'Cotter's Saturday' while the final line of the stanza is 'Come, let us worship God!' (p. 16). John Hodge Duffy contributed a poem which contained five stanzas on the poem, including this one on the father at evening prayer:

> Whilst o'er the Book divine he meekly bends,
> And turns and scans the page with rev'rent eyes,
> Whilst up to Mercy's throne his prayer ascends,—
> A thought of Burns shall with the scene arise (p. 90).

A number of the poems in this collection dwell on the figure of Highland Mary. A. E. G., of London, contributed 'Pastoral' in which he/she devotes about a quarter of this long poem to her, including a passage about the pledge the lovers made 'Beneath the starry witness of the sky./ The open Bible ratifies the oath' (p. 181). One of few who did so, he also celebrates Burns's use of satire. One stanza opens with the author extolling Burns's mirth, fun and frolic: 'While Laughter shakes his sides with jollity' (p. 183), but it is not all humor; before the end of the stanza 'Satire's biting tongue, with mocking smile, / Tunes her harsh notes' (p. 183).

William Shelley Fisher was another who focused on Mary; almost a quarter of his five-page contribution is devoted to her. Although she is not named, the lines

> Behold within the 'hallowed grove'
> How Nature weeps the wane of love! (p. 226)

with a phrase borrowed from 'Thou Lingering Star' leave no doubt as to the subject of the passage.

V. Y. of Edinburgh also sang the praises (and there were others in the collection too) of Highland Mary, of whom he/she writes, 'The peasant sat enfranchised on Love's throne' (p. 198). V. Y. makes the point that Burns's audience grew as time went on, using an oblique reference to 'Tam o' Shanter':

> Instead of peasant-audience, scant at best,
> When market-days called forth his ready jest (p. 198).

Burns did not, though, ignore his origins; he could still carry 'grandeur into cottage life' (p. 201). 'Had he no faults?' the author asks, and answers that the imperfections of nature are softened in moonlight:

> So with his faults amid the century
>   Which he has filled with beauty and delight,—
> Let them apart, in their own shadows lie:
>   The scene is not less bright (p. 202).

Several of the poems, indeed most of them, stress the profound influence which nature had upon Burns. William Sawyer drew attention to the fact that this love recognized not only the beauty of the sunset, but also 'the loveliness that lies/ In barren moors and ashen skies' (p. 209).

What is most striking about this collection, with its poems devoted to many aspects of Burns's life and works, is that not one poet singles out Jean for praise or comment—in fact I do not believe that the name Jean ever appears. Granted that Highland Mary is a more romantic topic, made so by Burns himself, but in a collection in which home life as exemplified in 'The Cotter's Saturday Night' is so admired, it appears odd that the poet's own domestic life should not have excited the praise of some of the poets whose work found expression in this volume.

Much more fun to read is the small collection put together by Samuel Lover under the pseudonym Ben Trovato, *Rival Rhymes, in Honour of Burns*. An author signing himself A Proverbial Philosopher contributed 'A Remonstrance to the Directors of the Crystal Palace', organizers, it will be recalled, of the above-noted competition. The poem opens, as the author would have it, by quoting himself: 'He is a bold man who dareth to tamper with the dead.' [19] Several lines later the statement is repeated, followed by 'Wherefore, then, dig up Burns for dignity posthumous?' (p. 15) and goes on to state:

> 'That waiting-room for unclad ghosts, before the presence-chamber of
>   their king.'
> This matters less for the Scotch than most of the ghosts in waiting;
> For the kilt is but cool wear, and they're better prepared to go naked;
> Nevertheless I say, 'Tamper not with the dead' (p. 16).

The scoffing at the high-serious tone of the Crystal Palace competition continued in 'Ode by an Amateur, an Ardent Admirer of Milton, on the Centennial Birthday of Burns', a spoof on 'L'Allegro':

> Hence, chroniclers of Time,
>   Makers of almanacs and strange predictions,
>   Held by the wise as fictions;
> Begone, and wallow in the river's slime
> To calculate the tides   (p. 45).

After a considerable warm-up, the author comes to Burns. Here we learn of his use of Scots that 'Nature in the natal hour, / Denied refined acoustic power' (p. 48). We all know Burns's own comment about his youthful reading, but the author of this poem reminds us of it after having devoted a stanza about Scotland and oats:

> But though oaten stop's [*sic*] forbid,
> Let no Scottish swain be chid,
> Who, while he takes his shepherd's crook,
> Also takes afield his book,
> That while his lambs enjoy their feed,
> He may enjoy his pastoral read   (p. 51).

One entry consists of a letter from 'Fergus McFash' to the Directors of the Crystal Palace describing how he came across what he maintains must be the earliest MS of Burns, written before 'he began to intermingle English so extensively in his productions' (p. 56); the letter is followed by verse which resembles a Scottish 'Jabberwocky'.

In addition to pseudonymous works there are parodies, thinly disguised with a mixture of letters and asterisks. For example, in the style of Thomas Campbell, who had published his 'Ode to the Memory of Burns' with *Gertrude of Wyoming* in 1808, we read:

> Such joy my own heart knew,
>   When it dwelt in mortal shrine,
> As it interwoven grew
>   Into brotherhood divine
> With the champions and the bards of the free,
>   And invoked upon my lyre
>   The succession of their fire,
>   That their mantle might attire
>   Even me (p. 30).

Among those parodied are, in order of appearance: Longfellow, with 'A Voice from the Far West'; Thomas Hood; Barry Cornwall; Tennyson, with 'The Poet's Birth: A Mystery'; Lord Macaulay (who is 'identified' as the author of *The Lays of Ancient Rum*), with 'The Battle of the Lake Glenlivit'. One passage in the poem is about a parade, and includes the following stanza:

> The Temperance lodges, two and two,
>   With fifes and drums and banners,
> But not a single man was there
>   Of the brave guild of Tanners.
> For tanners water will keep out
>   Even in the grave when lying,
> And will not choose to rot themselves
>   With water before dying (p. 107).

In proper academic form there is a footnote referring the reader to Hamlet's comment on tanners. The last poet to be parodied is Pope whose spirit recites a quick run-through of Burns's life, including quotations and references to poems, such as this when we are asked to admire:

> The poet's wit and tenderness and fire,
> The comprehensive mind, the varied power;
> To see the outstrech'd 'front of battle lower,'
> And triumph with a hero in the van—
> Or mourn 'The Mountain Daisy's' shorten'd span;
> Or give his pity to a startled 'Mouse,'
> And read a moral from its ruin'd house (p. 121).

If it was not so before the centenary celebrations, it certainly became *de rigeur* after it for Scottish poets to write at least one poem in praise of Burns. From a reasonably extensive reading of nineteenth-century Scots poetry, my guess would be that at least half the collections published until the end of the century contained a poem about the Bard.

This is only a part of the extraordinary outpouring of admiration, respect and love which this man and his poetry have engendered. Annually we usher in the new year to the strains of 'Auld Lang Syne', a song which I believe to

be the best-known non-political secular song in the world, not known to have
been written by Burns by most of those who sing it. Many toast in a new year
with a whisky named after a famous nineteenth-century clipper, but which was
itself named after an attractive girl in a short skirt seen by Tam on a midnight
ride past Alloway Kirk. There are relics true and false of the man; there are
forgeries of his work; as one may gather, there are poems aplenty about him.
All bear witness to the man who, two centuries after his death, continues to
astonish and delight us.

NOTES

1. G. Ross Roy, 'Robert Burns and the Brash and Reid Chapbooks of Glasgow,'
   Scottish Studies, edited by Joachim Schwend, Susanne Hagemann & Hermann
   Völkel, 14 (1992), 53–69.
2. Elizabeth Scot, *Alonzo and Cora, With Other Original Poems, Principally Elegiac*
   (London, 1801), p. 162.
3. *The Poems and Songs of Robert Burns*, edited by James Kinsley (Oxford, 1968), I,
   489.
4. Mrs. [Ann] Grant, *Poems on Various Subjects* (Edinburgh, 1803), p. 268.
5. John Gerrond, *Poems on Several Occasions, Chiefly in the Scottish Dialect* (Glas-
   gow, 1802), p. 48.
6. James Thomson, *Poems in the Scottish Dialect* (Edinburgh, 1801), p. 140.
7. [D. Bruce], *Poems Chiefly in the Scottish Dialect* (Washington [Pa.], 1801), p. 30.
8. *The Selector*, III, 40–43.
9. Robert Tannahill, *Poems and Songs, Chiefly in the Scottish Dialect* (London, 1815),
   p. 80.
10. Thomas Donaldson, *Poems, Chiefly in the Scottish Dialect; Both Humourous and
    Entertaining* (Alnwick, 1809), p. 82.
11. *Tranquility; A Poem. To which are added, Other Original Poems, and Translations
    from the Italian* (Dundee, 1810), p. 64.
12. Braine, *English Minstrelsy. Being a Selection of Fugitive Poetry from the Best English
    Authors; With Some Original Pieces Hitherto Unpublished* (Edinburgh, 1810), II,
    pp. 172–3.
13. Peter Forbes, *Poems, Chiefly in the Scottish Dialect* (Edinburgh, 1812), pp. 58–9.
14. Amédée Pichot, *Voyage Historique et Littéraire en Angleterre et en Ecosse*. 3 vols
    (Paris, 1825), III, 445–73.
15. Richard Gall, *Poems and Songs* (Edinburgh, 1819), p. xi.
16. [Hew Ainslie], *A Pilgrimage to the Land of Burns* (Deptford, 1822), p. 1.
17. George Beattie, *John o' Arnha': To which is added The Murderit Mynstrell, and
    Other Poems*. 5th edn (Montrose, 1826), p. v.
18. George Anderson and John Finlay (eds), *The Burns Centenary Poems: A Collection
    of Fifty of the Best* (Glasgow, 1859), p. viii.
19. [Samuel Lover], *Rival Rhymes, in Honour of Burns; With Curious Illustrative
    Matter*, edited by Ben Trovato (pseud. London, 1859), p. 14.

I wish to express my gratitude to the American Council of Learned Societies for a grant
which helped defray my expenses in getting to Glasgow where this paper was presented.

The Burns Cult and Scottish Identity in the Nineteenth and Twentieth Centuries

THE OBJECT OF THIS PAPER is to examine how the cult of Burns has been used by Scots in the nineteenth and twentieth centuries to bolster particular perceptions of Scottish national identity.[1] Along with Wallace, Bruce, Knox and the Covenanters, perceptions of Burns have been shaped and reshaped to give credence and authority to particular ideologies in Scotland. In other words, this essay is not so much concerned with the reality of the life and work of Burns, but more the representation of Burns as an emblem of imagined Scottish traditions and characteristics. It is not so much how Burns has shaped Scottish identity as how Scottish identity has shaped our visions of Burns. Whereas many Scottish historical icons have come and gone with changes in cultural and ideological fashions – a good example here is the way in which the Covenanters no longer occupy a central place in popular historical imagination as the nation has become more pluralistic in its religious values – Burns's power as an emblem of Scottish identity has remained undiminished over the two centuries since his death. Evidence of his centrality to Scottish self-perception is to be found in the constant references to the man and his works at key points in Scottish history in the nineteenth and twentieth centuries. Burns was consistently quoted by churchmen from the Disruption of 1843 to the unification of the churches in 1929.[2] At times of war, he was cited in sermons and in propaganda tracts. Visiting dignitaries were obliged to pay homage to his genius and practically all the leading personalities of Scottish society in this period, irrespective of political affiliation or social class, make some reference to him in their autobiographies. As a cultural icon of Scottish identity, the power of Burns has remained undiminished.

In order to understand the popularity of Burns from the early nineteenth century onwards, it is first of all necessary to place the phenomenon of the Burns cult in its appropriate historical context. The early nineteenth century was one of profound change and dislocation in Scottish society due to the impact of rapid industrialisation and urbanisation. For many contemporaries it appeared as if the traditions and national characteristics of Scotland were disappearing.[3] The three Scottish institutions which had survived the Treaty of Union in 1707 and in which much of Scottish national identity was vested were conspicuously failing to cope with the new demands of an increasingly industrial society. Whig lawyers such as Cockburn and Jeffrey looked to England for guidance in the development of law. The parochial school system of education had broken down in urban society which led George Lewis to complain in 1834 that Scotland was a half-educated nation. A Royal Commission of 1826 had exposed failings in the Scottish Universities which were unable to live up to the reputation that had been established in the halcyon days of the Scottish Enlightenment. Perhaps most seriously of all, the Scottish Kirk was bitterly divided. In 1843 the unifying force of Presbyterianism was shattered in the Disruption as three separate Presbyterian churches each claimed to be the true heirs of the Scottish Reformation tradition.

Such traumatic changes engendered a deep mood of cultural pessimism among the Scottish intelligentsia as to the future prospects for a distinctive Scottish national identity. Walter Scott moaned that 'what makes Scotland Scotland' was fast disappearing under a tide of modernity. Such pessimism was shared by Henry Cockburn who claimed that the growing communications between Scotland and England were making the Scottish language extinct. The Rev James Begg's prognosis was equally gloomy and he talked of the Scottish nation 'sinking under a combination of increasing evils'. Arguably, such fears and cultural pessimism culminated in 1853 with the formation of the National association for the Vindication of Scottish Rights which sought to halt the perceived decline of Scottish national identity.[4] The Association was similar to other anti-modernist and anti-industrialist groups which sprang up throughout Europe. Its outlook was essentially romantic and backward-looking and it is worth pointing out that the manifestation of this phenomenon in Scotland had no associations with pre-industrial conceptions of Britain, which should warn us against accepting any conclusions that British identity was forged by 1837. Britain, it would appear, was associated with modernism and industrialisation and not tradition and identity.[5]

It was during this period of rapid industrialisation and urbanisation that the Scots started to reinvent themselves. It was the era of Highlandism and tartanry, the romanticisation of the Scottish past, the sentimentalisation of rural life and the contribution of imperial Scotland to the British Empire. Much of this reinvention was manufactured by the new commercial middle classes who had been excluded from the traditional Scottish institutions through the power of aristocratic patronage. Not surprisingly, a key element in the reinvention of Scotland was that it was formed around a core of *laissez-faire* ideology in which characteristics such as thrift, self-help, temperance and hard work were presented as quintessential Scottish values. Evidence that such values formed a cultural hegemony in Scottish society can be illustrated by the political dominance enjoyed by the Liberal Party north of the border until after the First World War. Just as the cult of Sir William Wallace was used to propagate anti-aristocratic sentiment, so too was the cult of Robert Burns. Burns was a commoner, he had been let down by the aristocracy, and he showed that genius and talent were not the sole prerogatives of the aristocracy. Just as Highlandism was promoted because it was believed to be a purer and more traditional form of Scottishness, Burns was emblematic of an older, purer and uncorrupted Scotland, as yet untouched by industrialism and mammon. Burns and his world, as Andrew Noble has shown with his work on Christopher North, were corrupted to satisfy the sentimental and nostalgic needs of an industrialising nation.[6] The period witnessed a fad for collecting the relics of 'auld Scotia' before it passed into oblivion. Scott's gathering of the border ballads and the creation of numerous societies devoted to the preservation of historical manuscripts were evidence of a concern that Scottish identity was losing its distinctive national characteristics.[7] Consequently, for many in the nineteenth century, Burns's greatest achievement was to capture and preserve a dying language and way of life. Lord Rosebery at the centenary of his death stated:

> For Burns exalted our race: he hallowed Scotland and the Scottish tongue ... The Scottish dialect, as he put it, was in danger of perishing. Burns seemed at this juncture to start to his feet and reassert Scotland's claim to national existence; his Scottish notes rang through the world, and he thus preserved the Scottish language forever- for mankind will never allow to die that idiom in which his songs and poems are enshrined.[8]

To understand the veneration of Burns in the nineteenth century, it is necessary to take account of the ways in which Burns was moulded to accommodate the predominant *laissez-faire* ideology of the day. Freedom was more to do with middle-class individualism and anti-aristocratic sentiment than Jacobinism. Along with Wallace, David Livingstone and others, Burns was canonised into the broader 'lad o' pairts' mythology; namely that Scottish society was inherently democratic and meritocratic.[9] He was one of the many great Scotsmen who through honest endeavour had 'attained to high positions' in spite of great hardship and difficulties.[10] For Hector MacPherson and others, Burns owed his radicalism and democratic outlook to a Scottish tradition of Presbyterian democracy:

> Burns had intellectual breadth and religious susceptibility enough to appropriate what was best in the two phases of the religious thought of his time. Thus it happened that while the average Moderate looked upon Calvinism as represented by the Covenanters as a detestable fanaticism, an enemy to the amenities of social life, Burns paid tribute to their magnificent stand for liberty ... Burns, who had Covenanting blood in his veins, had no need to go to Rousseau for his democratic fervour. His 'A man's a man for a' that' owes infinitely more to Samuel Rutherford than to Rousseau.[11]

Although the middle class had attained the vote in 1832, Scottish society was still dominated, to a large extent, by the aristocracy. Anti-aristocratic sentiment formed one of the most potent political forces in nineteenth-century Scotland and Burns's radical sentiments were used to reinforce this. According to Charles Thomson, Burns's message was

> founded on the thoroughly Scottish sentiment, fostered by Scottish history from the days of Wallace to our own times, of the value of man as man, of the dignity of labour, whether physical or mental, as compared with the tinsel shows of privileged indolence. The scorn for the empty 'birkie ca'd a lord' and for the king-made dignities unbacked by merit, have persistently remained as Scottish qualities all down the ages, and they are becoming the qualities of men wherever thought has filtered down the humbler classes.[12]

The important point to emphasise here is that while Burns can be interpreted from a socialist perspective in the twentieth century, for most of the nineteenth century his work was used to give credence to *laissez-faire* liberalism. Burnsian notions of freedom and liberty and the dignity of mankind were ideally suited to Scottish middle-class self-perception and the erection of statues in his honour throughout the country reinforced the belief that talent was God-given and not the preserve of noble birth.[13] The achievement of Burns's rise from lowly birth was something that all Scots could aspire to emulate. According to Sir Arthur Conan Doyle,

> There was neither fortune nor title in the man's pedigree and yet he sprang from the salt of the earth, for he came from that lowland Scottish peasant stock which was one of the finest stocks that the world could show, if one might judge from its results.[14]

Burns could be used to promote notions that the dignity of hard work, the perseverance of toil and calm stoicism in the face of adversity were values that were intrinsic to Scottish society. Furthermore, while *laissez-faire* was a new ideology associated with modernity, its reinvention as embodying traditional Scottish values which had a long pedigree in Scottish history helped to give it an authority and legitimacy which remained unassailable in the nineteenth century.

Burns was praised for inculcating family values. According to Rosebery, Burns 'dwells repeatedly on the primary sacredness of the home and the family, the responsibility of fatherhood and marriage.'[15] The vision of family life in *The Cotter's Saturday Night* was an antidote to the widespread unease about moral degeneracy in the sprawling slums of urban Scotland. He was likewise praised for making respectable the old Scottish songs which contained language which was crude and vulgar and unfit for genteel company. Burns transformed the baseness of Scottish society into something sublime. While most acknowledged that the Bard had his own particular vices, even this could be put to good use, as Rosebery argued, 'To remind us all that we have feet of clay'.[16] The temperance league found that Burns could be used to endorse their message.

The Rev James Barr compiled extracts from the prose writing of Burns which he used to show that he warned against the evils of Strong Drink.[17] The wretchedness of drunkenness, Scottish society was warned, could visit even those as blessed with the gift of God as Robert Burns. As one of the most vociferous campaigners against the drink trade, James Barr never failed to include a liberal sprinkling of quotations from the Bard in his tirades against 'intoxicating liquor' in the House of Commons, a feat which never failed to impress his parliamentary colleagues.[18]

Burns was used by Churchmen of varying persuasions to extol the religious life. Evangelicals used the story of his life to illustrate the frailty of the human condition. His natural poetic simplicity was contrasted with the contortion of the too clever moderates. Burns and his ability to portray the perfection of creation, his humanity and charitable spirit were all highlighted by evangelicals. Burns could also be called upon for a critique of unthinking dogmatism.[19] In an anniversary sermon in 1946, James Barr stated that 'Of the person of Christ, Burns holds an exalted conception. From the excellent purity of His doctrines and precepts, he argues that He was from God'.[20] Burns was made a pious and religious man whose simplicity acted as a role model for Keir Hardie. Even the anti-vivisection and animal rights group of the nineteenth century used him as a champion of their cause.[21]

In the nineteenth century Burns was recast to mirror the predominant political values of the day. Although radicals in the eighteen-twenties had appropriated him for the cause, by the latter part of the nineteenth century strident Jacobinism was emasculated:

'A man's a man for a' that' is not politics – it is the assertion of the rights of humanity in a sense far wider than politics. It erects all mankind; it is the charter of self-respect … it cannot be narrowed into politics. Burns's politics are indeed nothing but the occasional overflow of his human sympathy into past history and current events.[22]

Likewise, Burns's Scottish nationalism was cancelled out by repeated reference to his British patriotism. In an era when Britain and the Empire were conceived by Scots as an imperial partnership between two distinct nations, Burns was hailed as a contribution to *British* literature. As Lord Rosebery explained to a Glasgow audience in 1896,

There seem to me to be two great natural forces in British literature. I use the safe adjective of British, and your applause shows me that I was right to do so. I use it partly because hardly any of Burns's poetry is strictly English; partly because he hated, and was perhaps the first to protest against, the use of the word English as including Scottish. Well, I say, there are in that literature two great forces of which the power seems sheer inspiration and nothing else – I mean Shakespeare and Burns.[23]

In the period before the First World War, the Scottish middle-class was able to recast Burns as an emblem of their own identity which reflected and promoted their own cultural values. Indeed, Burns was even given credit for much of the transformation of the nation from a feudal, backward and ignorant society into one which was intelligent, meritocratic, entrepreneurial and modern. According to one assessment,

> The influence of Burns on the imaginative literature of Scotland has been deep and abiding. Many Scotsmen have been so touched, moved and stirred by his writings, as to arouse an irrepressible feeling within them to compose verse themselves; and today there are many in the humble walks of life who can write passable and even animate verse and song, and appreciate the highest works of the imagination and elaborate faculties of the race. Burns has exercised much influence over the mind of the Scottish people by removing prejudice and superstition, fostering liberty and independence of spirit and greater freedom of thought.[24]

The Scottish middle-class were remarkably successful in their ability to 'see ithers as oursels' and in doing so turned Burns into a paradigm of Scottish bourgeois virtue. Burns was not the only victim: William Wallace was represented as a proto-Presbyterian fighter for *laissez-faire* individualism. Just as the cultural hegemony of liberal individualism can explain why the 'Kailyard' was so popular in Scotland and its colonies, it also accounts for the popularity of Burns. That is not to say that Burns was Kailyard, rather it is how he was represented in the nineteenth century.

As the dominant Liberalism of the nineteenth century gave way to the politics of class in the twentieth century, Burns was remoulded to suit those ends. Keir Hardie, Ramsay MacDonald, Tom Johnston and James Barr all used Burns and had their socialism influenced by him. According to Johnston,

> Our great democratic singer had no illusions about landlordism. He and his 'toiled with the ceaseless toil of galley slaves' and lived amid 'nakedness and hunger and poverty and want' that parasitical lairds should not only be well fed and well clad, but should have a plentitude of counters for their midnight gambling with 'the Devil's pictured beuks'.[25]

Just as many aspects of the radical Liberal tradition were incorporated into the political culture of the post-First World War Labour movement, so too were Burnsian notions of egalitarianism and liberty. The Co-operative movement featured Burns and his poetry in their advertisements to show that anti-capitalism in Scotland had a long and distinguished pedigree. Liberty was equated with freedom from poverty and capitalist exploitation, and egalitarianism lent itself towards international brotherhood. By making these links with Burns and the Scottish past, the Labour Party endeavoured to present Scotland as an inherently socialist society.

Nationalists, however, while maintaining Burnsian notions of liberty and egalitarianism, concentrated most effort into recasting Burns as an anti-Unionist Scottish patriot.[26] The theme of 'Bought and Sold for English Gold' was given as much prominence in nationalist circles as the sentiments which were associated with 'A Man's a Man for a' That'. Burns's anti-Unionist outbursts were widely circulated in the nationalist press and given considerable prominence. In spite of these exertions, however, neither a nationalist nor a socialist interpretation of the Bard and his work could overcome the largely sentimental and apolitical vision of Burns which dominated twentieth-century Scottish society. In part, this can be explained by the 'crisis' of national identity which hit Scottish society in the inter-war era.[27] Just as cultural pessimism accompanied the rapid urbanisation and industrialisation of the early nineteenth century, so too did it accompany the economic and social dislocation which followed in the wake of the First World War. The creation of the Saltire Society in 1936, as with the various historical clubs which appeared in the early nineteenth century, was the result of national insecurity and the desire to protect the nation's cultural inheritance. For most establishment literary figures, the Scots language was dead and the efforts of the renaissance futile.[28] Given the perceived wisdom that Scotland was losing its national distinctiveness, many sought refuge in the past where a clear and unambiguous vision of a distinctive Scottish identity could be found. Furthermore, as most new attempts to create a new and dynamic vision of Scottish culture and identity were associated with political nationalism, a sentimental appeal to the past was the only politically safe option open to the Scottish establishment. Burns had little or no vitality, other than to preserve in a fossilised manner a redundant literary tradition:

> It might have been thought that the genius of Burns would have opened up new paths in poetry for his countrymen; but the work of Burns is not the beginning of a period, but its climax and close. The Scottish muse has many things to her credit in the century and more since Burns died, but singly they are slight and innovate little upon the past.[29]

In short, the best and truest Scottish literature could only be found in the past.

David McCrone has recently examined the reasons behind the pervasiveness of the 'lad o' pairts' myth in Scottish society and has concluded that its longevity owes much to the fact that it can be appropriated for ideological use by both the left and the right, Unionists and nationalists.[30] For the left, it is evidence that Scottish society is inherently egalitarian, democratic and socialist. For the right it shows that the Scots are egalitarian, meritocratic and individualist. For both the nationalists and Unionists it is a source of pride that the nation has a superior education system. The fact that there is no ideological monopoly of ownership has meant that there is no vested political interest in debunking the myth. A similar case can be made about Robert Burns. Unionists have consistently refused to abandon Burns to a socialist or nationalist heritage. John

Buchan claimed that Burns was 'no parochial patriot. He was equally interested in the history and welfare of the wider unit, the British Empire'.[31] Another Unionist, the Earl of Home, pleaded with his audience of Burnsians to break free from the 'tyrannical fetish of party politics'.[32] So long as the man and his work can be appropriated by lots of different political factions and none has exclusive ideological ownership his centrality as a Scottish cultural icon is guaranteed. All agree on his greatness, but all agree to differ on what constitutes that greatness. However, the effect of this political stalemate renders the Bard as a safe apolitical emblem ripe for sentimental and nostalgic abuse. For many in the Scottish establishment, this has been an acceptable state of affairs for most of the twentieth century. Burns permits a safe celebration of Scottish identity which raises no awkward political questions, and this has been an enduring feature of the Bard's role in Scottish national identity.

Finally, on the shallowness of the Scottish establishment and its appreciation of the Bard, the last words should be left to George Malcolm Thomson and his scathing description of the embodiment of the Scottish bourgeoisie, the fictional Mr Gillespie Maclean:

> Mr Maclean does not neglect literature. It is an exploded delusion that the man of affairs, the stern practical man on whose work the prosperity of the country is built, has no interest in the higher activities of the mind. Every year on the twenty-fifth of January, he attends the dinner of the Burns Club of which he is a notable ornament. A busy man all his life, he has little opportunity to study the works of the national poet, but, after all, Burns was something more than the stringer of rhymes. He was an influence for good, a man whose heart was in the right place, a celebrator of the virtues of independence and equality (both very dear to Mr Maclean's heart). Besides, are not single copies of his work bought by American millionaires for fabulous prices? ... it is also true that Burns wrote in a language which Mr Maclean, especially since his sons came back from that English school, has been steadfastly seeking to forget ... As for those envious and presumptuous scribblers who dare to write poetry in that language which Burns made for ever his own, Mr Maclean has nothing but contempt for them. He has heard with a proper disgust that some of those lazy good-for-nothing scamps have overstepped the borderline of decency to the extent of questioning the supremacy of the bard in his art, of hinting that their own wretched little compilations can be placed on a level with the masterpieces of the great exciseman. The notion that poets can exist in modern times is an anachronism peculiarly revolting to Mr Maclean's fine historic sense; the idea that a man can, as it were, set up as a poet without the approval of a world-wide network of clubs and societies strikes him as dangerous and anarchical to a degree. There is, when he comes to look at it calmly, something both immoral and unmanly in the conduct of men who write verse which will never earn them a penny piece, when they might be employed in some useful occupation.[33]

NOTES

1. An expanded version of the themes covered in this paper is to be found in R. J. Finlay, 'Heroes, Myths and Anniversaries in Modern Scotland', *Scottish Affairs* (forthcoming).
2. See Graham Walker, 'Varieties of Scottish Protestant Identity' in T. M. Devine & R. J. Finlay (eds), *Scotland in the Twentieth Century* (Edinburgh, 1996).
3. See Finlay, 'Heroes, Myths and Anniversaries'.
4. Paul Scott, 'The Last Purely Scotch Age' in Douglas Gifford (ed.), *The History of Scottish Literature, Volume 3: The Nineteenth Century* (Aberdeen, 1988), 17.
5. Linda Colley, *Britons: Forging the Nation, 1707–1837* (Yale, 1992).
6. Andrew Noble, 'John Wilson (Christopher North) and the Tory Hegemony', in Gifford (ed.), *Scottish Literature*, 125–153.
7. See Marinell Ash, *The Strange Death of Scottish History* (Edinburgh, 1980).
8. Speech by Lord Rosebery at Dumfries on the centenary of the death of Burns, July 21, 1896.
9. David McCrone, *Understanding Scotland: The Sociology of a Stateless Nation* (London, 1992).
10. Quoted in *Chambers Biographical Dictionary of Eminent Scotsmen*, Thomas Thomson (Edinburgh, 1869), 2.
11. H. MacPherson, *The Intellectual Development of Scotland* (London, 1911), 177–8.
12. Charles Thomson, *Scotland's Work and Worth* (Edinburgh, n.d.), 433.
13. See for example, the speeches by the Paisley business community on the unveiling of a statue of Burns, September 26, 1896.
14. Quoted in Thomson, *Scotland's Work and Worth*, 433.
15. Lord Rosebery, speech in the St Andrew's Hall, Glasgow, July 21, 1896.
16. *Ibid.*
17. James Barr, *Lang Syne* (Glasgow, 1949), 275.
18. For example, see his speech in the House of Commons on the Gin trade to Western Africa, April 30, 1929.
19. See Gabriel Seton, *Robert Burns* (Edinburgh, 1908).
20. James Barr, *Lang Syne*, 277.
21. Keir Hardie, *Writings and Speeches* (edited by Emrys Hughes) (Glasgow, n.d.), 138–9.
22. Rosebery, Glasgow speech.
23. *Ibid.*
24. John Mackintosh, *History of Civilisation in Scotland, vol. IV* (Paisley, 1896), 181.
25. Thomas Johnston, *A History of the Working Class in Scotland* (Glasgow, n.d.), 61.
26. See, for example, *Scots Independent* 1928–33 for numerous references to Burns's Scottish nationalism.
27. R. J. Finlay, 'National Identity in Crisis: Politicians, Intellectuals and the "End of Scotland", 1919–39', *History*, 79 (1994).
28. *Scots Magazine*, 'Scottish Poets of Today' by Charles Graves, May 1926, 120–24, and 'The Importance of the Vernacular in National life' by Lady Margaret Sackville, April 1927, 14.
29. George Gordon, 'Scottish literature' in His Grace the Duke of Atholl *et al.*, *A Scotsman's Heritage* (London, 1932), 210.

30. McCrone, *Understanding Scotland*.
31. Speaking at the Annual Dinner of the Burns Club, Dumfries, January 1930.
32. Speaking at Sandyford Burns Club, Glasgow, January 1930.
33. G. M. Thomson, *The Rediscovery of Scotland* (London, 1928), 27–28.

Burns, The Elastic Symbol: Press Treatment of Burns's Anniversary, 1995 and 1996

THERE IS NO ESCAPING THE MEDIA in contemporary society. In Britain people watch on average twenty-five hours of television each week – the figure is slightly higher in Scotland – and listen to about eighteen hours of radio. In addition newspaper readership, although declining,remains substantial, with 321 copies per 1000 people being sold each weekday in the UK as a whole, a total which is exceeded in Scotland, where the figure is 366 per 1000.[1] People also buy local or evening papers and a wide range of magazines. The consequences of this situation, which is very much a phenomenon of the twentieth century, are many, but for the purposes of this essay what is crucial is that the media are an arena in which not only are information and entertainment offered to us, but also versions of reality are continuously constructed and reconstructed. Broadcasting and the press do not simply invite us to look through a perfectly formed transparent glass panel at the world but present us with a range of perspectives on that world. It is very difficult to measure conclusively the impact of media representations on our perceptions of reality, for the media are but one influence among several, but it will be the assumption here that media representations do have some effect, and that therefore the approaches to important aspects of our culture which they embody have an influence on how we view those aspects of that culture. But it is not a one-way traffic, for there is inevitably a constant interaction between real experience and media versions of it. Furthermore, audiences are not passive and homogeneous, but bring their own differing viewpoints to bear in their interpretations of media messages.

This paper began as an examination of the treatment of Burns Night in 1995: all of the Scottish morning newspapers and those English national tabloids which bring out Scottish editions were considered, as were the special programmes broadcast by the BBC and the commercial television companies which operate in Scotland. For reasons of manageability no attempt was made to look at local or evening papers nor to take account of general television output and radio broadcasts. Nor were English national dailies considered. After the paper was delivered, it seemed a good idea to extend the exploration into 1996, and to consider how Burns Night was marked in the year of the two hundredth anniversary of the poet's death. On this occasion not only were the Scottish morning papers and the Scottish editions of English papers considered but also all of the London-based dailies. However, broadcasting was not included in the survey, and therefore very little will be said about its contribution. There is extant in any case an excellent account of the varying approaches of television to Burns Night by practitioner and analyst Donny O'Rourke.[2]

The newspaper market in Scotland has in recent years been a highly competitive one. The Scots continue to buy indigenous morning and Sunday newspapers, with over sixty per cent of copies purchased being of Scottish titles. However, in the tabloid market the Scottish edition of the Murdoch-owned *Sun* has made substantial progress against its principal indigenous competitor, the *Daily Record*, and in mid-1995 was selling just under half the number of copies sold by the *Record*. In 1995 all of the English tabloid titles were bringing out overtly Scottish editions, which, in addition to signifying that fact in their titles, contained a more substantial journalistic input than had previously been the case. By the end of 1995 the *Daily Mail's* edition north of the border had more than doubled its circulation, aided by ruthless price-cutting against its principal competitor, the Scottish edition of the *Daily Express*, which, despite augmenting its journalistic resources, has failed to increase its market share, although it continues to sell more copies than the *Mail*. In the broadsheet sector there has not been the same effort to customise the product for northern consumption, but the price-cutting war initiated in 1993 by Rupert Murdoch's *Times* has put pressure on both the *Herald* and the *Scotsman* and led to a small but significant decrease in their sales.

Burns Night is a major Scottish anniversary – perhaps *the* major one – and therefore newspapers feel obliged to mark it in some fashion. The problem is how to do so in ways which appeal to differing readerships, and are not simply a tired repetition of what has gone before. While in broadcasting programmes inevitably have to engage to some degree with the poet's work, since they usually emanate from arts and features departments, this is not the case in the press, where the spectrum of possibilities is much wider, and ranges from the serious and literary to the downright frivolous.

Tabloid newspapers dominate the UK market, and the *Daily Record* leads the field in Scotland. In 1995 that paper marks Burns Night by printing a story which links the poet and tartan: alongside a large colour photograph of a television pop music presenter engulfed in a ridiculous plaid, kilt and bootees there is an article which informs the reader that tartan is now all the rage, though 'If Rabbie were alive today – when we remember his life and works – he'd be choking on his haggis'. The contrast with the approach of the *Sun* is startling: it runs no story, but uses the occasion to print – what is for it – a very long editorial, headed 'Nation is left in Bard state', alongside the Nasmyth head and shoulders. Readers are invited to consider what Burns would think of Scotland now – 'What would this man of vision make of his country today?'

The answer apparently is not much, and the leader goes on to attack Labour's devolution plans, and to argue for independence, a cause which the Scottish edition of the *Sun* has supported since 1992:

> When you toast Robert Burns this year, think not of the past, but of the future. And raise your glass to the freedom of Scotland.

What is clearly happening here is that Burns is being employed as part of the paper's campaign on behalf of the Scottish National Party, a campaign which some commentators have suggested is based on the cynical calculation that every vote for the SNP is a vote taken from Labour, and thus an indirect contribution to Conservative revival.[3] Since the *Daily Record* is the most faithful supporter of the Labour Party in Scotland, it can also be said that Burns is being used as an assertion of the Scottishness of the *Sun* against the England-dependent Labourism of the *Record*.

It might be expected that the *Daily Express*, which is the most overtly Conservative paper among those being examined here, would have felt obliged to make some kind of connection between Burns and Conservatism, even although this is a daunting task; the paper, alive to the problem, does not mention the anniversary at all, but more subtly runs a long piece by its Scottish political editor on the serious problems which he claims the SNP is facing.

One other tabloid, the *Mirror*, picks up the political aspect. In a relatively short editorial headed 'Burning Issue' (tabloid puns are blindingly obvious) it suggests that the English fail to understand the nature of Burns Night – 'an acknowledgement of the deep sense of independence many Scots feel from the rest of the United Kingdom' – notes, without great enthusiasm, that constitutional change is likely with the election of a Labour government, and speculates that this event will be followed by a special Burns Night. The *Mirror* is a Labour supporting paper – it is owned by the same company as owns the *Daily Record* – and, like the *Sun*, is happy to enlist the poet in its political cause. The *Mirror* also runs a story in its news pages which turns up elsewhere: a Dundee butcher, Gilbert Grosset, has apparently invented an aphrodisiac haggis; alongside a colour photograph of the gentleman in question, holding a basket of his new products, and his girl friend, the rather scantily dressed young lady is quoted as saying, 'It has certainly worked for Gilbert – after all the proof of the pudding is in the eating'.

This is an ideal tabloid story: it is loosely linked to the occasion, it is funny and it has sex. The Scottish edition of *Today* – another of Rupert Murdoch's newspapers, though one which was closed towards the end of 1995 – devotes most of a page to this same story, and fills the rest of the space with a piece about an alleged snub to Dumfries by a travelling exhibition planned for 1996. The *Daily Mail* has a – very brief – piece about the haggis, as does the Aberdeen *Press and Journal*, which solicits rather coy comments from some of Mr Grosset's customers. Curiously the Dundee *Courier* does not use the story, which originated from an agency based in the city, but that paper has always been rather puritan in its general approach. It marks Burns Night in meandering fashion through several diary items of no particular consequence.

Of the two nationally circulating Scottish broadsheets, the *Scotsman* makes far more of the occasion than does the *Herald*. The latter contents itself with a contrived piece in which a reincarnated version of the poet is interviewed by its popular music commentator, David Belcher: it appears that Burns is thriving in the modern multimedia environment and drives a 'Mitsubishi Shogun V6 3.5 litre four by four'. There are some witty sallies, not least at the Kelman school of social realism, but it is not a very substantial article. In the *Scotsman* a prominent space opposite the leader page is occupied by a cartoon in which a haggis, which bears a distinct resemblance to John Major, sits on a plate above the first line of the poet's 'Address ...', while on the back page Kenneth Roy offers a pocket guide to Burns's Ayrshire, and comments of Alloway, 'Most households in this prosperous suburb used to have at least two boats in the drive, but that was pre-recession. Edwin Muir suggested that the cottage in which Burns was born should be torn down as a service to his memory, but no one has been bold enough to implement this inspired proposal'. This is witty and entertaining – much more so than the rather obvious cartoon.

Arts pages have been expanding in the Scottish broadsheets, as has all feature material, as part of the response to the cut-price competition from south of the border. On one of these pages the *Scotsman* gives space to four Scots living abroad and invites them to reflect on the state of the nation. George Reid, former nationalist MP, argues for devolution as a half-way-house to independence within Europe, while Una Flett, a journalist living in Spain, suggests that, while devolution may induce regional dynamism, it can also produce corruption and little amelioration of poor economic circumstances. Frances MacEachen, who is managing editor of a Gaelic magazine in Nova Scotia, points out that her fellow Canadian Scots may have a great interest in Scotland's culture but little in its contemporary politics, while the poet Kenneth White casts a sceptical eye on the effect of Burns on Scottish literature and life, which he argues remain insular and unambitious.

This material is by far the most stimulating published by any paper on the anniversary, and is much more questioning than celebratory.

To judge from the evidence of January 1995, for the press Burns is a starting point, which can lead on to politics, culture and comic trivia. He is also very much on the agenda of both tabloid and broadsheet newspapers, which, in an age when there has been sharp divergence in the range of material covered by each type of publication, is unusual. In both he is seen as an opportunity to engage in a discussion of the future of Scotland which, it has to be said, is not a topic which is ignored for the rest of the year, but Burns Night clearly makes Scottish papers, and those that aspire to be thought of as almost Scottish, feel duty bound to tackle this topic yet again.

1996 was of course a special year, and in the run-up to 25th January press and broadcasting had already been covering several Burns stories: the problems which the International Festival based in Ayrshire ran into had been prominent towards the end of 1995, and when the BBC leaked details of claims which were going to be made in a television programme about the alleged discovery of new Burns poems, the ensuing critical argument attracted attention. Human interest items also begin to make their appearance: for example in mid-January the Glasgow *Evening Times* discovered a Scots–Italian caterer who, with the help of funds provided by Enterprise Ayrshire, had invented a haggis pizza, though whether it had aphrodisiac qualities was not revealed.

25th January saw the continuation of the various approaches already noted, with one important addition. In contrast to 1995, there was serious discussion of Burns's life and work, particularly in the *Herald*, which had devoted much of the space in its 'Weekend Extra' supplement the previous Saturday to the subject, offering a series of articles on various aspects of the poet's legacy. George Rosie and Ian Bell contributed pieces, which took a sceptical approach – scepticism now seems to be as much part of celebrating Burns as idolatry was previously. Rosie argues that in many respects the poet was a deeply unattractive character whose sexual activities reveal 'an unpleasant, calculating, and irresponsible lecher', an interesting post-feminist variation on the traditional Presbyterian disapproval of Burns's 'lapses'. The Aberdeen *Press and Journal* on the 25th prints a feature article which also explores Burns's sexual behaviour – 'There weren't many braw bricht Ayrshire lasses who escaped his amorous attentions' – but the tone is rather less censorious than the one adopted by Rosie, and there is a genuine attempt to link biography and song. Ian Bell in the *Herald* is more concerned to discuss the way in which the Burns cult – not the poet himself – detracts from the ability of the Scots to avert their eyes from the past and concentrate on the future; for Bell modern Scotland is 'that fictitious place whose chief industry is the mass production of self-doubt'. The piece turns into a sophisticated variation on the 'Burns was really a paid up member of the SNP before his time' approach, which was taken by several Nationalist spokespersons in 1996. On the 25th of the month the *Herald* gives a page over to an article by Patrick Hogg, the scholar who has claimed that he may have found some undiscovered politically radical poems; Hogg engages in close linguistic analysis of one poem in order to back his case. Curiously the Dundee *Courier*, which marks the 25th with Burns-related diary items, also comes up with an undiscovered work, a thirty-one line poem which a correspondent had suggested in an edition of the *Dundee Advertiser* of 1888 was declaimed by the poet to give vent to his feelings when, having been invited to an aristocrat's house near Edinburgh, he was told to dine with the servants; the *Courier* does not however offer a Hogg-style analysis of the sort published by the *Herald*. That paper for its part also runs an editorial, in which it argues forcibly that the teaching of Burns's work in schools must be sustained and developed:

The effort should be made and maintained by the public education system – indeed no better demonstration could be made of the worth of that system than its ability to protect values which carelessness would easily lose.

Anyone reading these words at the time they were printed could not fail to see the reference to the debate raging in Britain that week, following the decision by a Labour party front-bench spokesperson to send her son to a selective grammar school, a decision derided earlier in the week by the *Herald's* leader-writer, or to pick up the clear implication that the Scottish school system is superior to the one in England.

The role of education is also highlighted by the *Daily Express*, which prints the results of a random – and not very scientific – survey of young people's knowledge of Burns, and below it an article by John Hodgart, a teacher known for his championing of the Scots language, who argues that both the Scots language and the poet need to be taught and cherished.

The approach of the *Scotsman* is also serious but it concentrates less on the poems and songs and more on related matters, as it did in its 'Weekend' magazine the previous Saturday, when it ran pieces on the difficulties facing the would-be progenitors of a film and a musical about the poet, and asked various prominent Scots about their memories of Burns competitions: brief articles describe Burns suppers in Moscow, London and Kampala; the portraits of the poet are discussed and evaluated; there is an interview with the actor John Cairney who, ever since the premiere of Tom Wright's *There was a Man*, has had a close association with Burns. The obligatory sceptical note is sounded by Jim Gilchrist who calls for a five-year moratorium on all Burns celebrations – 'After which, perhaps our world can regard this remarkable man with an unjaundiced eye and the same wonderment with which he regarded his'. In an extended essay Kenneth Roy continues in similar vein, and focuses on the fact that while it was possible for the young Burns to extend his knowledge of literature, thanks to the generosity of Templeton the bookseller, whose shop the poet frequented when he was working in Irvine, there is no decent bookshop left in that town today: 'There is an explanation for this: no one has attempted the revolutionary task of educating the poor'.

As was noted above, MPs sought to cash in politically on the anniversary. So did the Scottish edition of the *Sun*. As in 1995, it uses the occasion to extol the nationalist cause, though instead of running an editorial, it hands over space to the SNP MP, Roseanna Cunningham, who does not waste the opportunity to enlist a new Ayrshire member posthumously. Elsewhere in the paper regular columnist Rikki Brown uses part of his piece to mount a crude attack on bourgeois frequenters of Burns suppers and to glory in his own ignorance – 'I'll bet they don't even know what his poetry is about – neither do I' – a perfect example of the *Sun's* skill in reflecting the insecurities, and confirming the prejudices, of its readers.

As to frivolity and insignificance, nothing appears which bears comparison with the aphrodisiasic haggis of 1995, but there are items about haggises being airlifted to Australia, and there is a piece in the Scottsh edition of the *Star* in which a handwriting expert is quoted as saying that the poet's plain signature suggests that Burns was emotionally reserved, had a mundane personality, and was mean with money!

The *Sun* dresses rugby player Kevin McKenzie in a kilt, and photographs him with a plate of haggis and two winsome barmaids. Both that paper and the Scottish edition of the *Mirror* run competitions with alcohol as the prizes, and both helpfully provide the answers to the questions they set. The *Record* for its part merely offers vouchers which reduce the price of a bottle of whisky; earlier in the week it had printed a feature piece about the failure of the Burns Festival and the town of Ayr to respond to the special occasion, which, the paper claims, is the two-hundredth anniversary of the poet's birth!

All of the English tabloids do something to mark 25th January in their Scottish editions – even if in the case of the *Mail* it takes the form of a belated report about the troubles of the Festival – but in the London editions of the same titles none of this material appears, although the *Express* does carry a very small Burns Supper item. The English broadsheets do not make much of the occasion: the *Guardian* runs a piece on the Festival, while the *Independent* prints a photograph of an engraving being included in an exhibition in Glasgow – both of these are also carried in the London editions of the papers. The *Telegraph* has a very minor item about the Festival, but that is not carried in the London edition. It is clear that Burns is a conspicuous example of the gap between the Scottish and London agendas: it was impossible to escape him in the Scottish and *soi-disant* Scottish press on 25th January, but in the metropolis he was almost invisible (although the *Guardian*, for one, made up for this omission a month later by running, in its weekend magazine, a long piece by Andrew O'Hagan, which explores the Burns cult and the ambiguous messages which the poetry still sends to us). In many other respects the two agendas differ, and beneath the agendas the general socio-cultural perspectives have moved far apart, a fact which is revealed most starkly in the contrasting editorial positions adopted by the broadsheet press, with the national Scottish titles much more liberal than the national English ones, the centre of gravity of which is firmly on the right of the political spectrum.

What emerges from the actual coverage examined here is the extraordinary power and suggestiveness of Burns and his work in the Scottish context. The work continues to be celebrated in its own right – though that is more likely to be the case in radio and television – but Burns has a resonance beyond poetry and song. Unlike so many of our major historical figures and events – Mary, Queen of Scots, Bonnie Prince Charlie, Flodden – he is not about defeat. The nostalgia which he can so easily evoke is counterbalanced by the robust survival and the universality of his work. Likewise, the feeling of tragic loss contrasts with the sense of remarkable achievement. Burns was clearly not classless;

indeed, as many commentators have argued, his most acute problems as writer and man stemmed from the uneasy and ultimately intolerable position he found himself occupying between classes.[4] But his poems and songs continue to appeal across social and cultural strata.

The resonance of Burns takes us into the realm of the symbolic, for he signifies central cultural and political aspects of Scottishness (to be semiotically correct he is a mixture of icon, index and symbol). He is an extraordinarily open and flexible, not to say elastic, symbol. Open symbols can be constructed and reconstructed and they can be trivialised out of all recognition, as some of the material considered here demonstrates all too clearly. But Burns has the advantage over other Scottish heroes, like Wallace and Bruce for example, that through his work he still has the ability to appeal to people directly and to pull them up short emotionally. Because he does that in the late twentieth century through work written in the late eighteenth century, he looks backwards but he also looks forwards. It is for us to decide whether we wish to employ him on our individual and national journeys into an unknowable future or whether we prefer to embalm him and ourselves in a nostalgic time-warp. Burns, the elastic symbol, and Burns the artist can accommodate either course of action; the decision remains ours, as it always did.

As for newspapers, they will continue to celebrate Burns and to use him for their own purposes, but even when these purposes seem remote from the poems and songs, that is an inevitable consequence of the huge load Burns carries as a national Scottish symbol. Within a few years there may well be constitutional change north of the Border, and it will be fascinating to watch how Burns the symbol is reconstructed by the media – and by all of us – in the very different Scotland which could then come into being.

NOTES

1. These figures are derived from data published in *World Press Trends, 1995* (International Federation of Newspaper Publishers, Paris) and produced by the Broadcast Audience Research Board (BARB), Radio Joint Audience Research (RAJAR) and Audits of Great Britain (AGB). Circulation data for English titles in Scotland are not officially available, but unofficial data are published regularly in *Scotmedia* magazine.
2. Donny O'Rourke, 'Supperman: Televising Burns', in Kenneth Simpson (ed.), *Burns Now* (Edinburgh: Canongate, 1994)
3. See Arnold Kemp, *The Hollow Drum* (Edinburgh: Mainstream, 1993).
4. See for example Kenneth Simpson, *The Protean Scot* (Aberdeen: Aberdeen University Press, 1988).

Burns in Japanese

A T THE OUTSET, I have to admit that I am laying myself open to a charge of presumption by speaking on the topic of Burns in Japanese. I have no scholarly qualifications, beyond a Grade C pass in the A-level exam, in Japanese; and I certainly am not tutored in the subtleties of Japanese poetry. However, I have at least an amateur's interest in and knowledge of the language, besides a fascination for the culture; and the present paper is intended as an answer to friends and colleagues over the last few years who have dropped gentle hints that the pursuit of Japanese studies is an unprofitable distraction to a Scots linguistic and literary scholar.[1]

Burns is renowned as the most universally appealing of poets; and it is a well-known fact that his work has been translated into a great variety of languages. However, poetic translation is a proceeding of infinite complexity; and the factors which influence its success or failure apply to translations of Burns as of other poets. Much more is required of a translator of poetry than the simple ability to understand the words the original poet used: the varying merit of the translations discussed in W. Jacks's classic study *Robert Burns in Other Tongues*[2] is ample proof that this alone is no guarantee of even the slightest measure of success. On any showing, a valid translation of a poem must itself be a poem, and a poem of comparable merit to the original. For this, the translator must be equipped with not only a sound knowledge of the vocabulary, grammar and so on of the original poet's language, but a high degree of competence in the literary exploitation of his own. Since a translation must reflect the qualities of the original in as specific a way as possible (possible, that is, with the resources of the target language and its associated literary tradition), the translator must also have a sufficient degree of sensitivity to literary merit in the original language to recognise the features of his source text on which its individual value depends. And since any poem, axiomatically, has its origin in the poet's own life experiences, and is therefore a product of his entire social and material culture as well as of his literary tradition and his own individual poetic gifts, the translator should, ideally, have sufficient understanding of all these factors to recognise, and when appropriate utilise in his translation, parallels from his own culture. Several factors can be recognised as contributing to the individual character of Burns's poetic corpus (besides the bedrock fact of his unique personality and poetic genius): one could cite a literary medium of unusual semantic and phonaesthetic potential, a strongly-emphasised literary debt to identifiable predecessors, a society in which complex and (arguably) in some respects pathological tensions were partly reflected in an unstable language situation, a peasant culture of a type familiar, with local variations, in Europe but not necessarily elsewhere. Neither individually nor cumulatively do these factors make Burns's poems in principle atypical as material to be translated: they are simply the manifestations which arise in this particular case of the universal problems of translation. Nonetheless, they are highly potent factors, presenting major challenges to a translator; and there is no guarantee that any individual translator can resolve them successfully.

Any language would, of course, afford to a translator its own individual range of possibilities for meeting these challenges. But *prima facie*, it must be said that Japanese, from several points of view, would seem to be about as unpromising a medium as the world affords for translating the poetry of Burns. Firstly, the dissimilarity between the languages is extreme. Speakers of English (or Scots) who acquire a degree of fluency in, say, German, French or Gaelic may be daunted at first by the differences in linguistic structure, at all levels, between the mother tongue and these "foreign" languages; but nothing demonstrates more clearly the essential relationship between languages of the Western Indo-European group than even the most superficial acquaintance with a totally unrelated language such as Japanese. On the level of morphology, nouns have no inflexions whatever, but verbs – and to some extent adjectives, which share the inflexional system of verbs – have a terrifying range of forms: no number or person distinctions, but a wholly un-European array of inflexions indicating 'causative', 'desiderative', 'potential', 'presumptive', 'alternative' and so on: as an artificial and perhaps unlikely, but perfectly possible, illustration, the conjugation of the verb *taberu* 'eat' could include a form *tabesaseraretakunakereba*, which would mean 'if (you) do not want to be made to eat'. On the level of syntax, the motto-text for learners is 'So shall the first be last and the last first': verbs invariably come at the ends of their clauses, the place of nouns in the clause structure is indicated not by prepositions but by *post*positions, and not only all adjectives but all adjective clauses precede their nouns, making the ordering of elements in the construction of a sentence almost precisely the mirror image of that in Romance or Germanic languages. (The sentence 'I wrote a letter to the girl I met on the boat' would be translated into Japanese as *Hune de atta zyosei ni tegami o kakimasita*[3], of which the elements mean literally 'Boat-on met girl-to letter-*obj* wrote.') The relative positioning of elements in clause and sentence structure of course gives equal difficulty to Japanese learners of English; as do such features of English, unknown in Japanese, as definite and indefinite articles, phrasal verbs, and the complex and subtle use of auxiliary verbs to mark tense and aspect.

It is not necessarily true that ease of translation, or adequacy of the result of an individual act of translation, is related in any simple way to the actual degree of linguistic similarity between the source and the target languages. An examination of Jacks's book will certainly suggest to any reader that German as a translation medium for Burns seems to make for renderings both more satisfactory as poetry and more faithful to the spirit of the originals than does French or Italian, and German of course belongs, as French and Italian do not, to the same branch of Indo-European as Scots. On the other hand, Marshak's translation of Burns into Russian, besides having the status of a landmark in the Russian literary canon, is said (having no knowledge of the language I cannot comment) to be remarkably accurate; and conversely the attempts which have been made at translating Burns into English, the language *maist lyk til ouris* (James VI), hardly deserve to be taken seriously. But when the difference between the source and the target languages is as extreme as in the case of Scots and Japanese, it must at the very least be conceded that a translator's preliminary qualification, adequate knowledge of the source language, must have been achieved at the cost of exceptional effort.

The mere fact of linguistic dissimilarity, important though it is, is of less moment than its corollary: poets writing in any given language necessarily develop stylistic conventions conditioned by the language's individual nature; and as the conventions which arise in mutually contrasting languages will themselves be in contrast, the translator's goal of trans-linguistic compatibility may be difficult or impossible of attainment. This would certainly seem to be true of any attempt to render Scots originals comprehensible to Japanese readers. Japanese is a syllable-timed language with a pitch accent (it is *not* a tone language like Chinese, to which it is genetically as unrelated as it is to European languages). As in the case of French, of which the same is true, this has led to a poetry based on syllable counting: the central requirement for poetry in both languages has traditionally been a fixed number of syllables per line. One item of Japanese culture which has acquired some degree of familiarity in the West is *haiku* poetry: poems of three lines containing five, seven and five syllables. (In English, which is a stress-timed language, the practice of writing lines with a set number of syllables is an importation from French, not necessitated by the rhythmic structure of the language and never, whether consistently observed or not, of fundamental importance to poetic prosody.) That is, there is no possibility of replicating or even approximating Burns's rhythmic effects in Japanese. This, though a major difference between the languages, is by no means sufficient in itself to preclude the possibility of successful translation: after all, precisely the same issue arises with every instance of poetic translation (in either direction) between French and English. But the catalogue of differences does not end there. The languages of the world show wide variations in size of vowel systems and complexity of permitted syllable structures. In both these factors, Japanese is among the simplest of languages: it has only five distinct vowels (Ayrshire Scots has nine [4]) and scarcely any types of syllable structure except V and CV (English is notoriously at the other end of the scale of complexity in this respect, allowing up to three consonants in the initial phase of syllables and as many as four in the final phase; and the same is true of Scots). In an absolute sense, that is, Scots has a far greater range of possibilities than Japanese for phonaesthetic effects in literature. In Scots, as in English, French and German, skilful use of rhyme has always been a conspicuous and productive poetic device: in Japanese poetry rhyme is very rarely used, for the simple reason that it occurs so readily that (one could almost say) more skill is required to avoid it than to use it. It is not to be imagined that the limitations of Japanese phonology have ever been an actual handicap to poets writing in the language: on the contrary, sound effects of various kinds are as conspicuous a part of the Japanese poetic tradition as of any other. Delicate patterning of recurring vowels and consonants is a common device; the frequency of homophones has led to a special literary trick involving a sort of pun, in which a word is used with both senses simultaneously present; and one of the most individual, most remarkable and (to a foreigner at least) most intriguing and charming features of the language is an extraordinary number of onomatopes and phonaesthemes. Almost every noise in nature can be expressed in Japanese: it may not seem particularly surprising that a duck says *gaa-gaa*, a sparrow *tyun-tyun*, a pheasant *horo-horo*, a cat *nyaa-nyaa*, a frog *kero-kero*, and so on; but a language which represents the sound of wind as *soyo-soyo* or *hyuu-hyuu*, thunder as *gara-gara* or *goro-goro*, and has at least five onomatopes for different kinds of rainfall (*potu-potu*, *para-para*, *sito-sito*, *zaa-zaa* and *zan-zan*); suggests walking at a brisk pace by *suta-suta*, strutting proudly by *toku-toku*, trudging heavily by *teku-teku* and skipping by *pyon-pyon*; and even has phonaesthemes to suggest the twinkling and glittering of stars (*pika-pika*, *kira-kira*), has surely something wonderfully distinctive [5]. But a Japanese translator confronted with a poet whose language offers as extensive and as individual a range of sound patterns as that of Burns, and who manipulates them with his degree of skill and subtlety, has no alternative but to find other ways, if any present themselves, of conveying the poetic effects which Burns gains by this means.

The dissimilarities of the languages are equalled at least by the contrasts between the poetic traditions. It would be absurd to attempt a summary of the characteristics of Japanese poetry in the time available (even if I had the necessary expertise); but perhaps its single most important feature, and one which seems at once to establish an unbridgeable gulf between Burns and Japan, is that the Japanese poetic culture emanated from, and for much of its history was consistently by, for and about, a social aristocracy. From the first emergence of a distinctive Japanese poetic tradition, the focus of literary activity was the Imperial court: in the *Penguin Book of Japanese Verse*, twelve of the first fourteen writers whose works are represented are 'Emperor —', 'Empress —', 'Prince —' or 'Princess —'; and the other two are 'Lady —' and 'A courtly lady'. The first great efflorescence of Japanese literature, in what is referred to as the Heian period [6] (the ninth to the twelfth centuries AD in European terms), was the product of one of the most extraordinary societies in the history of the world: an aristocratic class without political, military or administrative function, whose lives were devoted *entirely* to ceremonies, love intrigues, artistic creation and the development of aesthetic sensitivities. An Occidental reader who makes the acquaintance of the truly exquisite delicacy and refinement of the Japanese courtly culture of this period receives quite a shock on recalling that it was produced when Northern Europe was the stamping ground of the Macbeths, Cnuts and Edmund Ironsides of our own history! In Europe too, of course, royal courts have traditionally been centres of literary activity; but even in, say, Elizabeth Tudor's England or Louis XIV's France – let alone James IV's Scotland – the social and cultural barriers between the aristocracy and the commonality were never as profound as in Japan, nor did the aristocracies of Europe ever divest themselves totally from the social and political functions which kept them at least marginally in contact with the lives of the lower orders. (The nearest thing to an exception is perhaps eighteenth-century Versailles: a fact which speaks for itself in view of what ultimately happened to that regime.) By contrast, the greatest literary monument of the Heian period and one of the major literary works of the world, *The Tale of Genji* by Murasaki Shikibu (an enormous and probably unfinished work of prose fiction), gives almost no recognition to the fact that such things as commoners even exist: the characters pass their entire lives in the physically self-contained ambience of the Imperial court, and the hero's temporary banishment is seen as a catastrophe of devastating proportions. The conventions regulating the styles, techniques, functions, subject matter and underlying assumptions of literature established in the Heian period have influenced Japanese culture to the present day.

Japanese literature, that is, is almost entirely without a tradition of peasant poetry: a poet from the lower ranks of society would be a rarity in himself; and one whose poetic gifts were devoted to such things as celebrating the virtues of the common people and the joys of their domestic and convivial lives, or protesting against the oppressions of the poor by the privileged classes, would be totally foreign to the entire tradition of Japanese culture. (In the translation of Burns which I am going to discuss, his name on the title page is preceded by the words *noomin sizin* 'peasant poet', suggesting that even in contemporary Japan this requires to be pointed out as strange.)

Furthermore, the language in which Burns wrote poses immense problems in a Japanese context: one hesitates in principle to use the word 'insuperable'; but if not this, they are certainly the next thing to it. These problems are not merely linguistic. The idiosyncratic features of Scots which give it such remarkable potency as a poetic language are well-known; but it is salutary to remember that *every* language has its own peculiar characteristics. When Biagi renders 'stour' in *Mary Morison* as *polvere*[7], or de Wailly takes 'the Lord's house' in *Tam o' Shanter* to mean *le saint lieu*[8], it is not because translation from Scots is uniquely difficult or impossible, but simply because they have not done their homework properly. The difficulty of finding a way of saying 'Nou they're crouse an' canty baith' or 'When lyart leaves bestrow the yird' in another

language is no different in principle from any other problem of poetic trans-
lation: say, that of rendering *Les sanglots longs / Des violons / De l'automne*
into English. Similarly, it is of course true that Burns's poetic genius is manifest
in his own individual use of his medium; but this again is true of every great
writer. A translator of Burns has the particular difficulty that the unfamiliarity
of his language and his poetic tradition outwith Scotland, and the paucity of
materials and opportunities for learning Scots, make the preliminary task of
acquiring a working knowledge of the poet's medium a formidable one; but
this is a purely contingent difficulty: nothing in Burns's language, his literary
background or his individual poetic voice makes the task of translating his
work *in principle* any different from, or *intrinsically* any more difficult than,
that of translating, say, Wordsworth.

The relevant factor is not the linguistic structures of Scots, but its socio-
linguistic implications. The title of the Kilmarnock Edition is *Poems, chiefly in
the Scottish Dialect. Dialect*, note. I certainly am not going to raise here the
question of whether that is or is not the right term to apply to Scots: it was
the term Burns used; and its perfectly clear implication is that Burns was writing,
deliberately, in a non-standard tongue, socially and literarily less privileged
than another form. The plain fact of using Scots in the eighteenth century was
an act of subversion. It is this, and not any intrinsic difficulty in the language
itself, that makes the issue of translating from Scots inherently problematic:
non-standard languages exist in abundance, but ones which show the degree
of literary development of Scots and share its political implications are very
much harder to find.

Burns's contrastive use of Scots and English, and his modulations between
the two languages, are things which no translation known to me makes any
attempt to replicate. However, some European translators have at least tried
to find a counterpart to his Scots: he has been translated with great success into
Low German and Swiss German, for example, both of which have historical,
social and political overtones offering interesting points of comparison with
Scots. Neither the Japanese language nor its literary tradition affords any
equivalent to this. Japanese has local dialects, showing in some cases quite
extensive divergences: the language situation in Japan is much more like that
of a Western European nation-state, with a canonical standard and a variety of
non-standard forms of what is essentially a single language, than like most other
Asiatic countries. (We should remind ourselves occasionally that Europe is the
only part of the world where sequences of historical events have led to some
remote tendency for political and linguistic boundaries to coincide; and that
the notion of French as what they speak in France, German as what they speak
in Germany, and so on, naive even in terms of the actual situation in Europe,
is absurd if applied elsewhere – Japan being almost the only major exception.)
However, except in the very early stages of Japanese literary history, no attempt
was ever made to compose art poetry (as opposed to folk poetry) in the dialects –

still less to make literary capital out of the sociolinguistic contrast between the dialects and the standard. This is not because it is impossible to represent dialect variations in the Japanese writing system (as is true of Chinese), for this *can* be done at least to some extent: it is only recently that Japanese scholars have begun to use phonetic transcription instead of the Japanese syllabary for dialect studies. The reason for the absence of dialect literature is simply the incompatibility between the aristocratic ethos already discussed and the social implications of low-prestige speech. A poet whose medium is *essentially* a low-prestige one, and who wrote in it specifically to exploit that fact, could never have arisen in Japanese culture; and it is difficult to conjecture how this quality of Burns's language, so fundamental to his entire work, could even be suggested to a Japanese readership.

In summary, Burns in Japanese must lose not only his phonology, vocabulary and idiom with no possibility of their being replaced by anything even remotely similar, but also his status as a peasant poet and the socio-political implications inherent in his choice of language. Yet he *has* been translated, from well before the date of the translations which I am going to discuss. In the period following the ending of Japan's isolation in the nineteenth century, large numbers of Western literary and cultural texts were translated, including selections from Burns's poetry: a literary magazine entitled *Albion*, produced at Kyoto University, included translations and discussion of his work, and he appears to have enjoyed some degree of popularity in the first half of the present century. Some at least of his poems are still regularly taught in *Igirisu-bungaku*[9] classes. What, if anything, of Burns is left in a Japanese translation; and how, if at all, can the loss of so many characteristics be made good?

The translations which I will discuss in an attempt to answer this question are, with one exception, by Tadashi Itsuno, a distinguished scholar who taught English at Kyoto University. His collection of Burns translations appeared in 1959. The book is a small but finely-produced volume, with illustrations, an introduction, an extensive biographical essay and a short bibliography, in which the originals and the translations are printed on facing pages, and English glosses for the Scots words are given at the foot of each page. Most of the poems have brief introductory narratives: the prominence of these almost sugests that Itsuno has in mind a traditional Japanese literary form in which poems in a collection are linked by prose passages.

His rendering of *Bonnie Doon* illustrates his approach. This poem would perhaps make a particular appeal to a Japanese translator, as its mood is very similar to that of much Japanese poetry. (One respect in which Burns's works *could* harmonise with the Japanese literary tradition is the importance of love as a theme in his poetry: love has always been a principal inspiration for poetry in Japan. However, by no means all of Burns's love-poetry would strike a sympathetic chord in Japanese ears. The predominant mood of Japanese love poetry is either of regret for a lost love or anticipation of a love soon to be fulfilled; and in both moods, characteristically, the speaker's emotion is expressed in a restrained, allusive fashion, using references to nature (birds, flowers, weather, times of day and year, and so on) to evoke an emotional response. This particular poem would seem in those respects to be well attuned to Japanese sensitivities: on the other hand, *Corn Rigs are Bonnie*, for instance, probably would not: too frank and direct in its expression of the unequivocal joy of love, and too clearly focused in its description of the actual events.) A strong sense of identity with a particular place, suggested by the naming of an actual town or natural feature such as a river, is also frequent in Japanese poetry.

The translation conforms to the Japanese practice of syllable counting: alternate lines are of 7 + 7 and 7 + 5 syllables. (Every vowel belongs to a separate syllable, and *n* can, and when final always does, form a syllable by itself. Thus *Doon* is actually trisyllabic in Japanese: *du-u-n*. Interestingly, Itsuno uses a nonce spelling to suggest the foreign pronunciation: the syllable [du] never occurs in native Japanese words.) This is not a traditional Japanese verse form, but it is certainly a credible attempt to devise something comparable to the original stanza. Sound patterning is very much in evidence: one notes the line-initial alliteration in the first stanza, the interweaving of *a* and *u* in the third line, the near-parallel vowel arrangement in *hanayagu* and *kawayuku* at corresponding points in the first and third lines, the continuation of the *a-u* patterning in the third line with *utau* and the contrast of the three successive *o*s. The rhetorical questions in the original are not reproduced, but the concessive *satemo* 'indeed', repeated, emphasises the contrast with the clause introduced by *soreni* 'however'.

Watasi 'I' is underlined by the topic particle *wa* (obligatory in modern spoken Japanese but used only when desired in the poetic language), and as in the original, the equivalent to 'fu' o' care' is given an emphatic position at the end of the stanza. It is noteworthy that this, the first appearance of the speaker, is the only instance of the personal pronoun *watasi*: elsewhere 'I' is expressed by another form, *wasi*. To any ears *watasi*, being trisyllabic, is more conspicuous in the verse structure than *wasi*, and therefore more striking for the speaker's first appearance: however, the choice of pronouns has a further significance. One of the well-known features of Japanese is its difficult and elusive system of graded honorifics, manifest in pronouns and elsewhere: 'you', for example, can be expressed by the respectful *anata*, the familiar *kimi*, *omae* which can be either intimate or insulting, or the unspeakably rude *kisama*. *Wasi* is a 'low-class' pronoun appropriate for a peasant speaker. [10] What is possibly an example of Japanese double meaning is present in the word *hanayagu*: the first two syllables suggest the word *hana* 'flower', clearly appropriate here, though the word is not written with the character for 'flower' and therefore presumably not related to it.

A prose back-translation of the second verse – as will now be evident, the structures of Japanese and English are so unlike that the word-by-word translation supplied may not even be intelligible – would be something like 'Though I can hear the song of the bird in the tree-top, my heart is troubled and upset; I long with all my heart for the happy bygone days when my false love was true.' *Nagara* as a postposition meaning 'on (top of)' is a somewhat rare and poetic usage. *Mukasi* is a potent word, very like 'lang syne' in both range of meaning and emotive power. The sense of *kometa* appears to suggest a kind of intensity of inward feeling which neither 'with all my heart' nor 'devotedly' really conveys: it is the past form of a verb whose basic meaning (suggested by the character with which it is written) is 'put into'. The use of two passive verbs (the forms in -*reru*) in this stanza is probably deliberate: though neither has the speaker as its subject, the sense of her as victim is thereby reinforced. On the other hand, the force of *'thou'll* break my heart' (the second line in both stanzas 2 and 3 is the equivalent of this: *tizi ni*, of which the first word suggests a total fragmentation by being written with the character for 'thousand' repeated, is regularly used of broken hearts) is lost: the bird and its song are not seen as the agent of the speaker's heartbreak. (In Japanese poetry, however, the idea of sad thoughts aroused by a bird's song is of such common occurrence that the translator may not have thought it necessary to state the connection overtly.) *Suikazura* is a kind of honeysuckle (*Lonicera Japonica*) – an evergreen, as its name, which means literally 'winter-bearing', suggests: I do not know what emotional connotations, if any, it has to the Japanese mind; but it *may* be significant – the artistic culture of Japan, and China too, is such that no conjecture in this area can be dismissed out of hand – that the first of the two characters with which it is written is a combination of the sign for *blade* and that for *heart*!

In the very last line, the translator has added an implication not present in the original. The image of stealing the rose and leaving the thorn has a familiar significance in Europe which could also be recognised in Japan, but Itsuno has added a suggestion that the false lover (metaphorically of course) threw the thorn to wound the lady's heart: a conceit which certainly makes its own sense.

To a mere amateur like myself this certainly seems a skilfully-wrought poem, and the Japanese friends and acquaintances to whom I have shown it assure me that it reads very well. And undoubtedly, given what might be seen as the almost intolerable constraints of a wholly alien language and prosody, Itsuno has conveyed the sense of Burns's poem in terms which his own potential readers could appreciate.

The task of rendering *Auld Lang Syne* presents a specific difficulty in addition to those already discussed. *Bonnie Doon* is a supremely beautiful lyric; and though everybody in Scotland is familiar with the musical setting, the poem itself can perfectly well be appreciated without it. (Itsuno has translated the original version in ballad meter, not the version with the second and fourth lines of the stanzas extended to tetrameter for the music.) But *Auld Lang Syne*, as Burns left it, is a song pure and simple. (It almost goes without saying that there are Japanese words to the tune!) Can a song be translated by a version which is not written to be sung; and given that the music of Japan and that of Scotland are of course as dissimilar as everything else about the cultures, is it a meaningful venture to attempt a cultural transference of an artifact of which music is an essential part? These questions would lead us too far afield, and into regions where I would be hopelessly lost; and I therefore mention them only in passing.

The translation itself is sufficiently interesting. As before, Itsuno retains a metrical form based on traditional Japanese: for the verse, lines of 7 + 7, 7 + 5, 7 + 7 and 7 syllables; for the chorus, 7 + 5, 7, 7 + 7 and 7. (*Ippai* has four syllables: *i-p-pa-i*). *Mukasi-nazimi* is an established compound, serving very appropriately for 'auld acquaintance'. Itsuno follows Burns precisely in opening the song with a rhetorical question implicitly demanding a negative answer: the sense of the Japanese line is 'How could we ever forget old friends?' However, the first stanza has an un-Japanese feature: except for *mukasi-nazimi* it contains no concrete nouns whatever. This, I suspect, would make the translation seem much less emotive to a Japanese than the original is to a Scot: emotions in Japanese poetry are almost invariably expressed by association with something visible, audible or tangible. The refrain is addressed to a second person, though this is not obvious owing to the absence of person distinctions in Japanese: *noo* in the first line has the force of *n'est-ce pas?*, though more emphatic (the normal expression with this sense in Japanese is *ne*); and the line suggests 'Ye're my auld frein, shair ye are?'. *Doo de* ... suggests 'What about pledging each other in a drink?'

The second stanza is less abstract than the first. *Kakeru* (*kakete* is the present participle) is used of horses or people on horseback rather than meaning 'run' in the sense intended by Burns here: the implication is of covering a wide territory. The 'we' of the third line is suggested not by a pronoun nor by the repetition of *hutari* 'two people', the opening word of the stanza, but by *naka* 'companionship': the compound *nakayoku* in the first line contains the same word, the *yoku* part being an adverb derived from the word for 'good'. 'Mony a weary foot' is conveyed very neatly by the compound – compounding of words is a frequent feature in Japanese – *ukitabi*, from *uki* 'miserable, gloomy, troubled' and *tabi* 'journey'.

The remainder of the poem is consistent in style with the verses given. 'We twa hae paidled i' the burn' is rendered as *Hutari o-gawa de nakayoku asobi*, a line parallel in structure to *Hutari ko-yama o nakayoku kakete*: the closeness is still more evident in the written form, as the diminutive prefixes *ko-* and *o-* are written with the same character. The first three lines of the fourth stanza ('And there's a hand ...') all begin with the exclamation *saasa*, 'come on!' Just as all the stanzas in the original end with '— auld lang syne', so do all those in the translation end in *mukasi-nazimi* — ; a different verb or postposition corresponding to the 'and', 'for' and 'sin'' of the Scots. Though the theme and tone of this poem are perhaps less finely tuned to Japanese sensibilities than *Bonnie Doon*, the translation has been accomplished with comparable skill.

In the case of *Duncan Gray*, the challenge appears to have been to shape a fast-paced, humorous narrative to Japanese verse forms. Perhaps because this song, with its very Scottish brand of humour, was felt to be impossible even to attempt to naturalise completely, Itsuno has allowed himself a slight relaxation of the meter in places. The refrain can only make metrical sense if we regard the *ha, ha* as hypermetrical and attend only to the seven syllables of *ano kudoki-buri*; the foreign words seem to have enforced some irregularity: *Dankan Gurei* has seven syllables, so that with the subject particle the first half of the first line comes to the unusual number of eight, and correspondingly *Kurisumasu* (five syllables) also results in an eight-syllable section in the third line; and in at least one other half-line an eighth syllable occurs. *Ha, ha*, incidentally, is not among the usual Japanese onomatopes for laughter: the nearest to it is *ahaha* [11]. It is hard to imagine the sheer vigour of the Scots lines being conveyed in any translation, and certainly the measured pace of the Japanese does not attempt to do so; on the other hand, *ano kudoki-buri* has a strikingly, even obtrusively, colloquial ring; and Itsuno conveys a clear physical and emotional impression of Maggie in the first stanza with a word corresponding closely to 'looked asklent': *oppuri-tatete*, which combines an emphatic prefix with part of a verb meaning 'shake, toss [the head]', and a reference to a facial expression suggesting disdain. Unusually, the translation shows some signs of cultural naturalisation, incorporating references to Japanese traditional beliefs and altering a few of Burns's physical details. Itsuno conspicuously, and very entertainingly, alters 'doctors', by implication paragons of learning, to 'Buddhist priests'; and for 'Ailsa Craig' as a type of deafness, or rather lack of susceptibility, substitues a statue of Buddha! He could perhaps have avoided the metrical awkwardness of the names by naturalising them too (as many European translators have done: the poem in a Swiss version [12] opens *De Stöffi Schwarz hett d'Grite gern*); but clearly saw this as too radical a proceeding. The line corresponding to 'And O, her een they spak sic things!' has the sense of 'Though her heart was concealed one could understand from the expression of her eyes', and refers to a Japanese belief that whatever a person may say or do to hide his true feelings, a close look at his eyes will always give them away. Finally in the penultimate line, the significance of *matu* 'pine tree' though opaque to European readers would be clear to Japanese: the evergreen and long-living pine is a symbol of happiness (it is still customary to decorate the gates of houses with pine branches at New Year), and pine trees as they grow lean together like a married couple.

Itsuno's translation of *My Luve is like a Red, Red Rose* contrasts strongly with the version by Masao Hirai, emeritus Professor of English at Tokyo University and a distinguished Milton scholar. This is the only Burns poem (and the only Scottish poem, unless we count Byron as a Scot) in his anthology of poems in English with facing-page Japanese translations, published in 1989. Itsuno's word for 'you' is the archaic *sonata*, suggestive of a formal literary register; Hirai uses *omae*, in the modern language conveying intimacy. (The differing first-person pronouns have a separate significance: Hirai's *ore*, unlike Itsuno's *wasi*, is used only by men.) Similarly, 'June' in Itsuno's version is *huzuki*, the traditonal Japanese word for the seventh (not sixth) month of the lunar calendar; Hirai's *rokugatu* simply follows the modern Japanese practice of using the Western calendar and naming the months – disappointingly – 'one-month', 'two-month', etc. In these respects the language of Hirai's translation is less like that of classical Japanese poetry and more like the modern language than that of Itsuno's version: to some Japanese ears at least, his translation is for this reason much inferior to Itsuno's in poetic merit. Grammatically, too, his language is less elliptic and (though this may not be obvious) rather more like modern spoken Japanese: this may explain another feature in which his version differs from the earlier one, the absence of any consistent pattern of syllable-counting. However, Hirai maintains a poetic register by the repetition of the parallel phrases *akai bara da* and *amai ongaku da*: the implication of Burns's doubling of 'red' for emphasis is lost; but the phonetic similarity of *akai* 'red' and *amai* 'sweet' is probably Hirai's reason for selecting the ordinary word for 'red' rather than Itsuno's more intense, as well as more literary, *sinku*. Perhaps the most immediately obvious contrast between the two versions is that by the use of vocatives, the exclamatory particle *yo* and the interjection *oo*, the emphatic *itumodemo* and the idiomatic construction *umi to iu umi*, literally 'sea called sea', also used for emphasis, Hirai has conveyed a tone of emotional outpouring very unlike the (much more characteristically Japanese) restrained and subtle style of Itsuno's rendering. The word *inoti-gake* in the second stanza is also in keeping with this: the sense is 'I would sacrifice my life (for you).'

It has been observed by George Steiner [13] that Western translations from Chinese poetry, or Oriental poetry in general, show a certain uniformity of tone and mood which belies the variety in the originals. This he attributes to the fact that Western translators, having at best only a superficial knowledge of the exotic culture, accommodate their translations to a pre-conceived 'invention of China' rather than endeavouring to acquire the familiarity with the language and its culture which would enable them to recognise its native diversity. I cannot avoid the impression, though it may be due simply to my own lack of sophistication in Japanese, that the same criticism could be made of Itsuno's versions of Burns: he translates the contents of the originals with great skill and expresses them in very accomplished Japanese verse; but I see nothing of the exuberant variety in mood and style which is so characteristic of Burns. This is no doubt due at least in part to the sheer scale of the cultural gap already discussed; but another consideration may also apply. A distinction now well-established in translation studies is that between *source-oriented* and *target-oriented* translations. Briefly, the aim of translations of the first type is to produce something which will give its readers as clear an impression of what the original text was like as the structures of the target language will permit; that of the second, to compose in the translator's language a text comparable in content and in expressive power to the original but conforming fully to the criteria of literary merit accepted in the target language's associated culture. Even more simplistically, a source-oriented translator's first loyalty is to his original; that of a target-oriented translator, to his own literature. (I have suggested elsewhere [14] that a very good contemporary Scottish illustration of the difference between the two types is provided by the contrast between Robin Lorimer's and David Purves's translations of *Macbeth*.) The products of the two types of translation may not in the event differ as much as the contrasting approaches might suggest. Even a source-oriented translation cannot be excessively literal, or it will suffer from a linguistic oddity not present in the original (assuming, of course, that the original was not intentionally odd): that is, it will not give an impression comparable to that of the source text. Conversely, a target-oriented translator cannot claim unlimited licence to tailor cultural references and assumptions present in the original to the expectations of readers in the new culture, or else he runs the risk of losing contact with his source. But the distinction is nonetheless an important one. Itsuno's translations are very clearly target-oriented: he is writing for a Japanese audience; preferably with a knowledge of English (to read his English-language glosses for the Scots words), but relying essentially on their native language to understand and appreciate the translations. To make them acceptable, he was obliged to conform to Japanese conventions; and those simply do not contain a Burnsian cornucopia of poetic varieties. Even the practice of writing poems as long as *Auld Lang Syne*, let alone *Tam o' Shanter* (also included in Itsuno's collection) is foreign to Japan: some Japanese friends have told me that the translations seem strange for this reason alone. Whether Itsuno, or anybody else, *could* extend the boundaries of Japanese poetic conventions to the extent of incorporating Burns's range of styles I have no means of knowing; but he clearly did not see such an attempt as within his remit.

Nonetheless, it is a remarkable confirmation of Burns's universality that he has inspired such a sustained attempt at rendering his poems in a totally alien language and cultural tradition. And Itsuno's book clearly demonstrates that Burns can inspire translations of distinction in Japanese.

1. Bonnie Doon

Satemo hanayagu *Duun* no kisibe
Indeed splendid Doon's   shore

Saita   nagame no utukusisa
blooming scene   's beauty

Satemo kawayuku utau yo ko-tori
indeed charmingly sing (!) little-bird

Soreni watasi wa ukiomoi
however I (topic) sad-thought

Kozue   nagara no tori   no ne   kikeba
Tree-top on   's   bird 's sound if-hear

Tizi   ni   midareru waga kokoro
scattered in is-disordered my   heart

Adasi otoko no makoto o   kometa
fickle man   's   truth (obj.) devotedly

Tanosii mukasi   ga   sinobareru
pleasant past-time (subj.) is-longed-for

Tuma ni yorisoo tori no   ne   kikeba
wife to beside bird 's sound if-hear

Tizi   ni   midareru waga kokoro
scattered in   is-disordered my   heart

Wasi mo soo site   utatta mono yo
I   also so doing sang would (!)

ui   no sadame mo tuyu sirade
falsity 's fate   also at-all did-not-know

Kisibe sasurai   ikutabi   mita ka
shore wandering how-many-times   saw (?)

karamu sugata no siikazura
entwine shape 's honeysuckle

kotori   toridori koiuta   uta ya
little-bird various love-song sang (!)

wasi mo utatta koiuta   o
I   also sang love-song (obj.)

Kokoro ukiuki ubara   no hana o
heart cheerful wild-rose 's flower (obj.)

toge no eda   kara soto   tumeba
thorn 's branch from tenderly if-pick

Adasi otoko wa   hana   dake nusumi
fickle man   (top.) flower only stole

sutete   itta yo sono toge   o
thrown-away went (!) that thorn (obj.)

2. *Auld Lang Syne*

Mukasi nazimi   o   wasurete   naro   ka
past-time old-friend (obj.) being-forgotten may-become (?)

Omoidasaide   naru   mono ka
not-remembering become would (?)

Mukasi nazimi   o   wasurete   naro   ka
past-time old-friend (obj.) being-forgotten may-become (?)

Mukasi nazimi   o.
past-time old-friend (obj.)

Mukasi nazimi   d'ya, noo   koresa
past-time old-friend are not-so? 'my dear'

Mukasi nazimi   d'ya,
past-time old-friend are

Doo de   ippai   katane ni yaro   yo
how being one-cup pledge in may-give (!)

Mukasi nazimi   d'ya.
past-time old-friend are

Hutari   ko-yama o   nakayoku   kakete
two-people little-hill (obj.) in-friendship running

Hinagiku tunda ori   mo aru
gowan   picked time also is

Ima wa   ukitabi   sasurau naka   d'ya
now (top.) trouble-journey wander companionship is

Mukasi nazimi   mo.
past-time old-friend also

3. *Duncan Gray*

Dankan Gurei ga   kudoki ni kita yo
Duncan Gray (subj.) wooing to came (!)

Ha, ha, ano kudoki-buri.
Ha, ha, that wooing-way

Kurisumasu no yoru syuen   no seki de,
Christmas   's   night drinking-party 's place to

Ha, ha, ano kudoki-buri.
Ha, ha, that wooing-way

Magii atama o   oppuri-tatete
Maggie head (obj.) (much)-tossing

Iya-na   hito yo to   sirime   ni kakerya,
disagreeable person as with corner-of-eye in if-hang

Aresa, *Dankan* teasi   mo   dasezu,
Look! Duncan hand-foot even cannot-put-out

Ha, ha, ano kudoki-buri.
Ha, ha, that wooing-way

Kiite okure to inottya mire do
Listen please! (–) prayed try   but …

Nabiku mono ka yo kono isibotoke
yield   would (?) (!) this   stone-Buddha …

Donna wake ka wa   osyoo sa   ni kikyare,
what   reason (?) (top.) Bonze indeed to please-ask.

Otoko satoreba,   onna   ga   mayou,
Man   if-come-to-senses woman (subj.) become-lost …

Tutumu kokoro wa   memoto   de wakaru
veil   heart   (top.) eye-expression by understand …

Ima d'ya, medetai kono myooto   matu.
now is   joyous   this   married-couple pine-tree

4. My Luve is like a Red, Red Rose

(by Tadashi Itsuno)

Kawai   sonata wa huzuki no koro ni
charming 'you' (top.) June   's time in

Saita   sinku no bara no hana,
blooming crimson's rose 's flower

Kawai   sonata wa   hikute   mo tae-ni
charming 'you' (top.) play-hand also sweetly

kirei-na   sirabe no uta no kyoku
delightful tune   's song 's music

Atena sugata no sonata d'ya yue   ni
fair form   's 'you' is   reason in

Wasi no omoi   mo hukaku naru
I   's thought also deep   become

Wasi no kokoro ga   kawaroo   mono ka
I   's heart (subj.) can-change would (?)

Umi ga   higata   ni nareba   tote.
sea (subj.) tidal-beach to if-become even-if

(By Masao Hirai)

Ore no koibito yo, omae wa   akai bara da,
I   's beloved (!) you (top.) red rose are

Rokugatu ni patto   saita   akai bara da,
June   in suddenly blooming red rose are

Omae wa   maru de amai ongaku da,
You (top.) just-like sweet music are

Migoto-ni kanaderareta amai ongaku da.
splendidly played   sweet music are

Omae no utukusisa ni makemai   to
You 's beauty   in unsurpassable if

Ore no koi mo   inoti-gake, oo, ore no   kawaii koibito yo.
I   's love (top.) life-risk   oh! I   's   dear   beloved (!)

Itumodemo ore no kokoro wa   kawari wa   sinai,
For ever   I   's heart   (top.) change (top.) not-do

Tatoe   umi to iu umi ga   hiagaroo   to.
even-if all-the-seas   (subj.) can-dry-up if

NOTES

1. I record my grateful thanks to Naohiro Hirose and the other Japanese friends who helped me in my reading of the translations, and to Motoko Kajiyama and (most of all) Reiko Aiura-Vigers, who read the draft typescript and made many corrections and helpful observations.
2. Glasgow: James MacLehose & Sons 1896.
3. Except for proper names, I use throughout the *kunrei-siki* system of Romanisation, which is the one officially supported by the Japanese government. Though it is much less widely used than the Hepburn system, there are sound linguistic arguments for preferring it.

4. It goes without saying that I am familiar with Vol III of the *Linguistic Atlas of Scotland* and realise how simplistic this statement would be from the point of view of descriptive linguistics. It is perfectly adequate, however, from that of literary stylistics.

5. Of the thousands of amateur and professional singers who have performed Gilbert and Sullivan's *The Mikado* in the last hundred years, probably very few have ever realised that the words of a chorus in the opera are authentic Japanese, and include an onomatope of this class: *pira-pira*, referring to the fluttering of a flag.

6. From *Heian Kyoo*, 'city of harmony and peace', the new imperial capital on the site of modern Kyoto. The first syllable is pronounced like 'hay', not like 'high'.

7. *Virgil, Dante et al.;* Scotsoun Euro-Makars Series, vol. 1.

8. See Jacks, *op. cit.*, p. 365.

9. 'English literature' – but sometimes and by some people at least, *Igirisu* is used to mean 'Great Britain' or 'the United Kingdom' as opposed to *Ingurando*, which means England.

10. A somewhat odd feature in this context is that *wasi* is very rarely used by women. Some of my Japanese friends, on reading this translation, were surprised to realise that the speaker of the poem is female.

11. But *ihihi, uhuhu, ehehe* and *ohoho* are also onomatopes for different kinds of laughter. George MacDonald's wicked fairy (in *Little Daylight*) who laughs 'Ha, ha! He, he! Hi, hi!' and protests at being interrupted before reaching 'Ho, ho!' and 'Hu, hu!' would impress Japanese readers as a virtuoso of humorous reactions!

12. By August Corrodi. See Jacks, *op. cit.*, p. 159.

13. *After Babel* (OUP, 1975), 357–361. 'The more remote the linguistic-cultural source, the *easier* [italics mine] it is to achieve a summary penetration and a transfer of stylized, codified markers' (p. 361).

14. In a paper entitled 'When *Macbeth* becomes Scots', presented at a conference on translation at Liverpool University in August 1995 and submitted for publication in the Conference Proceedings volume.

Nature's Social Union and Man's Dominion: Burns the Poet after Two Hundred Years

BURNS DIED almost two hundred years ago. Why has it taken Scotland, and for that matter, the wider world, so long to take aboard that women have artistic, intellectual, and social rights which match those of any male, however well-known? Then again, can we expect to see Scotland, and the wider world, address by say the year 2000 or sooner some at least of the needs of the environment? If little is actually done now on behalf either of animals or the trees, can we justify citing the name of a Scottish writer two centuries ago who cared passionately about both? It hardly seems appropriate to throw yet more prejudice at the reputation of a born writer because he happens to have some beliefs which are different from those of the majority.

I propose to consider first some points relating to man's tyranny over other creatures. My title echoes what is possibly Burns's best-known short poem, 'To A Mouse'. 'To A Mouse' combines tender feeling and the ability to express much in few words. His concern is that in destroying the mouse's home and displacing the mouse he had broken the bond of 'nature's social union'. Man's abuse of power, accidental or not, over nature's creatures matters. Burns could also express real anger about indifference towards the natural world. Perhaps I can come up to date by touching on insights gleaned from my son. I belong to a generation of Scots which grew up indifferent, by and large, to such topics as vegetarianism, let alone animal rights. My son and his contemporaries have every right to feel radically critical about the indifference of our masters towards the exploitation of animals and the environment. My own notion is that there is more in common between their creative impatience and Robert Burns's attitude than between the poet's values and willed conformism now to what may be superficial late twentieth-century expectations.

An early love song, 'Now Westlin Winds, and slaught'ring Guns', combines in a surprising way the love of a man for a woman and outrage at the cruelty of the 'slaught'ring guns' directed against game birds:

> Thus ev'ry kind their pleasure find,
> The savage and the tender;
> Some social join, and leagues combine;
> Some solitary wander:

> Avaunt, away! the cruel sway,
> Tyrannic man's dominion;
> The Sportsman's joy, the murd'ring cry,
> The flutt'ring, gory pinion!

Who can ignore the protest of these lines?

In a letter to Mrs Dunlop sent from Ellisland and dated 21 April 1789, Burns refers to an incident which prompted the poem written 'On Seeing a Wounded Hare limp by me, which a Fellow had just shot at'. He expresses real anger at man's barbarity:

> Two mornings ago as I was, at a very early hour, sowing in the fields, I heard a shot, & presently a poor little hare limped by me, apparently very much hurt. You will easily guess, this set my humanity in tears and my indignation in arms. – The following was the result ... according to you just right, the very first copy I wrote. –
>
> On seeing a fellow wound a hare with a shot – [1]

A second copy of the poem entitled this time 'On seeing a Fellow Sound a Hare with a Shot-April-1789' was sent to Mr Alexander Cunningham in a letter in which Burns comments more elaborately on the occasion:

> One morning lately as I was out pretty early in the fields sowing some grass seeds, I heard the burst of a shot from a neighbouring plantation, & presently a poor little wounded hare came crippling by me. You will guess my indignation at the inhuman fellow, who could shoot a hare at this season when they all of them have young ones; & it gave me no little gloomy satisfaction to see the poor injured creature escape him. Indeed there is something in all that multiform business of destroying for our sport individuals in the animal creation that do not injure us materially, that I could never reconcile to my ideas of native Virtue and eternal Right.[2]

Mr Patrick Miller also received a copy of the same poem in a letter written on 21st June 1789, in which Burns condemns the 'assassinating of God's creatures'.

> As I was in my fields early one morning in this last spring, I heard the report of a gun from a neighbouring wood, and presently a poor little hare, dragging its wounded limbs, limped piteously by me. I have always had an abhorrence at this way of assassinating God's creatures without first allowing them those means of defence with which he has variously endowed them: but at this season when the object of our treacherous murder is most probably a Parent, perhaps the mother ... such an action is not only a sin against the letter of the law, but likewise a deep crime against the morality of the heart. We are all equally creatures of some Great Creator ... I think it is none of the least flagrant, that power which one creature of us has to amuse himself

by and at the expence of another's misery, torture & death. But to return to my Poem.

> On seeing a fellow wound a hare,
> Inhuman man! curse on thy barb'rous art,
> And blasted be thy murder-aiming eye;
> May never pity soothe thee with a sigh,
> Nor ever pleasure glad thy cruel heart![3]

His dislike of blood sports makes nonsense of the illustration of Burns fishing which is the title-page engraving of 'Dove's English Classics' edition of James Currie's *Life and Works of Burns* (1808). In her essay entitled 'Burns and Nostalgia', Carol McGuirk states:

> The picture illustrates a passage from Dr. Currie's biography, describing two travellers who came upon Burns one day: 'On a rock that projected into the stream, they saw a man employed in angling ... it was Burns.'[4]

Jean Armour strenuously refuted this comment of Currie's as she was well aware that Burns's abhorrence of blood sports included angling.

While Burns did not conform to the hunting and shooting political correctness of his day, he wrote sympathetically about the preservation of trees and the beauty of water be it river, loch or stream. In his Journal dated August 25 1787 he states,

> an uninclosed, half-proven country is to me more agreeable, and gives me more pleasure as a prospect, than a country cultivated like a garden.[5]

In 'Castle Gordon' he writes,

> Wildly here without control,
> Nature reigns and rules the whole;
> In that sober, pensive mood,
> Dearest to the feeling soul,
> She plants the forest, pours the flood.

While 'Written with a Pencil, standing by the Falls of Fyers, near Loch Ness' contains the following lines:

> Among the heathy hills and ragged woods
> The roaring Fyers pours his mossy floods;
> Till full he dashes on the rocky mounds,
> Where, thro' a shapeless breach, his stream resounds.
> As high in air the bursting torrents flow,
> As deep recoiling surges foam below,
> Prone down the rock the whitening sheet descends,
> And viewless Echo's ear, astonish'd, rends.

'The Humble Petition of Bruar Water to the Noble Duke of Athole' and 'On scaring some Water-Fowl in Loch Turit' are two other such poems. Burns is not only commenting on the wild beauty of the countryside but on the untouched places which are more natural and hold wildlife that is largely independent of man's schemes.

Where Burns was of his age was in regarding friendship as a primary value. Two hundred years after his death, one has only to think of the inspiring influence of his creative friendship with Allan Masterton, whom Burns met in 1787. This friendship between two brilliantly gifted men led to the perfect combination of Burns's words and Masterton's music in 'Willie brew'd a peck o'maut'. His friendship with Francis Grose gave us splendid lines, including

Thou art a dainty Child, O Grose!

and 'Tam o' Shanter', while the 'Elegy on Captain Mathew Henderson' came about through his friendship with Captain Henderson. As a result of Burns's close acquaintance with Clarinda, Mrs McLehose, a noted beauty of whom he saw much in Edinburgh in 1787–8, he penned the love song 'Ae fond kiss'. Burns sent the song to Mrs McLehose shortly after their last meeting in December 1791. She was to write in her journal 40 years later on 6 December 1831, 'This day I can never forget. Parted with Burns, in the year 1791, never more to meet in this world. Oh, may we meet in Heaven!'

In the 'Second Epistle to Lapraik', lines 85–90, Burns expresses his feelings about friendship:

> For thus the royal Mandate ran,
> When first the human race began,
> 'The social, friendly, honest man,
>   Whate'er he be,
> 'Tis he fulfils great Nature's plan,
>   And none but he.'

Whatever 'great Nature's plan' may be, it is scarcely surprising that people should be interested in the lives of the famous. It occurs to me that Burns is in one sense like Pablo Picasso. Worldwide, the Spaniard and the Scot both have certain associations. Some are with scandal, and it is natural for people to have a certain curiosity about scandal. Let me make a simple point which is behind everything I have written over the years about Burns. Sex and scandal are in a sense quite irrelevant to any student. Burns could be shocking, yes, but think of the positive side of what he achieved. Art and artistic creativity deserve attention first, whether given to the world by means of the words of Burns or the paintings of Picasso. Scandal and biographical speculation, whether spicy or dull, are intrinsically only of secondary importance, and trivial. Poetry and Art are what matter. Let us make use then, quite simply, of our eyes and ears. As it happens, neither Burns nor Picasso was free from human error. My claim is that despite their errors the creative work of each deserves to survive. And it is to their work that I feel a need to pay attention. Irony exists in Burns's love of the fiddle and Picasso's use of the guitar in painting and collage early this century. Picasso commented in 1949:

> We artists are indestructible; even in a prison, or in a concentration camp, I would be almighty in my own world of art, even if I had to paint my pictures with my wet tongue on the dusty floor of my cell.[6]

In a similar way, Burns is as much at home with the writing of poems and songs as Picasso with the creation of his paintings, sculpture and ceramics.

An issue any student of Burns is likely to come across sooner or later is his fluency in writing lyrics. His songs can be treated positively whether your individual training is in lyric or song, in words or music. As I understand it, words and tunes belong together in Burns's work, complementing each other. Whether the Bard is being bawdy or polite, it makes sense to heed his words and also the air he seems to have had in mind. Let me quote Adam Smith from *The Theory of Moral Sentiments*, earlier than *The Wealth of Nations* but with the same ability to focus clearly on key ideas:

> A well-contrived building may endure many centuries: a beautiful air may be delivered down by a sort of tradition, through many successive gener-ations; a well written poem may last as long as the world.[7]

Time and again, a beautiful air 'delivered down by a sort of tradition' and well written words by Burns give delight when placed together. In biographical terms, it is impressive that Adam Smith, a man of genius, took the trouble to seek to help Burns, another genius.

Burns is one writer among very many who writes in part out of a need to satisfy his own instinct and compelling need to play with words, to entertain himself. He explains in 'To J S****':

> Some rhyme a neebor's name to lash;
> Some rhyme, (vain thought!) for needfu' cash;
> Some rhyme to court the countra clash,
>   An' raise a din;
> For me, an aim I never fash;
>   I rhyme for fun.

Using one's skill 'for fun' is rather urgently needed in different professional contexts in 1996. There really is too much earnestness in the world of high education, and literature, at least, needs to be emancipated from the isms of the politically correct.

'I rhyme for fun' happens to be true equally of Burns at his best and of that other Scotsman, Byron, in his finest work, from *Beppo* to *Don Juan*. Candidly, despite changes in idiom, Byron's reading of the prevalence of mere conformist attitudes about literature – what he called 'Cant' – is still accurate. And of course Byron literally rhymes for fun. He doesn't call rhyming 'crambo-jingle', but he finds it entertaining. Now Byron is a few points closer to the all-important world of the canon than Burns is. Could Byron by any chance be right in deciding he prefers his own approach to that recommended to him by influential persons of the day? Let me make the point clearly. Byron suggests – some would still say wrongly – that much solemn nonsense clouds realism about good poetry. He wants such realism because he holds the view that life is full of unexpected surprises. Byron's is a poetry of experience. A similar claim can confidently be made for that of Burns. Clarity is a virtue Burns shares with Byron; it was an invaluable part of their Augustan inheritance in satire, and extends to song. Others will decide how much Byron's being born half a Scot and bred a whole one has to do with it. Byron and Burns are life-enhancing Non-conformists. Each is his own man not pinned down by any labels of convenience.

My theme, therefore, is that certain key ideas give unity to Burns's work. He loves nature, simplicity, and tender emotion. It will do him a disservice to dwell on the intellectual side as if he were Kant, Derrida or some such thinker. Energetic attack is in his satire, joy and beauty in his songs. The quality of Burns's best writing is such that his art will not only survive but be as vital in the twenty-first century as now.

NOTES

1. Letter to Mrs Dunlop, Ellisland, 21 April 1789, *The Letters of Robert Burns*, edited by G. Ross Roy (Clarendon Press: Oxford, 1989), vol. I, pp. 397–8.
2. Letter to Mr Alexander Cunningham, Ellisland, 4 May 1789, *The Letters of Robert Burns*, edited by G. Ross Roy (Clarendon Press: Oxford, 1985), vol. I, pp. 404–5.
3. Letter to Mr Patrick Miller, Ellisland, 21 June 1789, *The Letters of Robert Burns*, edited by G. Ross Roy (Clarendon Press: Oxford, 1985), vol. I, pp. 417–18.
4. 'Burns and Nostalgia', Carol McGuirk in *Burns Now*, edited by Kenneth Simpson (Canongate Academic Press: Edinburgh, 1994), pp. 45–6.
5. Brown, Raymond Lamont, *Robert Burns's Tour of the Highlands and Stirlingshire 1787*, (The Boydell Press: Ipswich, 1973), p. 17.
6. *Der Monat*, Berlin, December 1949.
7. Adam Smith, *The Theory of Moral Sentiments*, edited by D. Raphael and A. L. Macfie, (Indianapolis, 1982), p. 195.

'Castalia's Stank': Burns and Rhetoric

M Y TOPIC STANZA is taken from *The Jolly Beggars*. It comes near the end of that anarchist cantata. Among the core of 'randie gangrel bodies' invented by Burns, it is the Bard figure, who sings it. Having announced himself as the voice of the lower classes rather than the 'gentle folks an' a' that,' he rejects learned and mannerized verse by rejecting its mythological source for more immediate liquid stimulation:

> I never drank the Muses' stank,
> Castalia's burn an' a' that,
> But there it streams an' richly reams,
> My Helicon I ca' that. (p. 167) [1]

The specific example he uses to represent learned and mannerized verse happens to be the signature tune of James VI's courtly poetic Renaissance of the fifteen-eighties; the high-styled Castalian fountain, which he brings down to earth as a 'burn' happens to be the name of the group, led by that King as Maecenas and patron.

I intend, using this text as a fulcrum, to examine the simplifying tendency in Scottish literature, one symptom of which is the tendency to divide our poets into heroes and villains; those who conform to current ideals of Scottishness and those who do not. Burns is in the first class deservedly, James VI and his Renaissance, undeservedly, head the second as the almost complete excision of their contribution from the latest anthology of Scottish literature demonstrates. [2]

If the need to emphasise Scottishness encourages simplified, paradigmatic divisions, Burns's unique status as popular national poet – the voice of Scotland's own preferred vision of itself – intensifies the pressure to emphasise only those aspects of his genius which can be popularly understood – the romantic, spontaneous, simple, naturalist line as claimed here by the bard.

As the *Jolly Beggars* quotation shows, Burns encourages such a vision. Over and over again, he claims to be the poet of the heart and of easy inspiration. 'I rhyme for fun;' I am the 'hero of these artless strains, a lowly bard' celebrating the 'heart abune them a'.' It is no part of my remit to deny that this is a major part of Burns's greatness. Any critic, who has tried and failed to analyse the spellbinding effect of that list of trite images – rose, melody, seas, rocks and sand – which makes up 'My Love is Like a Red Red Rose' must know that Burns possesses the art of conveying and recreating simplicity to the highest poetic degree. Nor is it a power to which academics should condescend, though many do. My claim is that the popular myth delimits him within the bounds set by its own ecstasy, by seeking to contain him within that definition.

For, if we return to *The Jolly Beggars*, Helicon and Castalia, thinking first of the authorial point of view – things are not as simple as they seem. To begin with, let's listen to the opening of another Burns song –

> O were I on Parnassus hill;
> Or had o' Helicon my fill;
> That I might catch poetic skill,
>   To sing how dear I love thee. (p. 337)

Burns here praises the very type of inspiration damned by the bard in *The Jolly Beggars*. He is a dramatic poet, not a consistent logician nor a single-viewed politician. As much as MacDiarmid, he is great and contains multitudes. The craft of the neoclassicals; the rhetoric he was taught so assiduously by Murdoch is as important a line in his verse as the romantic.

The authorial perspective and the idea of dramatic voices remind us that *The Jolly Beggars* is composed by the poet Burns. The bard who speaks these lines does so as only one created voice among many in that anarchic cantata. If one then looks at verse forms, a curious fact emerges. The Heliconian stanza, derided by the bard, is the one used by the leading Castalian of all, James VI's own 'maister poete,' Alexander Montgomerie, in his long allegoric poem, *The Cherrie and the Slae* –

> About a bank with balmie bewes,
> Where nightingals their nots renews
>   With gallant goldspinks gay,
> The mavise, mirle and Progne proud,
> The lintwhite, lark and laverock loud,
>   Saluted mirthful May:
> When Philomel had sweetly sung,
>   To Progne she deplored
> How Tereus cut out her tongue
>   And falsely her deflorde;
> Which storie, so sorie,
>   To shew ashamd she seemde,
>   To heare her, so neare her,
>   I doubted if dream'd. (p. 46)[3]

Which stanza form does the narrator use to begin *The Jolly Beggars*?

> When lyart leaves bestrow the yird,
> Or wavering like the Bauckie-bird,
>   Bedim cauld Boreas' blast;
> When hailstanes drive wi' bitter skyte,
> And infant Frosts begin to bite,

> In hoary cranreuch drest;
> Ae night at e'en a merry core
> O' randie, gangrel bodies,
> In Poosie-Nansie's held the splore,
> To drink their orra dudies:
> Wi' quaffing, and laughing,
> They ranted an' they sang;
> Wi' jumping an' thumping,
> The vera girdle rang. (p. 157)

This signature tune of the Castalians with its intricate fourteen-line form, and complex rhyme-scheme is, then, rejected as too contrived and learned by the Bard-persona only after Burns has himself used it to introduce *The Jolly Beggars* in its entirety. A single Heliconian stanza also rounds off the Recitativo sections. That verse immediately follows the song in which the Bard has, literally, consigned all conscious artifice down the 'Stank:'

> So sung the BARD – and Nansie's waws
> Shook with a thunder of applause
> Re-echo'd from each mouth!
> They toom'd their pocks, they pawn'd their duds,
> They scarcely left to coor their fuds
> To quench their lowan drouth:
> Then owre again the jovial thrang
> The Poet did request
> To lowse his PACK an' wale a sang,
> A BALLAD o' the best.
> He, rising, rejoicing,
> Between his TWA DEBORAHS,
> Looks round him an' found them
> Impatient for the Chorus. (p. 168)

Rhetorically, as Burns the disciple of Murdoch and reader of Pope and Shenstone would know,[4] this is a witty form of the modesty topos, in which the artist claims no knowledge of the crafts of writing but does so in such a way that his more learned listeners know the opposite to be the case.

So where does this leave the neat oppositions favoured by a long line of Scottish Tradition critics? Led by Henderson,[5] they would have us believe that Burns the hero stands for simple verse, for everyman, the democratic intellect, the Scots language and folk song, while the Castalians as anti-type stand for stylised verse, for privilege and côteries, are the 'terminators' of Scots, and practise 'musick fyne.' If a comprehensive rather than dualistically opposed view complicates this vision in the case of authorial stance and verse form, how does it affect the other considerations of message, medium and mode?

Those who *are* reminded, in this way, of the muse of Montgomerie, another

Ayrshire poet, will know that *The Cherrie and the Slae* does not convey a message for nobles alone. As allegory, it is directed at Everyman. So, when the poet imagines a conflict between high romantic and theological aspirations – the Cherrie – and opposes them with lower romantic and theological aspirations – the Slae – he goes out of his way to stress that these choices face everyone. At the end of the poem, he refers to the successful completion of '*our* journey' and '*our* interprise' (Stanza 113, lines 4; 6) rather than 'his' quest and undertaking. This is because he, as one of the seed of Adam and Eve, had undertaken it on behalf of all fallen creatures. In the last stanza of all, therefore, it is fitting that he ask 'me with you and you with me' (Stanza 114, line 9) to join in praising God, the author of all (Stanza 81, line 4).

The whole point of Christian allegorization of classical epic was to draw it down from exclusive concern with one hero and the noble class so as to embrace every individual, however apparently inconsequential, in the spirit of Matthew 10: 29–31.[6] Complexity of mode confirms all-inclusiveness of message, making the Heliconian reference quite consistent for a radical cantata.

Even if this is accepted, surely the transition from message to medium confirms one form of Castalian treachery? Is James VI not the man who killed off the Scots language by going south and encouraging his Scots poetic entourage to write in English, thus necessitating the vernacular revival, as led by Burns? Once again, there is truth in this viewpoint but it is far from the whole truth. Who is this writing in 1585?

> The uther cause is, that as for thame that hes written in it of late, there hes never ane of thame written in our language. For albeit sindrie hes written of it in English, quhilk is lykest to our language, yit we differ from thame in sindrie reulis of poesie, as ye will find be experience.[7]

Historically, the first writer to adopt the currently politically correct stance of artificially boosting Scots against the Darwinian tendency of language to favour the strongest linguistic movement – in this case Anglicization – is James VI.

Why, then, did he sell out to English when he became king? That's too long and complex a question to answer here.[8] Broadly, however, he starts from the view that language is a sign system and therefore a means rather than an end. Poetically, Scottish writers have an advantage: Scots may have flourished and become a more subtle medium in the Middle Scots period but even the finest of Middle Scots practitioners – Dunbar, Henryson and Douglas – saw it as only one linguistic option among many. For Dunbar, James VI and Montgomerie as for Ramsay, Fergusson and Burns, our very advantage lay in NOT being delimited to English alone.

In *The Jolly Beggars* as in *The Cherrie and the Slae*, the principle of decorum pertains. In vernacular writing, the high style can be conveyed in latinate English and the Middle High style in English, leaving the normal or Middle Style for Anglo-Scots and reserving low style flytings for thick Middle Scots. Linguistic variety in subtlety is the preferred means of the poet. The Scots of James's Renaissance see themselves in a rhetorically superior not a nationalistically inferior position linguistically. This optimistic vision is inherited by Ramsay, when he claims two pen names to signify his broader linguistic inheritance – from Scots makar (Gavin Douglas) as well as English neoclassical (Isaac Bickerstaff).[9]

Inevitably an eighteenth-century anarchist cantata designed to champion society's rejects will use the lower styles of heavy Scots and Anglo-Scots more often than a late sixteenth-century allegory, composed by the king's poet-laureate. But the principle of decorous adaptation governs each. The Narrator as character in *The Jolly Beggars* may specifically reject that criterion – 'Life is all a variorum, We regard not how it goes, Let them cant about decorum' – but Burns obeys it throughout, even in his own couthy, low style. When the mercenary soldier sings as, literally, a man of the world or the highland lady adopts an elegiac stance, each sings, predominantly, in English because the Middle High style is the decorously appropriate mode for such serious topics:

> Soldier: I am a Son of Mars who have been in many wars,
> And show my cuts and scars wherever I come;
> This here was for a wench, and that other in a trench,
> When welcoming the French at the sound of the drum.
>
> (p. 159)
>
> Lady: They banish'd him beyond the sea,
> But ere the bud was on the tree,
> Adown my cheeks the pearls ran,
> Embracing my John Highlandman. (p. 163)

In this way, he manages to anticipate the Romantic movement without making Wordsworth's radical rejection of neoclassical artifice, rhetoric and poetic diction.

In similar fashion, the personified characters in the drama of *The Cherrie and the Slae* make their case in a variety of styles. Usually, the more serious and respectable personifications will use the higher ranges while the comic and vicious aspects of man's nature will rely on the lower. But the immediate ends of persuasive debate may override that general rule. Those who think the Castalians, especially in their allegories, wrote in English alone, should read them rather than accepting the lies of Henderson. Here, for example, is the way in which Coila's laureate bard, Alexander Montgomerie, may use couthy, proverbial Scots for dramatic effect. Here Experience, in fractious mood, enveighs against Will:

> Ye could not lucke as he alledgde,
> Who all opinions spearde.
> Hee was so frack and firie edg'd,
> He thought us foure but feard.

'Who panses, what chanses,'
Quoth hee, 'no worship wins;
To some best, shal come best,
Who hap wel, rack wel rins'.   (p. 73).

Finally, there is the question of musical mode. The popular view, as always, defines the bias correctly. David Daiches' comparison between the work done by Burns and Scott and that of Homer in reviving a national folklore is as thought-provoking as it is fair. The danger lies in believing that Burns's songs must, therefore, be set to simple old tunes for, of course, this is not a sustainable claim.

Montgomerie's *Cherrie and the Slae*, for all its 114 Stanzas, was almost certainly sung, as Helena Shire has argued.[10] With all its varied characters and James VI's known love of courtly performances, the possibility of its also having a dramatic cantata form seems strong. Amazingly, I have never seen it pointed out that James VI's Renaissance of the fifteen-eighties was, like the eighteenth-century movement culminating in Burns, a specifically musical revival. Why does James believe the vernacular may now claim to vie with Latin and even surpass it in some ways?

> ... as for them that wrait of auld, lyke as the tyme is changeit sensyne, sa is the ordour of poesie changeit. For then they observit not Flowing ... besydes sindrie uther thingis quhilk now we observe and eschew and dois weil in sa doing.' (p. 108)

Later on in the *Reulis* he explains that 'Flowing' means poetic rhythm as adapted to the rhythm of a tune. It is well known that many professional musicians were members of the Castalian band, giving a firm foundation in fact to C. S. Lewis's suspicion that he could 'hear the scrape of the fiddle and the beat of dancing on the turf'[11] in the work of Montgomerie and his fellows.

My own researches have shown that Montgomerie and the other Castalian lyricists used folk melodies as well as, or as a means of simplifying through counterpointing, the more rigorous forms of 'musick fyne.'[12] When this evidence is set beside research on Burns, variations on a theme rather than a clear opposition once more emerge. Jean Redpath's empirical evidence that Burns often proposed settings of an ambitiousness beyond the limits of the human voice has most recently been supported by Fred Freeman. His succinct description of Burnsian practice highlights how closely one Ayrshire bard imitates another across a bridge of almost two hundred years, when it comes to 'Flowing'. 'For Burns, composition (and editing) became, primarily, a matter of what he termed "ballad simplicity". With this in mind, he developed, paradoxically perhaps, elaborate theories regarding the appropriate music and language for a given song; the length and expression of syllables in a musical phrase ...'[13]

Far from the Castalians practising rarified, courtly music alone and Burns confining himself to folk song, the first group saw the benefits of including popular motifs while the poet of the people harboured a desire to be celebrated as a musical virtuoso by the musical experts of his day. This does not deny either the important contribution made by James's 'band' to the 'sang scule' tradition nor lessen the validity of Professor Daiches' Homeric comparison.

What it does achieve, I hope, along with all the other refinements-in-comprehensiveness I have suggested is the formulation of a necessary critical 'cautel.' If Scottish Literature Critics become too bound up with the adjective and so allow nationalist wish-fulfilment in retrospective oversimplification to obscure the essentially literary dimension of the craft to which they are quidditatively allied, then they may live easily in a politically correct Never Never Land where James VI is a villain and Burns a hero; *The Jolly Beggars* stands as a truly radical, romantically patriotic expression of popular spontaneous folk song in Scots while the Castalian Band practises effete manneristic exercises and 'musick fyne' while planning to sell out 'Scottis' for 'Inglis.'

Alternatively, they may listen to James VI rather than Kurt Wittig;[14] Montgomerie rather than Rory Watson; to Burns rather than his bard and think of two cantatas, decorously using the full rhetorical variety of the vernacular to explore, from different viewpoints, for different audiences in different times, the mysteries and miseries of existence for all of us, high and low, favoured and rejected. In the terminology of the classical rhetoricians, whom Carlyle perceptively defined as Burns's most powerful poetic influence, 'Varius sis' may be 'sed tamen idem.' Or, alternatively, what poets claim to share let not critics, or politicians, or sociologists break asunder.

NOTES

1. All Burns citations follow *Burns, Poems and Songs*, ed. James Kinsley (Oxford, 1969).
2. *The Poetry of Scotland: Gaelic, Scots and English*, chosen by Roderick Watson (Edinburgh, 1995).
3. Montgomerie citations follow *A Choice of Scottish Verse 1560–1660*, ed. R. D. S. Jack (London, 1978).
4. See *The Letters of Robert Burns*, ed. G. Ross Roy, 2nd edn (Oxford, 1985), 2 vols, I, 135 (No. 125 To Dr John Moore.)
5. T. F. Henderson, *Scottish Vernacular Literature*, 2nd edn (London, 1900) p. 333: 'Scottish vernacular prose as well as poetry virtually terminates with James VI'.
6. Verse 29: Are not two sparrows sold for a farthing? And one of them shall not fall on the ground without your father. Verse 30: But the very hairs of your head are all numbered.
7. James VI, *The Reulis and Cautelis to be Observit and Eschewit in Scottis Poesie* (Edinburgh, 1584/5). References are to *A Choice of Scottish Prose: 1550–1700*, ed. R. D. S. Jack (London, 1971) pp. 108–11.
8. See my argument in 'Of Lion and Unicorn: Literary Traditions at War' in *Of Lion and of Unicorn*, ed. R. D. S. Jack and Kevin McGinley (Edinburgh, 1993), pp. 67–99.

9. His entry in *The Journal of the Easy Club* shows that he first opted for Bickerstaff and later Douglas.

10. Helena Mennie Shire, *Song, Dance and Poetry of the Court of Scotland under King James VI* (Cambridge, 1969), pp. 171–2.

11. C. S. Lewis, *The Allegory of Love* (Oxford, 1936), p. 259.

12. See *Alexander Montgomerie* (Edinburgh, 1985), pp. 41–8.

13. Fred Freeman, 'Introduction' to *Robert Burns: The Complete Songs* Vol I (Linn Records, 1995) CD No. CKD 047.

14. Kurt Wittig, *The Scottish Tradition in Literature* (Edinburgh and London, 1958).

Hogg as Poet: A Successor to Burns?

W E TEND TO THINK of Hogg as the author of *The Private Memoirs and Confessions of a Justified Sinner* (1824), that is to say as a novelist of the first rank; but in his own time he was generally regarded as a poet rather than a novelist. Indeed, Hogg aspired to be regarded as Burns's successor in the role of poet to the Scottish nation. To this end Hogg convinced himself (wrongly) that he was born on 25 January; and his last major work was a book-length *Memoir of Burns*.[1] Furthermore, in his autobiographical *Memoir of the Author's Life*, Hogg goes out of his way to present the origins of his own poetic career as a kind of picking up of the torch in the aftermath of Burns's death.

> The first time I ever heard of Burns was in 1797, the year after he died. One day during that summer a half daft man, named John Scott, came to me on the hill, and to amuse me repeated Tam O'Shanter. I was delighted! I was far more than delighted – I was ravished! I cannot describe my feelings; but, in short, before Jock Scott left me, I could recite the poem from beginning to end, and it has been my favourite poem ever since. He told me it was made by one Robert Burns, the sweetest poet that ever was born; but that he was now dead, and his place would never be supplied. He told me all about him, how he was born on the 25th of January, bred a ploughman, how many beautiful songs and poems he had·composed, and that he had died last harvest, on the 21st of August.
>
> This formed a new epoch in my life. Every day I pondered on the genius and fate of Burns. I wept, and always thought with myself—what is to hinder me from succeeding Burns? I too was born on the 25th of January, and I have much more time to read and compose than any ploughman could have, and can sing more old songs than ever ploughman could in the world. But then I wept again because I could not write. However, I resolved to be a poet, and to follow in the steps of Burns.[2]

Hogg is getting a little carried away by his enthusiasm at this point: although he had been a semi-literate shepherd in his late teens, by 1797 he was in his late twenties and could write perfectly well. Indeed, he was already a published poet. However, a strong desire 'to follow in the steps of Burns' is unmistakable in this passage; and it may be that Hogg is here dramatising an incident that happened some years before 1797, placing it in the aftermath of Burns's death for artistic reasons. Be that as it may, the present paper sets out to try to trace the significance of Hogg's strong desire to be, and to be seen to be, a successor to Burns.

Hogg's first published poem, 'The Mistakes of a Night', appeared in *The
Scots Magazine* for October 1794. This might fairly be described as a poem
that draws heavily on aspects of Burns's style and aspects of Burns's subject-
matter. Written in the Christ's Kirk stanza often used by Burns, Hogg's poem
tells how Geordie mistakes his girl-friend's widowed mother for his girl-friend,
one foggy night.

> Awa' gaed Geordie hip and thigh,
>   Out-o'er the muir to Maggy:
> The night was neither warm nor dry,
>   The road was rough an' haggy:
> Wi' labour sair he reach'd the bit,
>   By chance there stood her mither;
> But Geordie ne'er observ'd the cheat,
>   They spak sae sair like ither,
>   That Friday's night.
>
> He kiss't her o'er and o'er again,
>   O'erjoy'd she was sae willin';
> An' vow'd if she'd reject his flame,
>   The very thought was killin'.
> Then aff into the barn they hye,
>   To spend the night in courtin';
> The widow's heart did sing for joy,
>   To think o' her good fortune,
>   That Friday's night.
>
> [...]
>
> At length the widow proves nae right,
>   Whilk soon as e'er she sa' man,
> She gangs and tells the hail affair,
>   To rev'rend Doctor C——d:
> Geordie appears on his defence,
>   Hears a' his accusation;
> But, conscious of his innocence,
>   He laughs at the relation
>   O' Friday's night.
>
> Says he, "'Tis false, this 'onest wife
>   "May be a man for me, Sir."
> Quo' she, "How dare ye for your life
>   "Attest so great a lie, Sir!"
> Says he, "If I a lie do tell,
>   "To elders, priest, or bellman;
> "Then may the miekle horned di'el,

> "Drive Geordie into hell, then,
>   "This very night."

However, 'the grand mistake' is cleared up, and:

> He married her, and brought her hame,
>   Upon a gude grey naggy;
> But often Geordie rues the time,
>   He cross'd the muir to Maggie
>   That Friday's night.[3]

As his poetic career developed, Hogg moved away from Burns's manner to strike out in directions of his own. This is hinted at in the passage from *Memoir of the Author's Life*, quoted above, which continues as follows:

> I remember in the year 1812, the year before the publication of the "Queen's Wake," that I told my friend, the Rev. James Nicol, that I had an inward consciousness that I should yet live to be compared with Burns; and though I might never equal him in some things, I thought I might excel him in others. He reprobated the idea, and thought the assumption so audacious, that he told it as a bitter jest against me in a party that same evening. But the rest seeing me mortified, there was not one joined in the laugh against me, and Mr. John Grieve replied in these words, which I will never forget, "After what he has done, there is no man can say *what* he may do."[4]

Hogg went on to write *The Private Memoirs and Confessions of a Justified Sinner*, among other things; so it might be thought that Grieve spoke with some justice. Be that as it may, it is abundantly clear from this passage that Hogg wishes to pick up from where Burns left off, to carry on the flame into the next generation. Equally, it is clear that Hogg does not aim to repeat *exactly* what Burns had done: he will continue Burns's work, but he will proceed in his own distinctive way.

What then, precisely, was the work of Burns that Hogg was proposing to carry on? We can approach an answer by looking at another passage from Hogg's autobiographical writings, a passage recording his first meeting with the young Walter Scott, a meeting that was to mark the beginning of a long but sometimes troubled friendship. Scott was visiting Hogg's native Ettrick Forest with a view to collecting and publishing the fragments of old ballads that remained there in oral tradition. Two volumes of Scott's authoritative *Minstrelsy of the Scottish Border* had recently appeared; and the third volume was in preparation. Scott was accompanied by Hogg's friend William Laidlaw; and the expedition was undertaken (among other things) to investigate 'Auld Maitland', a ballad which Scott suspected to be a modern forgery. Scott and his party sought out Hogg's mother, to hear her sing this ballad. Hogg gives an account of what happened next:

My mother chaunted the ballad of Old Maitlan' to him, with which he was
highly delighted, and asked her if she thought it ever had been in print? And
her answer was, "O na, na, sir, it never was printed i' the world, for my
brothers an' me learned it an' many mae frae auld Andrew Moor, and he
learned it frae auld Baby Mettlin, wha was housekeeper to the first laird of
Tushilaw. She was said to hae been another nor a gude ane, an' there are
many queer stories about hersel', but O, she had been a grand singer o' auld
songs an' ballads."

"The first laird of Tushilaw, Margaret?" said he, "then that must be a very
old story indeed?"

"Ay, it is that, sir! It is an auld story! But mair nor that, excepting George
Warton an' James Stewart, there war never ane o' my sangs prentit till ye
prentit them yoursel', an' ye hae spoilt them awthegither. They war made
for singing an' no for reading; but ye hae broken the charm now, an' they'll
never be sung mair. An' the worst thing of a', they're nouther right spell'd
nor right setten down.

"Take ye that, Mr. Scott," said Laidlaw.

Scott answered with a hearty laugh, and the quotation of a stanza from
Wordsworth, on which my mother gave him a hearty rap on the knee with
her open hand, and said, "Ye'll find, however, that it is a' true that I'm tellin'
ye." My mother has been too true a prophetess, for from that day to this,
these songs, which were the amusement of every winter evening, have never
been sung more.[5]

There is a distinction here between the living tradition of the folk, on the one
hand, and Scott's antiquarian interest in that tradition, on the other. There is
also a suggestion that Scott is in effect putting the old songs in a museum; and
that, by doing so, he keeps them as specimens but kills them as living things.

I should like to suggest that Hogg saw Burns as the person who had kept
alive the flame of the old oral tradition of the people; and that Hogg wanted
to become Burns's successor as the keeper of that flame. Hogg, in undertaking
this task, saw himself as offering an alternative to Scott's gentrified, antiquarian
interest in the auld sangs of the people.

In his *Familiar Anecdotes of Sir Walter Scott*, Hogg makes it clear that there
was much about Scott that he wholeheartedly admired; but in the second
paragraph he expresses one reservation:

The only foible I ever could discover in the character of Sir Walter was a
too strong leaning to the old aristocracy of the country. His devotion for
titled rank was prodigious and in such an illustrious character altogether out
of place. It amounted almost to adoration […].[6]

A little later comes Hogg's account of his dispute with Scott over *The Brownie
of Bodsbeck*, a novel by Hogg which is deeply out of sympathy with the brutal

tactics used by the Royalist forces that quelled the popular uprising of the Covenanters in late seventeenth-century Scotland. Scott took a different view and expressed his opinion forcefully in an interview with Hogg shortly after the publication of *The Brownie of Bodsbeck* in 1818. Hogg writes:

> His shaggy eyebrows were hanging very sore down, a bad prelude, which I knew too well.
>
> "I have read through your new work Mr Hogg" said he "and must tell you downright and plainly as I always do that I like it very ill—-very ill indeed."
>
> "What for Mr Scott?"
>
> "Because it is a false and unfair picture of the times and the existing characters altogether. An exhaggerated and unfair picture!"
>
> "I dinna ken Mr Scott. It is the picture I hae been bred up in the belief o' sin' ever I was born and I had it frae them whom I was most bound to honour and believe. An' mair nor that there is not one single incident in the tale – not one – which I cannot prove from history to be literally and positively true. I was obliged sometimes to change the situations to make one part coalesce with another but in no one instance have I related a story of a cruelty or a murder which is not literally true. An' that's a great deal mair than you can say for your tale o' Auld Mortality."
>
> [...]
>
> "Well well. As to its running counter to Old Mortality I have nothing to say. Nothing in the world. I only tell you that with the exception of Old Nanny the crop-eared Covenanter who is by far the best character you ever drew in your life I dislike the tale exceedingly and assure you it is a distorted a prejudiced and untrue picture of the Royal party."
>
> "It is a devilish deal truer than your's though; and on that ground I make my appeal to my country." And with that I rose and was going off in a great huff.
>
> "No no! stop" cried he "You are not to go and leave me again in bad humour. You ought not to be offended at me for telling you my mind freely."
>
> "Why to be sure it is the greatest folly in the world for me to be sae. But ane's beuks are like his bairns he disna like to hear them spoken ill o' especially when he is conscious that they dinna deserve it."
>
> Sir Walter then after his customary short good humoured laugh repeated a proverb about the Gordons which was exceedingly *apropos* to my feelings at the time but all that I can do I cannot remember it though I generally remembered every[thing] that he said of any import.[7]

This is a remarkable record of a conversation, showing as it does mutual respect and affection, combined with a passionate clash of loyalties. Scott's heart lies with 'the Royal party', Hogg's with the folk traditions of the people. Here as elsewhere, the egalitarian Hogg has much in common in these matters with his great predecessor, Robert Burns; but he finds himself in opposition to Sir Walter Scott's 'too strong leaning to the old aristocracy of the country'.

All this can be seen at work in the final pages of *The Private Memoirs and Confessions of a Justified Sinner*. The 'Editor' enters Ettrick Forest – Hogg's native territory – on an antiquarian trophy-hunt: he is going to dig up Robert Wringhim's grave and take away souvenirs. Throughout his narrative, the Editor's attitudes seem to echo not only Scott's antiquarian interests, but also Scott's gentlemanly good nature and common sense. In his expedition to Robert's grave the Editor is accompanied by Scott's son-in-law John Gibson Lockhart, by William Laidlaw, and by other members of Scott's circle. However, the expedition of the Scott-like Editor is hindered in the final pages of the novel by a character named James Hogg, a surly and unhelpful Ettrick shepherd.

Why does 'Hogg' seek to hinder the Editor's grave-robbing expedition? At a previous University of Strathclyde Burns conference, Carol McGuirk has suggested that the grave-opening in the *Justified Sinner* echoes accounts of the opening of Burns's grave in 1815.[8] Carol McGuirk's paper has been published, and I shall not repeat her arguments here: but her case seems to me to be entirely convincing.

This is not to suggest, of course, that Robert Wringhim is Hogg's portrait of Robert Burns. The point is rather to suggest that the two Roberts, Burns and Wringhim, are in their very different ways embodiments of aspects of the old popular culture of Scotland. By the 1820s, many of the gentry had come to hold attitudes of the kind exemplified by the Scott-like Editor in Hogg's novel. For such people, the old popular culture had become an object for antiquarian research rather than a vital, living thing. However, Burns and Hogg, the Ploughman and the Shepherd, were rooted in the old popular culture in a way that was direct and real. Scott, on the other hand, was a gentleman who became a sheriff, a laird, and a baronet; and as such he was less intimately connected than Burns and Hogg with what he would have regarded as the old peasant superstitions about witches and devils.

Recent events provide a parallel that helps to bring all this into focus. In the spring of 1995 there was much interest in Scotland in the fate of a souvenir of Sioux culture that had been kept in a Glasgow museum for about a century. By the late eighteen-eighties, the active resistance of the 'primitive' Native American tribes against the advance of 'civilisation' was dwindling; and that resistance suffered a catastrophic setback when the killing of the great war leader Sitting Bull was followed by the massacre of Big Foot and his followers at Wounded Knee in 1890. In the desperate days of the late eighteen-eighties, the old Native American culture flared to life in the Ghost Dance religion. Dancing in ghost shirts which gave them powerful protection, the Sioux and others looked forward to a new spring in which the whites would be swept away, the buffalo and other game would be restored in abundance, and the ghosts of dead Indians would return in all the vigour of youth.

A ghost shirt removed from the body of one of the massacre victims at Wounded Knee came into the possession of 'Buffalo Bill' Cody's Wild West Show; and when the Wild West Show visited Glasgow, this ghost shirt was acquired by the local museum as an interesting relic. A century or so later, it was seen by chance by a Native American visiting Scotland; and as a result moves were set in train by the Sioux people to reclaim the looted ghost shirt. A high-powered Sioux delegation visited Scotland in the spring of 1995 to press their case; and to judge from the correspondence columns of *The Scotsman*, the Sioux case was welcomed with warm sympathy in Scotland. In the spring of 1995, parallels between Wounded Knee and Culloden came readily to mind as Scots looked back two hundred and fifty years to the events of 1745–46.

When the ghost shirt was transferred from the Wild West Show to the Glasgow museum, it was handed over as a trophy, an interesting relic, a souvenir. When the Sioux delegation came to seek to reclaim it a century later, the ghost shirt was for them an object of the most profound cultural and spiritual significance, which had been looted from the dead body of an ancestor. That is essentially the contrast of perceptions articulated in *The Private Memoirs and Confessions of a Justified Sinner*, in the confrontation between the Editor and James Hogg about the opening of a grave at the heart of Ettrick Forest. And that is why Hogg aspired to be Burns's successor. Burns had kept Scotland's Ghost Dance going as a living thing, not as a museum piece; and Hogg wanted to carry on the dance.

Another perspective on these matters is made available by two twentieth-century fictions about what might be called the *Waverley* moment, the moment when an old traditional culture breaks down in the face of the advance of a more modern, more powerful culture. This is the moment explored in Kevin Costner's film *Dances with Wolves*, and in Chinua Achebe's novel *Things Fall Apart*. Whatever else might be said about it, *Dances with Wolves* certainly marks a great advance on the kind of old western that presents 'redskins' as barbaric and brutal savages. Perhaps, however, *Dances with Wolves* subtly patronises Native American culture by whitewashing it, by romanticising it. It might be argued that, as a result, *Dances with Wolves* neuters Native American culture, reinventing it in a form that has much in common with a safe and unthreatening theme park for the delectation of the mainstream culture. It might also be argued that Scott did something similar to traditional Highland culture during his organisation of the tartan extravaganza which was George IV's royal visit to Scotland in 1822. What we are talking about in these examples is what might be called the souvenir-hunting approach; and this is the approach of the Editor and his friends as they rob the grave at the heart of Ettrick Forest.

Things Fall Apart does something different. Faced with demeaning and blinkered Euro-centric assumptions that pre-colonial African tribal society was 'primitive' and 'savage', Achebe's novel constructs an alternative view of that society. This alternative view tries to give an honest, clear-eyed account of the old culture, an account which does not avert its gaze from such things as the routine abandonment of newly-born twins, the occasional violence of Okonkwo, the killing of Ikemefuna. Nevertheless, *Things Fall Apart* is an articulation and a celebration of the worth of traditional African culture, a celebration all the more powerful because it resists the urge to sentimentalise and romanticise.

When Burns articulates the values of the old Scottish popular culture, he does so in the *Things Fall Apart* way, not in the *Dances with Wolves* way; and Hogg wishes to follow Burns in that enterprise. *The Private Memoirs and Confessions of a Justified Sinner* is part of that project, and so is the *Memoir of Burns*. The *Memoir of Burns* seeks to provide a sympathetic but unsentimentalised and clear-eyed account of Burns – and this did not endear Hogg's text to a readership that would have responded more warmly to a contribution to the literature of the Burns cult.

Hogg's poetry likewise constitutes part of his attempt to continue Burns's work, to be Burns's successor. This emerges clearly from the pages of *A Queer Book*, a collection of poems by Hogg first published in 1832, and republished by Edinburgh University Press in 1995 as one of the first volumes in the new Stirling/South Carolina Research Edition of James Hogg. P. D. Garside, its editor, has written of the 'humour, quirkiness, variety, and virtuosity' of *A Queer Book*.[9]

Hogg's *Queer Book* poems inherit Burns's concern with both the folk tradition in Scottish poetry and the revival of the art tradition in Scottish poetry, a tradition going back to Dunbar and Henryson. For example, 'A Sunday Pastoral' relates to the folk tradition in that it is a poem of rural courtship; as P. D. Garside has suggested, this poem 'combines elements of Classical pastoralism with the Scottish vernacular tradition'.[10] Garside goes on to suggest that in 'A Sunday Pastoral' Hogg 'manages to explore the relation between sexual and spiritual experience in a daring and innovative fashion', a parallel being drawn in the poem between human sexual love and divine love. Like many of the other poems in Hogg's collection, 'A Sunday Pastoral' was heavily bowdlerised in *A Queer Book* of 1832. Indeed, it is only with Garside's edition of 1995, scrupulously edited from Hogg's manuscripts, that the full vigour, inventiveness, and virtuosity of *A Queer Book* has been allowed to emerge.

Many of the poems in *A Queer Book* are written in what Hogg called his 'ancient stile', a reinvented version of the Scots of Henryson and Dunbar. As with the 'Lallans' of Hugh MacDiarmid, Hogg's 'ancient stile' seems to serve to release the poet into a new freedom of imaginative inventiveness; but most of the 'ancient stile' was removed by the publishers of the *Queer Book* of 1832. Happily, the 'ancient stile' is restored in Garside's edition.

'The Goode Manne of Allowa' is a poem in the 'ancient stile' with a Dunbar-like quality of exuberance. The 'goode manne' rides a magical horse into the Firth of Forth, to seek treasure in wrecks on the sea-bed:

> And not one drop of salt watere
> Adowne his throppil ranne.

> But he rode als faire, and he rode als fre,
> Als if all swaithit and furlit
> In Mackintoshis patent wairre,
> The merval of this worlde.[12]

In 'Ringan and May' Hogg offers a re-working of Henryson's 'Robene and Makyne'. Garside argues that the '"ancient stile" undoubtedly allowed Hogg to be more daring in sexual terms: in fact, the two phases of the laveroke's (lark's) song [in 'Ringan and May'] are interpretable as paralleling courtship followed by consummation'.[13]

As these examples suggest, *A Queer Book* shows Hogg not only as a successor of Burns, but also in a sense as a precursor of the early MacDiarmid. The author of *The Private Memoirs and Confessions of a Justified Sinner* emerges from the new edition of *A Queer Book* as one of Scotland's major poets.

NOTES

1. Published in volume 5 of *The Works of Robert Burns*, edited by Hogg and William Motherwell, 5 vols (Glasgow, 1834–36).
2. James Hogg, *Memoir of the Author's Life* and *Familiar Anecdotes of Sir Walter Scott*, edited by D. S. Mack (Edinburgh: Scottish Academic Press, 1972), p. 11.
3. Quoted from James Hogg, *Selected Poems and Songs*, edited by David Groves (Edinburgh: Scottish Academic Press, 1986), pp. 1–3.
4. Hogg, *Memoir of the Author's Life* and *Familiar Anecdotes of Sir Walter Scott*, pp. 11–12.
5. Hogg, *Memoir of the Author's Life* and *Familiar Anecdotes of Sir Walter Scott*, pp. 136–37.
6. Hogg, *Memoir of the Author's Life* and *Familiar Anecdotes of Sir Walter Scott*, p. 95.
7. Hogg, *Memoir of the Author's Life* and *Familiar Anecdotes of Sir Walter Scott*, pp. 106–7.
8. Carol McGuirk, 'Burns and Nostalgia', in *Burns Now*, edited by Kenneth Simpson (Edinburgh: Canongate Academic, 1994), pp. 31–69 (pp. 50–53).
9. Hogg, *A Queer Book*, edited by P. D. Garside (Edinburgh: Edinburgh University Press, 1995), p. xxxiv.
10. Hogg, *A Queer Book*, ed. Garside, p. 268.
11. Hogg, *A Queer Book*, ed. Garside, p. 268.
12. Hogg, *A Queer Book*, ed. Garside, p. 60.
13. Hogg, *A Queer Book*, ed. Garside, p. 245.

Robert Burns and the Scottish Renaissance

ROBERT BURNS seems to have meant a lot to writers of the Modern Literary Renaissance. He was perhaps more important to them than any other figure of the literary past, Sir Walter Scott included. True, it was in a book about Scott that Edwin Muir's rift with Hugh MacDiarmid began (*Scott and Scotland*, 1936). True, too, the poetics and politics of Scott's historical novels are modified or rejected in the works of historical novelists like Neil Gunn and Fionn Mac Colla: Scott was a figure who meant enough to oppose. All the same it's with Burns MacDiarmid seems to identify in *A Drunk Man Looks at the Thistle* (1926), and with Burns he still feels compelled to grapple thirty years later in his book-length essay *Burns Today and Tomorrow* (1959). Here, in *A Drunk Man*, is MacDiarmid's appeal to the once and future king:

> Rabbie, wad'st thou were here – the warld hath need,
> And Scotland mair sae, o' the likes of thee! [1]

MacDiarmid may also have coined the slogan 'Not Burns, Dunbar', and devoted *Burns Today and Tomorrow* to a provocative reappraisal, but he is rather too interested in Burns for mere contempt. In the face of what he saw as sickly post-Burns versification and the curious Burns Clubs, MacDiarmid's polemic is targeted more at the vulnerabilities of particular poetic models, rather than Burns's work as such. 'Burns', MacDiarmid writes, 'knew that a nation's literature and its other arts can never rest on past achievements, but must go ever forward to cope with new needs and new difficulties', adding, with due self-consciousness, 'Yet the Scots poetry that has been written in the last 40 years by the so-called "new Lallans poets" has been cold-shouldered by the majority of Burnsians, who have shown a disposition lamentably different from that of Burns himself'. [2] With that in mind, it is surely more constructive to thank MacDiarmid for reminding people to read Dunbar, rather than blame him for suggesting to a culture perhaps not grown out of its monobook obsessions that there was more behind and beyond Burns. But, as Tom Leonard has shown in *Radical Renfrew* (1990), if MacDiarmid thought a post-Burns poet like Alexander Wilson of Paisley was something to be embarrassed about, he should have thought again. [3] Burns's example might encourage the pawky but it also inspired, in Wilson at least, satire vigorous enough for a prison sentence and then effective exile in America.

In *A Drunk Man* MacDiarmid invokes Burns approvingly, if 'approvingly' is quite strong enough a word for the hero-worship of the lines I quoted earlier, or for the Christ-comparison begun in the following:

> Mair nonsense has been uttered in his [Burns's] name
> Than in ony's barrin' liberty and Christ. (*CP* 84)

In these quotations from the poem – 'the warld hath need', 'mair nonsense has been uttered …' – at least two significant strands of response to Burns emerge, two broad preoccupations shared by MacDiarmid and his contemporaries. The first is the question of how much the values of the 'national bard' – whatever they may be – are needed to address social conditions in the world at large and in Scotland in particular. In MacDiarmid, Burns was used in fact to chastise the majority, the 'feck', of at least the male half of Scotland, who, against the phrase 'a man's a man for all that' he calls 'but zoologically men'. (*CP* 85) That is, he blamed the men of the 1920s *as opposed to Rabbie* for failing to wake up to what he saw as their cognitive and political slavery. It does seem to be men he was talking about here: in *A Drunk Man*, he doesn't care to bring women much into the conversation – one of the roles of the persona's wife is to terminate the work in fact – and the poem, in as much as it can be called a continuous single piece of work, is 'between us men, you understand'. In fact the poem's persona uses Burns's sexuality to justify his own sexual restlessness: 'I am like Burns, and ony wench, / Can ser' me for a time'! (*CP* 113)

The flipside of this interest in politicising Burns was the Renaissance writers' preoccupation with the Burns kitsch-cult. Why has so much nonsense been uttered in Burns's name, who utters it, what does that nonsense do to the body politic inside and outside Scotland, and whose interests are served by it? Muir, in his visit to Burns's birthplace in the mid-30s, offered the following analysis:

> To every Scotsman Burns is a familiar figure, a sort of household god, and most Scotsmen, I suppose, could reel off a few proverbial tags of his poetry, and one or two of his songs set to music. But that is all. This public effigy, in which the lover, the boon-companion and the democrat are the main ingredients, with a hard-working farmer in the background, but all subdued to respectability by time, is the real object of worship of the Burns cult. It is not a literary cult, but a social one. It has very little to do with Burns, and is concerned chiefly with the perpetuation of a myth. In that myth Burns becomes an ordinary man like his devotees, which he was not. He also becomes a successful lover and a free and glorious companion, which every-body would like to be. His myth is thus based on a firm foundation of sanctified illusion and romantic wish-fulfilment. This legendary figure is a Scotsman who took upon him all the sins of the people, not to redeem them, but to commit them as ideally as they should be committed, that is, freely and guiltlessly, in an imaginary world beyond good and evil, a Paradisal Kailyard with a harmless domesticated serpent; for even to the most respectable of

Burns's worshippers, to elders and ministers of the Kirk, Burns's sins are in a special category, and his fornications have the prescriptive right of King David's.[4]

Burns, in Muir's eyes, is popular because he is understood shallowly; even the 'decent classes' typified in Burns's day by the elders and ministers, and who were of course the targets of his poetry, have been able to knick-knackify him. The myth is cannily slippery, like that of other commodified popular figures. Burns is on the one hand 'perfect', a kind of Best Of album, hits only; on the other, his apparent personal excesses martyr and contain him – he's Jimi Hendrix or Marilyn Monroe.

Given the number of Scots who can quote a line or two of Burns and, even if they can't, feel some special ownership of him, i.e. that he *is* 'our national bard', no writer was more appropriate for Modern Renaissance resurrection. Walter Scott, though internationally popular and influential in his time and since, and though Scott was a novelist – most of the best Renaissance writers were novelists – would have been difficult to invoke in this way. As Tom Nairn and others have argued,[5] Scott's mythic structures tend towards calming matters down, anaesthetising the past, and making the present seem comfy: this may sanction the social change that's already going on – and the social change of the early nineteenth century was nothing if not fast-moving – but Scott is not your man if you want to connect revolutionary or at least progressive politics with Scottish nationalism, as some though by no means all of the Renaissance writers did. With a devolutionary spin on mainstream political consciousness today, and a greater willingness to look at the work of one who clearly offers more than unionist myths in his Scottish books, and more besides elsewhere, the situation is a little different, and Scott can now be mobilised by the right, as he always was, by the left (within a unionist framework), and by upper and lowercase nationalists, not to mention the unaligned. I am not sure that this could have happened in the '20s and '30s; Scotland itself is more relaxed with Scott than it has been for some time.

Burns, though, could be called upon for most or all of the things that the Renaissance writers in their different ways saw in themselves: individualistic radicalism, a social conscience, nationalism, and, perhaps, literary genius. The context of Burns's popularity, however, could not be matched in the twentieth century. MacDiarmid was working in the wrong form for many people actually to read him, and only the novelists of the Renaissance could get across to a potentally large audience. That potential was very rarely, if ever, fulfilled: if only they had been working in film! It is through libraries, the fragile continuities supplied by reprints, and the ambiguous means of the set text, that the Renaissance authors are as well known today as they are, and I would be interested in a measure of just how well known that is.

Perhaps the only writer of the '20s and '30s who really did make an impact with Burns then and there was Catherine Carswell. This she did with her provocative but substantial biography, *The Life of Robert Burns* (1930), and she was able to do it because, briefly, she had access to the popular media. As Thomas Crawford has recounted, extracts from *The Life* were published in *The Daily Record* in September 1930 and the response was quick and tumultuous.[6] The *Record* devoted column after column day after day, week after week, to readers' reactions, almost all of them negative, and aggressively negative at that. When Mrs Carswell was mailed a bullet and asked in the accompanying note to rid humanity of herself with it, this was untypical only in its physical extremism; verbal terrorists were everyday her correspondents. Critics and her few supporters by no means divided on party lines: as Thomas Crawford relates, John S. Clarke, the Labour MP for Maryhill, accused her of being a kind of professional graverobber, busy in 'the resurrection of the ghoulish remains of great men'.[7] Carswell had indeed touched a raw *national* nerve.

What didn't her readers like? The answer must surely be: Carswell's treatment of Burns's relations with women.

A rare female supporter got straight to the point: Carswell exposed 'the rotten truth', namely, that the women in Burns's life were 'the female victims of the poet's lust'.[8] A detractor, the Reverend Lauchlan McLean Watt, included at the top of his list of Burns's 'side-slips from virtue' 'the women who, carried off their feet by his passionate personality, bore children to him'.[9] In other words, some of the rare praisers and most of the many complainers all saw Carswell's Burns as someone who, with sexual charms nigh irresistible, actively preyed on defenceless women. Carswell's readers either liked that, because it showed what nasty things Men Really Are, or, much more commonly, they hated it, because it grossly over-emphasised what was unwholesome in their household poet.

Neither side seems to have got Carswell's Burns right. What is unusual about the book is the *mutuality* Carswell describes between Burns and his lovers, and the distinction they all make between desire and marriage. Burns does appear sexually haughty sometimes, and Carswell is critical when Burns thinks a girl plain, but he seems contemptuous of the formalisation of relations rather than contemptuous of women themselves. Carswell's women know fine well the difference between the mattress and matrimony and they are willing to run the risks of that knowledge.

Carswell sees desire as generally understood between men and women, as a given. For example, as a young man in Tarbolton, Burns is described as knowing 'as the girls knew ... that love was the single flower of life for poor country people' and, on the same page, 'It began to be whispered [i.e. *by the women*] that an hour with him in the dark was worth a lifetime of daylight with any other lad'.[10] Carswell describes Burns as thinking quite differently, though, about marriage, imputing this in part to Burns's experiences in Irvine where a woman preacher Elizabeth Buchan, and Burns's lover Jean Gardner, both enthused about 'free love'. More specifically, in refusing to wed Lizzie Paton when she bore him his first child, Burns is described by Carswell as easily being able to square his enjoyment of his newfound paternity and his continuing feelings of affection for Lizzie with his resistance to marrying her. Carswell candidly tells us he found Lizzy 'rough and uneducated to a disgusting degree' (*LRB 118*),[11] but that 'the issue between them had been as simple and indeterminate as her face, and that at no time had he led her to expect marriage.' (*LRB 118*) Carswell then gives Lizzie's side of things, and again there is a kind of down-to-earth acceptance of the incongruous nature of their relationship. It was not an affair between people who would make a good match – Lizzie is portrayed as certainly in love with Burns in a way that he does not reciprocate – but it was a liaison based, in an atmosphere of wellbeing, on a kind of desirous consent, a basis that, with its admission of female sexual enjoyment and its low estimation of the Church, Carswell's critics were unable to accept.

Carswell doesn't miss the material inequality of that kind of consent, though: the open-heartedness of Burns's women catches a ballad-like note that is more delicate than anything the elders could have hoped to detect. She says of Lizzy: 'She made no complaint. She had, it appeared, a clear – some called it a masculine – outlook on life. She admitted that she had not been taken advantage of or misled by promises. She had merely been heartily, perhaps hopefully in love'. (*LRB 119*) This emphasis on Burns making no promises is repeated in James Barke's novelisation of Burns's life, *The Song in the Green Thorn Tree* (1947), where Barke emphasises Burns's insistence on his having made no formal commitment to Lizzy. The same point is made when Burns conspicuously chastises a friend who, having sworn marriage to his now-pregnant lover, is unwilling to follow through with marriage. In Carswell's Burns, a promise was a promise, so you shouldn't make one if you couldn't keep one.

When Burns does think of matrimony, Carswell, no stranger to the extremes of marriage, gently laughs at him, seeing it as another form of immature dramatisation, like his earlier thoughts of becoming a soldier, like his nearly-realised self-image as a colonist in Jamaica, and like his love of the *Man of Feeling* pose. Burns's vulnerable silliness in love and in other things is not something I imagine Carswell's readers would have liked, and even the Marxist James Barke's account is more of a hagiography. For instance, Barke finds another way round the embarrassing Henry Mackenzie connection. In another of his Burns novels, *The Wind that Shakes the Barley* (1946), he defends Burns's enthusiasm for *The Man of Feeling* (1771) on the strength of the hero Harley's anti-empire stand, especially his view of injustices committed in the name of Britain in India.[12] Surely with an eye to the post-war struggle for Indian independence, Barke reports this as Burns's real justification for liking the book: 'When Robert had finished reading this passage he had to put the book down and go out. Here was the sensibility with social fervour to it! Here were words that scalded as no tears could scald. Here was truth that came as a flaming sword'. (*WSB 207*).

For Carswell, Burns is more suggestive. He was, she tells us, continually seeking external roles, images, and models to steady his own emotional instabilities. Jean Armour, she writes, 'had become the nucleus about which his recurrent dreams of marriage and a fireside and children of his own reassembled ... Jean went to Paisley – her parents having judged it wise to absent her from Mauchline for a time – but he thought of her none the less securely and passionately and honourably'. (*LRB* 141). Carswell's characteristic wit puts these already conventional, half-cottagey, half-abstract intentions in their place when she adds: 'Sitting one midnight in the same parlour where the singing had been, listening to the rats in the rafters, pondering over his difficult situation, he vowed himself formally and all afresh to a Scot[t]ish Muse that was clothed in flesh much resembling the flesh of Miss Armour, especially about the legs'. (*LRB* 141–2).

Carswell takes trouble to set her life of Burns in a national context, devoting the first chapter of the book to an analysis of eighteenth-century Scotland. The expectation is that her biography offers a way into post-Union Scotland as well as into Burns himself. Indeed, her sometimes tart anti-Enlightenment observations on what from the start she calls a 'backward country' may still ruffle the feathers of cock-robins, cuckoos and owls today (*LRB* 3). Perhaps more enduringly provocative, though, is her focus on Burns's relationship with his father rather than his mother. While Carswell champions folksongs, and notes the importance of a folksinging tradition to Agnes Burns neé Broun, she is clearly more fascinated with the overlap of life between Burns and Burns Senior.

In this way, while her Agnes seems to have very little independence of thought, the relationship between father and son in *The Life* is the subject of the most intense description. As if a father's treatment of his son was crucial to 'the Scottish psyche', Carswell also broadens out Burns's relationship with Burns Senior into a contemplation of national characteristics: 'If he [Robert] could have escaped from that second Scotland! But its God – the god of the [William] Burneses – was too powerful. Inscrutable, yet just, punishing guilt, yet pledged to wipe away all tears from penitent eyes, He lay in wait for him, compassed him about and dwelt within him. Rebellion was unthinkable. All a man could do was to play truant, and this Robert did. But in truancy there is no freedom'. (*LRB* 101).

In James Barke, Burns's father-figures are so important that Burns seems, to me at least, rather less interesting than the older men in his life. The first book, *The Wind that Shakes the Barley*, is dominated by William Burns and the second, *The Song in the Green Thorn Tree* (1947), by Daddy Auld, the minister of Machlin (*sic*). Like Carswell's account, Barke's reminds the reader very strongly of Burns's roots in the North-East. This is not just by the recounting of the factual details of Burns's ancestors in the Mearns. In a move that seems to pay a compliment to *the* novelist of that region, Grassic Gibbon, the opening of the first book echoes the prose of *Sunset Song* (1932), a book it is known

Barke loved. Barke's albeit light peppering of Scots, his long sentences, and his emphasis on the damp, on animal matters, and on the poverty of the North East, demonstrate an early use of the newly created prose-mythology of that region, evoking as it does in sub- 'speak of the Mearns' the world of almost two centuries before.

William Burns's trip south is described like this:

> They had tramped down through Perth and crossed the Tay and trudged on through the bare patches of Fife till they had stood on the shore of the gloomy Forth and had seen the reek of the Capital hang like a black cloud above the ridge of its rock even as royal Jamie the Saxth had seen it before he had gone slobbering South glad to be free of the stink and stench of its narrow wynds and closes. (*WSB* 19)

Just one sentence, that! To my mind, Barke's books, though, are marred by a kind of didacticism which, as Burns gets older, surfaces in Burns's conversation. Our poet, it seems, just couldn't resist a homespun class-analysis creeping into his discussions. His 'low-born' friends, too, increasingly operate as mere fan-club supporters: they are in awe of every poem he recites and so on. Rightly or wrongly, and as with Carswell's Burns, his middle-ranking and gentry friends are those Barke's Burns seeks out for advice. William Burns and Daddy Auld, though, fascinate the young Robin and clearly Barke, too, and though Burns crosses them he does so without a *feeling* of disrespect; their more complex character and characterisation seem to broaden Burns's character, and, for me, save Barke's novels from being mere curios. Read in the light of Barke's earlier novel *The Land of the Leal* (1939), where a stormy father-son relationship is powerfully evoked, the Burns novels can be seen as a continuation of the author's brooding preoccupation with fatherhood.

If Barke does initially graft *Sunset Song* on to Burns's life, it is surely in the recognition that Lewis Grassic Gibbon is himself using Burns's poetry in the book, in an interesting and perhaps surprising way. The novel's location, the country district of Kinraddie, is framed in the first chapter by Kinraddie's new minister, whom the author has self-mockingly named Reverend Gibbon. The Reverend calls Kinraddie 'the Scots countryside itself, fathered between a kailyard and a bonny brier bush in the lee of a house with green shutters. And what he meant by that you could guess at yourself if you'd a mind for puzzles and dirt, there wasn't a house with green shutters in the whole of Kinraddie'.[13] This is the last thing said in the first chapter. Like Carswell's first pages, Gibbon's book seeks a national context for what is to follow and positions that statement of intent early on. The two Gibbons, the Reverend and the novelist, jointly allude to two national phenomena, the nineteenth-century sentimental tales of the Kailyard, and George Douglas Brown's influential reaction to them, the novel *The House with the Green Shutters* (1901). But the allusion is also to Burns's poetry, in that 'There grows a bonie brier-bush in our kail-yard' is a Burns song.[14] This is an indication that Gibbon is locating and indeed limiting the matter of *Sunset Song* to an identifiably Burnsian rural society, only to go beyond it, as Chris is compelled to 'outgrow' it in the later books of the trilogy. The fact that the Reverend Gibbon makes these remarks at the expense of his flock, who, as the speaker amusingly enough reveals, won't get the allusion, is a pointer to the distance not just between the minister and his parishioners: in his regretful but assured commitment to Progress, Lewis Grassic Gibbon is, with the assumption of his readers' collusion, a cut above his farmyard subjects, too.

Burns's poems are used throughout *Sunset Song* to mark the distance Kinraddie's world is from the so-called real world about to encroach on it. They are also used to show how ignorant Gibbon's supporting characters are, and how ungenerous towards Burns's poetry. The stutterer old Pooty, for example, causes 'fair agony' among any audience whenever he recites 'To a Mouse', or, as the narration contemptuously says, 'some such-like poem' (*SQ* 30). But Pooty is destined to go mad by the end of the novel (there are rather a lot of mentally ill people in *Sunset Song*), and 'fair agony' is exactly what his donkey suffers when, failing to clap at its master's private Burns recital, it is severely beaten by him. This the narration regards as a 'fair entertainment' (*SQ* 184), and perhaps it is best not to be too precious about what may have moved away from any notion of the realistic, but for me the comedy is at the least uncomfortable.

The same voice, if it can be said to be one voice, is as misanthropic as it is cruel, and this surfaces when it comments on Burns and his poems. 'Auld Lang Syne', for instance, it regards as a 'sugary surge' (*SQ* 130), and in that criticism reveals one of the problems Gibbon breathlessly holds up in *Sunset Song*: the problem of 'community'. It is ironic that 'Auld Lang Syne', a song traditionally sung across the world in a spirit of brief fellow feeling; a song, more parochially, crucial to the national identity of Scots at 'their' festival, should be criticised by a voice which appears to be an amalgam of *typical* Kinraddie voices. This may be Gibbon himself ridiculing what he saw perhaps as a rather sentimental song, but to me it sends out another message altogether: it is as if the spirit of community is being shown collectively as it is expressed in the narrative voice to be turned against, paradoxically enough, the idea and assertion of community. In a similar way in Gibbon's next book, *Cloud Howe*, Robert Burns is remarkable as far as the narrating voice is concerned, not for the qualities of his poetry but as 'him that lay with nearly as many women as Solomon did, though not all at one time'. (*SQ* 202) For all its loquacity, the gossipy voice, here the sum total of what appears to be Segget society itself, is not quite as earthy and commonsensical as it likes to think it is: rather, as Muir's analysis of the modern-day audiences for Burns warned, void of self-awareness it speaks, despite its high opinion of itself and its dry humour, the language of repression, of resentment, of frustrated fantasy.

Even where Burns's poems avoid communal ridicule, they are used to chime in with the elegy to the dying countryside *Sunset Song* sings. Burns is presented as one of the last chances Kinraddie has of realising finer qualities like tenderness, but as we have seen with Pooty, that chance is always missed. To that purpose, Long Rob's open-air singing of 'Bonny wee thing, / Canty wee thing' (a variation on Kinsley 357), successfully interrupts the work of another Gibbonian daftie, Andy of Cuddiestoun. Andy is on the point of sexually assaulting Maggie Jean Gordon when Rob's song innocently but successfully diverts him (*SQ* 49). However, it is not long before this triumph of unknowing gentleness is undercut by Rob himself when, mistaking Andy for a dog skulking in the shadows, he hurls a rock at him (*SQ* 50). Andy's face is smashed, and it seems that even Rob, one of the emotional touchstones of the book, cannot escape his own brutishness.

Rob's compassion and knowledge is indeed set against his lack of fulfilment, a pattern into which his singing of Burns and other songs fits only too well. Rob is the lone farmer and miller, the would-be lover of the novel's heroine Chris, and the tragic ideologue killed in a war he passionately opposes. That he sings the songs of what appears to Kinraddie as a distant detached past is entirely in keeping with the elegiac role he has in the novel. These songs may still touch the heart that is open to them, but the narrator's heart, if not Gibbon's and the reader's, is clamped shut: 'You heard feint the meikle of those old songs now, they were daft and old-fashioned, there were fine new ones in their places, right from America, folk said, and all about queer blue babies that were born there, they were clever brutes, the Americans'. (*SQ* 186). In the face of the forces of progress sweeping over Kinraddie, a progress with worse effects unfortunately than The Blues, the world of the old songs, Gibbon would have us believe, is dying on its feet. In the context of the whole trilogy, Gibbon regrets, but I think accepts, the death of the countryside and its life. He seems at the same time to mock those who think Burns's songs 'daft and old-fashioned' and yet to accept that most people will think that.

Of those few who do think Burns worthwhile remembering, self-interest is too often the reason why. In the caricature of 'Hairy' Hogg, the corrupt and ape-like provost of Segget, Gibbon lampoons those who pitifully claim descent from Burns – 'you'd have thought the way he spoke that Rabbie had rocked him to sleep in his youth' (*SQ* 241) – and again lays emphasis on the backwardness of such thinking. Hairy Hogg, despite his hirsute appearance, vehemently denies Darwin's notion that humankind is descended from the primates, yet is very keen on more recent ancestry – 'ay, there still were folk had the power to rule, them that came of the Burns' blood' (*SQ* 264). In discussions of socialism, Hogg also uses Burns to defend the status quo: 'And Hairy said he thought Scotland was fair in a way, and if Burns came back he would think the same; and the worst thing yet they had done in Segget was to vote the Reverend Colquhoun to the pulpit – him and his Labour and sneering at folk, damn't he had said we were monkeys, not men' (*SQ* 293).[15] In all this, Gibbon shares with MacDiarmid a sense that Burns's work may have been excellent in itself, but that history, especially history perceived as zooming ahead with capitalism, has left Burns, his poetry and, most importantly, his world, isolated from the pressing needs of the here and now. In that, he is closer to Walter Scott and a philosophy of improvement than any other Renaissance novelist. But if Gibbon keeps the past down by relying on a bitter kind of nostalgia, and that earthy and gossipy narrating voice is itself consigned to yesterday as the trilogy proceeds, for all *A Scots Quair*'s insinuation that Burns's poetry is seen by most as ridiculous, outdated, and forgotten, Gibbon needs at least some of his readers to know the Burns allusions. The titles and the contexts of the songs within the novel are enough for anyone not knowing Burns very well to enjoy most of their richness, but that they *are* Burns's work adds another dense layer of association. In this way the alleged obsolescence of Burns's poetry becomes in Gibbon's hands something that is made to seem 'inevitable', but because Gibbon says this by allusion to Burns's work, it requires Burns's poetry still to be alive to understand it! Alive of course, like the country life Gibbon also seems to have hastily consigned to yesterday, it very much is.

The example of George Blake shows that other novelists did not feel the need to tie Burns to the sinking countryside as the 'modern world' arose, but that a spirit of elegy for a sense of communal life, even a community far-removed from the banks and braes of Ayrshire or the Mearns, haunted more than one writer in the Modern Renaissance, and Robert Burns was again a kind of marker for the melancholy of that. *The Shipbuilders* (1935) is based in Glasgow and follows the fortunes of a shipyard's owner Leslie Pagan and the life of the man who served alongside him during the First World War, the riveter Danny Shields. Burns is alluded to three times in the book, significantly near the beginning and then near the end. The first allusion is when Shields is walking back to his house after a drink:

> The tides of people flowing backwards and forwards along the Dumbarton Road delighted him. It was fine to see folks out and about, he thought: lads and their lassies, decent middle-aged and elderly couples making home from the Pictures, and bold files of girls abreast, many a bonny piece among them.
>
> The warmth of the human bond was astonishing. What was it Rabbie had said, speaking for the people? That bit about honest poverty and the guinea-stamp – a man's a man for a' that. And Rab, by God, was right! Folks were decent if you looked at them the right way: all plain bodies like himself, a wee bit misunderstood, but cheerfully going home along the Dumbarton Road to their decent beds. Danny began to think of Agnes. He was humming, almost singing, 'The Lea Rig' as he turned off towards Kingarth Street.[16]

At first it seems that Burns does have a place in the industrial heartlands: his poetry is known quite well by Shields who associates it with good feeling among men and women; in what is quite a sensual novel, Burns is thought of sensually; and as the intellectual MacDiarmid invoked him, so Danny the riveter can invoke him, as 'Rab' or 'Rabbie' – every man in Scotland, if not every woman, is on first-name terms with their national poet.

The good nature of this passage is transformed when Shields comes across his son, Peter, who is

> nasally intoning one of those mournful songs of negroid love in which he delighted; and as he passed the lighted mouth of the close Danny saw his first-born, shoulders hunched, hands in pockets, shuffling a dance for the entertainment of his friends.
>
> A spasm of the old anger seized him. His kindly feeling towards the world at large changed suddenly to a black contempt for that one young man – messing about with his fancy molls (*TS* 32).

As with Gibbon, Blake uses the Blues to pit against Burns, to mark a difference between a mature generation, connected to the scraps at least of its artistic and philosophical past, and its sons and daughters, cut free from all that and fast drifting towards the treacherous shallows of alien historyless America. In George Blake's version of events, Burns might be understood by those working in what were now 'traditional' heavy industries, but young people's loyalties, like their experiences of work or war, were radically different. It is a pity that Shields does not understand that he and his son may have a little more in common with the makers of the Blues than either seems to recognise, but the irony is not laboured by Blake. Danny's traditional values are also racist values as his 'black contempt' for black music shows. The book follows Shields's traumatic life when he is laid off by Leslie Pagan's firm, and when, to his shame, he has to rely on Peter, who lands a job as a commissionaire in a cinema. Scotland's economic transformation from apparently solid reliance on manu-facturing to certainly fragile dependence on service industries is neatly evoked in that switch of circumstances. Shields has to endure much more than that, though, including the break-up of his marriage, and when the book comes to a close he is still unemployed. But Blake wants to show that the new life Shields finally finds – with another woman and with children who really love him – compares handsomely with the rather arid comfortable life Leslie Pagan is to lead down south.

Burns is alluded to a second time a few pages before the end of the book, when Shields goes to an army reunion with Pagan:

> A hush fell when Danny Shields got up to sing, with tremendous gravity, 'Bonnie Wee Thing, Canny Wee Thing', and as they all joined in the lugub-rious chorus it was as if all the nostalgic sentiment were concentrated in that one room above a Glasgow pub, and as if the ultimate loveliness had been suddenly revealed to this unique body of hard-bitten men (*TS* 260).

This is a mournful and beautiful moment, an epiphany of male camaraderie in the same way that Long Rob's fieldsongs in *Sunset Song* are epiphanies of the observed solitary. If George Blake and Gibbon differ on the social context in which Burns is uttered, they agree that the poet is widely understood as a figure of the past incarnate. As part of this, both writers connect Burns to those who lived through or died in the First World War, as if that conflict marked the last generation who could be alive to Burns's thoughts and feelings. Epiphanies, by definition, are momentary, and when Shields stops singing, even 'this unique body of hard-bitten men' collapse into who they mostly are. After Shields's song, the reunion becomes

> more maudlin, more quarrelsome, more natural. Save those few who were teetotallers and those whose guard upon themselves and their attitude to the world could not be surprised, every man revealed himself for what he was (*TS* 260).

This feeling of final and enduring collapse is reiterated in the last allusion to Burns a page or two later. The men sing 'Auld Lang Syne', and to Leslie Pagan

> It was the song of parting, the song that marked an end. The Battalion would reunite next year and be happy in its way, but it would be a reunion different from this, for the minds and souls and circumstances of men must change in the course of twelve months. Some would be dead before the date came round again, some would be so bruised by events that they would forget the ancient loyalty and the warmth that comes of foregathering. He might himself, reflected Leslie, be so wrapped in the life of England that the secretary's circular would appear a negligible bidding to a scanty feast in a remote and unfriendly country. As for Danny ... (*TS* 262)

Despite this, Pagan's concerns for Danny, if not for his other comrades, are not as justified as he thinks, and this is where Blake so differs from Gibbon. Shields has found a new life in a once-broken but now re-made family, among children not his own and with a woman not his wife but all of whom he loves and all of whom love him. Blake emphasises the 'naturalness' of this (*TS* 240). Shields is certainly jobless, late-middle-aged and physically frail, and to that extent he warrants Pagan's anxiety, but the ex-riveter and his new family have a kind of self-reliance Pagan just can't understand. At home, Shields's new family will be as cheerful and as busy, albeit as financially precarious, as, at its best, Burns's family must have been. This is quite at odds with the rather sterile world Pagan is now to live in in his country house in the south of England, and it is poles apart again from the profound loneliness of *A Scots Quair* as it draws to a close. As Gibbon could be accused of a pessimism by turns mystical and coolly rationalist, Blake might be accused of being sentimental. That is one of the risks Burns ran, too. But to my mind Blake does manage to suggest that a delicate continuity of genuine feeling has been maintained between the world of Burns and the world of Danny Shields. In the end the connection is not through community but through *family* strength, with 'family' defined in an open and quite unorthodox way (on the example of *The Shipbuilders* Blake would not be interested in the recent reactionary mobilisation of the phrase 'family values'). The best of the world of the shipyard city, like the best of the world of the soldiers and their camaraderie, can't be sustained as such – that's all over – but an open family, as assorted as Burns's own family was, might be able to endure.

It is on the subject of a very odd open family that I'd like to conclude, and focus on perhaps the most unusual representation of the poet in the Modern Literary Renaissance: Burns's appearance in Heaven. In Neil Gunn's eerie novel *The Green Isle of the Great Deep* (1944), set in a Paradise that is half-dream, half-nightmare, it is in Burns's house that two fugitives from God's authorities take refuge.[17] They are the old man Hector and the young boy Art. Although the reader never knows Robert's second name, he is identified as an ex-poet, and, along with other internal evidence and the fact that it is on the record that Gunn intended him to be an echo of Robert Burns, many readers will take him to be such.[18] It is by no means an exact match: the compelling obliquity of so much in the novel is followed through in Robert's character. Though we can delight in Burns's appearance in Heaven at all (Holy Willie is no doubt cursing him from some other place), there are several even more surprising things about Gunn's portrayal of Burns that are worth consideration.

Burns's representation in a Gunn novel can be attributed in part to Gunn's identification with him. In fact they had more similarities in their lives than in their writing. The first most obvious connection is that both Gunn and Burns worked for the Customs and Excise. This meant that both travelled colossal distances in the course of their work, Gunn with the benefit of a motorbike not a horse, though after a few years he was given a more static position at a distillery in Inverness. Both Gunn and Burns could claim to know intimately the lands around them for tens of miles, and much further. As Government officers, they both had to be canny with their opinions – Gunn wrote under the pseudonyms Nial Guinne and especially Dane M'Neil whenever he had something politically sensitive to say. Professional involvement with whisky is another common denominator, and Gunn makes significant mention of Burns in his book-length essay *Whisky and Scotland* (1935), where, like Burns, he uses whisky as a symbol of Scotland's taxed freedom.

Although in their creative work the evocation of openheartedness, vibrant communal scenes, and a skilful flirtation with the supernatural, not to mention keen descriptive powers where landscape and the seasons are concerned, mean they have something in common creatively, Gunn's relationship with Burns is nevertheless ambiguous. In the essays of the second half of the 1920s, Gunn defends MacDiarmid's phrase 'Dunbar, not Burns', asserting in 'Defensio Scotorum', for instance, that the enemy of Scotland is 'those whose nationality consists of toasting Burns comically', and then suggesting that the kind of person who does that (rather than Burns himself) is 'that curious barren defeatist figure, the Anglo-Scot'.[19] Here, he sees Burns as certainly a halfway figure between Dunbar and the kailyard,[20] giving the impression that this is not a good thing to be, but in another essay, 'The Scottish Literary Renaissance Movement', he says of MacDiarmid that 'he is not only the finest Scots poet since Burns but ... he has poetically penetrated dimensions of the spirit that Burns never even conceived'.[21] He then adds, perhaps feeling he has gone too far: 'That doesn't mean that I am asserting that he is *greater* than Burns. Comparison of that sort is meaningless, as though it were being said that an orange is *greater* than an apple. But I do want thus to stake my critical faculty for what it's worth against those who find nothing but "a tootle on a penny whistle"'.[22]

Gunn's suspicion of Burns's followers, and his coolness about Burns's work itself, is helpful in understanding the portrayal of Robert in *The Green Isle of the Great Deep*. There is no doubt that Gunn associates Burns and poetry in general with a sense of freedom. God himself eventually expresses concern that Robert has made no poems since the cataclysmic rationalist revolution in Heaven (*GI* 243). All the same, Robert is part of the small conspiracy that evades Heaven's officials by eating the Green Isle's forbidden fruit. That is a furtive kind of defiance, though, and Robert is put to shame by the open-hearted dynamism of the little boy Art. By contrast Art, in publicly opposing the authorities and evading them, carries out a kind of art-terrorism. This, with the faith of frail Hector, and the near-martyrdom of Robert's wife, is what begins the counter-revolution and so gives the novel its eventually happy ending.

While marginalised figures overthrow the cruel neo-Enlightenment of the Green Isle, Robert seems able only to sit and worry. Grim and terse whenever he does speak, Burns, in life almost as famous for his witty conversation as his poems, in death is certainly not the man he was. When he finally does open his mouth for more than one sentence, to explain, at last with some eloquence, the history of the Green Isle, it is so unusual an action that Gunn signals it with its own chapter, 'Robert Talks' (*GI* 87). Again, the feeling is that the rationalist new world – and Robert is identified as in some sympathy with rationalism – has changed him almost beyond recognition. Indeed, this may go some way to explain why Hector himself never recognises this most familiar of Scottish faces.

As the novel develops, it becomes clear that Robert is acting in this surly manner under the strain of trying to protect his wife. He wants to contain their knowledge of the forbidden fruit to keep her out of the clutches of Gunn's proto- thought-police, but he is paralysed by his own paternalism. Perhaps closer to the real Burns than we might like to think, Gunn's Robert continues carefully contained transgressive behaviour while outwardly keeping his nose clean. Only when his wife is taken for questioning does Robert act with more outward bravery: he asks if he might go instead (*GI* 108). The authorities, true to form, refuse the offer and 'Mrs Burns' is taken for interview. Although the reader does not realise it straight away, she proves she is more than a match for her interrogators and it is she, rather than Robert, who helps bring down the Government.

But who is this 'Mrs Burns'? If you were expecting Jean Armour, in her late sixties when she died, to be the partner of the man Gunn describes as standing 'straight and quiet, slim and well built, a man perhaps in his early thirties' (*GI* 38), you will be disappointed. Rather, Gunn chooses Mary Campbell (*GI* 70).

Though Carswell and to a lesser extent Barke give Mary her due, Gunn's Mary is much more energetic than either portrayal: she is clever, determined, and brave. As I've hinted, there are the logistics of age behind the choice – Mary and Robert are both under 40 and can make a conventional couple in the Land of Youth. This also streamlines the plot as far as children are concerned – it would rather complicate things having Burns's infant and grown-up kids in the novel! – and Gunn's simplification concentrates one of the tragic under-tones of the novel, the loss of a single child. As earthly legend has it Mary, Robert explains, did indeed lose a baby and 'the boy Art brought back the memory of her son – our son – who was destroyed on earth' (*GI* 83). Though I'm not sure how worked out it all is, Heaven, it seems, has not accepted this son. For this reason, and although the child Art operates symbolically in the novel, there is psychological charge in Mary's immediate and desperate love of him: Art is 'innocence restored' but he is also a real child who literally cries out for the mother figure Mary is more than willing to provide. Gunn takes this further, for my tastes too far, when he says of Mary, 'Here at last was Woman, who for the warmth of life and for the love that sprang out of life and made life, would fight till the stars went down in their course and rose no more' (*GI* 201–02), but most of the time this explicit idealism does not get the better of the story's subtleties. Gunn's own childlessness, and the death of his premature son, cannot but add to the anguish of this aspect of the novel.

In that Hector is a Macdonald, and his working with Mary to liberate the Green Isle symbolically heals the old feud between that clan and the clan Campbell, we can see another reason why Mrs Burns is Mary, not Jean. Indeed, that Mary is a Highlander and Robert a Lowlander, a fact Hector immediately jokes about when they all first meet properly (*GI* 70), as if Gunn were saying the reader shouldn't make too much of it either, is another indicator of the gentle maturity of the novel: what were once serious divisions have become likeable idiosyncrasies. *The Green Isle* is rightly seen as a myth about artistic and political freedom, but these examples show that it also operates symbolically at more local levels, and most of the time with a light touch, even when dealing with the reunification of a supposedly divided nation.

I mentioned, though, that Hector never seems to recognise either Robert or indeed Mary as the people we know them to be. There are other instances where complete identification of the real-life people cannot be sustained. Mary, for example, though she says she is a Campbell, does not come from the Cowal as her earthly namesake is supposed to: she was born in the fictional town of Clachdrum, in the northern Highlands, where Hector himself was born (*GI* 70), though many years before him. Though it would have been good to have found all the loose ends of Robert's identity tied up, the central idea in the book of the near-death experience, the nightmare Hector and Art are having jointly as they writhe and all but drown in the river pool, argues against following up things too closely. Other characters on the island remind Art and Hector of people they know at home rather than world-famous figures – to Hector, God speaks Gaelic, to Art, God is a bit like Hector, and so on. The allusion to Robert Burns is sustained, but it is quietly done – he is just one of the several national images in the book, like the city on the Rock that is clearly a supernatural echo of Edinburgh. These myths are understood by their readers at a flickering level, with the intermittent logic of a dream: in short, in the way that most Scots understand Burns and Scotland itself.[23]

NOTES

1. *The Complete Poems of Hugh MacDiarmid* (Harmondsworth: Penguin, 1985), p. 85. Further references to this text take the form *CP* followed by the page number.
2. *Burns Today and Tomorrow* (Edinburgh: Castle Wynd Printers, 1959), pp. 4–5.
3. Tom Leonard (ed.), *Radical Renfrew: Poetry from the French Revolution to the First World War* (Edinburgh: Polygon, 1990). Cf. Leonard's selection of and introduction to this remarkable poet, pp. 8–32.
4. Edwin Muir, *Scottish Journey* (London: Flamingo, 1985) (originally published 1935), pp. 89–90.
5. Cf. Tom Nairn, *The Break-up of Britain* (London: NLB, 1977), p. 115.
6. Thomas Crawford, Introduction to Catherine Carswell, *The Life of Robert Burns* (Edinburgh: Canongate, 1990), pp. vii–xiii.
7. Quoted in Thomas Crawford, Introduction to Catherine Carswell, *The Life of Robert Burns* (Edinburgh: Canongate, 1990), p. ix.
8. *Ibid.*, p. ix.
9. *Ibid.*, p. x.
10. Catherine Carswell, *The Life of Robert Burns* (Edinburgh: Canongate, 1990), p. 103. Further references to this text take the form *LRB* followed by the page number.
11. *Ibid.*, p. 118.
12. James Barke, *The Wind That Shakes the Barley* (London: Collins, 1946), pp. 205–6. Further references to this take the form *WSB* followed by the page number.
13. Lewis Grassic Gibbon, *A Scots Quair* (London: Penguin, 1986), p. 31. *Sunset Song* was originally published in 1932, then republished with *Cloud Howe* (1933) and *Grey Granite* (1934) in 1946 in the single-volume trilogy, *A Scots Quair*. Further references to this take the form *SQ* followed by the page number.
14. James Kinsley (ed.), *The Poems and Songs of Robert Burns* (Oxford: Clarendon,

1968), no 587. Further references to this take the form 'Kinsley' followed by the ordinal number.

15. See also *SQ* 326 where Hogg states: 'What was it the poet Robert Burns had written? – an ancestor, like, of the Hoggs, Rabbie Burns. *A man's a man for a' that*, he wrote, and by that he meant that poor folk of their kind should steer well clear of the gentry and such, not try to imitate them at all, and leave them to manage the country's affairs'.

16. George Blake, *The Shipbuilders* (Edinburgh: B&W Publishing, 1993) (originally published in 1935), pp. 31–2. Further references to this take the form *TS* followed by the page number.

17. Neil M. Gunn, *The Green Isle of the Great Deep* (London: Souvenir, 1983) (originally published 1944), p. 93. Further references take the form *GI* followed by the page number.

18. Francis Russell Hart and J. B. Pick, *Neil M. Gunn: A Highland Life* (London: John Murray, 1981), p. 197.

19. Neil M. Gunn, 'Defensio Scotorum', first published in *The Scots Magazine*, April 1928, pp. 51–8, quoted here from Alistair McCleery (ed.), *Landscape and Light: Essays by Neil M. Gunn* (Aberdeen: Aberdeen University Press, 1987), p. 151.

20. *Ibid.*, p. 150

21. Neil M. Gunn, 'The Scottish Literary Renaissance Movement', first published in *Wick Mercantile Debating Society Journal*, April 1929, pp. 16–17, quoted here from Alistair McCleery (ed.), *Landscape and Light*, p. 90.

22. *Ibid.*, p. 90

23. Of course, Burns has been important to many writers since the 1940s. Eric Linklater's *The Merry Muse* (1959), for instance, uses the idea of a discovery of previously unpublished Burns poems to throw the modern-day Scottish literary scene into relief, with tragi-comic results, and Norman MacCaig's bicentenary anthology of new Scottish poetry, *Honour'd Shade* (1959), proved as controversial a collection as any this century when the editor declared in a tiny note: 'The absence of any notable name is not necessarily due to editorial negligence'. Ian Hamilton Finlay, not included in the book, might well have felt set upon. Perhaps the most touching reference to Burns in contemporary writing, though, and one which illustrates what will always be most valuable in Burns's work, is the reference made to him by Alasdair Gray in Gray's list of 'plagiarisms' towards the end of *Lanark* (1981). The reference is to the 1982 Panther edition:

> BURNS, ROBERT
> Robert Burns' humane and lyri-
> cal rationalism has had no im-
> pact upon the formation of this
> book, a fact more sinister than
> any exposed by mere attri-
> bution of sources (486–7).

Burns and Scottish Poetry

IT IS DIFFICULT, if not virtually impossible, to imagine English literature without Shakespeare, broad and generous as is England's literary heritage. It is absolutely impossible to imagine Scotland's literary heritage without Burns. In making this claim I am not comparing Shakespeare and Burns. Leaving aside the fact that Shakespeare's greatest poetry is meant to be spoken on the stage, mainly by kings and the great – or not so great – rulers of the past, while Burns wrote for the mind's ear – by far the subtlest way to enjoy poetry, in my view – there is the fundamental difference which distinguishes the two literary traditions.

Recently, a daughter who teaches English in a Southern English school found herself involved in a scheme where the pupils were exposed to a selection of contemporary work by English, Welsh and Scottish poets. The comparison most chose to make was between the English and the Scottish attitudes. One youngster seemed to put it particularly well when he described how he saw the difference: 'The Scots seem to be inside looking out. There's much more people poetry than in the English work.' 'People Poetry'. That is the outstanding characteristic of Scottish poetry down the ages, whether the hearty, peasant, humorous nonsense of 'Colkelbie's Sow' or, later, the gentle compassion in his comparison of the ways of mice and men so charmingly fabled by Robert Henryson, schoolmaster of Dunfermline.

While it is true that Dunbar, but more particularly Sir David Lyndsay of the Mount, did their share of celebrating the ways of kings and queens, the religious turmoils of the seventeenth century partially drove poetry underground. When it re-emerged in the eighteenth century, though stimulated by the threat to the sense of nationhood caused by the Union of 1707, Scottish poetry was already firmly people-orientated.

There are two kinds of artist: those who forge new forms or ways of expression; and those who take the forms already to hand and use them with greater richness then any of their predecessors had done. An analogy with music comes to mind. Two of the sons of the great Bach – Carl Philip Emanuel and Johann Christian – were innovators; the former both formally and with the personalization of expressiveness, the latter stylistically, giving an elegance to the *galant* manner which has, happily, been re-appreciated in our own day. Mozart, on the other hand, though greatly broadening and extending their use, took the forms that were to hand and by substituting genius for great talent, endowed them with a perfection not hitherto achieved.

And so it was in Scottish literature. Allan Ramsay – himself of fairly humble origin – and the other lesser literary figures around him, were essentially 'people poets'. Ramsay, indeed, through his anthologies and his library – the first circulating library in Scotland – wanted to make literature more widely available and was only thwarted by the clerical establishment from setting up a theatre in Edinburgh the better to reach the people through drama. He wrote about 'low-life' people – a brothel madame and a keeper of a tavern, for example – and he was unsparing with the verbal lash against the Kirk-Treasurer's man, whose sanctimoniousness oppressed the people.

Robert Fergusson, his successor, was even more of a people's man, and – as befitted the growing urban influence being brought about by the Industrial Revolution – more or less our first town poet. He, too, had no hesitation in applying the satirical lash to pompousness and social pretension.

The 'people' business – like the 'Standard Habbie' stanza they often favoured and which was imported from France – was used by one of the comic characters in Sir David Lyndsay's one surviving play 'Ane Satire of the Three Estates' – a comic masterpiece which surely couldn't have been Lyndsay's sole dramatic endeavour. So it was the practical poetic heritage which Burns came to heir. Like Mozart, Burns took the materials of his immediate predecessors and enriched them beyond anything hitherto imagined. There are two other significant links between Mozart and Burns. Mozart's opera 'The Marriage of Figaro', tilting ridicule at the unacceptable 'droit de Seigneur' privileges of the aristocracy, appeared in 1786, the same year as Burns's Kilmarnock poems, satirising the unacceptable practices of the Scottish establishment. Both were Freemasons, much favoured by socially conscious late-eighteenth-century intellectuals. And both paid for their temerity: Mozart through the withdrawal of Viennese upper-class support during the late seventeen-eighties; Burns by the growing coolness with which the Edinburgh upper classes came to regard him after the novelty of his year or so as 'the wonder of all the gay world', as Mrs Cockburn called him, began to wear off.

The notion that poetry had to be written in a high-falutin' manner and be about exalted topics, while a romantic fallacy already widely believed long before Romanticism ever raised its introspective head, was never one that fully pertained in Scottish poetry. Scotland never seriously succumbed to an Augustan phase. James Thomson, the leading Scottish Augustan, decamped to England and the circle of Pope beside the Thames. With so much cultural publicity focused on the Augustan English poetry of the time, it is hardly to be wondered at that, from time to time, Burns should have raised his eyes from his true preoccupation with the people, to emulate, almost always unsuccessfully, Shenstone's 'bosom-melting throe.'

Virtually anything can provide the subject-matter of poetry, and one of the reasons for Burns's astounding success with the Kilmarnock Poems was that they proved just that. The ways of country folk, and of the animals with whom the farmer necessarily worked in the closest contact, rather than, for example, the pampered lady at her toilet in front of her dressing-table mirror, were shown to reflect the basic values that matter in life. It is significant that out of all the stilted upper-class affectation – the Clarinda and Sylvander nonsense of Burns's affair with Mrs McLehose – there was finally distilled the one last note that summed it all up and rang true – the song, 'Ae Fond Kiss', a people's poem if ever there was one.

From the particular, Burns could draw the universal generality. Probably arising out of his love for an unattainable country lass, Alison Begbie, came the song 'Mary Morrison', with its heart-ache line celebrating the uniqueness of the beloved, 'Ye are na Mary Morrison' – thought by Hugh MacDiarmid to be just about the greatest line in Scottish poetry. And from the exposure of the secret lust of that poor old sanctimonious local Willie Fisher, came what is possibly the wittiest and most devastating denunciation of religious hypocrisy to be found in European, if not world, literature, 'Holy Willie's Prayer'. Burns's people's instinct rarely faltered – momentarily, perhaps in Edinburgh, when he was subjected to the patronising flattery of the social glitterati; and certainly in his over-enthusiasm for the French Revolution which ended, as most violent Revolutions do, in the establishment of a repressive and cruel dictatorship. But Burns was not the only poet to be carried away by the French Revolution's initial breath of democratic liberty. Wordsworth made the same mis-reading of the situation, though he at least lived long enough to be able to question his earlier unqualified enthusiasm before descending into stultified conservatism.

In his best work – and, ultimately it is only a poet's best work that really matters – Burns's democratic sincerity rang clear and true. That great Shakespearean actor, the late Lord Olivier, once remarked that sincerity was the hardest of all achievements for an actor to master. We live in an age where popular television-orientated culture is a monument to polished professional insincerity. We should therefore value the more the sincerity with which Burns characterised the nature of Scottish literature.

It was, I believe, a combination of his use of ordinary subject-matter and everyday imagery, coupled with this unflinching sincerity, that brought him, almost immediately, in 1786, the wide range of his readership. He was writing at a time when the old agrarian way of life and the time-honoured country values were being assailed by the very different social and economic conditions evolving from the Industrial Revolution. Burns perhaps seemed to enshrine the very qualities which were then regarded – and, indeed, have been ever since – as the fundamental qualities which constitute the Scottish character. It is difficult to find any other explanation for the phenomenon of the cult of Burns Supperism which established itself within a couple of decades of his death and, institutionalised by the establishment of the Burns Federation, has flourished ever since wherever in the world a handful of Scots find themselves gathered together around January 25th.

There was one aspect of Burns's life, however, where despite the fundamental understanding in the lyric 'Mary Morrison', Burns's sincerity can quite properly be questioned. I refer to his attitude to women. The women in Burns's life fit into three categories: family women, like his mother, her story-telling nursemaid companion, and his sisters and sister-in-law, Gilbert's wife; the upper-class ladies who were, quite simply, physically unattainable – Lady Winifred Maxwell Constable, Lady Elizabeth Cunningham, the sister of the Earl of Glencairn, Jane, Duchess of Gordon, the daughter of a Galloway nobleman, Mrs Maria Riddell, and even his mother-confessor, Mrs Frances Anna Dunlop. In this category, too, comes Margaret Chalmers, who nevertheless later told the poet Thomas Campbell that Burns had actually proposed to her, but that she had turned him down, and to whom he wrote in 1788: 'When I think I have met with you and have lived more of real life with you in eight days' – he had stayed at her father's house on his third Highland tour – 'than I can do with almost anybody I meet with in eight years – when I think on the improbability of meeting you in this world again – I could sit down and cry like a child.' Unattainable, indeed – she married a rich Edinburgh banker – but for her he surely felt a genuine love. Not so, for many of the other ladies in the second platonic category about whom he wrote songs. 'I am a good deal luckier than most poets,' he told Deborah Duff Davies, the 'Bonnie Wee Thing' of the song, 'When I sing of Miss Davies or Miss Lesley Baillie I have only to feign the passion. The charms are real.' But feigning the passion by one who declared that 'Woman is the blood-royal of life; let there be slight degrees of precedency among them, but let them all be sacred' perhaps came easier to Burns than to most. Then there is the third category, with whom his relations were not platonic: Jean Armour, later his wife – and she drew from him 'Of a' the airts the wind can blaw', the sincerity of which undoubtedly rings true' – possibly 'Highland' Mary Campbell, who did not inspire his song-writer's muse to its highest flights; and the women he used as what we would today call 'sex objects' – Jenny Clow, May Cameron, Anna Park (though she got a good song out of him), and Elizabeth Paton, his mother's serving girl and the mother of his daughter 'Dear-bought Bess', who also inspired at least one obviously heartfelt poem. So sincerity was not by any means always absent where his attitude to women was concerned. It is the best and most sincere love-poems and songs that really matter, not the feigned variety. Perhaps, like W. H. Auden in our own day, Burns had to write something, 'good, bad or indifferent every day', or he didn't 'feel well.'

But to return to the question of his influence. Now, as in his lifetime – despite, in the intervening years, such sentimental absurdities as 'The Star o' Rabbie Burns' and the often-stultifying attitude induced by the Burns Cult – it is the quintessential honesty of his poetry and its accurate capturing of the basic tenets of our Scottishness that has preserved his popularity among readers from generation to generation.

When we come to consider his influence – or rather the influence of his work – on later generations of Scottish poets, it is quite another story.

There was, for instance, the mistaken belief that it was his having been a ploughman, then later an Excise-man, that explained the secret of his genius. So, with vastly mistaken energy, a certain Mr Edwards, in 52 volumes, proceeded to collect a wide assortment of worker poets, categorizing them trade by trade. Virtually all of them were Burns clones, not only without the genius but without even much traceable literary talent. At a rather higher level of imitation, or at least model-copying, there were writers gifted in varying degrees – some, like James Hogg, a writer of imaginative distinction in other forms and literary fields; others, like Robert Tannahill, with some individuality and ability (albeit, in his case, 'a too-quick despairer', leading to his suicide). There was also, of course, a vast and now utterly forgotten horde of local versifying followers who thought the touch lay in the couthy use of the Doric.

Scots, like Gaelic, must come under increasing pressure in the years ahead. Gaelic, for the time being, like Welsh, has the support of special promotion by the most powerful media arm of our day, television, the same arm of the media that is exercising increasing pressure even against English as spoken in England, with its ever-increasing quantity of imported transatlantic material. The 'talkies' in the 'Twenties no doubt made some small impact against Scots and its dialects. But the BBC charter, when concerned only with sound radio, contained provision for the nurturing of local languages and dialects, a condition that it was obviously quite impractical to impose upon television. 'Market values' have now been, of necessity, let loose against 'the guid Scots tongue'. It has, indeed, been under sentence of death for many decades; yet is still in literary use. But for how much longer, who can say? Yet it seems unthinkable that a time should ever come when the people of Scotland would no longer understand the language of Burns, let alone that of Henryson, Dunbar and MacDiarmid.

The fact is that Burns virtually perfected the use of the poetic tools which lay to hand when he 'commenced poet', to use his own quaint phrase. Even quite gifted poets in later years who tried to don his mantle, like Stevenson (though, fortunately, not exclusively) or John Buchan, walked as if in antique guise; indeed, in literary fancy dress. It simply isn't possible to be sincere wearing the borrowed clothes of your literary ancestor. Hogg though much influenced by Burns and who, indeed, thought that the Ayrshire poet's mantle had descended on him, had himself a touch of genius, though it is only in our own times that his stature, both as poet and novelist, is being properly reassessed.

The link between the major influence on Scottish literature during the nineteenth century and Burns is a tantalisingly minor social one. The boy who became Sir Walter Scott was present at a social gathering where Burns was the centre of attraction and was able to supply him with the indentification of a poet which had slipped his memory. What Burns did for the Scots tongue,

Scott, through the Waverley Novels, did for Scotland's history. As a lasting influence on the preservation of our sense of nationhood, the two must be seen in tandem. We are apt to forget that the ordinary Scot did not have easy access to the history of Scotland before Scott popularised some of its main confrontation points through fiction. Thus the stemming of the tide which threatened to engulf Scotland as North Britain was achieved jointly by Burns and Scott, spreading knowledge both of the Scots language and the old Scots ways of rural life as well as the actions and decisions which shaped her destiny in the dubious years.

In any case, the first half of the nineteenth century was not a rich gleaning field for poetry in Scotland, the novel taking precedence in readership popularity. In the weedy rural sidewalks, of course, there were plenty of versifiers imitating Burns in form and content. Indeed, it was not until the middle of the century that the rural shadow of Burns was finally shaken off, poetically speaking. Urban and industrial influences began to be felt in the work of John Davidson and James Thomson ('BV'), the one born in industrial Greenock and the other in its then equally industrial neighbour, Port Glasgow. The work of neither showed any Burns influence, unless one counts anti-Calvinism, indeed anti-Religion, as to some extent a Burns influence. Although 'Standard Habbie' – which, incidentally, doesn't seem to work very well in English – chuntered on in the background, it no longer had any future-looking literary force. Nevertheless, Scots itself trickled on, not ineffectively, into the early years of the twentieth century in the work of such writers as Charles Murray, Violet Jacob, Marion Angus and Helen Cruikshank; no longer Burns-influenced perhaps. These ladies struck an original rather plangent note and demonstrated that the Scots tongue, whose demise had been prophesied since the eighteenth century, was certainly a gey long time a-dying!

It has been said that the creative energy flung into religious disputation in seventeenth-century Scotland and into cultural pursuits in the eighteenth, found its true expression in the nineteenth through engineering. There may be something in this, of course. Yet the great Scots concentration in providing engineering products for the world market – mainly, of course, a Glasgow and Clydeside preoccupation – did not in any way stem public enthusiasm for Burns's poetry. It has often been remarked of the English in recent years that they have never really taken to industrial urban society; that they believe the countryside to be their natural habitat. Thus, when they make money out of industry (or however), they buy themselves back into a kind of sanitised countryside; a countryside that has nothing to do with the hard work, low pay and constant battle with harsh elements of the real agricultural workers. The same social phenomenon probably also exists in Scotland. At any rate, Burns as a creative literary influence – though not, of course, as a source of delight to successive generations of readers – waned as the voices, mostly in English, celebrated, or denounced, an Industrial Society gathering in strength.

And so we come to our own century – 'the Age of Anxiety', as Auden called it; the decade of bloody wars, as many have experienced it; or 'The People's Century', as the BBC Television series called it. All are true definitions in their way.

In Scotland, what part has the Burns influence played in shaping our literature and our sense of nationhood which, during the last three quarters of the century, has, slowly but surely, been showing signs of renewed strength? On 'the-sense-of-nationhood' business, undoubtedly an enormous invisible influence, though difficult to quantify since impossible precisely to define, but on creative Scottish writing very little; beyond, perhaps, reminding Burns readers and the vast army of passive Burns-supperite attenders that in a master's hands the Scots tongue awoke and still awakes ancient, valid values deeper than the market-place 'value-for-money' attitudes increasingly urged upon us today.

The main influence on, and to a large extent the heart and centre of, the Scottish Renaissance movement, which flourished in Scotland from about 1925 to 1975 or so, has undoubtedly been Christopher Murray Grieve, the poet Hugh MacDiarmid. *Sangschaw* and *Pennywheep*, these two books of superb lyrics, are, broadly speaking, rural-inspired in content and imagery. 'A Drunk Man Looks at the Thistle', however, ranges widely over contemporary life and thought as it existed in the nineteen-twenties. 'Not Burns – back to Dunbar' was MacDiarmid's cry for many years.

For his own exquisite early lyrics the by-then-debilitated state of the Scots tongue as used so wonderfully by Burns was an insufficient tool; so MacDiarmid set about constructing Lallans, Plastic Scots – call it what you will – reviving words with latent imaginative potential out of Jameson's *Scots Dictionary*. Against all the odds, it worked. No one with an ounce of feeling for true poetry can fail to thrill to the lyric wonders of *Sangschaw* and *Pennywheep*, or be excited and impressed by the wit, the satire and the sheer energy of the 'Drunk Man'. But MacDiarmid's success and what he achieved in these early years, though surely imperishable, was built upon an intellectual structure poorly able to withstand the tides of chance and change and history. It had several flawed planks in its construction. It is, sadly, a well-proven fact that a language can only survive if it is used in commerce and the everyday business of life. The most obvious example of the failure of government legislation artificially to revive a language not so used is the lack of success in Eire of the long-standing official programme to revive Erse as the daily Irish tongue.

By the time MacDiarmid burst upon the Scottish scene, Scots had largely fragmented into a series of local dialects. Most non-Gaelic speakers by then spoke a kind of Scoto-English, the thickness of the dialect depending to some extent on education and social class.

I treasure and revel in our literary Scots as much as anyone; every word of it. And I applaud all who labour so enthusiastically on its behalf. But no matter how vigorous their endeavours, the artificial restoration of Scots as a used tongue is even less likely to succeed than the late-in-the-day efforts to lift Gaelic off the rather low-lying plateau where, happily, for the moment at least, it seems to have stabilised.

In his early days, MacDiarmid inveighed against the only Scots tides that showed any signs of stirring popular living Scots at all. I refer, on the one hand, to the honest efforts of the Burns Federation to stimulate interest in Burns's Scots among schoolchildren; and on the other, to the vibrant use of it, albeit in a thin, debased strain, by Scots comedians like Harry Lauder and Will Fyffe – 'Music Hall Scots', if you like. At least that kind of Scots was undoubtedly a people's tongue.

The faulty planks built into the MacDiarmid Scots Revivalist structure were, firstly, that he was a Communist who, in old age, even supported the brutal suppression by the Soviet Army of the Hungarian and Czech popular democratic risings; and that's a far cry from Burns's 'Liberty's in every blow/Let us do or die'. I got to know him very well in the post-war years because he lived in a house in the West End of Glasgow almost back-to-back with my father's house. I saw him frequently. Basically, I think he didn't much like people. Certainly he could not brook any suggestion that he might be wrong over some things, or that not everything he wrote was necessarily a manifestation of genius. Secondly, he ceased to practise what he preached, abandoning Scots in favour of a fairly rhythmless quotation-larded English sprawl. There have been many explanations for this curious reversion. The most probable, however, seems that told to me by Norman MacCaig. MacDiarmid, who was accidentally tossed from a London double-decker bus in the late twenties, lost his sense of rhythm as a result of the head injury sustained in that incident.

But this is not a lecture on MacDiarmid. It is, however, important to establish that great as are the Scots lyrics written between 1924 and about 1932 – and they are very great indeed – they are never likely to make him a popular poet. There has never been any question of it being 'move over Burns.' Whatever may be the future course of Scots, MacDiarmid's influence is to be found not so much on his use of the Scots tongue, as in the internationalising of Scots thought.

So low had the esteem in which Scotland held itself become that until the post-Second-War years, Scottish literature was not taught in Scotland's schools; not, at any rate, systematically and as a requirement. All that has changed for the better. Young people in future should come out of some Scottish schools at least able to understand what Burns was writing about. If I had a criticism to make of the work of the Burns Federation over the years – apart from its perhaps incidental encouragement of Burnsolatry, a mindless condition which has nothing to do with the merits of his poetry – it would be that for years they treated Burns as if he were an isolated phenomenon, springing fully armed to the forefront of Scottish letters. Obviously, that view is nonsense. Great poet that he is, it is simply not the case that he is so much better than all the other earlier Scots writers that none of them are worth reading. I hope this is an attitude which no longer prevails anywhere. 'Back to Dunbar' was thus not such a bad cry, if it could have been held to apply also to all the Makars.

It is probably true that Scotland's three greatest poets have been Dunbar, Burns and MacDiarmid. By far the greatest of the three, however, is Burns. It would appear from Dunbar's verse that, like MacDiarmid, he wasn't awfully fond of other people. Certainly, like MacDiarmid, Dunbar never was, nor ever can be, in any real sense a 'people's poet'. But he was a master technician, a creator of great bursts of verbal music: one of many of Burns's predecessors who should certainly still be studied and enjoyed by the general reader.

Finally, there is the influence of Burns, the man, to be considered. I once did a rough check in a library to try to find out who had inspired the greatest number of books in English. Leaving aside Jesus Christ as being a special case, numerically, Burns is rivalled only by Shakespeare and Napoleon. That was some years ago. Many of these Burns books, of course, are worthless: those that fulminate against strong drink as the cause of his death (it was a contributory cause, no doubt, but not the main cause); those which simply regurgitate the common facts of his life-story – and they still regularly keep appearing! There are those (a minority) which genuinely advance our knowledge of the facts of his life or result in an increased understanding of his work or the texts which contain it. All this regurgitation however, at least suggests that, whether conveyed in strictly factual form, in semi-fictional form, like the biography by Catherine Carswell, or wholly fictionally, as in the novels of James Barke, our interest in the man and his milieu seems to be more or less insatiable.

And no wonder: what a story it is! Born in an agricultural labourer's cottage – though Burns's father never thought of himself in quite such lowly terms – part of the thatched roof of which was blown off in a storm; smitten by the charms of love and poetry at an early age; as a boy, engaged in a heart-damaging labour in the fields; easily – perhaps too easily – successful with women; a hater of social injustice and an upholder of the rights and dignity of the ordinary man; an exposer of fake pretence and hypocrisy; fond of the good things of life, or such as he could afford; one with a talent for friendship, regardless of status or rank; one capable of making enormous mistakes and bitterly repenting them afterwards; here, if ever there was one, is a man whom nearly everyone who reads his story warms to and can identify with. Then again, some people like to assume that he would have supported this or that cause which happens to involve their own interest. Take religion, for example. When Burns was writing to his 'mother-confessor', Mrs Dunlop, knowing that she was of a religious turn of mind, he larded his letters with pietistic references; for example, 'I hope and believe, that there is a state of existence beyond the grave where the worthy of this life will renew their former intimacies'. Yet a few weeks earlier, to Alexander Cunningham, he was declaring: 'Of all Nonsense, religious Nonsense is the most nonsensical.' Probably his true beliefs were agnostical –

again, pretty well echoing the general modern view, so well expressed by Burns to Robert Muir on 7th March, 1788: 'If we lie down in the grave, the whole man a piece of broke machinery, to moulder with the clods of the valley, – be it so; at least there is an end of pain, care, woes and wants: if that part of us called Mind, does survive the apparent destruction of the man – away with old-wife prejudices and tales! Every age and nation has had a different set of stories; and as the many are always weak, of consequence they have often, perhaps always been deceived: a man, conscious of having acted an honest part among his fellow creatures; even granting that he may have been the sport, at times, of passions and instincts; he goes to a great unknown Being who could have no other end in giving him existence but to make him happy; who gave him those passions and instincts, and well knows their force.'

I usually find the biographies – now more often autobiographies – of 'the worthy of this life' – the goody-goodies – every bit as boring as the tales of the baddy-baddies. On the other hand, the story of Burns, the story of 'a man, conscious of acting an honest part among his fellow-creatures; even granting that he may have been the sport of passions and instincts' – particularly when he happens also to have been the greatest literary genius Scotland has produced – the story of such a man never ceases to absorb our interests and involve our deepest feelings.

The composer, Francis George Scott, used to say that the image of the dying Burns suggesting that he would shelter the sixteen-year-old girl Jessie Lewars, who was nursing him, moved him to tears. Tears are perhaps not so readily drawn from us now in these war-atrocity days – 'You cannot weep for everyone in the cemetery', as the Russian proverb has it. Even so – and again, a comparison with Mozart – I find the plight of a genius in mid-flight and on the verge of advancement which would have removed his material worries, as was the case with both men – infinitely touching: in 1791 Mozart, perhaps the greatest composer who ever lived, in Vienna; and Burns, the people's poet, in the Dumfries of 1796.

Burns in Dumfries

Here he moved and had what you'd call his being,
the smells of dirt and beer clinging to narrow wynds
that welcomed him when, taxed with excising miles
he left his horse in the corner of his mind's

preoccupation, to drink himself to his fellows,
soothing the degradation foosty barrels
dunted him raw injustice with; forgetting
the barked knuckles, the puppified drawing-room quarrels

the song that dirled his blood but couldn't be written,
only acted out of. As if he'd bet

the God he half-believed in that, without reins
and saddleless, he'd ride the white-thighed sweat

of shying, eager, red-cheeked Dumfries fillies
a gait where lords and lawyers couldn't meddle;
he who was up and away both man and master,
whom poverty couldn't catch in time to peddle

his pride for lost discretion. Remorse! Remorse!
systole and diastole, his heart kept pounding,
back to the generosity of his Jean
who patiently waited for him, never rounding

the whips of her anger on him, ready to bear him
over what gentler canter he needed next;
unsure of herself and his clever friends, content
to be what he always returned to, and only vexed

that he couldn't find whatever it was he wanted.
But what he found, oh the pity of it all!
left her behind in labour, and he not able to hear
the town band shakily playing the Dead March from *Saul*.

From *Collected Poems 1960–1990*

'Churches built to please the PRIEST': The Dialectics of Morality in Burns's Poetry

O N 18 JUNE 1787 in a letter to William Nicol, Burns wrote what has become an oft-remarked comment on his feelings about an earlier British poet. Burns writes:

> I have bought a pocket Milton which I carry perpetually about with me, in order to study the sentiments – the dauntless magnanimity; the intrepid unyielding independance [sic]; the desperate daring, and noble defiance of hardship, in that great Personage, Satan ... (I, 123)

A week earlier on 11 June in a letter to James Smith, Burns said, 'Give me a spirit like my favorite hero, Milton's Satan ...' (I, 121). When put together, the attitudes Burns reveals in these comments give us insight into Burns's quarrels with the dogmatic religious morality of his day. For Burns, heroism and perhaps the greatest human strivings are bound up with his reading of Milton's Satan – the 'unyielding independance,' 'daring, and ... defiance.' Significantly, this reading of Milton does not roundly condemn nor dismiss the 'author of all lies.' Indeed, Satan's attractiveness to Burns is that which has fascinated and appealed to audiences of *Paradise Lost* for centuries. This Satan, for all the trappings of cosmic malevolence, treachery and deceit, is quintessentially a human, all too human, figure engaged in intellectual, spiritual and ideological battle for an assertion of the integrity and primacy of the self, a hero who battles for among other things the principle of self-determination in the face of an authoritarian and absolutist system. Satan's dialogical conflicts with the Almighty are very much akin to Burns's own conflicts with the established and reigning religious morality of his day, for as Satan sees the angels and humans as races of worshippers created for the pleasure of the deity, so Burns sees religion as, in his words from 'Love and Liberty,' 'Churches built to please the PRIEST'.

As Carol McGuirk has noted in her book on *Robert Burns and the Sentimental Era*,

> The sentimental hero, who often seems patterned after Milton's Satan, continually tests the boundaries of the 'norm.' Sentimental heroes consistently

prefer ruling in the hell generated by their self-will to serving in a society upheld by a consensus of the vulgar, the timid, the law-abiding. (48)

In this respect, Burns indeed fits the mold of such a sentimental figure. We need only consider the relations between Burns, polite society, and the Kirk in such poems as 'A Poet's Welcome to his love-begotten Daughter' or 'The Fornicator' for validation of this analysis. In these poems Burns both defiantly and whimsically says 'so be it' to the social and moral disapprobation heaped upon him for engaging in the pleasures of the flesh. As companion pieces they reveal a Burns who at once sturdily and with integrity stands firm against a moral dictate of the purported 'religion of love' that in itself refuses to accept as valid one of the primary manifestations of love in this world. For Burns, fornication and love are many times one and the same. At the same time, as in the case of 'The Fornicator', Burns's light-hearted treatment of the subject, his essential comic vision, undercuts the seriousness with which the Kirk and society view such matters as premarital sex. This whimsicality is further reinforced by the fact that the poem is a song. This is not to say that Burns himself does not take the matter of fornication seriously, particularly since he lived in an age when birth control was hardly an exact science. In 'A Poet's Welcome' his rebellious paternal instincts conclude on a note of pride in being a father even though the child is born out of wedlock. In the last stanza he says,

> I'll never rue my trouble wi' thee,
>   The cost nor shame o't,
> But be a loving Father to thee,
>   And brag the name o't. – (45–48)

In a similar fashion, stanza four of 'The Fornicator' breaks from the merry romp through hormonal crime and punishment to a serious expression of the sentiment that underlies his activities with Betty Paton. He writes,

> But for her sake this vow I make,
>   And solemnly I swear it,
> That while I own a single crown,
>   She's welcome for to share it;
> And my roguish boy his Mother's joy,
>   And the darling of his Pater,
> For him I boast my pains and cost,
>   Although a Fornicator. (25–32)

Both implicit and explicit in these and other poems we can see that life on the socio-religious margins carries with it a certain degree of intellectual and emotional turmoil. There is the inevitable conflict that accompanies a refusal to go along with the moral status quo. Certainty, consistency and security accompany unquestioning acceptance of any system of belief. However, Burns in many instances appears to have no such luxuries, for as Thomas Crawford has noted, 'most of [Burns's] poems are made out of a highly inconsistent man's battle with the world' (xii). Indeed, if we read Burns's 'Epistle to a Young Friend' as being serious as opposed to ironic, the advice given there would appear to undercut Burns's own belief in the validity of his patterns of thought and behavior throughout much of his life. Echoing Ophelia, he advises his young friend to 'better reck the *rede*, / Than ever did th' *Adviser*' (87–88). Such advice, as an expression of self-doubt, would indicate that life on the social and moral margins carries with it the counterpart to the high-spirited emotions expressed in 'A Poet's Welcome' and 'The Fornicator' – namely a fundamental guilt and doubt about oneself. In orthodoxy is security in all forms. As such, this epistle can be viewed as a sermon premised on two issues Burns raises in stanza eight:

> The *fear o' Hell's* a hangman's whip,
>   To haud the wretch in order;
> But where ye feel your *Honor* grip,
>   Let that ay be your border:
> It's slightest touches, instant pause—
>   Debar a' side-pretences;
> And resolutely keep it's laws,
>   Uncaring consequences. (57–64)

Thus two notions of fear: fear of being punished by some moral authority, and fear of being punished by one's own authority *vis-à-vis* dishonouring oneself. This matter of honour receives slightly more explication earlier in the epistle. For instance, in stanza five Burns says to his young friend,

> Ay free, aff han', your story tell,
>   When wi' a bosom crony;
> But still keep something to yoursel
>   Ye scarcely tell to ony.
> Conceal yoursel as weel's ye can
>   Frae critical dissection;
> But keek thro' ev'ry other man,
>   Wi' sharpen'd, sly inspection. (33–40)

This particular stanza quite clearly paraphrases Polonius's advice to his son Laertes in Act One, Scene Three of *Hamlet*. Polonius says,

> Give thy thoughts no tongue,
> Nor any unproportion'd thought his act.
> Be thou familiar, but by no means vulgar ...
>   . . . .
> Give every man thine ear, but few thy voice.
> Take each man's censure, but reserve thy judgment.
>   (1.3.59–61, 67–8)

Honour and self-protection are the issues here, and they form essential elements of this scene in the play, for Laertes in his long-winded, cautionary advice to his sister Ophelia regarding her relationship with Hamlet tells her she 'must fear' Hamlet, his greatness and his will. Says he, 'Fear it, Ophelia, fear it, my dear sister .../ Be wary then; best safety lies in fear' (1.3.33, 42). A similar sentiment pervades Polonius's advice to her later in the scene: Hamlet's vows are to be held suspect, that her honour is at stake. When taken together, these issues are a call to trust no one but oneself and to fear the power of others. And these are fundamental themes in Burns's 'Epistle to a Young Friend'. As in the case of Shakespeare's play, Burns's advice preaches an essential mistrust of the world, hence leads to a stultifying and isolating philosophy of life. Leaving aside the very real possibility that Burns may be engaging in a bit of tongue-in-cheek irony with this epistle, the philosophy upon which it is premised is a matter of crime and punishment, and this takes two forms. First, insofar as religion and, broadly speaking, morality are concerned, fear, particularly as something that can be manipulated by institutions and powers beyond the individual's control, is that which is key 'To haud the wretch in order' as Burns says (58). The second fear, and for Burns apparently the more important of the two, is the fear of self-punishment. In other words, one's sense of honour and integrity appears to be paramount, superseding potentially the *'fear o' Hell'* (57). This is not to say Burns thumbs his nose at God, for in stanzas nine and ten he sees the natural necessity of 'the *Creature*' revering the 'Creator'. Rather, this aspect of his epistle centers squarely on pitting the individual and conscience in opposition to formalized, institutionalized dogma. As he says, '... still the preaching cant forbear, / And ev'n the rigid feature' (67–8). Thus, in this view, organized religion is not the solution but rather the problem. Another case of churches built to please the priest, to bestow upon the ecclesiastical class the power to control people's lives. In the face of this, Burns posits the apparently radical notion that one's conscience should be one's guide.

Conservatism, especially in its more extreme manifestations, whether in society or religion, tends to be a reaction against, and fear of, change and the forces that prompt it. Any system that is secure in and of itself can tolerate or be unconcerned with voices of opposition, with lawbreakers, with the ungodly. The fact that Burns could embrace and be reprimanded for so-called 'unacceptable behaviour' such as drinking and fornicating would indicate that Auld Licht Calvinist extremism itself held precariously to its function of social and moral control over the masses. Hence the need for punishing deviation from orthodoxy. The Calvinist prohibitions against many traditional forms of festivity and recreation coupled with an insistence on devoting one's energies to God would indicate that such behaviour gave rise to the prohibitions before the prohibitions gave rise to deviant behaviour such as drinking, dancing, fornicating and so on. Human behaviour itself constructs the codes and orders – the very ideologies that then condemn behaviour.

A thread running through these remarks thus far has been the interrelation of the social and religious realms. There is a certain class orientation involved in religious and moral doctrine. Thomas Crawford points out that in Burns's day there was 'a certain lack of support for the old [Calvinist] ideas amongst the educated and upper classes' (34). Put another way, this state of affairs indicates that the ruling elite could afford to distance themselves from, or utterly reject, religious dogma. Consequently, religion and its attendant morality can be viewed as a tool of social control that the elite can comfortably ignore with impunity. Curiously, for all his class-consciousness and orientation toward the poor and dispossessed, Burns intellectually sided with the upper classes on matters of religious liberalism. A fundamental tenet of religious thought is the question of how God shall be served. Burns's concern, however, centres on the question of how we as human beings function in this life, though this is not merely a *reactionary* response to religious doctrine, for his poetry certainly displays he was versed in old-school theology as well as that of the new, more moderate forms of his day.

Obviously, though, Burns was no fawning sycophant of the rich and famous. Clearly displayed in so much of his poetry is an outrage at socio-economic injustice, both personal and collective, stemming undoubtedly from the privation and hardship that he experienced from early in life. Yet significantly Burns does not seek refuge in orthodox religious consolations which rationalize personal circumstance as destiny, as God's will, as the earthly suffering that is a prerequisite for bliss in the hereafter. Indeed, to use John Weston's phrase, Burns's poetry from early on 'is full of protests of class inequality and assertions of his own worth in spite of his poverty' (40). The Muse is his god and poetry his theology. So in Burns's attacks on the social elite and on rigid orthodoxy we find a man taking umbrage at two prominent sources of the social control of the masses, the poor, and the powerless. It is thus no wonder that the terms of abuse and ridicule aimed at one group can just as readily be transferred to the other, for each group's power to control and at the same time to be above the law is anathema for Burns.

A beautiful case in point here is 'Holy Willie's Prayer'. In the persona of Holy Willie Burns demonstrates deftly and with savage insight just such a representative of a class who dictate codes of behaviour but who themselves feel no compulsion to practise what they preach. Further, specifically in the religious context, Burns lays bare the perverted moral logic inherent in the doctrine held by Willie. As Thomas Crawford puts it, 'once God has chosen him, it doesn't matter a jot whether a man lives a good life or not – he will be saved because he is one of the elect' (31). Willie knows full well that he 'deserv'd most just damnation' (15) on account of 'Adam's cause' (18), yet he also sees himself as being given divine immunity from the rules that encumber the rest of us poor sinners. Willie understands himself to be 'a chosen sample' who illustrates that God's 'grace is great and ample'. In other words, Willie comprehends his own moral failure but is not troubled in his conscience since he's sure of his destiny. This is self-centredness elevated to the realm of theology, for it presumes no less than Willie's smug assurance that he knows with absolute certainty the mind of God. We should all be so lucky. You might think, though, that a person who places such faith in the all-wise and just ways of God would rise above the petty call on the Almighty to curse Gaun Hamilton's 'basket and his store, / Kail and potatoes' (77–78). Then again, it always helps to have friends in high places. So Burns exposes the true impotence of those who wield so much control over human affairs. Their power resides in their ability to inspire fear in the herd, and this is a central theme in the 'Epistle to a Young Friend', as we saw earlier. Yet Burns in 'Holy Willie's Prayer' does more than skewer an arrogant hypocrite. Not far removed from Willie's bluster and bombast is the ideological underpinning that allows for such people. Burns's masterful use of irony showcases also the debauched and perverted system of value and belief that the Holy Willies of the world create as a haven for their own moral bankruptcy. Churches built to please the priest, indeed!

Burns articulates a similar sentiment in different words in his epistle 'To the Rev. John M'Math, Inclosing a copy of *Holy Willie's Prayer*, which he had requested.' In lines that reverberate out to condemn the religious hypocrites of the world, Burns says of himself,

> God knows, I'm no the thing I shou'd be,
> Nor am I even the thing I cou'd be,
> But twenty times, I rather wou'd be
>   An atheist clean,
> Than under gospel colors hid be
>   Just for a screen. (43–48)

At least atheists are not religious hypocrites.

Two stanzas later in this poem, Burns makes a devastatingly insightful comment on the true purposes at work in religious figures such as Holy Willie. Burns says of them that

> They take religion in their mouth;
> They talk o' mercy, grace an' truth,
> For what? – to gie their malice skouth
>   On some puir wight,
> An' hunt him down, o'er right an' ruth
>   To ruin streight. (55–60)

In other words, religion is none other than personal malice cloaked in metaphysical garb, elevated to the level of a universal absolute, and institutionalized as doctrine. With such a view of rigid religious orthodoxy, it is no wonder that a man of Burns's insight and temperament would prefer the warm society of the pub to the pinched and desiccated atmosphere of the Kirk. This is Blake's Little Vagabond with his innocence shattered and his barbs sharpened.

Burns sees an essential necessity in human immorality. Even Holy Willie himself is 'At times ... fash'd wi' fleshly lust ...' (38). Significantly, Willie's grammatical construction here centres on the use of passive voice, indicating that even the godly must contend with forces beyond their control. Similarly, the poet says this as well in his 'Address to the Unco Guid'. Here Burns comes to the defence of human weakness, immorality and imperfection, arguing in effect that a balance of good and bad is necessary for the equilibrium of human make-up. In stanza two he carries the banner for Folly, saying,

> Hear me, ye venerable Core,
>   As counsel for poor mortals,
> That frequent pass douce Wisdom's door
>   For glaikit Folly's portals;
> I, for their thoughtless, careless sakes
>   Would here propone defences,
> Their donsie tricks, their black mistakes
>   Their failings and mischances. (9–16)

And in stanza three Burns points out that the mighty and the Unco Guid are merely better in the 'art o' hiding.' Everyone, in this view, is immoral to one degree or another. 'To step aside is human,' the poet intones in stanza seven, hence Burns feels that human beings are in no position to pass judgement on each other, for God 'alone / Decidedly can try us ...' (57–58). So Burns sees the Unco Guid as having cut themselves off from significant and in many ways necessary avenues of human experience. He says that 'What's *done* we partly may compute, / But know not what's *resisted*' (63–63). Because of this, they don't know whereof they speak. The upshot of this outlook is that everyone must experience the bad, since it is an inextricable aspect of human existence. In short, Burns feels that we must not mutilate the self in an attempt to avoid what the systems tag as immoral.

This is not to say Burns excuses free exercise of passions as being something that we can't help doing. Rather, he has a philosophical and theological outlook on such behaviour. In a letter to Robert Muir dated 7 March 1788, Burns writes:

> Every age and every nation has had a different set of stories; and as the many are always weak, of consequence they have often, perhaps always been deceived: a man, conscious of having acted an honest part among his fellow-creatures; even granting that he may have been the sport, at times, of passions and instincts; he goes to a great unknown Being who could have no other end in giving him existence but to make him happy; who gave him those passions and instincts, and well knows their force. (I, 258)

In other words, God makes passions to give us pleasure, and therefore they are good. In 'A Prayer, in the Prospect of Death' Burns takes a similar notion and addresses it squarely at the deity. Here, God has formed Burns 'With passions wild and strong' (10). And significantly, the vision of God in stanza five is one of a forgiving rather than a vengeful deity. Burns concludes with the lines:

> Where with *intention* I have err'd,
>   No other plea I have,
> But, *Thou art good*, and Goodness still
>   Delighteth to forgive. (17–20)

This dichotomy of spirit and flesh, religion and passion, is in many ways central to Burns's philosophy. The apparent conflicts between Auld Licht and New Licht theology are just that – apparent. As 'The Holy Fair' so poignantly demonstrates, the Auld Licht/New Licht dichotomy is a false one, a distinction without a difference. Even the relatively liberal theology of New Licht Calvinism is still a theology, a moral doctrine, an ideology of priestly power. It matters not except in the smallest of circles that (stanza fifteen) 'Smith is anathema to the bigoted Evangelicals: [that] they cannot stand him because he emphasizes such irrelevant matters as moral living and good works instead of blind "faith"' (MacLaine, 'Burlesque' 32). In contradistinction to all the religious theorizing and moralizing, Burns later, in stanza nineteen, writes:

> Leeze me on Drink! it gies us mair
>   Than either School or Colledge:
> It kindles Wit, it waukens Lear,
>   It pangs us fou o' Knowledge.
> Be't *whisky-gill* or *penny-wheep*,
>   Or onie stronger potion,
> It never fails, on drinkin deep,
>   To kittle up our *notion*,
>   By night or day. (163–171)

Burns thus pokes 'ironic fun of the fact that a few drinks can magically turn ignorant, inarticulate men into glib (but specious) experts on any subject – especially on Scots Calvinist theology' (MacLaine, 'Burlesque' 32). Whisky is a kind of muse for the unlearned and the ignorant, giving everyone an opinion but no one a final say on matters – just like the quarrelsome ministers divided over the fine points of theology. In this poem, spatially as well as philosophically, the ale house is ranged against the church, and we need not look too far to see, as David Daiches put it, 'Burns starts from the coldly theological and moves rapidly down to the physical and earthy' (123). If anything, the human orientation in this poem toward the physical and earthy moves to the concluding point of '*Houghmagandie*.' This in itself would suggest that in the passions for drink and particularly sex are intimate links with the life force itself, with notions of fertility as opposed to the cold, arid and life-hating theology of the Fair. This is not to say Burns roundly and absolutely condemns all that theology stands for. His tool of attack is comedy, not invective. In this case, the comedy is essentially conservative in nature because Burns hardly advocates any sort of warfare directed at the priestly class and their ideologies. Rather, to borrow Crawford's phrase, we are presented with a 'richly humorous spectacle of peaceful coexistence' (71). Burns is shrewd enough to realize that despite the onerous and odious nature of such religious dogma, be it Auld Licht or New, the real world does and must accommodate *all* sorts from the spectrum of human belief and behaviour. Obviously, though, Burns takes sides. He can appreciate the human comedy of both the saintly and the sinners, but the ideology of the pub is in the end more forceful and seemingly more desirable than the doctrines of organized religion.

Such a necessary coexistence of sacred and profane, social and antisocial, achieves its supreme treatment in 'Love and Liberty', Burns's Dantean cast of comic characters each telling his or her story within the confines of the privileged space of Poosie-Nansie's pub. Despite the generally low social station these bar-flies inhabit, there is the element of admirableness, even heroism, in their marginal status. Carol McGuirk is one of the more insistent on seeing a fundamental and sentimental heroism at work beneath the hedonism and debauchery of this assemblage of society's flotsam and jetsam. Essentially, she sees in the jolly beggars a process of self-determination by which they have devised their fates. In her words, 'the defense of characters in emotional rebellion from social norms has social and ethical dimensions ... Burns's beggars refuse to feel as society decrees that they should; ... they embrace instead a stubborn, and not especially idealistic, individuality' (16). In essence, she views the beggars' lives on the social margin as a matter of pride for these people, who have freely chosen to be social outcasts – people who emphatically do not whine and moan about their condition.

The extent to which the anti-social sentiments expressed by and embodied in the beggars reflect Burns's own rebellious and potentially anarchic sentiments has been the subject of some debate. At face value, the poem would appear to reject any and all systems of socio-political and religious order that seek to channel human behaviour in specific directions. Indeed, David Daiches reads the ending of the poem as representing 'the final and most extreme repudiation of social institutions' (207). However, this is not necessarily Burns's own embrace of anarchy even though the culminating jab directed at courts and churches undoubtedly reflects the realistic and cynical attitudes of the poet who himself was more than once the victim of the hypocrisies and injustices of the systems he (or more properly here, his Chorus) rails against. Significantly, particularly in light of Burns's own understanding of the necessity for the liberated individual to live with and function in and around social order, the beggars in this poem do not get portrayed in utopian or sentimental terms, despite their obvious appeal as vital beings. Clearly, though, Burns empathizes with this motley crew, since he and they are 'victims of the same kinds of social and economic injustice and hypocrisy' (MacLaine, 'Jolly Beggars' 140). Between poet and characters there is a common bond of down-to-earth humanity. Indeed, the physical deformities, the drunkenness, the hedonism of the Jolly Beggars and their links to spiritual deformities can be read in Bakhtinian terms as links to the material bodily lower stratum and hence to connotations of fertility, and this is a point also operative in 'The Holy Fair'. Yet Allan MacLaine has argued that the narrative voice of 'Love and Liberty' is essentially a conservative one, that the radical expressions in the poem are offset by the Burns who 'is also the author of the socially orthodox recitatives' ('Jolly Beggars' 139). Central to this thesis is MacLaine's reading of the Doxy's song beginning at line 57, which he sees as constructing a character who lives innocently in a world of illusion ('Jolly Beggars' 134). In essence, many if not most of the songs in the poem can be read ironically. To quote MacLaine's idea here, 'Burns admires the defiant spirit of his beggars, and he half envies their total irresponsibility; but he also gently satirizes them by letting them speak in their own voice in such a way as to bring out the absurdities of their heroic or romantic pretensions, the illusory nature of their vaunted "freedom", and the actual squalor of their lives' ('Burlesque' 35). Thus true 'freedom' is not possible. This is not to say that Burns advocates everyone's strict adherence to social and moral codes. Rather, the point here is that the amoral and asocial attitudes and behaviour of the beggars must exist in a dialogical relation with their social and moral opposites, for each gives meaning to the other. The Jolly Beggars' tavern is a 'refuge' in every sense of the term from what the external environment represents, though it cannot remain a 'home' *per se*. The external world presumably is where all the Beggars must eventually go. Poosie-Nansie's place is not nor can it be an island unto itself. In light of Mikhail Bakhtin's notion of Carnival, Poosie-Nansie's pub, like all such places, is a socially licensed locus of so-called 'deviant behaviour', a place and method of release, an illusion of anti-social, amoral liberty where normal rules of social and moral behaviour are temporarily suspended. In this world laughter, lechery and drunkenness construct an alternate world in opposition to the socio-political realm and its own church in opposition to that built to please the priest. The world of these Jolly Beggars is a festive arena where there is a reaffirmation of the life force in the face of all the social and moral rules that deny life and liberty. For us as audience, the Beggars' carnival is spectacle, whereas for them and their ilk it is life itself. And though the reality behind what these Beggars represent is at best a social and moral safety valve for desires and pent up passions for liberty, nevertheless the spirit and organized disorder of Poosie-Nansie's pub represent a temporary though significant suspension of socially acceptable truth, hierarchies, ranks, socio-religious hypocrisies and coercions, and all else that make the social and moral orders in fact orderly. The Beggars' world consecrates a view of freedom by liberating this cast of characters from a prevailing ideology and world view, from accepted truths and conventions, from a monological outlook on life. The Beggars are liberated from the banal necessities which govern the society outside the pub. Burns's comedy illustrates the multifaceted richness of life, but the comedy of the Beggars' world does not completely negate the values of society. If anything, the ideology of the pub paradoxically invigorates the world which exists in opposition to the pub. A comment Bakhtin made concerning laughter applies perfectly well to Burns's essential outlook in 'Love and Liberty', 'The Holy Fair', and other poems of this kind. Bakhtin says,

> True ambivalent and universal laughter does not deny seriousness but purifies and completes it. Laughter purifies from dogmatism, from the intolerant and the petrified; it liberates from fanaticism and pedantry, from fear and intimidation, from didacticism, naivete and illusion, from single meaning, the single level, from sentimentality. (123)

As such, Burns's comedy and satire along these lines are in fact quite philosophical, forms of truth unto themselves.

The essential transitory and illusory nature of the Beggars' so-called 'liberty' points back to the inevitability and inescapableness of the world outside the pub door. The laughter and satire directed at this world and simultaneously at the world of the Beggars certainly points up the deficiencies of both realms without completely dismantling either. The true notion of liberty that the poem advances is not the wholesale adoption of the Beggars' world nor its wholesale abandonment. Rather, liberty here exists in the endless dialogical interrelationship between both worlds. The authoritarian perspectives of court and kirk here and in many of Burns's poems must exist in such dialogue with their antitheses. Authoritarian discourse attempts to thwart dialogue, but it cannot. Order and anarchy, kirk and flesh exist as contending yet mutually necessary opposites.

In sum, Burns accepts, in contrast to religious doctrine, the need to embrace this world with all its pleasures and frustrations. He seeks to find his purpose in and through this realm. This is not to say he is overly bound to the material realm, for in so many of his poems he extols the virtue of simple poverty. For Burns, human love, the passions, and physicality in all their manifestations bring about the complete realization of people's humanity. Concern with the material and the bodily does not imply his rejection of the metaphysical realm, however. Rather, Burns rejects the astringent dogmas of religion that refuse to accept as valid the behaviours that give Burns life's pleasures in this world.

WORKS CITED

Bakhtin, Mikhail, *Rabelais and His World*, translated by Helene Iswolsky (Bloomington: Indiana UP, 1984).

Burns, Robert, *Burns: Poems and Songs*, edited by James Kinsley (Oxford: Oxford UP, 1969).

——, *Letters*, edited by J. De Lancey Ferguson; second edition edited by G. Ross Roy (Oxford: Oxford UP, 1985).

Crawford, Thomas, Burns: *A Study of the Poems and Songs* (Stanford: Stanford UP, 1960).

Daiches, David, *Robert Burns* (Edinburgh: Spurbooks, 1950; reprinted 1981).

MacLaine, Allan H. 'Burlesque as a Satiric Method in Poems and Songs of Burns', *Scottish Literary Journal* 13 (1986): 30–46.

——, 'Radicalism and Conservatism in Burns, *The Jolly Beggars*', *Studies in Scottish Literature* 13 (1987): 125–143.

McGuirk, Carol, *Robert Burns and the Sentimental Era* (Athens, GA: U. of Georgia P., 1985).

Shakespeare, William, *Hamlet. The Complete Works of Shakespeare*, edited by Irving Ribner and G. L. Kittredge (New York: John Wiley & Sons, 1971).

Weston, John C. 'Robert Burns's Satire', *The Art of Robert Burns*, edited by R. D. S. Jack and Andrew Noble (London: Vision P, 1982), 36–58.

'Sacred Freedom': Presbyterian Radicalism and the Politics of Robert Burns

IN DISCUSSING THE POLITICS of Robert Burns, it is advisable to proceed with a degree of diffidence. As the poet's most recent biographer reminds us, 'Burns's politics were ... never less than moderately confused'.[1] To attempt to abstract a rigorously coherent political philosophy from Burns's work would be a futile project. As well as contradictions and ambivalences in the poetry, there are tensions between the poetry and the biography to which the student of Burns's politics must attend. For one thing, there is the question of how the poet of universal human brotherhood should have been ready to contemplate becoming a slave-driver in Jamaica. Samuel Johnson's indignant query – 'how is it that we hear the loudest yelps for liberty among the drivers of negroes?' – would have possessed an uncanny prescience had Burns gone ahead with the Jamaica project.[2] Given such contradictions, it is best to avoid seeking a definitive account of Burns's politics, and to be aware that the subject admits of various approaches.

One approach in particular has dominated the study of Burns's political work in the twentieth century. Overwhelmingly, critics have viewed Burns's political poetry as part of a democratic historical moment whose climactic expression was the French Revolution of 1789. Writing in 1907, Hector Macpherson set the tone by discussing Burns as 'the incarnation of the new [Revolutionary] spirit'. Subsequent critics have followed this lead, including Christina Keith, who avers that 'Liberty, Equality and Fraternity are the keynotes of all Burns's social thought'; Howard Brogan, who refers to the poet's 'revolutionary idealism'; and W. J. Murray, who finds that the poet's political ideals 'were, broadly speaking, the ideals of the French Revolution'.[3]

I intend to pursue a rather different approach to Burns's political poetry. When we consider that much of Burns's best political work was written three or more years prior to the fall of the Bastille, it is easy to appreciate Marilyn Butler's contention that critics have 'overstated the links of Burns with the French Revolution'.[4] Burns's support for the French Revolution was in fact somewhat belated – it dates from late 1792 – and not altogether solid, suggesting that the popular image of 'Burns the Jacobin' is impressionistic at best. Commentators habitually quote Cockburn's account of the Revolution's impact on

Scotland ('Everything rung, and was connected, with the Revolution in France
...'), but few record his scepticism regarding the existence of genuine Scottish
Jacobins – 'we had wonderfully few proper Jacobins'.[5] 'French principles', it
must be remembered, were not simply swallowed whole by British radicals,
but were absorbed into indigenous traditions of radical discourse. Too often
in Burns criticism, a vague gesture towards the 'ideals of the Revolution' has
concealed a failure to engage with the structure of political debate in Burns's
Britain.

In 1897, however, an alternative approach to Burns's political work had been
outlined – ironically, by a critic whose explicit concern was with the literary
effects of the French Revolution. In *The French Revolution and English Litera-
ture*, Edward Dowden argued that the 'French' ideals to which Burns responds
in the 1790s were ones with which, as a Scots Presbyterian, he was already
familiar: 'by the fact that he belonged to the democratic Presbyterian Church
and sympathized with the party of spiritual revolt, Burns was fitted to be a
spokesman of the passions of the time'.[6]

Now, while Dowden's remark has been fleetingly endorsed by one or two
critics – notably A. B. Jamieson and Alan Bold – it has never been taken up as
the basis of a sustained analysis of Burns's politics.[7] This is unfortunate, for,
with this remark, Dowden suggests how we might move beyond the superficial
image of 'Burns the Jacobin' and begin to explore the historical provenance of
Burns's political ideas and idioms. What stands against Dowden's thesis is
Burns's often antagonistic relationship with the Scottish kirk, as evinced most
emphatically in the kirk satires. But the kirk satires represent a very Presbyterian
phenomenon: the competent layman's attack on priestcraft. In the epistles to
McMath and Goldie, Burns is participating in a tradition of anticlericalism (or
'priest-skelping' as he calls it) which has deep roots in Presbyterian culture,
particularly in Burns's own part of Scotland. As Walter McGinty has empha-
sised, Burns criticised the kirk very much from the position of an insider.[8]

Moreover, the fact that Burns welcomed the liberalising 'New Light' currents
within eighteenth-century Presbyterianism should not be read as a rejection of
the Presbyterian heritage. If the New Lights jettisoned much of the theological
baggage of Calvinism, they by no means relinquished their claim on Presby-
terianism's libertarian past. In their commitment to freedom of conscience and
the right of private judgement the New Lights saw themselves as renovating
the true founding principles of Protestantism.[9] As the kirk satires indicate,
Burns, too, regarded the New Lights as a reforming force, a 'candid, lib'ral
band' ('To the Rev. John McMath'), renewing the assault on superstition and
priestcraft. Tellingly, when Burns discusses his Old Light adversaries, he em-
ploys the stigmatizing terminology of Roman Catholicism.[10] Burns attacks the
Old Lights not for being too Protestant, but for not being Protestant enough.
In many respects, then, the kirk satires rather reinforce than diminish Burns's
Presbyterianism. Burns's passionate irreverence, his readiness to speak out

against figures of authority – be it ministers, M. P. s or monarchs – can be seen as a very Presbyterian characteristic. This is perhaps what Edwin Muir was getting at when he cited the poet's 'ribaldry' and 'blasphemy' as evidence that Burns was 'a very Protestant poet'.[11]

On a broader, social level, Dowden's suggestion of a religious basis to the radicalism of Burns's time is highly pertinent. Historians have long perceived a nexus between eighteenth-century radical politics and Presbyterian/Dissenting religion: we think of the activities of Price and Priestley in England; the emphatically Presbyterian nature of the Volunteering and United Irish movements in Ulster; and the strong Covenanting Presbyterian input into Scottish radicalism.[12] Similarly, the ideology of the radicals often owed less to secular theories of natural rights than to political theology. Radicalism drew on long-standing denominational – especially Presbyterian – discourses which emphasised the contractual nature of government and the duty to resist 'tyranny'. Roy Foster's comment in relation to Ulster radicalism in this period holds good for lowland Scotland: 'what should be borne in mind is not only the percussion of events … from the early 1790s, but also the Presbyterian tradition of libertarian republicanism that long antedated 1775 or 1789.'[13] In what follows, I shall give a brief outline of this tradition of Presbyterian political thought, before going on to assess its impact on Burns and his poetry.

The association of Presbyterianism with political radicalism reflects the pattern of development of the Calvinist Reformation. Whereas Lutheranism tended to develop through the sponsorship of princes, and so remained politically quiescent and deferential to the civil power, Calvinism developed in open conflict with hostile Catholic courts in Scotland as in France. Repudiating the right of the monarch to intervene in matters of spiritual moment, Calvinism stood for limited government in defiance of monarchical absolutism. Moreover, Calvinism drew its support from social classes – the bourgeoisie, artisans, peasants – which were excluded from existing power structures. It gave these groups a share in ecclesiastical power by adopting a partially democratic system of government by church courts (Presbyterianism). And increasingly, given its hostile relationship with the crown, the kirk asserted the civil and political competence of the people, their right to resist bad government.

The theory of justified resistance was developed by Presbyterian thinkers in a series of polemical works, often written in times of armed rebellion: George Buchanan's *De Jure Regni Apud Scotos* (1579), written after the deposition of Mary; Samuel Rutherford's *Lex Rex: The Law and the Prince* (1644), written during the Presbyterian resistance to Charles I; and Alexander Shields's *Hind Let Loose* (1687), written during the later Covenanting struggles. In these seminal works, the right to resist is put forward as part of a contractarian theory of government, in which sovereignty is seen to be vested in the people as a whole.

In developing their political philosophy, Presbyterian theorists drew on two key resources. Firstly, they drew on the biblical concept of the 'covenant'. Government is represented as a covenant or contract between ruler and ruled, by which the people undertake to render obedience only so long as their ruler governs in the public interest. Buchanan speaks of government as 'a mutual contract between the king and the people',[14] while, for Alexander Shields, 'Government is nothing else but a mutual stipulation between Kings & People'.[15]

Secondly, Scottish resistance theorists employed arguments derived from the structure of Presbyterian church government. The Presbyterian understanding of ecclesiastical authority – whereby a fully competent lay community delegates a conditional authority to its ministers – is extended into the civil sphere. Again, this results in a contractarian scenario, in which government wields an authority which is not absolute, but conditional on its acting for the good of the public. Where authority – either civil or religious – is not used for the good of all, the people are held to be justified in resuming direct control. Allegiance must be conditional, not absolute:

> [I]n Conscience, we are no more free to Prostitute our Loyalty and Liberty absolutely, in ouning every Professor of the Magistracy; than we are free to Prostitute our Religion and faith implicitely, in ouning every Pretender to the Ministry.[16]

That is, the Protestant right of private judgement in matters of faith has as its corollary the right – and indeed the duty – to scrutinise one's political leaders and call them to account.[17]

Importantly, Covenanting political theory was not confined to a few Scottish extremists. The ideas of the Scottish resistance theorists were taken up during the constitutional crises of the late seventeenth century. Contractarian ideas were expressed in John Locke's *Two Treatises of Government* (1690), a work which Quentin Skinner has called 'the classic text of radical Calvinist politics',[18] and in countless Whig resistance tracts of the years around 1690.[19] In this way, the contractarian political theory of the Presbyterians – often conjoined to the highly compatible idiom of European 'civic humanism' – became part of the mainstream of political debate in eighteenth-century Britain.[20] Above all, it influenced the 'Real Whigs' and 'Commonwealthmen' (as discussed by Caroline Robbins in her seminal study of political radicalism, *The Eighteenth-Century Commonwealthman*[21]). And, through such figures as Francis Hutcheson (who speaks of government as 'a mutual agreement or contract' between governors and people), contractarian political theory exerted a strong influence on the thinkers of the Scottish Enlightenment, and on the radical reformers of the seventeen-eighties and nineties.[22]

The intellectual basis of early-modern British radicalism, then, was a long-

standing tradition of 'social contract-resistance theory'[23] associated primarily
with non-Anglican Protestant denominations. In the context of eighteenth-cen-
tury politics, contract theory was concerned less with the question of cashiering
the monarch than with that of ensuring the independence of the House of
Commons and the 'balance of the constitution'. Nevertheless, the principles of
eighteenth-century radicalism remained firmly Buchananite: that government
is for the good of the people; that authority ascends from below; that sovereignty
resides in the people, who retain the right to scrutinise and ultimately to cashier
their government.

To what extent, and by what means, was Burns exposed to contractarian
political thought? Growing up in Ayrshire, Burns was exposed to a vigorous
oral culture which celebrated the memory of the seventeenth-century Cove-
nanters and their struggle against the 'tyranny' of successive Stuart monarchs.
Burns's mother was of Covenanting stock and from her Burns 'would have
absorbed much Covenanting lore'.[24] While Burns came to find certain aspects
of the Presbyterian heritage rebarbative, he remained responsive to the appeal
of the Covenanters (his Jacobite leanings notwithstanding). As early as 1785,
an entry in the first Commonplace Book shows Burns expressing his pride at
coming from 'a country where civil, and particularly religious Liberty have
ever found their first support, and their last asylum',[25] while, a decade later,
Burns composes a poetic tribute to the Covenanters ('The Solemn League and
Covenant').

As well as this exposure to Covenanting legend – to 'many rueful, bloody
stories / Of tyrants, Jacobites and tories' ('A Fragment – On Glenriddel's Fox
breaking his chain') – Burns was familiar with the large body of Presbyterian
literature which circulated in Ayrshire, at least some of which was of a historical
and political nature.[26] In addition to this, Burns acquired his political education
partly in those institutions of Presbyterian popular culture, the debating society
and the Masonic Lodge, where he no doubt encountered political ideas of a
contractarian or 'Real Whiggish' cast. Similarly, many of Burns's associates
among the Ayrshire New Light – Dalrymple, McMath, McQhuae, McGill –
had been educated at Glasgow University, one of the major centres of contrac-
tarian Real Whig thought in the British Isles.[27]

In addition to these local influences, we must note Burns's reading in British
Augustan literature. Critics have tended to restrict the significance of Burns's
literary reading to questions of stylistic influence, ignoring possible ideological
implications. Many of Burns's favourite Augustan writers were vehement Real
Whigs, drawing on a Presbyterian/Dissenting body of political ideas. Thomson,
Akenside, Addison and Fielding were all perceived by contemporaries as
poets of Liberty, champions of opposition Whiggism and fierce critics of Old

Corruption.[28] It was from these authors (as well as from more explicitly political writers like 'Junius') that Burns absorbed that Real Whig idiom – of 'liberty' and 'independence' pitted against 'corruption' and 'luxury' – which pervades his political writings, and to which his regional religious background had already exposed him. Burns was steeped in Real Whig politics long before he read radical political writers of the 1790s such as David Steuart Erskine, or 'Timothy Thunderproof' in *The Bee*.

The Presbyterian roots of Burns's political radicalism are perhaps most evident in his early political satires, in which Burns exercises his right to call his political leaders to account and to scrutinise their moral conduct. Under Calvinism, as we have seen, the people are encouraged to scrutinise the moral worth of their leaders, both civil and religious – to 'mind the Kirk an' State affairs' ('The Twa Dogs'). In his political satires Burns looks behind the robes of office as his kirk poems look beneath the 'holy robes' of the clergy.

A Calvinist critique of public corruption is at the centre of poems such as 'The Author's Earnest Cry and Prayer', and 'The Twa Dogs'. The latter poem takes the form of a dialogue between two dogs on the social inequalities which exist among mankind. When Luath, a ploughman's collie, speculates on the great public virtue which the average Member of Parliament appears to possess, he is emphatically disabused by the more knowing Caesar:

> Haith lad, ye little ken about it;
> *For Britain's guid!* guid faith! I doubt it.
> Say rather, gaun as PREMIERS lead him,
> An' saying *aye* or *no's* they bid him:
> At Operas an' Plays parading,
> Mortgaging, gambling, masquerading:
> Or maybe, in a frolic daft,
> To HAGUE or CALAIS takes a waft,
> To make a *tour* an' take a whirl,
> To learn *bon ton* an' see the worl'.
>
> There, at VIENNA or VERSAILLES,
> He rives his father's auld entails;
> Or by MADRID he takes the rout,
> To thrum *guittarres* an fecht wi' *nowt*;
> Or down *Italian Vista* startles,
> Wh-re-hunting amang groves o' myrtles:
> Then bowses drumlie *German-water*,
> To make himsel look fair an' fatter,
> An' clear the consequential sorrows,

> Love-gifts of Carnival Signioras.
> *For Britain's guid!* for her destruction!
> Wi' dissipation, feud an' faction! [29]

Caesar's damning verdict on the governing elite is one of a series of moralising salvoes which Burns directs against upper-class dissipation, against those who 'riot in excess' ('Epistle to Davie'). Partly, Burns is expressing the classic Protestant opposition to wasteful consumption.[30] But these lines point also to a more specifically political concern with the corruption of the legislative branch of government by the executive branch. In 'The Twa Dogs', the M.P.'s lavish lifestyle has neutralised his ability to represent the people; his pleasures are financed not only by rents from his property but by angling for ministerial patronage, 'gaun as PREMIERS lead him, / An' saying *aye* or *no* 's they bid him'. The M.P. described by Caesar is the servant, not of the people but of the executive; he is working not 'for Britain's guid', but to please the 'PREMIER'. Burns is already alive to the condition which he later described as 'a system of corruption between the Executive Power and the Representative part of the Legislature'.[31]

In 'The Author's Earnest Cry and Prayer, to the Right Honorable and Honorable, the Scotch Representatives in the House of Commons',[32] the constitutional concerns which are adumbrated in 'The Twa Dogs' become the central focus of the poet's attention. Adopting the persona of a 'simple Bardie', Burns implores the Scots M.P.s to work for the repeal of the Wash Act of 1784, which had placed severe excise duties on Scotch whisky, and was popularly regarded as an anti-Scottish measure. The tone of the poem is mainly jocular, but that does not diminish the stinging rebuke implicit in the circumstance of a 'simple Bardie' having to exhort his upper-class representatives to perform their civic duty and fight Scotland's corner in the British parliament. That the Scottish members have so far proved reluctant to trouble the House with Scotland's grievances is put down to their involvement with the system of parliamentary patronage:

> Does ony *great man* glunch an' gloom?
> Speak out an' never fash your thumb!
> Let *posts* an' *pensions* sink or swoom
>   Wi' them wha grant them:
> If honestly they canna come,
>   Far better want them.
>
> In gath'rin votes ye were na slack,
> Now stand as tightly by your tack:
> Ne'er claw your lug, an' fidge your back,
>   An' hum an' haw,
> But raise your arm, an' tell your crack
>   Before them a'.

Sensing that the appeal to public duty will not be sufficient to move Scotland's representatives to action, Burns then plays on their instinct for self-preservation, threatening an eruption of popular violence if the M. P. s fail to secure redress for Scotland:

> Arouse my boys! exert your mettle,
> To get auld Scotland back her *kettle*!
> Or faith! I'll wad my new pleugh-pettle,
>   Ye'll see 't or lang,
> She'll teach you, wi' a reekan whittle,
>   Anither sang.
>
> *   *   *   *   *   *   *
>
> An' L—d! if ance they pit her till 't,
> Her tartan petticoat she'll kilt
> An' durk an' pistol at her belt,
>   She'll tak the streets,
> An' rin her whittle to the hilt,
>   I' th' first she meets!

Clearly, Burns's political horizon allowed him to envisage a resort to arms when the covenant between government and people was being breached.

Among Burns's lesser-known prose works, and one which throws light on the issues raised in 'The Author's Earnest Cry and Prayer', is a letter sent to the *Edinburgh Evening Courant* in 1789, written under the pseudonym of John Barleycorn. This is an open letter to Prime Minister Pitt, composed on behalf of the Scottish distillers, in protest at a new round of prohibitive whisky duties. These duties threatened to ruin, not the distillers alone, but farmers, cotters and all who worked the land, 'from the landlord of a Province down to his lowest hind'. Now, Burns was in no doubt as to why this 'most partial tax' had been imposed on the Scots. It was designed, he says, 'to favour a few opulent English Distillers, who ... were of vast Electioneering consequence'. The interests of Scotland had been 'sacrificed, without remorse, to the infernal deity of Political Expediency!'.[33] Again, the corrupting influence of Westminster politics was threatening the welfare of Scotland.

Burns's alienation from the corrupt politics of the capital is evident as much in the style as the substance of the early satires. It is crucial to the success of poems like 'A Dream' or 'The Author's Earnest Cry and Prayer' that the speaker should address his exalted audience in a low, unvarnished style. Such a style testifies to the speaker's independence from courtly pretence and hypocrisy. He demonstrates his integrity through the irreverence of his style, his use of 'a raucle tongue'. The style of the early satires is an expression of political dissent, comparable in significance to the 'opposition poetics' cultivated by various English republican poets after the Restoration of Charles II. Steven Zwicker has shown how poets like Marvell cultivated a plain-spoken, often irreverent style as part of their dissident 'country' politics, and eschewed a high courtly style as indicative of moral depravity and corruption. This was a poetics which took its stand on such concepts as 'the authenticity of satiric bluntness' and 'the equation of immorality and stylistic excess'.[34] We can perceive just such principles at work in the political satires of Burns's early period; the use of 'plain, braid Scots' promises a 'plain, braid story' ('The Brigs of Ayr'). The familiar, irreverent style which Burns employs was identified by contemporaries as characteristic of Presbyterianism and its 'levelling' doctrines. In *The Scotch Presbyterian Eloquence*, an episcopalian satire first published in 1692 but reprinted throughout the eighteenth century, Presbyterian writers and preachers are chastised not only for incendiary political doctrines but for the offensive 'rusticity' of their language and their familiar and irreverent treatment of persons of quality.[35]

Perhaps the most licentious, and certainly the most controversial, blast of irreverent 'Presbyterian eloquence' among Burns's early satires is 'A Dream', the mock laureate ode to George III.[36] Despite an equivocal reference to the Pretender, this is a poem which reminds us that anti-Hanoverianism was as much a radical Whig as a Jacobite principle by the seventeen-eighties. Burns challenges George III's absolutist pretensions in the name, not of the exiled dynasty, but of a sovereign people. As in 'The Author's Earnest Cry and Prayer', Burns adopts the deliberately lower-class persona of the 'humble poet', and again he uses a provocatively uncouth idiom, his independence from the courtly standard of speech signalling his independence from court corruption. Reversing the conventional role of the laureate, Burns's speaker 'winna flatter' but chooses instead to admonish: he advises the king to reform parliament ('rax Corruption's neck'), reduce taxation, and improve the quality of his ministers,

> ... chaps, wha, in a *barn* or *byre*,
> Wad better fill'd their station
> Than *courts* yon day.

Implicit is the principle of the covenant: the notion that the king has duties and that his subjects, however humble, may call him to account. To demonstrate that this particular monarch is in pressing need for such counsel and admonition, Burns alludes caustically to the loss of the American colonies:

> 'Tis very true, my sovereign King,
> My skill may weel be doubted;
> But *Facts* are cheels that winna ding,
> An' downa be disputed:
> Your *royal nest*, beneath *Your* wing,
> Is e'en right reft an' clouted,
> And now the third part o' the string,
> An' less, will gang about it
> Than did ae day.

This stanza brings into focus a crucial aspect of Burns's politics: his support for the American Revolution. Indeed, the American Revolution is arguably more significant than the French as an influence on Burns. The American Revolution is the political event which dominates Burns's early satires (vide 'When Guildford good', 'Address of Beelzebub', 'A Dream'); but even in the seventeen-nineties, it is America, and not France, which Burns hails as the paradigm of the progressive society:

> But come, ye sons of Liberty,
> Columbia's offspring, brave as free,
> In danger's hour still flaming in the van:
> Ye know, and dare maintain, The Royalty of Man.[37]

Now, a neglected point about Burns's pro-Americanism is that it again inscribes him in this cultural matrix of Presbyterian radicalism. As J. C. D. Clark has argued, contemporaries viewed the American Revolution largely as a war of religion, a revolt of Scots-Irish Presbyterianism and Rational Dissent against a high-handed (almost 'popish') Anglican state.[38] British sympathizers pointed to the Quebec Act of 1774, by which George III had sanctioned not only the Catholic religion but high-handed governing practices in one part of his North American dominions, and to the rumour that the crown was seeking to erect an episcopalian establishment in the colonies, as evidence of a 'transatlantic conspiracy ... against both civil and religious liberty'.[39] George III was seen to be presiding over a recrudescence of high Anglicanism and arbitrary government. In this scenario, the Americans were cast as the modern Covenanters, keeping the flame of liberty alive in defiance of a high-handed monarch and a subservient parliament. The colonists were reasserting the principles of 1688: that government is a covenant between ruler and ruled, and that the people have a right to dissolve their system of government and create it anew when that system works against the public good. 1776 was a re-run of 1688.[40]

That Burns interpreted the American Revolution in this politico-religious framework is evident from a letter he sent to the *Edinburgh Evening Courant*, on the centenary of the Glorious Revolution:

> Who would believe ... that in this our Augustan age of liberality and refinement, while we seem so justly sensible and jealous of our rights and liberties, and animated with such indignation against the very memory of those who would have subverted them, who would suppose that a certain people, under our national protection, should complain, not against a Monarch and a few favourite advisers, but against our whole legislative body, of the very same imposition and oppression, the Romish religion not excepted, and almost in the very same terms as our forefathers did against the family of Stuart! I will not, I cannot, enter into the merits of the cause; but I dare say, the American Congress, in 1776, will be allowed to have been as able and as enlightened, and, a whole empire will say, as honest, as the English

Convention in 1688; and that the fourth of July will be as sacred to their posterity as the fifth of November is to us.[41]

For all his sentimental Jacobitism, Burns clearly perceives the American Revolution as an event dynamised by political theology, carried out 'in the very same terms' as the resistance to the Stuarts. This passage, which ties in with Burns's celebration of the Covenanters, identifies Burns as one of those radicals who were 'prepared to talk of the crises of the late eighteenth century as a replay of those of the seventeenth'.[42]

With the contractarianism of Burns's political satires in mind, I should like, finally, to assess Burns's attitude towards the British constitution. On several occasions, particularly around the winter of 1792/93, Burns stated his attachment to the British constitution. A letter to Graham of Fintry sees Burns declaring: 'To the British Constitution, on Revolution principles, next after my God, I am most devoutly attached!'[43] Such remarks appear to be at odds with Burns's strongly-held reformist opinions, and critics have been wont to treat them as, in Paul Scott's phrase, 'prudent insincerities'.[44] But are they not rather honest expressions of Burns's radical position, albeit given a maximally uninflammatory spin; if anything, prudent sincerities?

For let us be clear as to what Burns is endorsing. Burns is not declaring his attachment to the constitution as it presently stands, nor to the constitution as an immemorial and organically evolving body of customary practices. Quite unequivocally, Burns's attachment is to the constitution as established on the revolution principles of 1688. The crucial question now becomes: what does Burns understand by 1688? What is the scope of Burns's revolution principles? 'Revolution principles', of course, is a notoriously slippery term, covering a range of positions within eighteenth-century British politics.[45] Essentially, however, there was a 'conservative' and a 'radical' reading of 1688. The conservative reading is perhaps best represented by Burke, for whom 1688 had in fact changed very little: the crown had merely been transferred to another branch of the same royal family; the king still ruled by divine sanction, and the duties of passive obedience and non-resistance remained in force. In contrast to Burke, eighteenth-century radicals argued that 1688 had established the constitution on a contractarian basis and confirmed the people's right to resist bad government. For Wilkesite radicals, pro-Americans, and seventeen-nineties reformers, 1688 had confirmed 'the natural rights of resistance and popular sovereignty'.[46]

We can gauge which interpretation of 1688 secured Burns's assent by turning again to the *Edinburgh Evening Courant* letters. For Burns, the Revolution was a transformative event; it altered the 'relation between King and subject'; it established the British government 'on covenanted terms', and the king now owed his throne 'to the call of a free people'.[47] For Burns, 1688 had established the British constitution on a new basis – that of consent and contract. Importantly, in his second letter to the *Courant*, Burns extends the concept of the covenant to comprehend, not merely the relation between ruler and ruled, but also the relation between component territories of a given polity; he refers to the Union of 1707 as having 'solemnly covenanted' the relationship between Scotland and England.[48]

Burns's 'Revolution principles' thus comprehend the far-reaching concept of government as a covenant between rulers and ruled. As we have seen, Burns regarded the British constitution as having departed dangerously from its original principles, perverted by a 'system of corruption'. Whether the constitution had, in Burns's eyes, become sufficiently unbalanced as to jeopardise the welfare of the British people or of one of the component nations (as it had done in the case of America and as it often seemed to be doing in the case of Scotland), remains a moot point. What a poem like 'The Author's Earnest Cry and Prayer' does make clear, is that Burns's contractarian view of the British constitution allowed him to envisage circumstances which would justify popular resistance to government and even, perhaps, Scottish rejection of the Union. Far from representing a failure of nerve, then, the conditional attachment to the British constitution which Burns expressed in the winter of 1792/93 is fully in line with the radicalism of the early satires. In early 1793, to declare one's support for the British constitution, *on revolution principles*, was a standard gesture of even the most committed British radicals, as the pages of the *Northern Star*, the newspaper of the revolutionary United Irishmen, abundantly witness.[49]

To conclude, then, it remains unfortunate that Burns's run-ins with the kirk have obscured the extent to which his own political philosophy is grounded in his religious inheritance. His politics are shaped by two complementary strands of Presbyterian thought: on the one hand, the New Light, with its subjection of all forms of authority to the tribunal of the individual reason; on the other, the traditional contractarian political theory long associated with Presbyterianism. These influences are evident in Burns's repeated avowal of 'revolution principles', in his support for the American Revolution, and, above all, in his satirical attacks on political corruption. The whole framework of assumption on which Burns's political satires rest recalls the contractarian principles of Presbyterian thought: that authority ascends from below; that government is a contract, and political power a trust; and that even the humblest members of society are competent to censure their governors. That Burns deplored certain aspects of Calvinism – its harsh soteriology, its emphasis on faith over works – should not blind us to his sincere identification with the Presbyterian political inheritance:

> THE Solemn League and Covenant
>   Now brings a smile, now brings a tear.
> But sacred Freedom, too, was theirs;
>   If thou 'rt a slave, indulge thy sneer.[50]

NOTES

1. Ian McIntyre, *Dirt and Deity: A Life of Robert Burns* (London, 1995), p. 123.
2. Samuel Johnson, *Taxation not Tyranny*, in *Political Writings*, edited by Donald J. Greene, The Yale Edition of the works of Samuel Johnson (New Haven, CT, 1977), pp. 401–454 (p. 454).
3. Hector Macpherson, *A Century of Intellectual Development* (Edinburgh, 1907), pp. 182–183; Christina Keith, *The Russet Coat: A Critical Study of Burns's Poetry and of its Background* (London, 1956), p. 186; Howard O. Brogan, 'Satirist Burns and Lord Byron', *Costerus*, 4 (1972), 29–47 (pp. 42–3); W. J. Murray, 'Poetry and Politics: Burns and Revolution', in *Studies in the Eighteenth Century*, ed. by R. F. Brissenden and J. C. Eade (Canberra, 1979), pp. 57–82 (p. 59).
4. Marilyn Butler, Review of Ian McIntyre, *Dirt and Deity: A Life of Robert Burns*, *London Review of Books*, 8 February 1996, p. 9.
5. Henry Cockburn, *Memorials of His Time* (Edinburgh, 1856), pp. 80–82.
6. Edward Dowden, *The French Revolution and English Literature* (London, 1897), p. 146.
7. A. B. Jamieson, *Burns and Religion* (Cambridge, 1931), p. 114; Alan Bold, *A Burns Companion* (London, 1991), p. 94.
8. Joseph Walter McGinty, 'Literary, Philosophical and Theological Influences on Robert Burns', 2 vols (unpublished doctoral thesis, University of Strathclyde, 1995), II, 299, 386.
9. McGinty, II, 331–334.
10. In a letter to Agnes McLehose Burns attacks her minister for 'assuming ... the dictatorial language of a Roman Pontiff', *The Letters of Robert Burns*, ed. by J. De Lancey Ferguson, 2nd edn, edited by G. Ross Roy, 2 vols (Oxford, 1985), I, 232; he invariably refers to the Old Light minister of Mauchline as 'Daddy' (that is, 'Father') Auld; and he terms the Mauchline kirk session 'the Inquisition' (*Letters*, I, 41).
11. Edwin Muir, *Scottish Journey* (Edinburgh, 1979), p. 46.
12. John Brims, 'The Covenanting Tradition and Scottish Radicalism in the 1790s', in *Covenant, Charter, and Party: Traditions of Revolt and Protest in Modern Scottish History*, edited by Terry Brotherstone (Aberdeen, 1989), pp. 50–62.
13. R. F. Foster, *Modern Ireland: 1600–1972* (Harmondsworth, 1989), p. 265.
14. George Buchanan, *The Art and Science of Government among the Scots, Being George Buchanan's 'De Jure Regni apud Scotos'*, translated by Duncan H. MacNeill (Glasgow, 1964), p. 96.
15. Alexander Shields, *A Hind Let Loose* (n. p., 1687), p. 35.
16. Shields, p. 269.
17. For an extended discussion of Presbyterian political theory, see Liam McIlvanney, 'Robert Burns and the Calvinist Radical Tradition', *History Workshop Journal*, 40 (1995), 133–149 (pp. 136–139).
18. Quentin Skinner, *The Foundations of Modern Political Thought*, 2 vols (Cambridge, 1978), II, 239.
19. Lois G. Schwoerer, 'The right to resist: Whig resistance theory, 1688 to 1694', in *Political Discourse in Early Modern Britain*, edited by Nicholas Phillipson and Quentin Skinner (Cambridge, 1993), pp. 232–252.

20. For the combination of Calvinist and civic humanist discourses in early modern Scottish thought, see David Allan, *Virtue, Learning and the Scottish Enlightenment: Ideas of Scholarship in Early Modern History* (Edinburgh, 1993), and McIlvanney, 'Radical Tradition', pp. 137–8.

21. Caroline Robbins, *The Eighteenth-Century Commonwealthman: Studies in the Transmission, Development and Circumstance of English Liberal Thought from the Restoration of Charles II until the War with the Thirteen Colonies* (Cambridge, Mass., 1959).

22. Francis Hutcheson, *Philosophical Writings*, edited by R. S. Downie (London, 1994), p. 192. See also, Ian McBride, 'The school of virtue: Francis Hutcheson, Irish Presbyterians and the Scottish Enlightenment', in *Political Thought in Ireland Since the Seventeenth Century*, edited by George Boyce, Robert Eccleshall and Vincent Geoghegan (London, 1993), pp. 73–99.

23. Richard Ashcraft and M. M. Goldsmith, 'Locke, Revolution Principles, and the Formation of Whig Ideology', *Historical Journal*, 26 (1983), 773–800 (p. 786).

24. William Donaldson, *The Jacobite Song: Political Myth and National Identity* (Aberdeen, 1988), p. 73.

25. Quoted in James Mackay, *Burns: A Biography of Robert Burns* (Edinburgh, 1992), p. 156.

26. McIlvanney, 'Radical Tradition', pp. 138–9.

27. Robbins, pp. 17, 185, 214, 303, 356.

28. See the discussion of these figures in Robbins.

29. Robert Burns, *Poems and Songs*, edited by James Kinsley (Oxford, 1969), p. 114.

30. Max Weber, *The Protestant Ethic and the Spirit of Capitalism*, translated by Talcott Parsons (London, 1930; reprinted 1992), pp. 163, 171.

31. *Letters*, II, 208. Burns seems here to be echoing the Earl of Buchan's description of 'a system of corruption, established and digested early in this reign', *Essays on the Lives and Writings of Fletcher of Saltoun and the Poet Thomson* (London, 1792), p. xxxiii.

32. *Poems and Songs*, p. 149.

33. *Letters*, I, 371–375.

34. Steven N. Zwicker, 'Lines of Authority: Politics and Literary Culture in the Restoration', in *The Politics of Discourse: The Literature and History of Seventeenth-Century England*, ed. by Kevin Sharpe and Steven N. Zwicker (Berkeley and Los Angeles, 1987), pp. 230–70.

35. Gilbert Crokatt and John Monro, *The Scotch Presbyterian Eloquence; or, The Foolishness of their Teaching Discovered from their Books, Sermons and Prayers, And some Remarks on Mr Rule's Late Vindication of the Kirk*, 4th edn (London, 1719), pp. 3–4, 29, 90.

36. *Poems and Songs*, p. 212.

37. 'Ode [For General Washington's Birthday]', *Poems and Songs*, p. 580.

38. J. C. D. Clark, *The Language of Liberty 1660–1832: Political Discourse and Social Dynamics in the Anglo-American World* (Cambridge, 1994).

39. Clark, p. 277.

40. Clark, pp. 317–335.

41. *Letters*, I, 334–5.

42. J. G. A. Pocock, 'Introduction' to Edmund Burke, *Reflections on the Revolution in France*, ed. Pocock (Indianapolis/Cambridge, 1987), pp. vii–lvi (p. xiv).

43. *Letters*, II, 169. See also the subsequent letter to Fintry (*Letters*, II, 172–175), the letter to Erskine of Mar (*Letters*, II, 207–210), and the poetic toast given at a meeting of the Dumfries Volunteers ('INSTEAD of a song, boys, I'll give you a toast').

44. The phrase was used by Scott in his paper to the bicentennial Burns Conference at the University of Strathclyde, 12 January 1996.

45. For a discussion of the term as applied in the early eighteenth century, see J. P. Kenyon, *Revolution Principles: The Politics of Party, 1689–1720* (Cambridge, 1977).

46. Kathleen Wilson, 'Inventing Revolution: 1688 and Eighteenth-Century Popular Politics', *Journal of British Studies*, 28 (1989), 349–386 (pp. 362, 386).

47. *Letters*, I, 334.

48. *Letters*, I, 373.

49. See, for example, the declaration of the Presbyterian congregation of Drumbo, *Northern Star*, 16–19 January 1793, p. 3; or the similar declaration by the Randalstown Masonic Lodge, *Northern Star*, 26–30 January 1793, p. 4.

50. *Poems and Songs*, p. 634.

Burns and the Union of 1707

NO READER of the letters or poems of Burns can doubt the depth and sincerity of his patriotism, his commitment to Scotland and his concern to preserve and celebrate in literary form a version of its past in which he believed. A passionate attachment to the ancient house of Stuart and the Jacobite cause comes across loud and clear in numerous poems and songs. A potent example is the poem the lines of which were engraved onto the glass pane of a window of a Stirling inn late in August 1787, and probably the day after he had visited Bannockburn and 'said a fervent prayer for old Caledonia over the hole in a blue whinstone, where Robert de Bruce fixed his royal Standard':[1]

> Here Stewarts once in triumph reign'd,
> And laws for Scotland's weal ordain'd;
> But now unroof'd their Palace stands,
> Their sceptre's fall'n to other hands.

The 'other hands', of course, were the Hanoverians, described as 'grovelling reptiles', 'a race outlandish':

> An idiot race, to honour lost;
> Who know them best despise them most.

Stirling was part of Burns's itinerary on a Highland tour during which he had paid homage at various sites which were resonant with echoes of a pre-Georgian Scottish past. At first sight Burns's views on the Union of 1707 seem fairly straightforward as well. The familiar words of the second and final stanzas of 'Such a parcel of rogues in a nation' seem unambiguous in their meaning and pour unforgiving scorn on the Scottish Commissioners who treated for parliamentary union and those members of the Scottish Estates who ratified the twenty-five Articles of Union:

> What force or guile could not subdue,
> Thro' many warlike ages,
> Is wrought now by a coward few,
> For hireling traitors' wages.
> The English steel we could disdain,
> Secure in valor's station;
> But English gold has been our bane,
> Such a parcel of rogues in a nation!

O would, or I had seen the day
That treason thus could sell us,
My auld grey head had lien in clay,
Wi' BRUCE and loyal WALLACE!
But pith and power, till my last hour
I'll mak this declaration;
We're bought and sold for English gold,
Such a parcel of rogues in a nation!

Read aloud or put to music, this is powerful language. It swells the heart and lifts the head. Poems and songs like these provide Scottish patriots with a menu of memorable lines. And, because they were attributed to Scotland's national poet (although there are doubts about whether the theme or the refrain were those of Burns), they have a certain legitimacy.[2]

But we should be careful: what is good patriotism is not necessarily good history. Slogans are rarely an adequate guide to the past. And certainly the Union issue was more complicated than the simple notion of a nation 'bought and sold for English gold' suggests. This will be briefly demonstrated below.

It is important to establish that in writing what he did about the Act of Union of 1707, Burns was operating within a well-established popular political and cultural tradition. The air 'A Parcel of Rogues in a Nation' dates back to the early 1700s and perhaps even to the Union itself. The nationalist sentiment, the deification of Bruce and Wallace and even the words owe not a little to the image of degenerate and unprincipled Scots parliamentarians which had emerged in much popular poetry and doggerel as well as several songs in 1706, as the details of Union were debated and settled during the final months of the Scottish parliament. A slightly later example of the genre is Allan Ramsay's 'Poem to the Memory of the Famous Archibald Pitcairne MD', written in the emotionally fraught aftermath of 1707. In the poem Ramsay's hero, Archibald Pitcairne, on his way to paradise,

Observ'd a pool of boyling gold,
On which did float, those who their country sold.
They howl'd and yell'd and often curs'd the gods,
Who had not made them vipers, asps or toads.[3]

And what has been ably documented by a number of scholars was the emergence, first underground, and later publicly, of a popular Jacobite sentiment which was not only anti-commercial, but also anti-Union as the Stuart cause became entwined with that of Scottish patriotism and liberty. It was during the first half of the eighteenth century that what have been described as the 'talismans of nascent Scottish nationalism' were invented: the ancient and legitimate Stuart dynasty, martial greatness, the corrupt Union and the hostile English, and the two national heroes, Robert Bruce and William Wallace.[4]

These, of course, were symbols to which Burns had frequent recourse. For him, they seem to have had a particular and real personal purchase, owing to his family's connections with the Episcopalian and strongly pro-Jacobite north-east, prior to the move to Ayrshire: 'My Fathers rented land of the noble Kieths of Marshal', he wrote with some pride in 1787, 'and had the honour to share their fate.'[5] By this time, although Jacobitism in any meaningful political sense was virtually moribund, it was finding a new use as a source of Romantic nationalist inspiration which Burns was able to recreate to provide Scots with a usable if mythical version of their past.[6] By the mid-nineteenth century this had become an important, if politically neutered, feature of Scottish cultural identity much loved by Queen Victoria and, as has often been remarked, by manufacturers of shawls and shortbread.

The economic and social context in which such cultural productions appeared is readily described. Although we have no accurate measure of public opinion in the eighteenth century, such evidence as is available indicates that incorporating union with England was not a prospect favoured by the vast majority of urban Scots (less is known of the rural districts), thousands of whom petitioned against it. In Stirling, Glasgow and elsewhere, copies of the draft Articles were burnt, although at Dumfries the wrath of the 'common people' may have been directed against a threatened rise in excise duties on ale rather than against the union itself.[7] Nevertheless it does appear that while some of the proposed Articles were amended in the light of Scottish complaints, and the future of the Church of Scotland was secured by a separate Act, the settlement itself was distinctly unpopular. There was certainly widespread dissatisfaction about its failure to produce the promised benefits prior to the later 1720s and 1730s, the consequence of which was that the Jacobite risings of 1708 and 1715 took place amongst a population who had little sympathy with the British government. Poverty and under-employment provided an ideal breeding ground for festering anti-English xenophobia from which opposition to the British state and its agents could periodically erupt, as happened in the Shawfield disturbances of 1725, when in Glasgow and other towns in Scotland mobs protested against the imposition of the malt tax.[8] Less spectacular but more insidious was the anti-Englishness which made life difficult and eventually impossible for English workers who came north to build and begin to operate Carron ironworks, or who were employed as overseers by Robert Owen at New Lanark. Scottish mill workers, Owen reported, would not work under English supervision. One of the facts of Scottish life in the eighteenth century was that while the Scots learned fast, and, of course, could later boast many innovators and inventors, English expertise was essential during the early stages in the modernisation of Scottish society.

Popular indignation was further aroused by rumours that English monies had eased the passage of the Articles through the Scottish parliament. The publication in 1714 of a pirated edition of the *Memoirs* of the Jacobite George

Lockhart of Carnwath provided welcome confirmation that palms had been greased. In a brilliantly written account of the events which led to the Union of 1707, few political figures of any note escaped the savagery of Lockhart's pen. At the heart of his vitriolic attack, however, was the discovery that some £20,000 sterling had secretly been made available by Queen Anne to the Earl of Glasgow for, in Lockhart's words, 'promoting his Countrie's Ruine and Misery'. Even more damaging, at least in the eyes of Lockhart and his sympathisers, 'all the persons (excepting the Duke of Atholl) on whom [the money] was bestowed, did Vote for and promote the Union'. He was driven to conclude then 'that the money was designed and bestowed for bribing of Members of Parliament'.[9]

This, of course, is an interpretation of the Act of Union of 1707 which for many Scottish people rings true. What it means in effect is that, in a squalid and shameful deal, Scotland's political elite – Burns's 'parcel of rogues' – bartered Scotland's political independence in return for pensions and places. The implications are profound and have sustained, and continue to sustain, those for whom 1707 was an act of national betrayal, a wrong which will only be made good when Scotland is freed of English shackles. But we would do well to remember that Lockhart had a vested interest in portraying the Union settlement in a dishonourable light. If the legitimacy of the Union could be challenged, so too, after 1713, could the legitimacy of the first Hanoverian monarch, George I. The Stuarts might then be restored to their rightful place on the throne of Scotland. It was a cause in which Lockhart was engaged from 1714 until 1728 when he reluctantly made his peace with King George II.

This is not the time to re-open the debate about the causes of the Union of 1707. In order to bring the focus of this essay back onto Burns, however, a brief summary of current perceptions of its causes is required. There are several schools of thought on the Union, including that which comprises nationalist-inclined writers and a small number of historians who argue that political management and bribery played a major role in bringing about the settlement of 1707.[10] This, however, is only one perspective. It is also a partial and flawed interpretation.

There is no denying the fact that a variety of what can justifiably be called bribes were offered to members of the Scottish Estates in 1706 (although there are historians who argue that most of the monies involved were used to pay salary arrears to various officers of state). Pensions were asked for and obtained, as were promotions in the army; Acts of the pre-Union Scottish parliament which secured certain private rights in the form of tax advantages were preserved; a number of special interest groups – coal owners, saltwork proprietors, grain producers and cattle traders for example – insisted upon and obtained guarantees for the future which usually took the form of tax concessions. The Equivalent – that sum of money which was to repay the massive amounts of capital (with interest) lost by Scots in the Darien adventure – was written into the Articles as well. The Alien Act passed in London in 1705 threatened to cut off Scottish trade with England (a 'formidable economic bludgeon'); fears that English naval and military might could also be brought to bear add to an equation which suggests that the best cards were in English hands.[11]

But two points need to be emphasised. First, the evidence that any of Queen Anne's bounty changed more than a handful of minds when it came to voting is simply not to be found. The Duke of Hamilton almost certainly succumbed, and as leader of the Country Party he was an important figure, but he stands out, not quite alone, but few others followed him. It is almost impossible from this distance of time to do other than speculate why Scottish parliamentarians voted as they did on the Union issue, but a detailed analysis of voting patterns in the Scottish Estates during 1706 reveals that the principal variable determining voting practice on the Articles of Union was party, not payment. What has also been found is groups of parliamentarians on both sides of the Union fence voting on the basis of principle.[12]

Secondly, what is missing both from Lockhart's Jacobite-inspired attack on the motives of his contemporaries who accepted rewards and from the assessments of modern commentators who feel or affect moral outrage about the events of 1706 is an acknowledgement that bribery in the form of sums of money, treating, preference, or other forms of patronage was part and parcel of the machinery of government in Scotland and England at this time. It oiled the party machine, it made government easier, but it was not the driving force behind issues of substance. Nor should it occasion any surprise or much disappointment that individual and sectional interests were looked after – secured – in the Articles of Union. These were important practical considerations, the resolution of which was vital, given the realistic fears there were that the Scottish economy and its component parts might succumb to superior competition from England until Scotland had time to adjust to the post-Union trading environment.

Refinements to the Articles of Union, however, simply sugared the pill of incorporating union, and made it easier to swallow. The prescription for medication came from two other main sources. First, England, or in the short-run, English Whigs. The Tories were less enthusiastic. The leader of the English Tories in 1700, Sir Edward Seymour, had remarked that union with Scotland would be like marrying a beggar, and 'whoever married a beggar could only expect a louse for her portion'. Although in cultural terms there was considerable convergence between the two nations over the course of the second half of the seventeenth century in particular, it is mistaken to assume that England was a single political entity united in its desire to participate in an alliance with the Scots. Such an arrangement would be costly and troublesome, not least because Scots would expect to share the spoils of England's expanding commercial empire. English Whigs, however, recognised that if Scottish Whig MPs were enabled to represent their constituencies at Westminster, they could bolster support for their English counterparts. Closer ties with the Scots, too, would remove English fears of a Scottish alliance of Scotland with France at a time when England's army was fighting abroad, embroiled in the War of the Spanish Succession. Linked with this, Scotland, under King William and Queen Anne, had begun to assert her parliamentary independence and had demanded the right to conduct her own foreign policy and to choose a successor to Anne. From the point of view of the British monarch the dual monarchy, the regal union of 1603, was becoming unworkable. This was not a uniquely Scottish problem or indeed one which was confined to the British Isles but was one faced by the Bourbons and the Habsburgs as well as the Stuarts. 'Composite monarchies' – where a single ruler exercised authority over a number of territories – were commonplace throughout early modern Europe. Imposed and negotiated unions were nothing new: what happened between Scotland and England was simply a British variant of a European phenomenon which had long been debated by political philosophers. For many Englishmen the satisfactory resolution of tensions inherent in the British regal union would strengthen English aspirations for an empire of the seas which would rival the power of the universal French monarchy under Louis XIV.[13]

Related to this are Scottish attitudes to union. It can be argued that the second major driving force towards union came from within Scotland itself, in the persons of men such as the earls of Stair, Mar and Marchmont, and lesser but loquacious individuals like William Seton of Pitmedden, younger. Furthermore, there are grounds for believing that their support for union with England resulted not from treachery or betrayal but from a realistic assessment of Scotland's situation and best interests. This included the recognition, however reluctant, that Scottish 'independence' in the later seventeenth and early eighteenth centuries was a chimera. Thus, reflected Sir John Clerk many years later in his *History of the Union* which he wrote in part to counter Lockhart's 'silly' account of 1714, 'As to this Sovereignty, I own I could never conceive in what it consisted ... except within her own [Scotland's] confines'. 'Independency' was 'at best a meer shadow and an empty name'.[14] These were uncomfortable realities with which Clerk, both a North Briton and a patriotic Scot, wrestled for much of the rest of his life. They are dilemmas which find no place in Burns's verse, although privately he does appear to have been aware of Scotland's unenviable but by no means unusual situation.

The Scottish elite at the turn of the eighteenth century – landowners, merchants, traders and lawyers – were highly ambitious and determined to eliminate poverty and unemployment through increased trade. They sought what in contemporary parlance was described as 'opulence'. In this they were not alone. Worldwide, nations were contending for what Andrew Fletcher called the 'golden ball' of overseas trade.[15] It was this imperative which had taken the Scots into the daring and ambitious Darien venture, the attempt to found an overseas colony in the Isthmus of Panama and open a trading route to the Pacific.[16]

In part the scheme foundered because King William sided with London merchants against those of Scotland, cruelly exposing the conflicts of interest which existed within the regal union of unequal states. What its failure also revealed, however, in what was an age of muscular mercantilism where the great European powers were striving against each other in order to expand overseas empires and establish secure trading routes, was that Scotland, a small, relatively poor and in terms of sea power a weak nation, could not easily achieve her aims alone. What was needed was the protection of a larger neighbour. This may not have been palatable but it was nevertheless almost certainly true and recognised by contemporaries such as Seton of Pitmedden.

In his published *Speech in Parliament On the First Article of the Treaty of Union*, Seton made a number of astute and clinically accurate observations, including the unworkability of the existing arrangement *and* of the disadvantages to Scotland of the *status quo*. Adopting a comparative and an historical perspective, he argued that 'Every Monarch, having one or more Kingdoms, will be obliged to prefer the Counsel and Interest of the Stronger to the Weaker'; 'No Money or Things of value can be purchased in the Course of Commerce but where there is a Force to protect it', and 'This nation being poor ... and without force to protect its commerce cannot reap great advantages by it', and so on.[17] Union, he argued, would bring commercial advantage and benefit to both countries; it would also guarantee Scotland's liberty, property and religion. Too easily overlooked are the concerns there were in presbyterian circles (excluding the anti-union Covenanters) about, in Colin Kidd's words, 'Louis XIV's ambitions to create a Counter-Reformation Catholic empire in Western Europe'.[18] Union, in this sense, provided a Protestant bulwark against the threat of Rome.

Scottish national ambition then led some influential Scots in the direction of closer British union – which, it is worth adding, was something several leading Scotsmen had sought for decades. Indeed, somewhat ironically, given Burns's association of Jacobite sentiment with Scottish liberty, it was the Stuart King James VI who had been one of the earliest and most ardent proponents of incorporating union. A 'union of traid', with Scots having unhindered access to England and English markets, was a long-standing Scottish aspiration, articulated for example by Sir Thomas Craig in 1605. It was achieved in 1707 after an overwhelming vote in favour of the 4th Article which opened England's commercial empire – the greatest in the world – to the Scots. It was the most strongly supported Article and one which attracted a substantial number of votes from the opposition. Union in Scotland had its critics, not the least voluble of whom were the Jacobites who now despaired of a Stuart return to the throne, but across the Irish Sea in Dublin the *Dublin Gazette* published in envious detail the concessions gained by the Scots in 1707 in an arrangement which enraged Jonathan Swift and other Irishmen, who judged that England had ignored their superior claims for parliamentary union.

In sum, there were a variety of motives behind the Union of 1707. Contrary to the more sceptical and even cynical assessments of the personalities who brought it about, not all of those who supported incorporation were lacking in honour or genuine consideration of Scotland's interests. Those politicians who used the situation to feather their own nests were not admirable, but their actions are understandable. With their support, through the autumn of 1706, Queensberry and his followers fashioned a settlement which would conceivably be to Scotland's advantage, and was almost certainly less to Scotland's disadvantage than might otherwise have been the case. To date no plausible, albeit hypothetical, alternative has been convincingly advanced. Too many historians, particularly those of a nationalist persuasion, have failed to acknowledge the achievements of the stubborn and far from pliant Scottish parliamentarians, who ensured the future of the Scottish church and several other major Scottish institutions such as the legal system and the rights and privileges of the royal burghs. The incorporating union of 1707 was not a *diktat*. It was an early modern example of *realpolitik*, a practical agreement between unequal partners, born and made of political, economic and strategic necessity, which was underpinned by a common bond of language and a growing convergence of cultural interests.[19]

And ultimately it served the needs of most Scots during the eighteenth century. Without spelling out in any detail the economic consequences of the Union,[20] what should be emphasised is that the opportunities which the Union presented were seized by enterprising Scots, whether in trade, manufacturing, politics or the arts. Scots benefited disproportionately at Westminster and in finding employment in the service of the British empire overseas.[21] Of course, there was dislocation and pain as Scottish rural society was transformed, perhaps more rapidly in the second half of the eighteenth century than anywhere else in western Europe as thousands of cottars and sub-tenants on the land were driven off to find work in manufacturing in planned villages and the burgeoning towns of Glasgow, Greenock and Kilmarnock.[22] But the appearance of a rampant capitalism in Scotland was not as a result of Union; the Union was the channel through which Scottish entrepreneurial vigour was released.

Later eighteenth-century Scotland was a dynamic society which was clearly reaping the rewards of incorporation within the British Hanoverian empire. In spite of periodic troughs in economic activity and the vagaries of the weather and the acute distress that bad harvests or the dislocation of trade could bring and of which Burns was acutely aware, household living standards were rising.[23] Yet it was just at this time that Burns was beginning to produce some of his most potent patriotic songs and poems, chief amongst them being 'Robert Bruce's March to Bannockburn' (written in 1793), better known as 'Scots Wha

Hae'; other similarly-inspired productions appeared in 1794, most notably the 'Ode For General Washington's Birthday'.

Is the implication of this that Burns was a political nationalist, committed to overturning the British parliamentary union? If so, he was very much out of step with most of his contemporaries. Burns was not a political philosopher or an economist, although he had read and admired Adam Smith's *Wealth of Nations* in 1789.[24] Dugald Stewart, Professor of Moral Philosophy at Edinburgh, noted Burns's Jacobitism but reflected that he 'did not appear to have thought much on such subjects, nor very consistently'.[25] Indeed, of his attachment to the Stuarts, Burns confessed that 'except when my passions are heated by some accidental cause, my Jacobitism was merely by way of, *vive la bagatelle*'. It was such an event – presumably an over-zealous assault on the House of Stuart during the annual celebration of the dispatch of James VII and his replacement by William III – that prompted his reasoned defence of the Stuart kings but also the admission that for their failures in 1715 and 1745 'I bless my God most fervently'.[26] This is not surprising. All the indications are that Jacobitism in Scotland, even before 1745 but certainly after 1746, was largely of the sentimental and symbolic variety. Jacobite songs lacked steel and the genuine oppositional linguistic force which marks many of their Irish counterparts. By the 1780s and 1790s the romantic elements of the failed Stuart risings had been incorporated into the national consciousness but, unlike 1745 when Charles Edward Stuart had been persuaded that a Stuart restoration would be more likely to succeed if this was linked to a promise to revoke the Union, the issue of parliamentary union had for the most part lost its political purchase. Burns's nationalism was retrospective and his Jacobitism rose above party consideration.[27] He conceded as much in a letter to Alexander Cunningham, when, almost apologetically (he promises to send words to the Jacobite air 'There'll never be peace till Jamie comes home') he observed that 'When Political combustion ceases to be the object of Princes & Patriots, it then ... becomes the lawful prey of Historians & Poets'.[28]

Recent work by Murray Pittock has purported to demonstrate the strength of Jacobite support in Lowland as well as Highland Scotland, not only in 1715 but also in 1745 and 1746.[29] Recruits to the Jacobite army have been sought and counted and found to have been around in considerable numbers. Yet what as yet has not been measured is the extent of support there was, even in the Episcopalian centres of the east and north-east, for the Hanoverians and for the Union. Early indications, however, suggest that this was substantial, and furthermore that it was deliberately orchestrated on carefully chosen occasions, principally the monarch's birthday. Unlike their English counterparts, which appear more commonly to have been private affairs, restricted to municipal elites, such celebrations in Scotland were open, very public and often spectacular occasions, attended by large crowds who were drawn by drums, bells and the grandeur of the spectacle, as well as in some cases by the prospect of free drink.[30] The biggest crowds on the streets of many Scottish towns were Hanoverian rather than Jacobite. The strength of popular loyalism in Britain for most of the eighteenth century, and in Scotland from mid-century (and earlier), should not be underestimated.[31]

Thus when looking at eighteenth-century Scotland and the post-1746 period in particular, commentators ignore at their peril the strength of support there was for the Hanoverians, for the Protestant succession and indeed Union. It has long been recognised that several strands were woven into the tangled fabric of Scotland's post-Union national identity. One which until recently has been largely overlooked is the 'English-oriented North Britishness' of Scottish culture, its 'intense admiration of English liberties, laws and institutions'.[32]

The conviction that the Union should be preserved and made to work was not held solely by those towards the top of the social and political order. Sections of the working classes in Scotland, growing conscious in some trades of the need to organise to protect their interests on a national rather than a local basis, were becoming increasingly British in their outlook. The first instance of this may have occurred in 1756, when members of the Aberdeen-based Woolcombers' Society began a correspondence with their English brethren.[33] By the turn of the nineteenth century, cross-border links had been forged in a number of trades.

Political reformers in Scotland adopted a distinctly British agenda. During the campaign for burgh reform in the 1780s and amongst the political Radicals of the 1790s, the nationalist dimension was notable by its virtual absence. Thus, in December 1792, delegates at the first Scottish Convention of the Friends of the People anxiously distanced themselves from the so-called 'Irish Address', sent by the United Irishmen, which was overtly nationalist in content. At the third National Convention, it was agreed to forge closer links with English radical societies; and an appeal from Belfast that the Scots should join with the nationalist United Irishmen was ignored. As John Brims, the foremost scholar of the Scottish Radical movement of the period, has remarked, 'the Scots reformers ... consistently declared that their objective was to reform the British constitution ... they had no aims to renegotiate, far less dissolve the parliamentary union with England'. There were exceptions – Thomas Muir and Lord Daer are the best-known examples, but theirs was a minority movement. In general, however, potentially the most fearsome adherents of the Scottish radicals – the common people – were more often democrats and Jacobins than nationalists and Jacobites. By and large Scottish Radicals fought on a British battleground.[34]

Burns certainly engaged with the Radical movement in Scotland and in the song 'For a' that and a' that' offered a universal hymn in praise of human dignity. He may have been playing a more active if as yet unsubstantiated underground role after 1793, although he strongly denied this in what is one of the clearest statements of his political principles, in its urgency and importance

stripped bare of Burns's usual linguistic self-indulgence.[35] Whether his decla-
ration of uncompromising loyalty to King George III, his adherence to the
Revolution of 1688 and his distaste for post-Revolutionary French aggrandis-
ement were genuine is another matter, although his enrolment by the end of
January 1795 in the local volunteer force, the Dumfries Loyal Natives, a
self-financing body of men whose purpose was to repel the threatened French
invasion, seems to indicate that it was likely to have been. It is conceivable that
fears for his employment and liberty as the authorities rounded up suspected
revolutionaries persuaded him to adopt such a prudent course of action, but if
not, historians of the period would certainly recognise in Burns's stance and
actions a plausible political animal of the time: a modestly radically-inclined
loyalist Foxite Whig whose criticisms were not of the constitution itself but of
its corrupt and unrepresentative operation.

There is little evidence in his letters to suggest that Burns was particularly
interested in the practicalities of the Union or that he had strong views about
it. He did write to William Pitt in 1789 about the favoured tax regime of the
English distillers which caused considerable outrage in Scotland. In this letter
he reflected on the 'tragic scenes' whereby the 'ancient nation of Scotland' had
been drawn into union with England but had been betrayed by the imposition
of higher than anticipated excise duties.[36] The tone of the letter is conciliatory,
however, even light-hearted, and it was on an issue – the revenue – which ever
since 1707 had periodically raised Scottish hackles. In this respect the Union
never disappeared from the political agenda, not least because contained within
it were rough edges which could lead to eruptions of national or sectoral
irritation. After the 1740s however, these were never serious enough to foment
a challenge to the Union itself. The Union was there to stay, and indeed there
were interest groups within Scotland who argued against tax and other alter-
ations on the grounds that these would be in breach of its Articles which should
be amended only with 'the consent of the people of Scotland'.[37]

In attempting to resolve the question of Burns's attitude to the British union
it is important to distinguish the protean poet, self-consciously the national
bard, from the man. The evidence suggests that Burns the citizen was uncertain
about his position. This can be seen in a well-known letter he wrote to Mrs
Francis Dunlop in April 1790. It begins with a passionate outburst of patriotic
fervour: 'Alas! have I often said to myself what are all the boasted advantages
which my country reaps from a certain Union, that can counterbalance the
annihilation of her Independence, & even her very Name!' when, all too often,
'England' was used instead of 'Britain'. But then he asks, 'tell me, my friend,
is this weak prejudice?'[38]

Hurt national sensitivities and carefully-articulated outrage which was tem-
pered with good grace and some mild self-searching are hardly indicative of a
deeply-seated nationalist agenda. It seems reasonable to suppose, given his
constant personal striving for financial security and the preferment through

which he could achieve this happier state, that Burns would have been acutely aware of the compromises that nations as well as individuals necessarily have to make in the messy business of eking out a living. Contradiction was no stranger to a man who could express discomfort in his work in 'grinding the faces of the Publican & the Sinner on the merciless wheels of the Excise' but also communicate unalloyed joy on his promotion – just reward for his diligence and carefully cultivated connections.[39]

To conclude: Burns, Scotland's national poet, collected, edited and wrote some of the best patriotic songs and poetry we have. As works of art they stand up to rigorous critical analysis. But we need to bear in mind their origin and function. It is doubtful if they were calls for action, and indeed it has been suggested that from 1787 Burns saw his role as '"Scotland's bard" increasingly in terms of song-collecting'.[40] Carol McGuirk ended an important essay on Burns with the reflection that 'We want him to be a camera, not a poet; we want his Scotland to be "real"'.[41] There is a case for saying that in his personal and poetic enthusiasm for Jacobitism and a canon of Scottish heroes (and a single heroine, Mary, Queen of Scots) Burns's portrayal of Scotland's past lacked realism. Unwittingly Burns may even have contributed to the creation of what, after Sir Walter Scott's 'achievement' of turning 'the Scottish past into an ideologically neutral pageant', has become 'the debased canon of Scottish history which still dominates the national memory'.[42] It does us no good to take seriously, at least without substantial qualification, the idea that Scotland is a nation which was 'bought and sold for English gold'. At best it is only partly true. It is also a cop-out; it is an easily-recounted myth which in some hands has formed the basis of what purports to be a respectable historical analysis. But ironically, given that it tends to be those of a nationalist persuasion who argue such a case, it actually undermines the cause they quite properly seek to uphold. It contributes to the 'we wuz robbed' or inferiorist school of Scottish history. Yet what recent scholarship in a number of disciplines has revealed is that later seventeenth-century Scotland was beginning to emerge as a vibrant society, in economic, political and cultural terms; part of the process of growing self-awareness and the aspiration to achieve national greatness was a recognition in some quarters that closer ties with England and even emulation of some English practices might be to Scotland's advantage. Together these factors provided the basis of her eighteenth-century success. It is sadly ironic and testimony to the poverty of the Scottish history curriculum in too many of our schools that Scotland's national poet should also have been adopted as its historian when what he was really engaged in was recording and transforming a particular version of its past.

The proposition that Scotland was cheated of its independence by a clutch of unscrupulous men satisfies the worst Scottish prejudices, but it fails to engage us intellectually. It conceals the complexity of the forces which drove Scotland and England into incorporating union and evades the big question: how was a small country such as Scotland to survive and flourish in a threatening world which seemed to offer the Scots few if any viable alternatives? The problem still confronts us today no less than it did Andrew Fletcher, Sir John Clerk and others in the first decades of the eighteenth century who were attempting to create a modern society modelled on the best that was to be found in England and Europe, but without losing sight of Scotland's virtues.

What is intriguing is that, through Burns, large numbers of Scots celebrate the myth of betrayal and loss when what might reasonably be acknowledged is a considerable Scottish success. But Burns both in himself and in his poetry was more than a Scot: he was a Briton too, and on more than one occasion gloried in it.[43]

NOTES

1. *The Letters of Robert Burns*, edited by G. Ross Roy (Oxford, 1985), I, 151.
2. *The Poems and Songs of Robert Burns*, edited by J. Kinsley (Oxford, 1968), III, 1403.
3. Quoted in A. M. Kinghorn and A. Law, 'Allan Ramsay and Literary Life in the First Half of the Eighteenth Century' in A. Hook (ed.), *The History of Scottish Literature, Volume 2: 1660–1800* (Aberdeen, 1987), 66.
4. M. G. H. Pittock, *The Invention of Scotland: The Stuart Myth and the Scottish Identity, 1638 to the Present* (London, 1991), 43.
5. *Letters*, I, 134.
6. For a brilliant discussion of Burns's Jacobite poetry see W. Donaldson, *The Jacobite Song: Political Myth and National Identity* (Aberdeen, 1988), 72–89.
7. Sir John Clerk, *History of the Union of Scotland and England*, edited by D. Duncan (Edinburgh, 1993), 192.
8. C. A. Whatley, 'How tame were the Scottish Lowlanders during the Eighteenth Century?' in T. M. Devine (ed.), *Conflict and Stability in Scottish Society, 1700–1850* (Edinburgh, 1990), 8–10.
9. D. Szechi, ed., *'Scotland's Ruine': Lockhart of Carnwath's Memoirs of the Union* (Aberdeen, 1995), 259.
10. The school is best represented in W. Ferguson, *Scotland's Relations with England: A Survey to 1707* (Edinburgh, 1977); P. H. Scott, *Andrew Fletcher and the Treaty of Union* (Edinburgh, 1992).
11. The most recent survey of the debate about the causes of the Union of 1707 is C. A. Whatley, *'Bought and Sold for English Gold'? Explaining the Union of 1707* (Glasgow, 1994).
12. A. Macinnes, 'Studying the Scottish Estates and the Treaty of Union', *History Microcomputer Review* (Fall, 1990).
13. See J. Robertson (ed.), *A Union for Empire: Political Thought and the British Union of 1707* (Cambridge, 1995).
14. Clerk, *History*, 199–200.
15. *Fletcher of Saltoun: Selected Writings*, edited by D. Daiches (Edinburgh, 1979), 120.
16. D. Armitage, 'The Scottish Vision of Empire: Intellectual Origins of the Darien Venture', in Robertson, *A Union for Empire*, 97–118.

17. An edited version of Seton of Pitmedden's *Speech* is printed in Whatley, *'Bought and Sold for English Gold'?*, 48–50.
18. C. Kidd, 'Religious Realignment Between the Restoration and Union', in Roberston, *A Union for Empire*, 146.
19. This topic is dealt with admirably by R. L. Emerson, 'Scottish Cultural Change 1660–1710 and the Union of 1707', in Robertson, *A Union for Empire*, 121–44.
20. See T. M. Devine, 'The Union of 1707 and Scottish Development', *Scottish Economic & Social History*, 5 (1985).
21. L Colley, *Britons: Forging the Nation, 1707–1837* (Yale, 1992), 101–32.
22. For a detailed analysis of the process of rural change in Scotland, see T. M. Devine, *The Transformation of Rural Scotland: Social Change and the Agrarian Economy, 1660–1815* (Edinburgh, 1994).
23. J. Treble, 'The Standard of Living of the Working Class', in T. M. Devine and R. Mitchison (eds), *People and Society in Scotland Volume 1: 1760–1830* (Edinburgh, 1988), 188–226; for a longer and more detailed study, see A. J. Gibson and T. C. Smout, *Prices, Food and Wages in Scotland, 1550–1780* (Cambridge, 1995).
24. *Letters*, I, 410.
25. Stewart is quoted in I. McIntyre, *Dirt & Deity: A Life of Robert Burns* (London, 1995), 123.
26. *Letters*, I, 333–4.
27. K. G. Simpson, *The Protean Scot: The Crisis of Identity in Eighteenth-Century Scottish Literature* (Aberdeen, 1988), 212; L. Leneman, 'A New Role for a Lost Cause: lowland Romanticisation of the Jacobite Highlander', in L. Leneman, ed., *Perspectives in Scottish Social History: essays in honour of Rosalind Mitchison* (Aberdeen, 1988), 113.
28. *Letters*, II, 82.
29. M. Pittock, 'Who were the Jacobites? The Pattern of Jacobite Support in 1745', in M. Lynch (ed.), *Jacobitism and the '45* (London, 1995); see too M. Pittock, *The Myth of the Jacobite Clans* (Edinburgh, 1995).
30. R. Harris and C. A. Whatley, 'Loyalty and Royalty: Celebration of the King's Birthday in George II's Britain', paper read at the 'Jacobitism, Scotland and the Enlightenment: Focus on the North' conference, Eighteenth-Century Scottish Studies Society, University of Aberdeen, 1995.
31. H. Dickinson, *The Politics of the People in Eighteenth-Century Britain* (1995), 255–86.
32. C. Kidd, 'North Britishness and the Nature of Eighteenth-Century British Patriotisms', *The Historical Journal*, 39, 2 (1996), 373, 377.
33. W. H. Fraser, *Conflict and Class: Scottish Workers, 1700–1838* (Edinburgh, 1988), 47.
34. J. Brims, '"The Scottish Jacobins", Scottish Nationalism and the British Union', in R. A. Mason (ed.), *Scotland and England 1286–1815* (Edinburgh, 1987), 247–65.
35. *Letters*, II, 172–5.
36. *Letters*, I, 373.
37. M. Fry, *The Dundas Despotism* (Edinburgh, 1992), 143.
38. *Letters*, II, 24.
39. *Letters*, II, 135, 145.
40. D. Low, *Robert Burns* (Edinburgh, 1986), 105.

41. C. McGuirk, 'Scottish Hero, Scottish Victim: Myths of Robert Burns', in Hook, *History of Scottish Literature, Volume 2*, 236.

42. C. Kidd, 'The canon of patriotic landmarks in Scottish history', *Scotlands*, 1 (1994), 7.

43. T. C. Smout, 'Problems of Nationalism, Identity and Improvement in later eighteenth-century Scotland', in T. M. Devine (ed.), *Improvement and Enlightenment* (Edinburgh, 1989), 5.

Contrary Scriptings: Implied National Narratives in Burns and Smollett

THE *Swann Report* of 1985 asserts, 'The English language is a central unifying factor in being "British", and it is the key to participation on equal terms as a full member of the society.'[1] This perspective on the British polity presumes the hegemony of a single language, in this case, English, as necessary to both the unity of Great Britain and to the condition of equal membership among its constituent nations. It also implies that a hegemonic English culture informs the British society on offer for this fullness of participation. The *Report* does not write the end of 'ane auld sang', but instead produces a text of it perhaps only slightly more anxious than the eighteenth-century original it echoes. It rescripts the same Anglocentric narrative for the future history of Britain that the Enlightenment literati, lairds, and magnates of Scotland bought into with the intent, ironically, of preserving some Scottish national identity in the wake of the Union. Linda Colley admirably relates the eighteenth-century 'invention of Britishness' in the drive to forge the nation of Britain.[2] To the English, the terms Britain, British, and British Empire, served primarily as signifiers for England, English, and English Empire, a United Kingdom that assimilated Scottish and Welsh identity. Enlightened Scots, however, while supporting the concept of Britain, advanced a different one signified in their version of forging the nation. This narrative scripted a Britain in progress towards a sublated British culture, an ultimately non-Anglocentric Britain with a transcendent culture synthesized from and constructed by the contributing nations, primarily Scotland and England. Robert Crawford has recently foregrounded the goal of their project, a culture that would exhibit what Colin Kidd, recounting the literati's subversion of Scottish constitutional history in aid of it, aptly calls 'a genuinely inclusive pan-Britannic whig identity' and, of course, one resisted by the English, most noisily by Wilkesites, who feared a non-Anglocentric Britain.[3] Somehow constituent national cultures would continue to exist, presumably, as the non-English cultures, in fact, did, in some minimal, what Tom Nairn calls 'subnational' condition.[4] The rub, however, was an immediate Anglocentrism, the need to become English enough to beat the English at their own game, an inevitable but expectedly transitional episode in their narrative of a sublated Britain. Contrary, presumably, to their conscious expectations, as R. D. Grillo writes, 'the effect of the unification of Britain on the dialects of England, and the languages of Britain, has been devastating. "English," as

Granville Pierce ... puts it, "is a killer."[5] And it kills the national culture of the Others as well. The Anglocentric narrative dominated eighteenth-century Scottish discourse about Britain and the '*British* Empire,' the latter itself a Welsh term, as Angus Calder notes, revived by an enlightened Scot, Samuel Veitch.[6] The literary endeavours of Tobias Smollett and Robert Burns, I think, are situated at the heart of the discourse on forging the nation and can speak to us most effectively from that site. Smollett's *Humphry Clinker*, published in 1771, embodies the Scottish Anglocentric narrative's most powerful literary articulation. Burns's poetic project, as I shall call it, offers one of the major contrary scriptings. It implies and inscribes a compelling, dialogic narrative of a Great Britain retaining and nurturing national cultures, each one understanding, even appropriating from, but always also contesting the Others' dialects, languages, and values within a decentred polity called Britain. This narrative scripts an invention of Scottishness and the equivalent in Other national cultures as an alternate way toward forging the nation, a narrative generally unattended if not resisted by both contemporary and later generations.

Smollett, argues Robert Crawford in his excellent *Devolving English Literature*, living in England and there 'Schooled in Scotophobia,' achieved literary triumph by writing 'the eighteenth-century's greatest novel on the theme of prejudice'.[7] *Humphry Clinker*, indeed, takes on English prejudice against the Welsh, Irish, and Scots and the reciprocal prejudice of each against the English. The novel, by exposing the various prejudices and pitting them against each other, projects the ideal of an emergent but yet unrealized, prejudice-free Great Britain. Its text figures the sublated Britain advanced by his various literary projects, including, as James Basker shows, an envisioned Academy of British Letters.[8] The pens of Matt Bramble and his nephew, Jery Melford, especially, provide in the novel satirical representations of English, Scottish, Irish, and Welsh cultural characteristics – social, ideological, political, sociological, economic, aesthetic, topological, geographical, domestic, familial, linguistic, moral, medical, climatic, religious, philosophical – which they resolve through contrasting encomia. The novel foregrounds, of course, English and Scottish matter, and certainly its detailed and loving traiting of Scottish customs, institutions, topography, and scenery rhetorically seeks to reduce English ignorance of Scotland as well as recommend Scottish virtues.[9] Tabby, Matt's genealogically-proud, penny-pinching, husband-hungry sister, Jery writes, 'was so little acquainted with the geography of the island, that she imagined we could not go to Scotland but by sea' (206). Tabby, of course, is represented as Welsh, so Jerry makes clear her ignorance extends to the English as well. He continues, 'If the truth must be told, the South Britons in general are woefully ignorant in this particular. What, between want of curiosity, and traditional sarcasms, the effect of ancient animosity, the people at the other end of the island know as little of Scotland as of Japan' (207). The novel's glowing rendition of the Highlands, this 'Scottish paradise' (244), in Matt's terms – its landscape, supposed abundance of food (despite some residual poverty), natural resources and sturdy, army-recruitable clansmen – in fact, constitutes, as Peter Womack argues,[10] an early contribution to the invention of the Highland myth – indeed an early advert for Scottish tourism in general.

If the novel's rhetoric attempts to dispel English ignorance of, and prejudice against, Scotland, it also presents the concept of a sublated Great Britain as an achievement that will benefit all the constituent nations, especially Scotland. Smollett's peppering of the text with the terms *South* and *North Briton*, predominantly Scottish usages in the eighteenth century, enforces a presupposition in favour of the concept which finds symbolic articulation in the synthesis of cultures, nations, and social ranks represented in the multiple marriages ending the novel. The philosophical debates between Matt and Lismahago especially serve to foster the idea that Scottish and English cultural differences form a dialectic capable of synthesis in a sublated British culture. In the debate rhetoric Lismahago can voice Scottish grievances with the Union – English assumptions that economic and social improvement (that ubiquitous Enlightenment term) began only with the Union, when it had already begun and would have continued without the Union (266), a thesis now generally accepted by scholars;[11] English reproaches against Scottish poverty (266); British Parliamentary corruption and Scottish under-representation, with its continual tempting of the Scottish delegation to venality (198–99, 226); English ability, because of greater financial resources, to out-bribe the Scots for military and other promotions (185, 198); English disdain for the Scots language, which Lismahago, quite contrary to the literati's theories, propounds as the original English language from which contemporary English had declined (193 ff.);[12] English as well as Scottish (at least among the majority of the literati) under-valuing of the dangers of unbridled commerce and freedom of the press (198–99, 269).[13] Lismahago's bill of particulars obviously participates in the rhetorical strategy of disabusing the English. Matt writes, 'I must own, I was at first a little nettled to find myself schooled in so many particulars. – Though I did not receive all his assertions as gospel, I was not prepared to refute them; and I cannot help now acquiescing in his remark so far as to think contempt for Scotland, which prevails too much on this side the Tweed, is founded on prejudice and error' (268).

At the same time, however, the arguments between the Scotsman and the Welshman are just as rhetorically contrived to convince the Scots that a sublated Britain, although replete with problems in its current, unfinished state – failing to pension adequately such gallant soldiers as Lismahago, fiscal cards being stacked in favour of the English (198), and, not least, failing to prevent Wilkes-like outbreaks of anti-Scotticism (198) – should remain Scotland's goal. Matt's rejoinders to Lismahago are necessarily weak to allow Scottish complaint to enjoy maximum rhetorical effectiveness. Lismahago's contentiousness, rudeness, and arrogance, even grudging acceptance of the present faulty workings of the British system as something to be expected, serve as the primary means to undermine any suggestion he ultimately opposes the idea of even the current stage of a united Britain. Indeed, referring to the military, he acknowledges the opportunity it offers to the Scots: '"I am a gentleman; and entered the service as other gentlemen do, with hopes and sentiments as honourable as ambition inspires"' (185). Despite its current limitations, the expense of living in Scotland on his pension prompts Lismahago to consider emigration to the American colonies, an opportunity that most eloquently endorses the advantages offered even by the current Britain, the empire, and the anticipated future – especially for the Scots. The downside of working for the ideal, but presumed an interim necessity, is that the Scots must defer to English culture, starting with preferring English and its Southern pronunciation to Scottish. Matt makes the case very exactly, and I must quote at some length to register the pragmatic appeal of his argument:

> The first impression which an Englishman receives in this country, will not contribute to the removal of his prejudices; because he refers every thing he sees to a comparison with the same articles in his own country; and this comparison is unfavourable to Scotland in all its exteriors, such as the face of the country in respect to cultivation, the appearance of the bulk of the people, and the language of conversation in general. – I am not so far convinced by Mr. Lismahago's arguments, but that I think the Scots would do well, for their own sakes, to adopt the English idioms and pronunciation; those of them especially, who are resolved to push their fortunes in South-Briton. – I know by experience, how easily an Englishman is influenced by the ear, and how apt he is to laugh, when he hears his own language spoken with a foreign or provincial accent. – I have known a member of the house of commons speak with great energy and precision, without being able to engage attention, because his observations were made in the Scotch dialect, which (no offence to lieutenant Lismahago) certainly gives a clownish air even to sentiments of the greatest dignity and decorum. – I have declared my opinion on this head to some of the most sensible men of this country, observing, at the same time, that if they would employ a few natives of England to teach the pronunciation of our vernacular tongue, in twenty years there would be no difference, in point of dialect, between the youth of Edinburgh and of London. (225–26)

Matt's own anglicized contempt for Scots (his recommendations to the 'most sensible men' were, in fact, already being implemented[14]) along with his estimation of current English prejudice, if not against Scotland, certainly in favour of things English, prompt the immediate agenda of anglicization Matt proposes for reaching a sublated Great Britain. This agenda is reinforced by the comic, indeed satiric, rendering of Scottish dialect in the characters of Lismahago and Micklewhimmen and of uneducated Welsh dialect in those of Tabby and Win Jenkins.

Smollett's Anglocentric model for Britain (however temporarily it would be in place) reinforces the Scottish literati's dominant discourse on the subject. His novel provides mainly a literary vehicle and, perhaps, a wider, at least, English, audience for the favoured ruling-class narrative of Scotland's national future. The literati, committed to their stadial view of societal development from savagery to commercial civilization (the former stage represented in the novel by the American Indian episodes Lismahago relates and the latter by the various encomia of commercial progress Jery and Matt primarily deliver), subverted, as Colin Kidd demonstrates, the traditional constitutional histories of Scotland's past in favour of the presumably more progressive history of England and its enlightened and unsurpassed constitution, which the Scots could now enjoy as they became anglicized and joined in constructing the future British culture. It is this commitment to Scotland's participation in a commercial British future that underwrites Smollett's and the literati's anglicizing project, beginning with the presumed first step of granting ascendency to the English language itself. The points scored by the Select Society in 1761 recur monotonously in enlightened Scottish discourse: 'As the intercourse between this part of Great Britain and the capital daily increases, both on account of business and amusement, and must still go on increasing, gentlemen educated in Scotland have long been sensible of the disadvantages under which they labour, from their imperfect knowledge of the ENGLISH TONGUE, and the impropriety with which they speak it.'[15] Although undoubtedly patriotic, as recent studies have made clear,[16] with their assault on the Scots language and their relentless narrating of a sublated British culture, the enlightened Scottish ruling class inevitably trapped themselves into a 'denial of indigenous national culture.'[17] Anglicization could not be adopted without assimilation, as Sir John Sinclair, echoing Matt Bramble, clearly understands and applauds in his *Observations on the Scottish Dialect* of 1782: 'the time, it is hoped, will soon arrive, when a difference, so obvious to the meanest capacity, shall no longer exist between the two countries by nature so intimately connected. In garb, in manners, in government, we are the same; and if the same language were spoken on both sides of the Tweed, some small diversity in our laws and ecclesiastical establishments excepted, no striking mark of distinction would remain between the sons of England and Caledonia.'[18] Sinclair thinks language change has lagged behind changes in dress and mores; he even downplays the very diversity of law and religious establishment so prominently touted in the Treaty of Union; any anticipated sublation, however, seems to have disappeared with acquiesence in an overwhelmingly Anglocentric Britain.

Smollett's *Humphry Clinker*, in effect, promotes the narrative of a sublated Britain, but its anglicizing thrust, however patriotically intended, also portends an inevitable, ultimate Anglocentricty. Jery and Matt praise what they observe as the retention of Scottish culture and both clearly want to see it preserved (e.g. 214–15). At the same time Matt fairly bubbles with admiration of the literati and important lairds, whom he identifies by name and often meets in the course of his travel in Scotland. He effusively details the trade, commerce, manufacturing, agribusiness and industry – all denominated improvement – that their anglicizing homiletics have produced. Matt's oft-quoted reference to Edinburgh as a 'hot-bed of genius' (227) must be taken with his lesser-known reference to Glasgow as 'a perfect bee-hive in point of industry' (238). The hot-bed and the bee-hive, the genius and industry combine to produce English-style manufacture and improvement. And Smollett projects the imperial features of a currently Anglocentric Britain onto Scotland itself. 'It cannot be expected,' Matt writes, 'that the gentlemen of this country [Scotland] should execute commercial schemes to render their vassals independent; nor, indeed, as such schemes suited to their way of life and inclination; but a company of merchants might, with proper management, turn to good account a fishery established in this part of Scotland – Our people have a strange itch to colonize America, when the uncultivated parts of our own island might be settled to greater advantage' (248).

Tom Nairn may overstate the case against the literati when he claims that 'The Enlightenment intelligentsia sold out its birthright – its roots in the Scottish-national-popular community – for the sake of its pottage of tedious abstractions'[19] and, one must observe, abstractions written in what they considered standard English. Their narrative of a sublated Britain of the future allowed countless numbers of Scots to leave Scotland (rarely to return, as Lismahago acerbically notes, 267–68) and to thrive in the Anglocentric reality of Britain even as they scripted themselves, in Linda Colley's words, as 'heroes of a national and imperial epic'[20] in the making. But their narrative never became historically enacted. The Scottish whig tradition underwriting it, in Colin Kidd's analysis, was both unable 'to sustain a strong sense of Scottish nationhood' or to generate a 'genuinely British identity (though this also stemmed from a lack of English commitment to a British idea which was more than either an alternative name for England or a euphemism which disguised the nature of the English core's imperial relationships with her assorted peripheries).' A 'wounded but operative Scottish national tradition' remained, Kidd observes, but the 'ideological consequences,' he continues, were 'the triumph of Anglo-Britishness; the dismal failure to construct a wholeheartedly "national" British identity different in form from loyalty to crown or to Empire; and a continuing Scottish national identity weakened by a loss of ideological coherence.'[21] By 1793, in his *An Account of the Highland Society of London*, even Sir John Sinclair was reasserting a Scottish distinctiveness he had been undermining in his 1782 *Observations on the Scottish Dialect*. 'National peculiarities are of great use,' he writes, 'in exciting a spirit of manly emulation ... It is in the interest of the United Kingdom to keep alive those national, *or what, perhaps, may now more properly be called local distinctions* of English, Scotch, Irish and Welsh.'[22] Robert Burns's poetic project, long anticipating

Sinclair, makes most sense when understood and read as an alternative to the monologic authoritative narrative of the literati. Its narrative, if adopted historically, might also have failed, but it had and retains the strength of avoiding the Anglocentric trap, for it did not presuppose a sublated Britain with a uniform culture. It scripted, instead, a narrative of vigorous multinational cultures, focusing on Scotland's, contained within an entity or polity called Britain that was united, not 'uniformed,' through the British constitution and, in Scotland's case, the Treaty of Union.

'Almost everything that Burns ever wrote,' Thomas Crawford writes perceptively, 'was political, in the broadest sense of the word.'[23] In the narrow sense, of course, Burns wrote poems addressed to specific political situations interesting him, 'The Heron Ballads' and 'The Author's Earnest Cry and Prayer', for example. Despite the anti-French Revolutionary climate of the 1790s, moreover, Burns also took explicitly political pro-Revolutionary actions – poetic and otherwise – that inevitably caused him trouble, evoking the famous letters to Robert Graham of Fintry and John Francis Erskine of Mar defending and explaining his loyalty to Britain.[24] A poem like 'Does Haughty Gaul', however, hardly suggests Burns retreated from previously enunciated pro-liberty principles, as some readers infer. It rather makes the narrowly political point that united Britons will correct British political ills: 'Be Britain still to Britain true,/Amang oursels united;/For never but by British hands/Must British wrongs be righted' (13–16).[25] Moreover, the poem ends with an equally narrow political point – British support for the monarch, and hence government, rests on constitutional recognition of the needs and liberties of the British citizen: 'Who will not sing, God save the King,/Shall hang as high's the steeple;/But while we sing, God save the King,/We'll ne'er forget The People' (929–32). His writings addressing contemporary politics in the narrow sense indicate that Burns's poetry presupposes the political status of the Union and the British constitution, a presupposition which allows poetry favouring both the French Revolution and the defence of Britain against threatened French invasion.[26] In the broadest sense of the term, however, Burns's poetry as a whole constitutes both a Britannic and Scottish political agenda – that of proposing a non-anglicizing cultural identity and future for Scotland within a British polity in which England must inevitably retain superiority of size in geography, population, and economic resources, but not uncontested moral and cultural authority. My intent in what follows is not to offer literary interpretations of specific Burns poems. It is rather to lay the groundwork for interpreting the Scottish ideology inscribed in Burns's work as a whole – the Scottish agenda enacted rhetorically in what I am calling Burns's poetic project. That project is not, I think, founded on what Iain Crichton Smith considers a 'disquieting,' unhealthy Scottish chauvinism,'[27] but on a Scottish cultural nationalism engaged in dialogue with English and Other cultures.

Burns's poetic project is dialogic in the important Bakhtinian sense that it sets up cultural multiplicity and contestation, both within and between cultures, as the historically preferable norm. Dialogue assumes otherness and difference, two or more entities engaged in the give and take of conversation, and each with valid claims to simultaneous existence. As Michael Holquist points out, 'Instead of a teleology whose course is a movement from one unitary state to another, Bakhtin's historical masterplot opens with a deluded perception of unity and goes on to a growing knowledge of ever-increasing difference and variety that cannot be overcome in any uniting synthesis.'[28] In a dialogic world the centripetal, monologic drive of systems of values, unitary language, or any cultural force struggles with centrifugal drives insisting on their own significance, and this condition Bakhtin observes occurs historically, becoming more pronounced as history unfolds. Referring specifically to language as an emblem of historical dialogism, Bakhtin writes, 'The world becomes polyglot, once and for all and irreversibly ... The naive and stubborn co-existence of "languages" within a given national language also comes to an end – that is, there is no more peaceful co-existence between territorial dialects, social and professional dialects and jargons, literary language, generic languages within literary language and so forth.'[29] Unity in this polyglot world does not occur as a synthesis of dialectic but by what Bakhtin calls polyphony or unity of the second order. This higher unity, note Gary Morson and Caryl Emerson, 'is roughly analogous not to a set, but to a set of sets, with the important exception that a set of sets may be closed, whereas a polyphonic unity is necessarily open.' In Bakhtin's own terms, polyphonic unity is 'unity not as an innate one-and-only, but as a dialogic *concordance* of unmerged twos or multiples.'[30]

Burns's poetic project assumes even an externally dialogic form in that it consciously shapes itself as a rejoinder to the literati's anglicizing project, intruding into their dominant discourse about Scotland and Britain and urging a challenging, alternative discourse. Burns dialogism rejects anglicization, clearly recognizing England as an Other in the British polity. To Mrs. Dunlop he writes in 1790: 'Alas! have I often said to myself, what are all the boasted advantages which my Country reaps from a certain Union, that can counterbalance the annihilation of her Independence, & even her very Name! ... Nothing can reconcile me to the common terms, "English Embassador, English Court, & ['] And I am out of all patience to see that [e]quivocal Character, Hastings empeached by "the Commons of England"' (Letter 397). The literati's anglicizing project only contributed to Scottish marginalization in a Britain where England's sheer size and population tended to absorb other national cultures. Containing the English sphere of influence, however, did not mean denying or ignoring English culture, but rather using and decentring it. As many scholars, most notably Thomas Crawford, have pointed out, Burns's poetry borrows heavily from English as well as non-English and classical authors, and it often adapts English poetic structures.[31] Burns's poetic project engages English and other British cultures in a carefully dialogic manner.

Bakhtin argues that 'there exists a very strong, but one-sided and thus untrust-worthy, idea that in order better to understand a foreign culture, one must enter into it, forgetting one's own, and view the world [entirely] through the eyes of this foreign culture.' This process may be imaginatively necessary, but it cannot become the goal, as it did for the literati, or one's own culture disintegrates. Creative understanding, according to Bakhtin, is the goal, and '*Creative understanding* does not renounce itself, its own place in time, its own culture; and it forgets nothing.' In a 'dialogic encounter of two cultures,' he contends, 'each retains its own unity and *open* totality, but they are mutually enriched.'[32] The size difference between the two nations meant for Burns, I think, that Scottish culture could prosper, never mind achieving superiority in quality, only as a dialogic, contesting culture. The 'Epistle to J. Lapraik, An Old Scotch Bard' may serve as an emblem of such dialogic contesting running through Burn's writings. The self-depreciating '*Rhymer*' who has 'to Learning nae Pretence' (51) valorizes a diversity of poetic voices, giving equal time to the obscure Lapraik and to both English and Scottish poets of learning who in Burns's day enjoyed an all-British, indeed international stature. In a carni-valesque tone, the Rhymer exclaims, 'Thought I, "Can this be *Pope*, or *Steele*,/or *Beattie's* wark"' (21–22) and later installs Lapraik (and himself by implication) in a Scottish pantheon headed by Ramsay and Fergusson.

The dialogic presuppositions of Burns's project even shape the criteria set for including songs in the *Scots Musical Museum* and the *Select Collection of Scottish Airs*. Burns's letters repeatedly assert the Scottish character of the collections, which I will comment on further later, but they also are remarkably sensitive to cultural enrichment. Referring to 'The Yellow-Hair'd Laddie' in a letter to Thomson, Burns urges him to 'set the air to the oldest Songs to that tune, "The yellow-hair'd laddie sat on yon burn brae"' but to 'place in letter-press after as an English set, – "In April when primroses paint the sweet plain"' (Letter 554), and he exerts effort to supply Thomson with a 'variety of English Songs,' despite 'Despairing of … [his] powers' to do so, 'turning over old Collections to pick out songs of … which the measure is something similar to what I want, & with a little alteration so as to suit the rhythm of the air exactly' (Letter 646). And as Burns is adapting from the English song culture, he is consciously aware of English attempts to adapt from the Scottish. Commenting on 'The Banks of the Tweed' in his 'Remarks on Scottish Song', Burns observes, 'This song is one of the many attempts that English composers have made to imitate the Scottish manner, and which I shall, in these strictures, beg leave to distinguish by the appellation of *Anglo-Scottish* productions. The music is pretty good, but the verses are just above contempt.'[33] Burns's letters on song are equally alert to Irish possibilities. In 1792 (?) Burns writes to Johnson, 'If we cannot finish the fifth volume any other way – what would you think of Scots words to some beautiful Irish airs?' (Letter 513), and in 1793 he approves of Thomson including five songs, 'though they certainly are Irish' (Letter 557).

Moreover his discussion of some songs in 1794 indicates Burns's awareness of
the mutual borrowings between the Irish and the Scots. 'In the neighbourhood
& intercourse of the Scots & Irish, & both musical nations too, it is highly
probably that composers of one nation would sometimes imitate, or emulate,
the manner of another' (Letter 647).

Dialogic relations with English and other British cultures meant for Burns's
project mutual cultural enrichment, but in place of the literati's anglicizing, it
sets a positive promotion of national cultural identity. On the most basic level
such promotion entailed a vigorous contesting of Scottish against English cul-
ture. And in this context of dialogic contesting, I suggest, the potential liability
of being a small nation Burns valorizes into the concept that small is beautiful
and can be better – carried most powerfully in the images of a less opulent
Scottish economy and in a moral refusal to use wealth as a sign of worth. In
his 1787 letter to Mrs. Dunlop, Burns lays out the conditions: 'An integritive
character, honest pride, and my poetic fame, will, I hope, ever ensure my
welcome with those whose esteem I value: the trappings and luxuries of upper
station, I have seen a little of them in Edinburgh – I can live without them –
I shall never blush for my own poverty, nor the poverty of my Country' (Letter
90). Burns's poetic project in no way advocates poverty or proscribes wealth.
Rather it rejects the equation of human worth with wealth and title: 'Ye see
yon birkie ca'd, a lord,/Wha struts, and stares, and a' that,/Though hundreds
worship at his word,/He's but a coof for a' that./For a' that, and a' that,/His
ribband, star and a' that,/The man of independent mind,/He looks and laughs
and a' that' ('For a' that' 17–24). It is precisely, however, such an equation that
has overtaken the literati and the Scottish ruling classes, Burns's poetry asserts,
and that has driven them to seek wealth and title at the cost of the Scottish
people and Scottish cultural identity. As the allusions to 'ribband' and 'star' in
'For a' that,' suggest, Burns's poetry associates this moral degeneracy primarily
with the English – an infiltration started with the Union and fostered by the
literati's anglicizing project.

'English gold has been our bane' (15), writes Burns in 'Such a parcel of rogues,'
and this charge resonates in many poems – 'To James Smith,' 'The Twa Dogs,'
and 'For a' that,' to name merely three examples. In his 1783 letter to James
Burness, recording the effects of recession in Ayrshire, Burns writes, 'Even in
higher life, a couple of our Ayr shire Noblemen, and the major part of our
Knights & squires, are all insolvent. A miserable job of a Douglas, Heron, &
Co.'s Bank, which no doubt you have heard of, has undone numbers of them;
and imitating English, and French, [and] other foreign luxuries & fopperies, has
ruined as many more' (Letter 14). Burns's insistence on 'honest poverty'
constitutes a direct rejoinder to the literati's anglicizing project and its promotion
of wealth through anglicized modes of improvement – unchecked commerce,
trade, and King Harry the ninth-type government patronage. Their pro-
ject promised, as Robert Crawford demonstrates, to 'promote cultural and

commercial success,' enabling 'Scots to ... "attain in society a greater portion of influence and fame." '[34] Ironically, its appeal to immediate personal aggrandizement invited a contradictory flight from, rather than a building up of, Scotland, contributing, in effect, to the inevitable triumph of an Anglocentric Britain. Robert Adam complains in 1755 of his need for 'a greater a more extensive and more honourable scene I mean an English Life,' for 'Scotland is but a narrow place.' A later letter to his sister suggests the chilling arrogance Burns's honest poverty was contesting: 'I often think what a pity it is that such a genius [as I] should be thrown away upon Scotland where scarce will ever happen an opportunity of putting one noble thought in execution. It would be a more extensive scheme to settle a family also in England and let the Adams be the sovereign architects of the United Kingdom' – which clearly means England for Robert Adam.[35] Set Adam's Anglocentred perspective against the decentred Scottish perspective Burns conveys amidst the hilarious trappings of heraldry he devises for his personal seal: 'At the bottom of the Shield, in the usual place –

"Better a wee bush than nae bield" ' (Letter 620)

Burns's poetic project claims for Scotland rather homely, unglamorous cultural values – what Thomas Crawford summarizes as fulfilment of physical desire, comradeship, regard for the uniqueness and sanctity of individual human beings, and the honest man[36] – but encodes them as an appealing alternative to glamorous imperial values so readily anglicized into greed and overweening ambition. In effect, it constructs a future Scottish national culture characterized by personal and social integrity which it expresses pithily in terms like 'honest poverty' and renders representationally again and again in figures like the cotter, the farmer who salutes his old mare, Maggie, on New Year's Day, poor Mailie, the poet addressing the unco guid, the poet exposing religious hypocrisy, the poet addressing a mouse, a louse, and a daisy, the auld and new brigs of Ayr, even the humble petition of Bruar Water for some enlightened improvement. Very few, if any, of such poems, select details from Burns's historical milieu merely for the sake of verisimilitude. Nearly all are contrived rhetorically as models for a cultural future. Even the cotter, perhaps especially the cotter, who as a social reality could hardly be found any longer on newly rack-rented estates, represents a moral type in search of a historical antitype.[37] This prefigurative rhetoric underwrites Burns's almost obsessive textualizing of Scottish geography, topography, and monuments. It prophetically grants a Scottish culture the power to invest Scotland's natural and civic environment with a moral and social significance that allows it to contest the terrains Other, especially English, cultures have celebrated. His letters detailing his Highland tours, his Commonplace Book, and his poems resonate with this idea, but it receives poetic rendering with full mythic status in 'The Vision', whose very title asserts its prefigurative design calling for the poet and Scotland to enact culturally the values the apparition reveals. The poem, although inserted most significantly almost at the centre of the Kilmarnock edition, remains generally underappreciated.[38] Again the vigour with which the mythification of Scottish terrain recurs (think merely of Joyce's Dublin as a comparable case) constitutes a first stage in an envisioned program of making Scotland's landscape an alternative locus of transcultural, at least British, value, a goal the literati's anglicizing of national cultural identity contemptuously dismissed. Henry Mackenzie is illustrative. Writing in the last instalment of the *Mirror*, he comes down on the side of English monopoly: 'With us, besides the danger of personal application, these local characters and public places are hardly various enough for the subject, or important enough for the dignity of writing. There is a sort of classic privilege in the very names of places in *London*, which does not extend to those of *Edinburgh*. The *Canongate* is almost as long as the *Strand*, but it will not bear the comparison upon paper; and *Blackfriars-wynd* can never vie with *Drury-lane* in point of sound.'[39]

Classic privilege for the literati extended most completely, of course, to the English language itself, which formed the basis of their anglicizing project. Scholars have commented extensively on the literati's dedicated and often unintentionally humorous pursuit of purity in spoken and written standard English. What has not achieved sharp focus is the deliberately Lallans contesting of English Burns's poetic project entails. Despite his several claims at inadequacy in English, Burns's letters and his standard English poems demonstrate as admirable a command of the language as Joseph Conrad's. Critical sneering at poems like 'A Dirge' really suggests not Burns's inability in standard English but our exasperation with the Shenstone-type English Burns's skill in standard English enabled him to produce. Despite his adeptness at writing the standard English prevalent in his day, Burns deliberately refused it as his regular poetic language. He pointedly subverts standard English by titling both the Kilmarnock and Edinburgh editions of his poetry, *Poems, Chiefly in the Scottish Dialect*, by providing a glossary and pronunciation guide for both editions, and by asserting somewhat flamboyantly in the dedication to the Caledonian Hunt prefacing the Edinburgh edition, 'I come to claim the common Scottish name with you, my illustrious Countrymen; and to tell the world I glory in the title.'[40] The literati were not much interested in the common Scottish name and lionized him in Edinburgh primarily because the use of Scottish dialect indicated Burns was a 'heaven-taught ploughman' and therefore living evidence that ancient, 'barbarous' Scotland was on a cultural par with other nations in their 'barbarous' stage, able to have produced epic poetry like that ascribed to Ossian. Since modern Scotland, however, was advancing into the civilized, commercial age, the ruling class demanded a modern anglicized poetry. Reviewers and the literati hounded Burns to modernize, to drop the Scots and write in good British English. The anglicizing British-is-English assumptions underlying their advice stand out most blatantly in Lord Buchan's famous Anglo-British comment: 'Burns appeared to me a real *Makar* a *Creator* a *Poet* & I wished him to assume the language as well as the character of a Briton & to throw off the masquerade garb of Allan Ramsay, whom, he so greatly surpassed.'[41]

The point of Burns's poetic project, however, was precisely that to be properly British the Scots needed to be properly Scottish, and this presupposed for Burns a vigorous Scottish language. Burns undoubtedly played up to and also with the literati during his storming of Edinburgh. Yet he remained persistently, even doggedly, committed to Scottish, perhaps hoping to convert the literati from their anglicizing project. Instead, his refusal to take their advice and write in standard English cost him their support and a promising literary career. Indeed, his turn to song following the Edinburgh edition of the poems steered his poetic project almost exclusively to advancing the future of a Scottish language and culture. Burns's collection and rewriting of old Scottish songs and his writing of new ones to old airs superficially associates his activity with the current antiquarian rage in Britain.

Burns's design, however, did not share the literati's antiquarian love of the past for its own sake, and it was geared to a nationalistic cultural agenda rather than their patriotic nostalgia.[42] The song-work promoted the idea of a useable past, one enabling a future Scottish culture, a continuation, indeed a constant reinvention of Scottish identity. In his letters Burns represents himself as merely a poetic dabbler about to leave off rhyming until 'meeting with Fergusson's Scotch Poems,' when he 'strung anew' his 'wildly-sounding, rustic lyre with emulating vigour' (Letter 125). Although more than able in English and well read in the English literary tradition, Burns deliberately chooses a Scottish identity and a poetic project that holds out the possibility of promoting an on-going Scottish culture, whatever the fate of his own poetry. As he tells Mrs. Dunlop, 'The appellation of, a Scotch Bard, is by far my highest pride; to continue to deserve it is my most exalted ambition. – Scottish scenes, and Scottish story are the themes I could wish to sing' (Letter 90). The song-work, including a great deal of the anonymity it often involved for himself and others, advances the ambitions of his poetic project by providing, in published, hard-copy form, the very material conditions necessary for a future Scottish culture, a future Scottish story. Burns clearly suggests this goal in his request that James Hoy obtain a copy of the Duke of Gordon's verses to 'Cauld kail in Aberdeen': 'I beg a copy of his Grace of Gordon's words ... which you were so kind as to repeat to me. – You may be sure we won't prefix the Author's name, except you like; tho' I look on it as no small merit to this work [the *Museum*] that the names of many of the Authors of our old Scotch Songs, names, almost forgotten, will be inserted' (Letter 145). His preface to the second volume of the *Museum* is merely one indication that a major purpose of publishing the song collections is to make visible and accessible the facticity of a continuous Scottish culture, 'to preserve the productions of those earlier sons of the Scottish muses, some of whose names deserved a better fate than has befallen them.' In contrast to the literati's interest in the past as a way of wrapping an anglicized future in a nostalgic Scottish patriotism, Burns's song-work offers the basis for a continuing renewal of Scottish identity within a palpable, lived Scottish culture that unites all social ranks. Although Burns denominates 'the common people' as 'nature's judges' of the song-work,[43] his persistent pestering of all ranks of people from rustics to dukes for song words and airs translates his song-work into the compelling signifier of a socially united Scottish culture. And just as compelling for Burns is the concept that the song-work and his own independent poems serve as scriptings for that future Scottish culture. Commenting to John McMurdo in 1793 on the ballad he presents to McMurdo's daughter, Burns writes: 'I assure you, I am not a little flattered with the idea, when I anticipate children pointing out in future Publications the tribute ... of respect I have bestowed on their Mothers. – The merit of the Scots airs, to which many of my Songs are, & more will be, set, give me this pleasing hope' (Letter 571). It is precisely this concern for a Scottish future and its thriving that prompted Burns to support the antiquarian activities of Captain Francis Grose. When Burns first met him in 1787 Grose had already published in six volumes *The Antiquities of England and Wales* (1773–87). The proposed *Antiquities of Scotland* (2 volumes, 1789, 1791) would make the completed work, by title alone, a powerful statement for a decentred Britain with foregrounded multinational, contesting cultures. Burns reinforces just this point in 'On the late Captain Grose's Peregrinations thro Scotland', a poetic rendering of the Englishman from Middlesex in a text shot through with Scottish diction.

Burns was, of course, extremely adept at the Scottish language he advocated. As he writes in 'To William Simpson, Ochiltree,' 'In days when mankind were but callans,/At *Grammar, Logic*, an' sic talents,/They took nae pains their speech to balance,/Or rule to gie,/But spak their thoughts in plain, braid lallans,/Like you or me' (115–20). And the famous letter to William Nicol (Letter 112) amply demonstrates that he could do 'braid lallans' in prose as well as verse.[44] Yet, as many scholars have well noted, the poetic 'braid lallans' in Burns's poetry ranges variously from very braid to hardly Lallans at all. A clue to the significance of Burns's practice is offered in one of his letters to Thomson. Despite his multicultural awareness in producing the *Museum* and *Scottish Airs*, Burns declared his disinterest in the *Scottish Airs*, if Thomson was 'for *English* verses,' insisting on 'at least a sprinkling of our native tongue' (Letter 507). Burns's term 'sprinkling' here, I think, points to the way Scottish functions in the poetic project. The linguistic situation of eighteenth-century Scotland was almost a paradigm of Bakhtinian heteroglossia – Lowland Scots, with a variety of spoken dialects, ecclesiastical English, official or 'paper' English, English pronounced with a Lowland 'burr', Gaelic, and the many varieties of languages particular to social rank, the professions, and the crafts.[45] All of these in Bakhtin's terms, 'are *different languages*, even from the point of view of abstract socio-dialectical markers,' but, again in Bakhtin's terms, 'these languages ... [are] not dialogically coordinated in the linguistic consciousness of the individual,' who normally passes 'from one to the other without thinking,' who does not normally 'regard one language (and the verbal world corresponding to it) through the eyes of another language (that is, the language of everyday life and the everyday world with the language of prayer or song, or vice versa.)' The 'national literary language of a people,' however, Bakhtin observes, can be constructed as an 'organized microcosm that reflects the macrocosm ... of national heteroglossia,' setting up within itself a dialogical unity of 'several "languages" that have established contact and mutual recognition with each other.'[46]

Burns's poetic project, I suggest, was laying the foundation of just such a national literary language for Scotland. The language of his poetry and the songs, with its range and mix of Scottish diction, idiom, and syntax jostling with standard English, as Raymond Bentman and others have made eminently clear, does not so much reflect eighteenth-century spoken Scottish as constitute 'a literary language, combining elements of older Scottish diction, contemporary colloquial Scottish of various dialects, spoken sophisticate Scottish, spoken English, and literary English.'[47] The literary language is indeed a 'Variorum-sprach,' to use Robert Crawford's delightful term. Nevertheless, quite contrary to Crawford's argument, it in no way forms 'a *Lingua Britannica*' which 'in its constantly shifting mix, illustrates how a truly "British" language might have operated.'[48] What it forms instead, I think, is a proto-Scottish print-language, a visual language, which, in Benedict Anderson's terms, is 'above the spoken vernaculars' and creates 'unified fields of exchange and communication' among speakers who might find it difficult or even impossible to understand one another in conversation but who become 'capable of comprehending one another via print and paper.'[49] The 'livid reality' of national identity, Kathleen Wilson argues, is one of representation, not one of direct communal solidarity.[50] As 'fellow-readers,' to use Anderson's terms again, however many they are and however dispersed through Scotland, they are, 'connected through print' and they form, 'in their secular, particular, visible invisibility, the embryo of the nationally imagined community.' And it is precisely such an imagined community for Scotland that Burns's poetic project seeks to set forth, rhetorically configuring for his readers a Scottish version of what Simon During so aptly called the 'civil Imaginary.'[51] Anderson makes clear that 'Print-language is what invents nationalism, not a particular language *per se*,' and nationalism is the self-conscious awareness of an imagined community, '*imagined* because the members of even the smallest nation will never know most of their fellow-members, meet them, or even hear of them' but only construct or imagine a communion with them through a shared print-language.[52] Burns's sprinkling of Lallans, sometimes lightly and sometimes heavily, contributes, in the printed texts of the song books and of his own poetry, to building a Scottish print-language that could visually and orally contest the hegemony of standard English and, indeed, reduce it to merely one of several contesting languages and dialects making up a dialogical print-Scottish worthy of the rich heteroglossia of the Scottish nation. The point comes across with emblematic and comic acuity in 'The Dream,' a mock birth-day-ode to the king, whose title again suggests a content not yet historically realized, in fact, as Christopher Whatley makes clear, a content of the kind authorities tolerated in print only because of the carnival occasion.[53] The poem, chattily lecturing his Britannic majesty, a Hanoverian ruling from London, to give 'auld *Britain* peace' (46), is represented as coming from a loyal Scottish poet who enjoys the democratic freedom to address the monarch in an utterly familiar style through a heteroglossic text of standard English heavily weighted with Scottish Lallans.

Burns's poetry offers a gold mine of contestation among Scottish, English, classic, European, and non-European matters – a wondrous intertextuality of quotations, traditions, dictions, idioms, dialects, languages, meanings. His texts do not produce, I suggest, the agonistic of conflicted tongues heard by Thomas Crawford nor the Smollettian dialectic of synthesized literary traditions sought by Carol McGuirk.[54] Instead they orchestrate a polyphony of voices contesting languages, literary traditions, and cultures. Burns's poetic project is dialogical through and through, internally within and between poems and externally within and between Scottish and other cultures. It scripts a future Scottish national culture that is inherently diverse – an imagined community whose lack of uniformity would appal Tobias Smollett, whose last and dying years, despite his anglicizing in aid of a sublated British culture, nevertheless were spent, perhaps fittingly, outside of Britain. Kenneth Simpson has written the most persuasively, I think, of Burns's varying roles and poses, a poetic strategy he considers a reflection of the protean eighteenth-century Scot undergoing the dissociation of sensibility caused by the Union. Burns, he thinks, 'became trapped behind the roles he so readily created.'[55] I would suggest instead that these roles register the rich profusion of personal and cultural possibilities, opportunities, and identities made available to both individuals and Scottish society by the dialogic – indeed postmodern – world Burns's poetic project scripts. This paper serves merely to suggest the many possibilities for exploration that Burns's dialogism offers. Alan Bold misleadingly argues that Burns 'looked back in ecstasy and did not take the future of Scotland into account.'[56] It can be argued that dominant Scottish discourse since the Union has instead looked back in ecstasy while enacting the literati's rather than Burns's implied national script, and this possibility may cause some subconscious guilt that the 'great tartan monster' and the annual Burns Supper orgies seek to absolve. If this is so, tartanry and toasts to the 'Immortal Memory' yet also serve to keep alive the possibility of attending to Burns's script.[57] Dialogism, Michael Holquist reminds us, 'conceives history as a constant contest between monologue and dialogue, with the possibility of reversions always present.'[58] Morson and Emerson refer to Bakhtin's concept of unfinalizability, 'an all-purpose' signifier of 'his conviction that the world is not only a messy place, but is also an open place.' In Bakhtin's own words, 'Nothing conclusive has yet taken place in the world, the ultimate word of the world and about the world has not yet been spoken, the world is open and free, everything is still in the future and will always be in the future.'[59]

NOTES

1. Quoted in R. D. Grillo, *Dominant Language* (Cambridge: Cambridge University Press, 1989), 107.
2. *Britons: Forging the Nation 1707–1837* (New Haven and London: Yale University Press, 1992), 1. See also Gerald Newman, *The Rise of English Nationalism* (New York: St. Martin's Press, 1987). Much has recently been written on the activities of the literati and ruling class. See, for example, the essays in *Sociability and Society in Eighteenth-Century Scotland*, edited by John Dwyer and Richard B. Sher (Edinburgh: Mercat Press, 1993); Angus Calder, *Revolving Culture* (London: I. B. Tauris & Co Ltd, 1994); the essays in *Wealth and Virtue*, edited by Istvan Hont and Michael Ignatieff (Cambridge: Cambridge University Press, 1983); the essays in *Scotland in the Age of Improvement*, edited by N. T. Phillipson and Rosalind Mitchison (Edinburgh: Edinburgh University Press, 1970), 107–124; Nicholas Phillipson, 'The Scottish Enlightenment', *The Enlightenment in National Context*, edited by Roy Porter and Mikulas Teich (Cambridge: Cambridge University Press, 1981), 19–40; David Spadafora, *The Idea of Progress in Eighteenth-Century Britain* (New Haven and London: Yale University Press, 1990); David Daiches, *Literature and Gentility in Scotland* (Edinburgh: The University Press, 1982).
3. See Kidd, *Subverting Scotland's Past* (Cambridge: Cambridge University Press, 1993) 272. On Wilkes see Colley, 116–117. For Robert Crawford's discussion, see *Devolving English Literature* (Oxford: Clarendon Press, 1992).
4. *The Break-Up of Britain* (London: New Left Books, 1977), 156.
5. Grillo, 23.
6. Calder, 19.
7. Robert Crawford, 57
8. See *Tobias Smollett: Critic and Journalist* (Cranbury, NJ: Associated University Presses, Inc., 1988) and also 'Scotticisms and the Problem of Cultural Integrity in Eighteenth-Century Britain', *Sociability and Society*, 81–90.
9. All quotations are from *Humphry Clinker* in the Georgia edition, edited by Thomas R. Preston (Athens and London: University of Georgia Press, 1990) and cited in the text.
10. See *Improvement and Romance: Constructing the Myth of the Highlands* (London: Macmillan, 1989), 83–85. See also Hugh Trevor-Roper, 'The Invention of Tradition: The Highland Tradition of Scotland', *The Invention of Tradition*, edited by Eric Hobsbawm and Terence Ranger (Cambridge: Cambridge University Press, 1983), 15–41.
11. See T. M. Devine, *Exploring the Scottish Past* (East Linton: Tuckwell Press, 1995) and R. H. Campbell, 'The Englightenment and the Economy', *The Origins and Nature of the Scottish Enlightenment*, edited by R. H. Campbell and Andrew S. Skinner (Edinburgh: John Donald, 1982), 8–25.
12. See Preston, Introduction xxxii, xxxvii.

13. On the literati's attitude towards commerce, see Istvan Hont, 'The "rich country-poor country' debate in Scottish political economy', *Wealth and Virtue*, 271–315; Peter Stein, 'Law and Society in Eighteenth-Century Scottish Thought', *Scotland ... Improvement*, 148–168; Phillipson, 'Scottish Enlightenment', *National Context*, 19–40; Nairn, 120–129.

14. See Basker, 'Scotticisms'.

15. Quoted in Janet Adam Smith, 'Some Eighteenth-Century Ideas of Scotland', *Scotland ... Improvement*, 111.

16. See, for example, Robert Crawford; *Sociability*; Calder.

17. John Dwyer, Introduction, *Sociability*, 5–6.

18. Quoted in Robert Crawford,, 25.

19. Nairn 120; see also N. T. Phillipson, 'Scottish Public Opinion and the Union in the Age of the Association', *Scotland ... Improvement* 127–147.

20. Colley, 178.

21. Kidd, 272.

22. Quoted in Colley, 374. See also Robert Crawford, 24.

23. *Burns* (Edinburgh and London: Oliver and Boyd, 1960), 238.

24. See Letters 530 and 558 in *The Letters of Robert Burns*, edited by G. Ross Roy, 2nd edn, 2 vols (Oxford: Clarendon Press, 1985), vol. 2. Further references to the *Letters* are to this edition and appear in the text by number only.

25. All quotations from Burns's poetry are from *The Poems and Songs of Robert Burns*, 3 vols, edited by James Kinsley (Oxford: Clarendon Press, 1968) and are cited by line number in the text.

26. For a concise and judicious account of Burns's attitude to the French Revolution, see Thomas Crawford, *Boswell, Burns and the French Revolution* (Edinburgh: The Saltire Society, 1990).

27. 'The Lyrics of Robert Burns', *The Art of Robert Burns*, edited by R. D. S. Jack and Andrew Noble (London and Totowa, NJ: Vision and Barnes and Noble, 1982), 22.

28. *Dialogism: Bakhtin and his World* (London and New York: Routledge, 1990), 76.

29. *The Dialogic Imagination*, edited by Michael Holquist, translated by Caryl Emerson and Michael Holquist (Austin: University of Texas Press, 1981), 12.

30. *Mikhail Bakhtin: Creation of a Prosaics* (Standford, Cal: Stanford University Press), 255–56.

31. See, for example, Carol McGuirk, *Robert Burns and the Sentimental Era* (Athens, GA: University of Georgia Press); R. D. S. Jack 'Burns as Sassenach Poet', *Burns Now*, edited by Kenneth Simpson (Edinburgh: Canongate Press, 1994), 150–166; Thomas Crawford, *Society and the Lyric* (Edinburgh: Scottish Academic Press, 1979); Thomas Crawford, *Burns*.

32. Quoted in *Prosaics*, 55–56.

33. 'Remarks', *Works* (London: Henry G. Bohn, 1842), 520.

34. Robert Crawford, 36. Crawford is quoting from William Barron (1774).

35. Quoted in Smith, 'Ideas of Scotland', 108

36. See Thomas Crawford, *Burns*, 337–39

37. See John Strawhorn, 'Everyday Life in Burns's Ayrshire', *Burns Now*, 13–29.

38. See, however, Thomas Crawford's excellent revaluation of 'The Vision', *Burns*, 182–193.

39. Quoted in David Craig, *Scottish Literature and the Scottish People 1680–1830* (1961; reprinted Westport, Conn.: Greenwood Press, 1976), 48–49.

40. Textual Introduction, *Poems*, 3:97.

41. Quoted in McGuirk, 72.

42. See Newman, 52–55 for these distinctions.

43. Preface, *Works*, 547–58; for excellent discussions of the songs, see Mary Ellen Brown, *Burns and Tradition* (Urbana and Chicago: University of Illinois Press, 1984); David Daiches, *Robert Burns* (New York: Rinehart & Company, 1950), 248–78; Thomas Crawford, *Burns* and *Society and the Lyric*; James Kinsley, 'The Music of the Heart', *Critical Essays on Robert Burns*, edited by Donald Low (London: Routledge & Kegan Paul, 1975), 124–36.

44. Burns's pro-Scottish dialect had some few supporters among the literati. See, for example, Robert Crawford, 24.

45. The linguistic complexity of eighteenth-century Scotland has received serious attention. See, especially, David Murison, 'The Language of Burns', *Critical Essays*, 54–69; Jack, 'Sassenach Poet'; Daiches, *Robert Burns*, 1–33; Thomas Crawford, *Burns*, passim; the essays in *Scotland and the Lowland Tongue*, edited by J. Derrick McClure (Aberdeen: Aberdeen University Press, 1983).

46. *Dialogic Imagination*, 296, 295

47. *Robert Burns* (Boston: Twayne Publishers, 1987), 15.

48. Robert Crawford, 106, 107.

49. *Imagined Communities*, revised edn (London: Verso, 1994), 44, 6. See also the essays in *Nation and Narration*, edited by Homi K. Bhabha (New York: Routledge, 1990); Terry Eagleton, 'Nationalism: Irony and Commitment', *Nationalism, Colonialism and Literature* (Minneapolis: University of Minnesota Press, 1990), 23–39.

50. 'Citizenship, Empire, and Modernity in the English Provinces, *c.* 1720–1790', *ECS*, 29 (Fall: 1995): 72.

51. See 'Literature – Nationalism's Other? The Case for Revision', *Nation and Narration*, 138–153.

52. Anderson, 44. Andrew Noble has written persuasively on Burns's nationalism. See, especially, 'Burns and Scottish Nationalism', *Burns Now*, 167–192; 'Versions of Scottish Pastoral: The Literati and the Tradition 1780–1830', *Order in Space and Society* ed. Thomas A. Markus (Edinburgh: Mainstream Publishing Company Ltd, 1985), 263–310.

53. 'Burns, Kirk and Community in Later Eighteenth-Century Scotland', *Burns Now*, 109–110.

54. See Thomas Crawford, *Burns*, 193–216 and McGuirk, xxiii.

55. 'Robert Burns: "Heaven-taught ploughman"?' *Burns Now*, 90. Among his other excellent discussions, see, especially, *The Protean Scot: The Crisis of Identity in Eighteenth-Century Scottish Literature* (Aberdeen: Aberdeen University Press, 1988), 185–246

56. 'Robert Burns: Superscot', *Art ... Burns*, 234.

57. For similar readings see Brown, 118 and Carol McGuirk, 'Burns and Nostalgia', *Burns Now*, 31–69.

58. Holquist, *Dialogism*, 75

59. *Prosaics*, 36 and quoted in *ibid.*, 37.

Burns and the *Siècle des Lumières*

*J*e *vois avec plaisir qu'il se forme en l'Europe une république immense d'esprits cultivés, la lumière se communique de tous côtés*: thus Voltaire, writing to the Russian Ambassador, Prince Gallitzin, on 14 August 1767 (Littré, 1889). This expression *lumière* means here a combination of 'intellect', 'knowledge', and 'critical understanding'. Voltaire and his fellow liberal writers in France regarded themselves as *lumières*, intellectuals combating the darkness incident to autocratic government, also superstition and enthusiasm in religion, and spreading for society the benefits of advances in the arts and sciences. They welcomed the appearance of intellectuals with similar attitudes and agendas in other countries, from as far afield as Russia and America, and together they thought of themselves as forming a republic of letters. Their talents earned them privileged positions among the upper classes, or a haven, as in the case of Voltaire at Ferney, in France but on the French–Swiss border, from which they could criticize the existing order and herald the acceptance of their progressive views by more and more ranks of society. The lateral and vertical penetration in French society of the *lumière* movement, or Enlightenment as we say in English, has been closely and helpfully studied by the historian Daniel Roche (1978, 1995), and we await the results of such research for Scotland, but it is not too far-fetched to claim that Burns's career as a writer can be perceived usefully in relation to the proponents of *lumière*.

One French-speaking intellectual, however, refused to be co-opted by the 'little troop' of the *philosophes*, as the leaders of the *lumière* movement called themselves. This was Rousseau: a republican-minded Swiss Protestant, who convinced himself that culture corrupted human nature, and expressed this thought so memorably that his readers were also half-convinced; who constantly stressed virtue, transparency, candour, and love in human relations to an audience of intensely self-aware exponents of self-interest and social artifice; who denounced luxury in an age of expanding consumerism and social inequality; and who counselled a return to Nature in idealistic, lyrical terms, when urban, also commercial or manufacturing, bases for living were more and more common. Above all, Rousseau was a highly persuasive propagandist for sensibility as the core human capacity, and communitarianism as the true but increasingly-endangered human condition. His readers were often swept away by his anti-Cartesian identification of the root of authenticity in life: *Exister, pour nous, c'est sentir; notre sensibilité est incontestablement antérieure à notre intelligence, et nous avons eu des sentiments avant des idées* (Rousseau, *Profession de foi du vicaire savoyard*, *Émile*, 1762/1963: IV; May, 1967: 98; Grimsley, 1967; Gay, 1967, 1969).

The publication of these views in 1762, above all the stress on the self-sufficiency of the *lumière internelle* in religious faith, and the appearance of the democratic manifesto of the *Contrat social* (1762/1963) in the same year, both imprudently acknowledged by Rousseau, resulted in punitive legal action. His books were condemned, and his arrest was sought in France, also his native city Geneva turned against him. Forced into hiding, Rousseau believed the *philosophes* with Voltaire at their head had betrayed him, and he engaged in a bitter quarrel with Voltaire.

All this is interesting you may now be prepared to admit, at the same time asking, what has it to do with Burns, only a child at this time? The answer comes in the unfolding of this essay.

The Scottish literati, counterparts in certain ways of the *philosophes*, were intensely interested in the literary careers of Voltaire and Rousseau. In Paris as Secretary of the British Embassy, David Hume made a determined effort to rescue Rousseau from persecution. He brought him to England in 1766, secured a pension for him from George III, and found him a refuge near the Peak district of Derbyshire. Tormented by paranoia, Rousseau came to believe Hume was conspiring with his enemies to silence him and bury him in obscurity in England. Accordingly, he ran away from England back to France, and was protected until his death in 1778 by nobles whose culture he had vilified.

Adam Smith, Hume's best friend, had championed Rousseau as a writer in the first *Edinburgh Review* of 1755–6, and as Voltaire's guest at Ferney in 1766 he probably heard a firsthand account of the quarrel with Rousseau. He certainly quizzed Hume about Rousseau in 1766–7, and advised him not to publish anything about their quarrel, advice Hume was not to take, making public his side of the story in an *Exposé Succinct de la Contestation Qui S'est Elévée entre M. Hume et M. Rousseau*, which appeared both at Paris and London in 1766. Hume hung on his wall in his Edinburgh homes in the Old and New Towns the portraits Allan Ramsay had painted of him and his paranoid protégé that occasioned the latter's tormented broodings in the autobiographical dialogues, *Rousseau juge de Jean-Jacques* (1780–2/1959). This story must have been well known to Smith and the other literati, such as Hugh Blair, fully advised by Hume about his difficulties with Rousseau.

Those acquainted with Smith or entertained by him heard of his enthusiasm for Voltaire as a corrector of the vices and follies of men. Once when a superficial thinker was called a Voltaire, he banged his fist on his table, and declared: 'Sir, there is only one Voltaire'. Smith is also reported to have declared in company that by the 'attraction of sentiment, and force of conviction, Rousseau drew the reader into the heart of reason and truth', and that 'his Social Contract will avenge him for all the persecution he suffered' (Ross, 1995: 212; Streminger, 1994: 541–63).

Rousseau's sufferings came to an end at Ermenonville, 86 kilometres from Paris, where he died on 3 July 1778. This developed into a centre of pilgrimage, with the resting place of his ashes on the Isle of Poplars becoming a shrine for throngs of devotees of Rousseau that included Franklin, Robespierre, Marie Antoinette, and Napoleon. Voltaire had returned to Paris in 1778, and it is said that his death there on 30 May was hastened by exhaustion brought on by the public acclaim to which he was exposed. The campaigns of his last years to correct major injustices of the French legal system had aroused great popular support. Abroad in the English-speaking world, in the pamphlet war attendant on the revolutionary struggle in America, both Voltaire and Rousseau were often cited for their opposition to oppression and as sources of ideas of reform (Bailyn, 1992: 27). When revolution came to France, both writers were hailed or execrated as leading contributors to the ferment that brought down the *ancien régime* (Schama, 1989). In this fashion, their light continued to shine after their deaths, the rays reaching rural Ayrshire where Burns developed a writing career that combined display of both the mocking laughter of Voltaire and the tears of Rousseau.

Between 1765 and 1768, Rousseau was quarrelling with Voltaire and Hume, and Burns from his sixth to ninth year was benefiting from formal elementary schooling in English under John Murdoch, a rather priggish eighteen-year-old educated at Ayr Grammar School and Edinburgh, hired by Burns's father and others to teach a school at Alloway. Burns made 'rapid progress' in reading selections from Arthur Masson's *Collection of Prose and Verse* (1749). These introduced him to English classics by Shakespeare, Milton, and Dryden, and the work of eighteenth-century poets such as Addison (more noted, of course, as a prose writer), Thomson, Gray, and Shenstone, much admired by their contemporaries. Later in life, Burns recollected to Dr John Moore that the Scottish tales and songs of a family servant (Betty Davidson) 'cultivated the latent seeds of Poesy,' but that the first 'Composition' he took pleasure in came from Masson's *Collection*: Addison's *Vision of Mirza*, and his hymn beginning, 'How are Thy servants blest, O lord!' Burns particularly remembered a half-stanza which was 'music to [his] boyish ears':

> For though in dreadful whirls we hung,
> High on the broken wave. (CL 249)

This acknowledgment suggests that Burns experienced a pleasurable response to art, 'Composition', in the form of language directed at evoking heightened states of feeling with religious or erotic overtones, a vein cultivated in French prose with enormous success by Rousseau. Elsewhere, in the letter to the same correspondent, Burns associates Shenstone and Gray, other poets found in Masson's *Collection*, with 'drawing the tear' (CL 246–7), that is, arousing pathetic feelings.

Many critics have deplored this turn in Burns's literary education, arguing that it led to such effusions as his 'Epistle to Mr Tytler of Woodhouselee, Author of a Defence of Mary Queen of Scots,' which combines imagery of the tear and light in a disastrous fashion:

> Tho' something like moisture conglobes in my eye,
>   Let no man misdeem me disloyal;
> A poor, friendless wand'rer may well claim a sigh,
>   Still more if that Wand'rer were royal.
>
> ...
>
> Now life's chilly evening dim shades on your eye,
>   And ushers the long dreary night;
> But you like the star that athwart gilds the sky,
>   Your course to the latest is bright. (PS i. 332–3)

To be sure, the poet very wisely did advise the recipient: 'Burn the above verses when you have read them,' but he also produced revised versions and sent one to another supporter of the Stuarts (PS iii. 1233).

However, Murdoch's choice of an English literature textbook, and possibly his teaching, introduced Burns at a highly impressionable age to examples of the artistic cult of sensibility or sentimentality, which suggested to him ways of extending the range of his poetry and rendering its emotional appeal more complex. We are much indebted to Carol McGuirk (1985) for opening up a productive line of criticism by taking a positive view of Burns's interest in the English literature of sentiment or sensibility. To be noticed here is the further French example of such literature provided by Rousseau, whose inner light was so often employed to analyze and reveal refinement of feeling, and give it a fascinating psychological and philosophical framework, as an additional development of the sentimental tradition.

As matters turned out, John Murdoch was also responsible for putting Burns in a position to read French. Burns's father took over the education of his children from 1768, after the family had moved from Alloway to the farm of Mount Oliphant. The emphasis was on religious instruction, with attention to contemporary science buttressing Christianity; factual information about history and geography; and practical skills such as arithmetic. Then in 1772, Murdoch returned to Ayr to teach the English school, and the following year Burns was sent to be a boarder with him for three weeks, to review English grammar. This was the last formal schooling Burns received, and the intention was to prepare him to teach his siblings at home.

Gilbert, Robert's brother, remembered that Murdoch himself at this time was learning French:

he communicated the instruction he received to [Robert], who, when he returned, brought home with him a French dictionary, and the *Adventures of Telemachus* in the original. In a little while, by the assistance of these books, he had acquired such a knowledge of the language, as to read any

French author in prose. This was considered a sort of prodigy, and, through the medium of Murdoch, procured him the acquaintance of several lads in Ayr, who were at that time gabbling French, and the notice of some families ... where a knowledge of French was a recommendation. (quoted in Mackay, 1992: 47)

Murdoch's choice of a textbook, Fénelon's novel, *Les Aventures de Télémaque* (1st edn 1699; English trans. John Ozell, 1715), though not a landmark work of the *siècle des lumières*, was certainly admired for its liberal and progressive ideas in the eighteenth century. A case has even been made that its author was a *sensibilité frémissante* worthy of comparison with Rousseau, though this has been scorned in relatively recent discussion (Kearns, 1979: 132). It was widely read, and in 1746 was the first French issue of the Glasgow printer and publisher Robert Urie (Brumfitt, 1967: 327). Burns is likely to have been charmed by this novel of the wanderings of the young Telemachus, searching for his father Odysseus among the islands and realms and exotic places of the Mediterranean, and receiving lessons from his companion old Mentor en route, on human nature, society, and nature at large.

Book XII presents plans for a Utopian state on the Sallentine Plain, at the heel of Italy. There will be freedom of trade – Adam Smith anticipated long before the appearance of the *Wealth of Nations* – but luxury goods are to be excluded as encouraging softness, and the keynote of the approved life style is a 'noble et frugale simplicité.' Mobility of labour is to be favoured, and the humble and rustic ways of cultivators of the soil are to be respected, as well as the productivity of artisans, also families are to be encouraged to raise a hardy, patriotic, and pious youth trained to defend the state in time of war (Amsterdam, 1719 edn). Ancient Sparta is the model for much of this exposition of ideal social policy, together with elements from Plato's *Republic*. The novel was clearly aimed at providing for Fénelon's pupil, the duc de Bourgogne, Louis XIV's heir, an alternative to the Sun King's policies of maintaining a luxurious court to dazzle his nobles, and indulging in ruinous and bloody military aggrandizement. Rousseau expanded on Fénelon's themes of the threat to virtue from luxury and empire-building, and went on in the Utopian vein to outline the social and political conditions necessary for maintenance of civil and religious liberty, not in the princely state of the *Aventures*, but in a small-scale democracy. Burns seems to have followed Rousseau in taking these directions, and they led him to welcome the democratic American revolution, also the initial stages of the French one (CL 214, 488). The recent controversy over the claim of new attribution to Burns of political poetry written *c.* 1793 (Hogg, 1996: 10) will require further work to be done on his democratic and Rousseauistic sympathies.

His early exposure to French left him with the trait of introducing French words or phrases into his poems and prose discourse, especially when addressed to superiors in rank. To Margaret Chalmers, a slightly older lady of some literary and musical culture, he admits in 1787: 'Still my motto is – I DARE! My worst enemy is *Moimême*' (CL 235). To Robert Ainslie, his crony but also a lawyer, he boasts, notoriously, of a sexual exploit with Jean Armour: 'I took the opportunity of some dry horse litter, and gave her such a thundering [e]scalade [attack using a ladder, according to Littré] that electrified the very marrow of her bones' (CL 331). Dugald Stewart considered this trait Burns's only affectation (quoted, PS iii. 1535). Burns was probably making the point that he too was man of some cosmopolitan culture.

From his prose writings we have only tantalising glimpses of which French authors of the *siècle des lumières* he had read or was about to read, though we know that there was a general public demand for French books and translations in Scotland in Burns's time (Howard, 1959). In the Journal of his tour of the Border Marches in 1787, he recorded that he beat a Mr Foreman 'in a dispute about Voltaire' (quoted, Snyder 1932: 236). What was this about – Voltaire's philosophy or his writings or his reputation or what? Burns owned a copy of *La Pucelle* (CL 687), Voltaire's scandalous version of Chapelain's epic on Joan of Arc. This poem had its place in the history of Voltaire's fight for religious toleration, for the Chevalier de La Barre had been mutilated and crucified in 1765 for refusing to doff his cap at a religious procession, singing blasphemous songs, reciting a verse of *La Pucelle*, also possessing a copy of Voltaire's *Dictionnaire philosophique*, which was burned with him. Voltaire fought unsuccessfully to vindicate La Barre, and helped his companion d'Etallonde escape to refuge in Prussia (Topazio, 1967: 22).

Burns's stuffy, but well-meaning old friend, Mrs Frances Anna Dunlop of Dunlop, once made a revealing proposal to him: 'I have been told Voltaire read all his manuscripts to an old woman and printed nothing but what she would have approved' (CL 130). Aiming at the role of censor, moral and perhaps linguistic, was she unconsciously recognizing that in his way Burns had a Voltaire side as the champion of humanity, justice, and toleration? She was successful in deflecting him in 1789 from a plan to print a satire directed at the Auld Licht 'fanatics' persecuting the New Licht Ayr minister, Dr William McGill, author of a heterodox *Practical Essay on the Death of Jesus Christ* published in 1786 (PS iii. 1306–7). They were his old enemies the 'holy beagles, the houghmagandie pack' (CL 110), who had disciplined him for his fornication with Elizabeth Paton and Jean Armour:

> Several of these reverend lads ... have come thro' my hands before; but I have some thoughts of serving them up in a different dish. – I have just sketched the following ballad ['The Kirk's Alarm'] ... If I finish it, I am thinking to throw off two or three dozen copies at a Press in Dumfries, and send them, as from Edin[burgh] to some Ayr-shire folks on both sides of the question. – If I should fail of rendering some of [Dr McGill's] foes ridiculous, I shall at least gratify my resentment in his behalf. (CL 176)

In the event, however, Burns did not have Voltaire's confidence in his social standing and the power of his pen, and he ruefully concluded that he had too many enemies already to take a public stand on behalf of another victim of rigid Calvinist persecution. It seemed to Burns on this occasion that 'humor is the peck of a sparrow, and satire the pop-gun of a school-boy' (CL 95).

Nevertheless, 'The Kirk's Alarm' goes off with a bang and can join company fittingly with Voltaire's witty attacks on the bigots and numbskulls who seemed to him dangerous enemies of reason and natural feelings:

> Orthodox! Orthodox! –
> Wha believe in John Knox –
> Let me sound an alarm to your conscience;
> There's a heretic blast
> Has been blawn i' the wast.
> That what is no' sense must be nonsense –
> Orthodox! that what is no' sense must be nonsense.
>
> Dr Mac! Dr Mac!
> You should stretch on a rack,
> To strike evil doers wi' terror;
> To join faith and sense
> Upon any pretence
> Is heretic, damnable error –
> Dr Mac! 'tis heretic, damnable error.
> . . .
>
> Calvin's sons! Calvin's sons!
> Seize your spiritual guns,
> Ammunition you never can need;
> Your hearts are the stuff,
> Will be powther enough,
> And your skulls are storehouses o' lead –
> Calvin's sons! your skulls are storehouses o' lead.
>
> (PW ii. 209–13)

This vigorous poem circulated only in manuscript and as an unauthorized broadside (*The Ayrshire Garland*, ?1789), and was first published posthumously in Glasgow in the chap-books series edited by Thomas Stewart (1799). It was presented in book form by Stewart in 1801, along with the more celebrated and more successful religious satires, 'The Holy Tulzie' and 'Holy Willie's Prayer', which were written in the period 1784–5, when Burns was farming at Mossgiel. Both were kept out of the Kilmarnock edition of the poems in 1786 to avoid scandal over such satires on religious illiberality.

Indeed, the spirit of Voltaire is not strongly present in Burns's first book, and that of Rousseau predominates. This is not surprising since in addition to some wariness over publishing his satires, Burns was still exalted with the inspiration of sentimental literature. As he wrote on 15 January 1783 to his former schoolteacher, John Murdoch, who had introduced him to it:

> My favourite authors are of the sentimental kind, such as Shenstone, particularly his Elegies, Thomson, [Mackenzie's] Man of feeling, a book I prize next to the Bible, [his] Man of the World, Sterne, especially his Sentimental journey, McPherson's Ossian, &c, these are the glorious models after which I endeavour to form my conduct ... (CL 55)

He does not mention Rousseau by name in this list nor among the writers he describes in print in 1786 as his models, though now we find the Scottish literary tradition represented by Ramsay and Fergusson, in the Preface to the Kilmarnock *Poems, Chiefly in the Scottish Dialect*. But surely we find Rousseau's spirit in the opening poem of 'The Twa Dogs', as if the beast fable tradition developed by La Fontaine (which Burns said was 'in the way of my trade': CL 433) had been taken up by a witty, Scottish Jean-Jacques who depicts a dialogue between a Newfoundland dog, symbolically given the name Caesar, evoking the rich and powerful master who owns him, and a working collie, Luath, linked by his name to Ossianic poetry, owned by a ploughman identified as a 'rhyming, ranting, raving billie.' The dogs digress about their masters, and we are treated to the Rousseauistic paradox that the rich and powerful are unhappy and unhealthy despite all their advantages, whereas the poor for all the oppression they suffer are wonderfully contented in their own family and social life (*Émile*, 1762/1963: 316–7). Simple, virtuous life at home is shown off to advantage, by contrasting the desperate search for diversion by one of the master race going on the Grand Tour:

> At Operas an' Plays parading,
> Mortgaging, gambling, masquerading:
> Or maybe in a frolic daft,
> To HAGUE or CALAIS takes a waft,
> To make a *tour* an' tak a whirl,
> To learn *bon ton* an' see the worl'.
>
> There, at VIENNA or VERSAILLES,
> He rives his father's auld entails;
> Or by MADRID he takes the rout,
> To thrum guittars an' fecht wi' nowt;
> Or down *Italian Vista* startles,
> Whore-hunting amang groves o' myrtles:
> Then bowses drumlie *German-water*,
> To mak himsel look fair and fatter,
> An' purge the bitter ga's an' cankers,
> O' curst *Venetian* bores and chancres.
>
> *For Britain's guid*! for her destruction!

> Wi' dissipation, feud an' faction!
>
>   (K 1786/1911: 17–18)

In the first 'Epistle to John Lapraik,' we find Burns's profession of poetic faith, which can be connected with the Savoyard priest's profession of faith in natural religion, beginning with the recognition that he is 'no great philosopher,' and emphasizing that his appeal is to the heart (*Émile*, 1762/1963: 228). Burns wrote:

> I am nae *Poet*, in a sense,
> But just a *Rhymer* like by chance,
> An' hae to Learning nae pretence,
>   Yet, what the matter?
> Whene'er my Muse does on me glance,
>   I jingle at her.
>
> Your Critic-folk may cock their nose,
> And say, 'How can you e'er propose,
> 'You wha ken hardly *verse* frae *prose*,
>   'To mak a *sang*?'
> But by your leaves, my learned foes,
>   Ye're maybe wrang,
>
> What's a' your jargon o' your Schools,
> Your Latin names for horns and stools;
> If honest Nature made you *fools*,
>   What sairs your Grammars?
> Ye'd better taen up *spades* and *shools*,
>   Or *knappin-hammers*.
>
> A set o' dull, conceited Hashes,
> Confuse their brains in *Colledge-classes*!
> They *gang in* Stirks, and *come out* Asses,
>   Plain truth to speak;
> An' syne they think to climb Parnassus
>   By dint o' Greek!
>
> Gie me ae spark o' Nature's fire,
> That's a' the learning I desire;
> Then tho' I drudge thro' dub an' mire
>   At pleugh or cart,
> My Muse, tho' hamely in attire,
>   May touch the heart.
>
>   (K 1786/1911: 198–9)

The Kilmarnock volume ends with 'A Bard's Epitaph' which is inspired by the 'Epitaph' for the young country poet placed by Thomas Gray at the conclusion of the 'Elegy Written in a Country Churchyard'. Burns is attracted by this device of self-projection. The nineteenth-century editor William Scott Douglas may well be right, however, that Burns discarded as his conclusion another poem, 'Elegy on the Death of Robert Ruisseaux'. The name in the title is the French word for streams, and thus a pun on 'Burns'. It also reveals that Burns thought of himself as a kind of Rousseau. In fact in the first Commonplace Book there are some 'Egotisms from my own sensations', among which is listed the following:

> I sometimes think the character of a certain great man I have read of somewhere is very much *apropos* to myself – that he was a compound of great talents and great folly. N.B. To try if I can discover the causes of this wretched infirmity, and, if possible, to mend it.

Rousseau certainly combined 'great talents and great folly,' and Burns was conscious both of his own genius and the follies he was led into by his pride and passions. His discarded 'Elegy', to be sure, does not make so much of this as of his Voltaireian proclivity for lashing back in satire at what oppressed him:

> Now Robin lies in his last lair,
> He'll gabble rhyme, nor sing nae mair,
> Cauld poverty, wi' hungry stare,
>   Nae mair shall fear him;
> Nor anxious fear, nor cankert care,
>   E'er mair come near him.
>
> To tell the truth, they seldom fash't him,
> Except the moment that they crush't him;
> For sune as chance or fate had hush't 'em –
>   Tho' e'er sae short –
> Then wi' a rhyme or song he lash't 'em,
>   And thought it sport.
>
> Tho' he was bred to kintra wark,
> And counted was baith wight and stark,
> Yet that was never Robin's mark
>   To mak' a man;
> But tell him he was learn'd and clark –
>   Ye roos'd [praised] him then!
>   (PW ii. 261–2)

His way prepared by the growing success of the Kilmarnock volume, Burns went to Edinburgh in late November 1786 and visited there apart from his tours of the Highlands and the Borders until February 1788. He received the encouragement, patronage, and condescension of the established men of letters, including Henry Mackenzie, author of the sentimental (and Rousseauistic) novels he had revered, *The Man of Feeling* (1771) and *The Man of the World*

(1773). Despite the worldly wisdom of his professional legal life, which belied the sentimentalism of the heroes of his fiction, Mackenzie swallowed the bait of the Preface to the Kilmarnock *Poems*, and hailed Burns as 'this Heaven-taught ploughman' (*Lounger*, 9 December 1786). Perhaps Burns's greatest triumph came at the meeting of the Grand Masonic Lodge of Scotland on 1 February 1787, when the toast was given: 'Caledonia, and Caledonia's Bard, brother Burns' (Daiches, 1952: 239).

Burns used the word 'lights' (connected with the usage *siècle des lumières*) to refer to the Edinburgh men of letters he encountered. Generously, he saluted them in a letter to Hugh Blair, the leading critic, as 'permanent lights of genius and literature,' and contrasted the 'meteor-like novelty' of his own appearance in the great world. Prophetically, he also wrote that 'abuse or almost even neglect will not surprise me in my quarters' (CL 288). Like Rousseau, he proved to be prickly and sensitive, and was judged to be lacking in deference and accommodation by some of these same Edinburgh men of letters, the recognized 'lights' of his time. However, from that group, perhaps only Adam Smith (whom Burns admired but probably did not meet: CL 136, 428), through his contributions to moral philosophy and political economy, has continued to throw some light on the baffling problems of understanding human nature and society. And Burns, after the period of abuse and neglect, seems to us to have caught up what he required of the essence of the great French spirits of his time such as Voltaire and Rousseau, and to gleam through his poetry in our time with ever-brightening light.

REFERENCES

a) Writings of Robert Burns

CL = *The Complete Letters of Robert Burns*, edited and introduced by James A. Mackay (Ayr: Alloway Publishing Ltd, 1987).

K = *Burns: Poems Published in 1786*, Oxford Miscellany Series (London: Henry Frowde, 1911) – facsimile reprint of *Poems, Chiefly in the Scottish Dialect* (Kilmarnock: John Wilson, 1786).

PS = *The Poems and Songs of Robert Burns*, edited by James Kinsley, 3 vols (Oxford: Clarendon Press, 1968).

PW = *Poetical Works of Robert Burns*, edited by William Scott Douglas. 2 vols in 1 (Glasgow: Scottish Daily Express, 1935).

b) Other Sources

Bailyn, Bernard (1992), *The Ideological Origin of the American Revolution*, enlarged edn, Cambridge, Mass.: Belknap/Harvard.

Brumfitt, J. H. (1967). 'Scotland and the French Enlightenment', in *The Age of the Enlightenment: Studies Presented to Theodore Besterman*, edited by W. H. Barber *et al.* Edinburgh: Oliver & Boyd, 1967.

Daiches, David (1952), *Robert Burns*, London: G. Bell and Sons Ltd.

Hogg, Patrick (1996), 'Robert Burns under the Microscope', *The Herald*, Thursday 25 January, p. 10.

Howard, Alison K. (1959), 'Montesquieu, Voltaire and Rousseau in Eighteenth-Century Scotland: a checklist of editions and translations of their works published in Scotland before 1801', *The Bibliothek*, 2: 40–63.

Fénelon, François de Salignac de la Mothe (1719), *Les Aventures de Télémaque*. Amsterdam: Les Wetsteins.

Gay, Peter (1967), *The Enlightenment: An Interpretation*; vol. 1 *The Rise of Modern Paganism*. (1969); vol. 2 *The Science of Freedom*. London: Weidenfeld and Nicholson.

Grimsley, Ronald (1967), 'Jean-Jacques Rousseau', *The Encyclopedia of Philosophy*, editor in chief Paul Edwards. New York: Macmillan & The Free Press. London: Collier-Macmillan.

Hume, David (1766), *A Concise and Genuine Account of the Dispute between Mr Hume and Mr Rousseau*, London: T. Becket and P. A. DeHondt.

Kearns, Edward John (1979), *Ideas in Seventeenth-Century France*. Manchester Uiversity Press.

Littré, Émile (1889), *Dictionnaire de la langue française*. 4 t. Paris: Hachette [Supplement, 1923].

McGuirk, Carol (1985), *Robert Burns and the Sentimental Era*. Athens: University of Georgia Press.

Mackay, James A. (1992), Burns. A Biography of Robert Burns. London: Headline.

Mackenzie, Henry (1786), [Review of the Kilmarnock Burns], *The Lounger*, 9 December.

Masson, Arthur (1749), *A Collection of English Prose and Verse, from Several Authors of Established Credit*, 2nd edn, Aberdeen.

May, Georges (1967), *Rousseau par lui-même*, Paris: Seuil.

Roche, Daniel (1978), *Le Siècle des lumières en province: académies et académiciens provinçaux 1680–1789*. Paris: Mouton. (1995). *La France des lumières*. Paris: Fayard.

Ross, Ian Simpson (1995), *The Life of Adam Smith*, Oxford: Clarendon Press.

Rousseau, Jean-Jacques (1762/1963), *Émile* [including 'The Creed of a Savoyard Priest'], translated by Barbara Foxley. London: Dent/Everyman. (1762/1963). *The Social Contract and Discourses*, translated by G. D. H. Cole. London: Dent/Everyman. (1780–2/1959). *Oeuvres complètes, i. Les Confession; Rousseau juge de Jean-Jacques*, edited by Bernard Gagnebin et al. Paris: Gallimard.

Schama, Simon (1989), *Citizen: A Chronicle of the French Revolution*. Toronto: Vintage.

Snyder, F. B. (1932), *The Life of Robert Burns*, New York: Macmillan.

Streminger, Gerhard (1994), *David Hume: Sein Leben und sein Werk*, Paderborn: Ferdinand Schönigh.

Topazio, Virgil W. (1967), *Voltaire: A Critical Study of His Major Works*, New York: Random House.

Voltaire (1784–9), *Oeuvres complètes*, edited by Beaumarchais. 70 t. Paris: Kehl.

Burns and Superstition

Life is a fairy scene; almost all that deserves the name of enjoyment, or pleasure, is only charming delusion; and in comes ripening Age, in all the gravity of hoary wisdom, and wickedly chases away the dear, bewitching Phantoms.[1]

'I AM naturally of a superstitious cast',[2] wrote Robert Burns in 1787. What follows is a brief investigation of the accuracy of his assertion. The topic might appear somewhat superfluous given the existence of such poems as 'Halloween', 'Address to the Deil' and 'Tam o'Shanter' from the hand which also preserved that wonderful ballad 'Tam Lin', but it is one which has, so far, received comparatively little critical attention. A preliminary consideration of Burns's attitude towards superstition will highlight his part in a profound historical process which was central to the experience of eighteenth-century Scotland, the consequences of which continue to resonate in the country of the bard's birth on the two hundredth anniversary of his death.

Superstition was, if not an obsession, at the very least a central concern of writers of the Scottish Enlightenment. David Hume, penning 'Of Miracles' (1748), stated that his purpose was 'to silence ... bigotry and suspicion and free us from their impertinent superstitions'.[3] He flattered himself that he had discovered an argument 'which if just, will ... be an everlasting check to all kinds of superstitious delusion, and consequently will be useful as long as the world endures'. Elsewhere he contemptuously remarked,

> Does a man of sense run after every silly tale of witches or hobgoblins or fairies, and canvass, particularly the evidence? I never knew anyone that examined and deliberated about nonsense who did not believe it before the end of his inquiries'.[4]

Adam Ferguson (1767) believed that ignorance was the mother of superstition. He described the superstitions of the indigenous population of North America as 'grovelling and mean' while cautioning that this was a subject 'on which few nations are entitled to censure their neighbours'.

> When we have considered the superstitions of one people, we find little variety in those of another. They are but a repetition of similar weaknesses and absurdities, derived from a common source, a perplexed apprehension of invisible agents, that are supposed to guide all precarious events to which

human foresight cannot extend ... Superstition being founded in doubts and anxiety is fostered by ignorance and mystery.[5]

Dr Johnson (1773) was of the opinion that the superstitions of the Hebrideans had virtually been 'extirpated' by the efforts of the ministers.[6] There is no doubt that Johnson and Boswell are too often quoted; indeed the bottle labelled *J & B* should be corked and allowed to languish in a dark cellar for a generation. But the impact and influence of *Journey's* publication cannot be exaggerated. Johnson's belief in the triumph of literacy over orality made him implacably opposed to what he considered to be the wilder claims of James Macpherson on his Ossianic sources. 'One generation of ignorance effaces the whole series of unwritten history', he opined. 'Written learning is a fixed luminary, which after the cloud that had hidden it has past away, is again brought in its proper station. Tradition is but a meteor, which, if once it falls, cannot be rekindled'.[7] He thus, significantly, linked orality and superstition.

Like Johnson, Boswell (whose *Tour* was published in 1785 ten years after the appearance of the *Journey*) was greatly interested in such topics as second sight, a belief in which, he noted, was often attributed to superstition. Characteristically Boswell pointed out that second sight was not peculiar to the *Gaidhealtachd*, sensibly observing that 'to entertain a visionary notion that one sees a distant or future event, may be called *superstition*; but the correspondence of the fact or event with such an impression on the fancy, though certainly very wonderful, *if proved*, has no more connection with superstition than magnetism or electricity'.[8]

Enlightenment flayers of superstition, if they did not actually use the term, tended to insert the word 'credulity' as a code for an attack on the same commodity. Thus William Robertson the historian asserted (1759) that the first nine hundred years of Scottish History constituted 'pure fable and conjecture and ought to be totally neglected or abandoned to the industry and credulity of antiquaries'.[9]

Lord Hailes in 1773, expostulated,

> let it be considered that Thomas the Rhymer is not forgotten in Scotland nor his authority slighted even at this day. Within the memory of men his prophecies and the prophecies of other Scottish soothsayers have not only been reprinted, but have been constituted with a weak, if not criminal, curiosity.[10]

The foregoing is a random sampling of the views of certain Scots (Johnson excepted) who wrote before the Kilmarnock edition appeared. Suffice it to note that virtually every major writer had something to say on the subject of superstition thus distancing themselves from the Scottish past and – it must be said – from the Scottish vernacular present. The trouble with the label 'Enlightenment' is that its corollary is darkness. We are reminded of *Corinthians* – 'God commanded the light to shine out of darkness' or as the

Lorimer translation of the New Testament has it 'lat licht shine oot o the mirk'.[11]

The denial of eighteenth-century contemporaries is too readily echoed by their scholarly critics. The Scottish historian perusing current studies in the Scottish Enlightenment too often has the uneasy feeling that he or she is contemplating an unfamiliar landscape, that the Scotland being described is unrecognisable, that he or she is, in a word, being conned. Too many students of the Enlightenment [12] (though admittedly not all) are still prone to follow the writers of the Enlightenment themselves who depicted a Scotland somehow benighted during the first sixteen hundred years of her existence – a wretched, barbaric, anarchic, superstition-ridden, blood-soaked kingdom frozen in darkness until the first rays of a new dawn caressed her blighted landscape at the Union of the Crowns in 1603 to gradually bathe her in dazzling light following the Union of the Parliaments in 1707. Enlightenment studies therefore have a tendency to be not just elitist but anti-Scottish in the sense that by definition they exclude over 95% of the population of Scotland who were not aware that an Enlightenment was underway during their very own lifetimes. The majority of the Scottish population was consigned to the pit of darkness and the code-word used by contemporaries to place them there was 'superstition' which embraced the beliefs, customs and practices of the people at large.

Most of Burns's educated contemporaries would have agreed with Voltaire – 'Superstition sets the whole world in flames – philosophy quenches them'. Perhaps Burns would have been readier than most to concur with another of Voltaire's aphorisms – 'it is one of the superstitions of the human mind to have imagined that virginity could be a virtue.' [13] These two quotes raise the question of what superstition actually means. *Superstitio* in Latin just means any non-Roman belief.[14] Today the word connotes someone else's belief and is almost always used in a pejorative sense; for that reason it is generally avoided by modern ethnographers and folklorists.

In English, superstition conveyed a religious belief or practice founded upon fear or ignorance, the sense in which Hume used it in 'Of Miracles' and the meaning which was also understood by his polemical fellow-countrymen throughout the seventeenth century. Adam Smith in *The Wealth of Nations* distinguished science as 'the great antidote to the poison of enthusiasm and superstition'.[15] According to the *Oxford English Dictionary* the word by 1794 had acquired the sense of an irrational or unfounded belief or 'an unreasonable or groundless notion'. Thus, although the term had been in circulation for several centuries it acquired its modern meaning in the course of the Enlightenment debate.

That debate was by no means new. Throughout Europe a battle royal had raged between the elite and subordinate classes from about 1450 onwards during which period catholic and protestant countries alike had seen church and state conspire in the suppression of popular culture. In that struggle the Enlightenment furnished the final prolonged skirmish.[16]

In the nineteen-thirties the American anthropologist Robert Redfield developed his ideas on the 'Great Tradition' of the educated elite and the 'Little Tradition', or the non-exclusive tradition, of the people at large.[17] His terminology was actually anticipated by Burns in his emotive letter to Creech of February 1793 asking him to send twenty copies of the recently published two-volume edition of the poems, 'as I mean to present them among a few Great folks whom I respect and a few Little folks whom I love'.[18]

For over three hundred years the Scottish authorities attempted to suppress, confine, or control the popular culture of the country. The medieval church had disapproved of the May Day celebrations including the Robin Hood plays. Protestant reformers attempted to outlaw bards, minstrels, dancing, wakes and festivals, while not neglecting to interest themselves in the bedroom activities of the Scots. No aspect of the behaviour of the subordinate classes was left untouched by these calvinist ayatollahs and sanctimonious merchants of gloom. As is well known, their petty-minded interferences continued into Burns's own lifetime, yet despite their best efforts they failed. For example, they had targeted ballads as sources of subversion and satire since the 1540s yet the ballad tradition was as buoyant and vibrant as ever when Burns reaped his bountiful harvest in the last years of his life for the collections of James Johnson and George Thomson.

In the eyes of the corbies in clerical garb 'superstitious' was the adjective to describe any non-presbyterian – and especially any faintly papist – belief. It was therefore highly ironic that when deism raised its ugly head at the end of the seventeenth century those self-same arbiters of popular pastimes and pursuits suddenly turned their own arguments on their heads and emphasised the reality of fairies, elves and witches in order to prove the existence of God. Such, almost incredibly, was the motivation behind publications like *Satan's Invisible World Discovered* (1685) by George Sinclair, professor of natural philosophy at Glasgow University and designer of water pumps for the coal-mining industry, and *The Secret Commonwealth* (1692), a treatise on fairy belief by Robert Kirk, minister of Aberfoyle and translator of the psalms into Gaelic.[19] In turning full circle, the wheel had also described a revolution in mentality – at least to modern eyes since the Sinclairs and the Kirks of proto-Enlightenment Scotland would not have distinguished any inconsistencies in their own, or their predecessors', attitudes.

Where then did Burns stand in this debate? In truth he did not have a great deal to say about it. To judge from his creative work and his correspondence the supernatural was less central to Burns than it was to Scott or Hogg or Stevenson. In this regard much has been made of Robert's remarks in the famous and ever-quoted letter to Dr John Moore of August 1787 referring to his mother's maid, Betty Davidson, remarkable for her ignorance, credulity and superstition – she had, I suppose, the largest collection in the county of tales and songs concerning devils, ghosts, fairies, brownies, witches, warlocks, spunkies, kelpies, elf-candles, dead-lights, wraiths, apparitions, cantraips, giants, inchanted towers, dragons and other trumpery.[20]

Betty thus fulfilled for Burns the function which was to become essential to a number of Scottish writers, namely that of female tradition-bearer; Hogg had his mother, Scott his mother and his aunties and Stevenson his Cummy. Writing to Alexander Cunningham and well fortified with 'a nipperkin of Toddy ... just by way of a spell to keep away the meikle horned Devil or any of his subaltern Imps who may be on their nightly rounds' he displayed, in equal measure, his inebriation, his cronyisms and his gentle mocking of the spirit world:

O, thou Spirit! whatever thou art, or wherever thou makest thyself visible! Be thou a Bogle by the eerie side of an auld thorn, in the dreary glen through which the herd-callan maun bicker in his gloamin route frae the fauld! – Be thou a BROWNIE, set, at dead of night, to thy task by the blazing ingle, or in the solitary barn where the repercussions of thy iron flail half affright thyself, as thou performest the work of twenty of the sons of men, ere the cock-crowing summon thee to thy ample cog of substantial BROSE! – Be though a KELPIE, haunting the ford, or ferry, in the starless night, mixing thy laughing yell with the howling of the storm & the roaring of the flood, as thou viewest the perils & miseries of Man on the foundering horse, or in the tumbling boat! – Or, lastly be thou a GHOST, paying thy nocturnal visits to the hoary ruins of decayed Grandeur, or performing thy mystic rites in the shadow of the time-worn Church while the Moon looks, without a cloud, on the silent, ghastly dwellings of the dead around thee; or taking thy stand by the bed-side of the Villain, or the Murderer, pourtraying on his dreaming fancy, pictures, dreadful as the horrors of unveiled Hell, & terrible as the wrath of incensed Deity![21]

Here is Burns in typical ironic mode, the trumpery not tempered by the toddy.

A similar playfulness pervades 'Address to the Deil' although there is some room for argument as to how the poem should be read. Many in 1785–6, when the piece was composed, would have been incensed at Burns's flip attitude towards the deil, indeed just as angry as if he had questioned the existence of God himself. The poem is, of course, comic and the tone is set by the sense of bonhomie at the commencement of the address. There is no question but that many of the bard's contemporaries had similar experiences to his reverend granny who heard Auld Clootie in the weather and expected him to haunt glen and castle. Rab himself could explain any devilish activity as a cause of nature whether the devil appeared as a 'rash-buss' or a drake on whistling winds. But people still believed that Auld Nick[22] would sour the butter in the churn or bring about the destruction of travellers on moor or at ford. A particularly interesting stanza though one which we perhaps nowadays do not linger over is

> Thence, mystic knots mak great abuse,
> On *Young-Guidmen*, fond, keen an' croose;
> When the best *warklum* i' the house,
>   By cantraip wit,
> Is instant made no worth a louse,
>   Just at the bit.[23]

The reference here is to what were known in French as *les novements d'arquillettes*, knots tied by witches, obviously through diabolical influence, to cause impotence. Such a fate allegedly befell the legendary Martin Guerre. It was believed the spell could only be lifted by finding the original knots, in leather, threads, ropes or whatever, and untying them.[24] Although the practice is quite well attested from the Continent the reference in Burns's stanza is the only one so far known to me from Scotland.

The comedic element which has been detected in the 'Address' is not entirely absent at the height of the witch-hunt, a phenomenon which was unquestionably regarded with deadly seriousness. *News from Scotland* (1591), which describes the events surrounding the North Berwick witches, includes a tale of the schoolmaster from Prestonpans, John Cunningham, whose schemes to seduce a young girl were foiled by her mother, and who ended up as the unwilling recipient of the fond attentions of a cow.[25] The trial of Isobel Gowdie at Audearn in 1662 related how the devil used to beat his disciples but the victims sometimes resisted – 'Bessie Wilson would speak crusty, and be belling again to him stoutly'[26] – in other words she gave as good as she got! There is an element of the pacificatory in the 'Address' comparable to the convention of north-east fishermen who referred to the Gyre Carlin – the winds of winter – as Gentle Annie, or to the Gaelic custom of addressing the devil as Donald Dubh. Both David Daiches and Thomas Crawford have commented on the fine balance in 'Tam o'Shanter', 'between mere supernatural anecdote and the precisely etched realistic picture',[27] on Burns's recognition that he himself 'emancipated man of the eighteenth century though he was – could, in the appropriate circumstances, feel some of the terrors that afflict the superstitious and the simple-minded'.[28] The same points could be made of the 'Address'. In both poems the laughter is nervous. It was easy enough to banish the devil at the nappy but once transposed, like Tam, to the harsh reality of a tempestuous Scottish night, Auld Nick was still not far enough removed in time or space. Eight years after Burns's death a woman in Kirkcudbright was accused of witchcraft, while stray cases continued to be reported throughout the nineteenth century.

By the late eighteenth century a steady stream of tourists was entering Scotland intent on distinguishing superstitions among the peasantry and, of course, they found them. They were inspired by Johnson and Boswell but ultimately by Martin Martin who, almost a century earlier, had ensured that folk belief was an essential item on any serious wanderer's itinerary.[29] Thus Robert Heron in 1792, on a visit to Galloway of which he was a native, described superstitious practices, the circulation of Percy's *Reliques* and the long winter nights when Brownies and 'Gyar Carlins' could be heard curling on frozen lochs.[30] The original 'chield' among us 'taking notes, an faith, he'll prent it' was Captain Francis Grose, the comical – and boozy – practitioner of the 'Antiquarian trade' who eagerly consorted with the devil's crew in 'auld, houlet-haunted' biggins and ruined kirks.[31] The very act therefore of contributing a manufactured piece of superstition – 'Tam o' Shanter' – to Francis Grose's second volume of *Antiquities of Scotland*, was itself ironic; the mode of publication was part of the joke and thus Burns contributed as surely as Sir Walter Scott has allegedly done to the Scottish mythos and to the expectations of Scottish tourists.

Before leaving 'Tam o' Shanter' it is worth recalling that Burns recounted three tales of Alloway kirk to Francis Grose.[32] They remind us that it is a great pity that Burns did not record as many folk tales as he did ballads and songs. In his letter to Grose he adopts the Man of the World position, lightly mocking the daft notions of a former era. The second tale is always quoted since it clearly forms the basis of the poem. Had the other two tales been used then Tam would have been a farm-servant carrying home his ploughing irons. Attracted by a light in Alloway kirk he found the place deserted save for a caldron containing a stew made of the heads of unchristened children and the limbs of malefactors. The resourceful ploughman emptied the contents in the fire and placed the caldron over his head thus wearing it as a helmet all the way home. Another of his stories, which Burns could allegedly 'prove to be equally authentic', had a shepherd boy visiting Alloway kirk to find a company of men and women transforming stalks of ragwort into flying horses by which means he was transported to a wine cellar in Bordeaux. He woke up drunk and alone to explain in his best Ayrshire French that he was a herd-boy in Alloway and he somehow returned home with the next wine consignment. Burns had already alluded to the widespread belief in 'ragwood nags' in the 'Address'. It is fortunate for his readers that he exercised more discretion in selecting materials for 'Tam o' Shanter' than he did for 'Halloween', an extraordinary poem in the sense that it is extraordinarily disappointing. Commentators have suggested that it is invaluable as a source for the folklorist but in fact it is not. It starts out well:

> Upon that *night*, when Fairies light.
> On Cassilis Downans dance,
> Or owre the lays, in splendid blaze,
> On sprightly coursers prance.[33]

The text is generously supplied with footnotes and there are some interesting allusions to Halloween customs such as nut prognostication but the poem rapidly deteriorates into an excuse for houghmagandie. The promise of the title is not fulfilled – 'a night when Witches, Devils, and other mischief-making beings are all abroad on their baneful midnight errands: particularly those aerial people, the Fairies, are said on that night, to hold a grand Anniversary'. The poem is a monument to wasted opportunity. On the other hand it may be that in a clumsy fashion Burns was attempting to satirise the antiquarian predilection for seeking custom in folk activities, stressing instead the replacement of the traditional past by the carnal present.

What then did Burns make of superstition? Sometimes he can disappoint. In one of his preaching letters he says,

> ... away with old-wife prejudices and tales! Every age and every nation has had a different set of stories; and as the many are always weak, of consequence they have often, perhaps always been deceived.[34]

It does not bode well for the topic under discussion when Robert declares to Anna Dunlop, 'I have ever looked on Mankind in the lump to be nothing better than a foolish, headstrong, credulous, unthinking Mob; and their universal belief has ever had extremely little weight with me'[35] Where is the tireless individual who expended so much energy collecting the ballads and songs of the folk tradition? This is the same man who shared with James Candlish a 'pride of despising old women's stories',[36] the same who occasionally seemed to forget that he self-confessedly admired the old Scots proverb, 'Better be the head o' the Commonality, as the tail o' the Gentry'.[37] There must be a useful paper to be written on Burns's use of proverbs, always one of the great repositories of the wisdom of the folk.

But we end up where we began. Was Burns 'naturally of a superstitious cast'? Did he side with the Little Folks whom he loved as opposed to the Great Folk whom he respected? Where did he ultimately stand in the battle of the Folk which was fought out over so many centuries? Here it is pertinent to recall that Burns spoke in many voices.[38] His ideas about superstition seem to have depended upon the person he was addressing. On this topic, as on so many others, he was ambivalent. Yet, in his letter to John Moore about Betty Davidson and her superstitions, in the greatest single autobiographical statement that he ever made, and which has been taken at face value by every single commentator on the bard, he concluded his near Rabelaisian list of the members of the secret commonwealth with a very important statement:

> This cultivated the latent seeds of Poesy; but had so strong an effect on my imagination, that to this hour, in my nocturnal rambles, I sometimes keep a sharp look-out in suspicious places; and though nobody can be more sceptical in these matters than I, yet it often takes an effort of Philosophy to shake off these idle terrors.[39]

There, loud and clear, is the articulation of the tension at the very heart of the

Enlightenment. He was, perhaps, a superstitious sceptic. He was clearly not in the thralls of 'Superstition's Hellish Brood' but no more did he believe himself when he wrote to James Smith

> This life, sae far's I understand,
> Is a' enchanted fairy-land.[40]

He knew that the phantoms would soon conspire to destroy the enchantment, sensing that where the Reformation had failed, the agrarian transformations, which so bedevilled his own agricultural enterprises, would succeed in combination with such powerful allies as philosophy. Yet the latter commodity could never be such an absolute weapon in his armory as it was in that of Davie Hume. Burns remained true to his roots, steeped in tradition. His commitment to folk culture is evident in his use of language or in the vast knowledge of music, ballad and song which he displayed in his correspondence with James Johnson and George Thomson. He had many other concerns apart from superstition; it was not as central to his thought as it was to that of the *philosophes*. Yet in the final summation, bearing in mind the great tensions in Enlightenment Scotland which have earlier been suggested, like love and poesy, or freedom and whisky, Robert Burns and superstition 'gang thegither'.

NOTES

1. *The Letters of Robert Burns*, edited by J. De Lancey Ferguson; 2nd edn edited by G. Ross Roy (Oxford, 1985), I, 245.
2. *Letters*, I, 93.
3. *The Philosophical Works of David Hume*, edited by T. H. Green and T. H. Grose, 4 vols (London, 1874–5), iv, p. 93.
4. Quoted in Ernest Campbell Mossner, *The Life of David Hume* (Oxford, 1970), p. 293.
5. Adam Ferguson, *An Essay on the History of Civil Society 1767*, edited by Duncan Forbes (Edinburgh, 1966), p. 90. See also p. 182.
6. *Johnson's Journey to the Western Islands of Scotland and Boswell's Journal of a Tour to the Hebrides with Samuel Johnson, LL.D.*, edited by R. W. Chapman (Oxford, 1970), p. 97.
7. *Johnson's Journey*, p. 101.
8. *Boswell's Tour*, p. 424.
9. William Robertson, *The History of Scotland During the Reigns of Queen Mary and James VI*, 3 vols (London, 1809), I, 205–6.
10. David Dalrymple, Lord Hailes, *Remarks on the History of Scotland* (Edinburgh, 1773), quoted in *The Romance and Prophecies of Thomas of Erceldoune*, edited by James A. H. Murray (*Early English Text Society*: London, 1875), p. xlii.
11. *The New Testament in Scots*, translated by W. L. Lorimer (Edinburgh, 1983).
12. The best introduction to the subject is probably *A Hotbed of Genius The Scottish Enlightenment 1730–1790*, edited by David Daiches, Peter Jones, Jean Jones (Edinburgh, 1986; reprinted 1996).

13. *The Oxford Dictionary of Quotations* (Oxford, 1980), p. 561.

14. Robin Lane Fox, *Pagans and Christians* (New York, 1989), p. 32.

15. Adam Smith, *An Inquiry into the Nature and Causes of the Wealth of Nations*, edited by R. H. Campbell, A. S. Skinner, W. B. Todd, 2 vols (Oxford, 1976), II, 796.

16. On this see Peter Burke, *Popular Culture in Early Modern Europe* (London, 1978), Mikhail Bakhtin *Rabelais and His World* (Bloomington, 1984). On Scotland 'Calvinism and the Survival of Folk' in Edward J Cowan (ed.), *The People's Past: Scottish Folk, Scottish History* (Edinburgh, 1980; reprinted 1991), pp. 32–57.

17. Burke, *Popular Culture* pp. 23–29.

18. *Letters*, II, 185.

19. George Sinclair, *Satan's Invisible World Discovered* (Glasgow, 1685), *The Secret Commonwealth and A Short Treatise of Charms and Spells by Robert Kirk*, edited by Stewart Sanderson (Folklore Society, 1976).

20. *Letters*, I, 135.

21. *Letters*, II, 145–6.

22. Kinsley, III, 1129 finds the derivation of Nick, from Nicholas, obscure. I understand it to be inspired by none other than Niccolo Machiavelli.

23. *Poems*, I, 170.

24. Natalie Zeman Davis, *The Return of Martin Guerre* (London, 1983), p. 21; Vern L. Bullough, 'Postscript: Heresy, Witchcraft and Sexuality in *Sexual Practices and the Medieval Church*, edited by Vern L. Bullough and James Brundage (Buffalo, 1982), p. 217.

25. *Criminal Trials in Scotland from 1488 to 1624*, edited by R. Pitcairn (Edinburgh, 1833) I, 213–223.

26. Pitcairn, *Trials*, III, 600.

27. David Daiches, *Robert Burns* (Edinburgh, 1950; reprinted 1981), p. 260.

28. Thomas Crawford, *Burns A Study of the Poems and Songs* (Edinburgh, 1960; reprinted 1965), p. 221.

29. Martin Martin, *A description of the Western Islands of Scotland* (London, 1696 reprinted by James Thin, 1976).

30. Robert Heron, *Observations made on a Journey through the Western Counties of Scotland 1792* (London, 1793), p. 228.

31. *Poems*, II, 494.

32. *Letters*, II, 29–31.

33. *Poems*, I, 152. The Downans of the poem recalls the Downie Hills near Auldearn mentioned in Isobel Gowdie's trial. Such nomenclature seems to have signified fairy hills in Scotland, as Burns explained – 'certain little, romantic, rocky, green hills', *Poems*, I, 152.

34. *Letters*, I, 258. I think Ian McIntyre, *Dirt and Deity: A Life of Robert Burns* (London, 1995), p. 437 underestimates Burns's capacity for preachifying.

35. *Letters*, I, 349.

36. *Letters*, I, 99.

37. *Letters*, II, 74.

38. Kenneth Simpson, *The Protean Scot: The Crisis of Identity in Eighteenth-Century Scottish Literature* (Aberdeen, 1988), pp. 185–218.

39. *Letters*, I, 135.

40. *Poems*, I, 180.

Burns and the Scottish Critical Tradition

FOR MANY YEARS it has been a well-recognised critical priority to dislodge readings of Robert Burns's poetry from the entangled mythology of Burns the man. The poet's biography, however, is not the only place to provide for Burns an inflation of context. We find a manifestation of this in an area which has been surprisingly little noticed. Many people – both general readers and students – turn for their first critical approach to Burns to a handful of authoritative twentieth-century critics of Scottish literature in general in whom they find discussion of Burns within the terms of his nation's literary and cultural profile. Such historical placement is, of course, an important area of critical investigation but what I intend to question is certain aspects of the attempts of the generalist critical tradition to give shape to Scottish literary history and to locate Burns within this. It is a remarkable fact that this tradition includes some of the finest critical minds Scotland has produced but that much of the most specialised and fruitful work on Burns in the last thirty five-years has been achieved by scholars who have had virtually to ignore many of the large-scale conclusions of the generalists.

G. Gregory Smith in his *Scottish Literature: Character and Influence* (1919) is the father of the modern Scottish critical tradition in his attempts to explain the worrying discontinuities in Scotland's literary history.[1] He identifies among a number of key debilitating tendencies in Scottish literature what he calls the 'retrospective' or 'historical' habit where Scottish writers are seen to return rather incestuously to a set of forms and themes which have been well-tried by their national predecessors.[2] Of this tendency, Gregory Smith says, 'only two writers, Burns and Scott, have done anything to loosen this … grip – both unconsciously, and the former with no permanent aid to the victim'.[3] Here we have a strange dislocation of Burns in particular. His achievement manages to transcend (to some extent) the unhelpfully parochial dispensation of the Scottish literary climate (the materials of eighteenth-century Scots poetry, with its strongly signalled elements of historical continuity, is a key piece of evidence in Gregory Smith's postulation of the 'historical habit') but he is unable to leave any real legacy to Scottish literature. Clearly, the two facts which condition Gregory Smith's view here are Burns's manifest success as a poet and the seeming terminus in Scottish poetry which he represents. In an attempt to square the notion of the successful Burns and an unhealthy Scottish literary climate Gregory Smith declaims:

Before him, even though the literature suffered from the dulling habits to which attention has been drawn, some change might have come … some fresh outlook, at the bidding of writers not so richly endowed as he was, and he himself in other circumstances, might have used his powers to such an end. He made the best, the very best of what had been and there the matter ended. He completed the edifice, and men admired, and have gone on admiring and declining the hope of admiring anything else.[4]

Here we have Gregory Smith finding a location for Burns's problematic genius which emerges as a kind of highspeed performance. Having already rendered Burns 'unconscious' (to the limitations of the Scots poetic materials he is working with), Gregory Smith now presents Burns the cheerfully oblivious joyrider racing through the barren plain of eighteenth-century Scots poetry and spoiling everyone else's fun as he uses up all of the road. In rather futile fashion (given that Burns simply brings about the inevitable exhaustion of Scots poetry much more quickly than otherwise might have been the case), Gregory Smith speculates that some change, some liberation of what he calls vaguely 'outlook', might have come about in Scots poetry but for the over-awing power of Burns. Burns is also, then, the pied piper whose hypnotic performance those who follow cannot resist. If the Scottish 'historical' mentality presents Burns with a handicap in terms of limited dynamic direction to begin with, Burns returns the favour with interest by building even higher the walls around the narrow enclosure that is the eighteenth-century Scots poetic tradition. If the Scottish literary tradition is bad for Burns – and what other inference can be drawn from Gregory Smith's claim that 'in other circumstances' Burns might have found a greater range in literature? – then he too is bad for the Scottish literary tradition in taking its tendency to historical folly to its ultimate conclusion. Gregory Smith slyly confirms this in his witty reference to the Burnsomania of the nineteenth century with its monumental Burns. In a hilarious throwaway manoeuvre, Gregory Smith actually has Burns completing his own monument or 'edifice' himself. This manipulation is typical of Gregory Smith throughout his book. He observes a more or less concrete phenomenon – in this case the Burns of the cultists – and infers that this phenomenon follows inevitably from the nature of the literature which inspires it. But Gregory Smith, like many Scottish critics since, overplays cause and effect. In particular, he looks at effect and assumes one overarching, inherent and directly identifiable native cause. In the most prosaic matter of fact, it is, of course, true that Burns is 'responsible' for his ratpack of sentimental followers, but he is not the inevitable cause of their existence. They choose him, he does not choose them. The reason for Gregory Smith's tight model of causation is basically because of a predisposition toward believing in a kind of cultural integrity or holism where the health of Scottish literary culture is read according to the perceived health of all its parts taken together and the ability of these parts to engender meaningful continuity. When breaks in continuity or malcontinuities occur, such as happens with the bastardised use of Scots (frequently Burnsian Scots) for emasculatingly sentimental purposes in the nineteenth century, then a tendency toward sterility is read in the whole system.

Gregory Smith's 'historical habit' is a rather one-dimensional concept as it is an attempt to label a more or less innate tendency in the Scottish literary psyche without real reference to the myriad internal and external circumstances which account for the shape of Scottish literary history. However, it is easy to see how he arrives at his shorthand. To some extent, the familiar appearance and primitivist polemicism of eighteenth-century Scots poetry allows the slur of the 'historical habit'. One thinks of Allan Ramsay's disingenuous claims in the preface to *The Ever Green* to be promoting the Scots poetic tradition as it had been – free of alien cultural pollution, or Robert Fergusson's bombasts against the Italian influence on Scottish music, or Burns's participation in his image as primitive bard. This polemicism, though, never actually extended to Ramsay, Fergusson or Burns accepting the linguistic resources of England and Europe as contraband (though their smuggling in of such goods has often blinded critical pronouncements to the linguistic complexity of all these poets). Gregory Smith is the first modern voice to devalue eighteenth-century Scots poetry by concentrating on its strongly accented 'Scottish' features and reading its developmental impossibility which is seemingly confirmed after Burns. What Gregory Smith has an inadequate grasp of is that many forms or modes of literary and artistic expression do indeed have their vogue and then die. This is perhaps inevitable in the case of many of the most visible features of eighteenth-century Scots poetry (for instance, the standard habbie is bound to depreciate as the new lyrical vehicles of Romanticism arrive from the end of the eighteenth century). Gregory Smith, though, over-extends the notion of superannuation so that it represents a *priori* weakness and so that Burns emerges as a curiously unsatisfactory manifestation of an unsatisfactory literary culture. As well as the vagaries of literary fashion, what Gregory Smith's view fails to take into account is the way in which Burns *does* fruitfully energise literary consciousness in Scotland after him (to take a simple example, the debt of Hogg's *Memoirs and Confessions of A Justified Sinner* to 'Holy Willie's Prayer'). He also passes silently over the wider factors influencing Scottish literature after Burns such as the socio-political climate of nineteenth-century Scotland which leads to the lobotomy of Burnsian poetic consciousness and the admittedly difficult question of the failure of Scotland to produce much of any kind of meaningful poetry (if one discounts the claims for Byron) in the early nineteenth century.

The tendencies of Gregory Smith toward huge dissatisfaction with the *cul de sac* achievements of Burns and Scottish literary history in general are continued in those who follow him in the generalist critical tradition. In his highly influential *Scott and Scotland* (1936), Edwin Muir ranges over the wide terrain of Scottish literary culture and offers comprehensive reasons for its shape. Muir explains in his introduction that he seeks to explain what Scotland did for Walter Scott. In a startling conclusion which chimes with Gregory Smith's appraisal of Burns, Muir says of Scott, 'Scotland did not have enough life of its own to nourish a writer of his scope; it had neither a real community to foster him nor a tradition to direct him'.[5] For Muir the underlying reason for the huge inadequacy of Scottish culture in these respects lies in what he famously labels the 'dissociation of Scottish sensibility' where the emotional and intellectual apparati of the Scots are prised apart due to the dominance of English in Scotland after the Reformation as the language of the head and the relegation of Scots as the language of the heart. The dystopian outcome is that the Scottish people are in receipt of two languages neither of which is complete or what Muir calls 'homogenous'.[6] This represents a reworking of what Gregory Smith had identified as Scottish parochialism or the inability to go beyond the most immediate native experience. In Muir's theory the Scots are locked into their withered historical experience, as their 'natural' language, which means not simply the Scots language but the Scots language used for the full range of expressive, intellectual and artistic purposes, has been smashed and this can never be recovered. Muir's linguistic theory has had incredible vogue – one can still hear versions of it being taught in Scottish universities today – but it is very crude. Its most spectacular crudities emerge in Muir's treatment of Burns. Burns songs are grist to Muir's mill. He says of 'A Red Red Rose' that this 'is sentiment, sentiment at its very best but nothing more'.[7] For Muir, 'A Red Red Rose' lacks an 'intellectual' component. Muir 'proves' this by comparing the song to the sixteenth-century Scots lyric, 'My heart is heigh above', in which he finds 'all the aspects of love, sensual, romantic, and spiritual', and this for Muir represents a 'holistic' treatment of love.[8] Now it seems entirely possible to me to identify in 'A Red Red Rose' 'spiritual love' and indeed an intellectualism in its large nature symbolism but the point really at issue for Muir is that it contains no reference to God, unlike the sixteenth-century lyric. This is disingenuous. He observes the shift from the medieval religious mindcast to the more materialist outlook which follows and adduces a peculiarly Scottish problem as he wishes to maintain that the Scots lose God more utterly than elsewhere due to Calvinism. Lurking behind his strained reading also is his chagrin that Burns – Scotland's foremost poet – should be writing a folksong (for this is how he naively defines 'A Red Red Rose').

For Muir western literature has a fairly clear developmental or teleological history which is disrupted in Scotland by the loss of true religious and linguistic sensibility. This disruption involves an inevitable fracturing of the proprieties of literary development which Scotland can never compensate for. Muir sees the evidence for this in Scottish puritanism's snuffing out of drama which he sees in England as a supremely humanist mode involving the working out of moral and philosophical conflicts. In Scotland the official Calvinist establishment provides no space for this metaphysical mind and metaphysical literature. As if this were not oversimplification enough, Muir proceeds to claim that the Scottish 'dramatic urge' goes underground into folk poetry such as the ballads which cannot from their decentred cultural location provide the dramatic urge with full sustenance. It is this reading of broken Scottish literary history which leads Muir to the most ridiculous estimation of 'Tam O'Shanter' ever to be published. He sums the poem up as 'a joke followed by an explanation', a description he derives from the notion of the poem's relation to Scottish Calvinist society.[9] For Muir, it is a peculiar piece of Scottish fantasy 'governed over by a Protestant Pope of unreason'.[10] That is to say, Tam's 'wild ride' or release in the poem is ultimately explained away in the poem by drunkenness, and this, for Muir, shows the stamp of Scottish puritanism. The poem is not a true piece of fantasy, which would allow the possibility that Tam's supernatural adventures might have actually happened. With an eye on the poem's sources in oral and folk-tradition, Muir proposes that it is 'wild irresponsible fantasy ungoverned by intellect'.[11] This reading, so skilfully consistent with Muir's grand narrative of Scottish cultural history, represents a comprehensive dismissal. It undermines Burns's status as a true literary artist and it is also highly condescending to the traditional folk materials informing the poem. For Muir these folk materials include the Scots language – by the eighteenth century, according to Muir, merely a dialect. Discussing the 'pleasures are like poppies spread' passage of the poem, he offers a famous diagnosis. He says:

> I had often wondered why Burns suddenly dropped into English at this point and for a long time I put down the whole passage as an unaccountable blemish, until I saw that it was the touch that made the poem perfect, the one serious reference that gave all the rest proportion. The point to be noticed, however, is that when Burns applied thought to his theme he turned to English. The reflection in this passage is neither deep nor original, but in the context it is quite adequate. And it is clear that Burns felt he could not express it in Scots, which to him was a language for sentiment but not for thought. He had no language which could serve him equally for both.[12]

Muir is here disabled by his rather flat principle of socio-linguistic holism which he demands in relation to a national literature. He makes no allowance for the register-hopping, the form-hopping even, which any sensible reading of 'Tam O'Shanter' must allow and which is such an important feature of western literary history in general from the eighteenth century at least. Muir talks of the 'pleasures' passage as giving the rest of the poem 'proportion'. By this he implies that Burns himself is dismissing Tam's wild ride adventure as a simple folk-vision which is not to be taken seriously. In one limited sense this is true. Burns provides a modern sceptical voice to qualify Tam's experiences. But this should not be taken merely as an index of fissures in specifically *Scottish* experience. It is the response of the European Enlightenment to traditional folklore in general. At the same time, it is not mere dismissive scepticism. It is what one might call 'synthetic scepticism' or affirmative scepticism in that 'reflection' as Muir denotes it in 'pleasures are like poppies spread' actually accords with Tam's experiences. The seeming real world with its pleasures and its natural phenomena is just as difficult to pin down as the folk-view of the world's nature with its witches and ghosts. What Burns is doing, then, is presenting a remarkably harmonised poem which accords equal status to the 'folk-view' and to the 'modern' view. Muir implies in effect that Burns is never actually easy in his recourse to folk-materials when his lengthy usage of these actually identifies him as being in the vanguard of the Romantic movement. Burns is not switching flatly between Scots and English, the folk and the literary. He is harmonising these in a highly democratic fashion according to his confident predilections as a cultural nationalist, countryman, and a man who is well versed in British literature and philosophy. Muir's pessimistic portrait of Burns and his awkward Scottishness is guided, as I have commented, by his observation of the huge cultural disruptions in Scottish history. This 'disruption' is in one sense undeniable. The Reformation and the relationship with England *do* 'alter' Scotland's cultural and literary directions, but the problem with Muir's treatment of these is that he is absolutist in identifying their effects. He takes up a critical stance where, as with Gregory Smith before him, the lacunae and differentials he sees in Scottish literary history lead him to read what Scotland *does* produce as divorced from a truly essential or organic tradition. This stance, though, is an over-idealisation of the true context in which any literary artist struggles with cultural conflict and a mental and expressive freedom which can never be anything like as foreclosed as Muir alleges.

One of Burns's finest modern critics is also, along with Gregory Smith and Muir, one of the three central definers of the cultural narratives of the generalist critical tradition. This is David Daiches. His *The Paradox of Scottish Culture* (1964) is a very astute description of the diverse cultural strands of eighteenth-century Scotland and, at the same time, a canonising consummation of the generalist tradition's pessimistic identification of deep psychocultural pollution and confusion in Scottish literature.[13] Where Gregory Smith diagnoses psychocultural insularity and Muir diagnoses psychocultural destruction, Daiches diagnoses national schizophrenia. He finds the definitive version of this in the eighteenth century when, due to the synthetic mental and cultural compromises forced on them by the newly formed British state, Scots have great difficulty in exercising more free or natural means of cultural expression. The 'paradox' of Scotland, then, is that its 'modern' development from the eighteenth century occurs on the back of a loss of integrated or properly focused culture. It is in this context that Daiches places Burns:

> He had begun as a local poet, and his most brilliant early poetry reflects his response to local church politics and other aspects of his life as lived in his immediate environment. It was produced for friends who shared his reactions. He soon widened his aim and sought to be a national rather than a

merely local Scottish poet. But the materials for Scottish poetic tradition were not really to hand. Burns drew on what resources he could, both Scottish and English, and developed a variety of styles and idioms reflecting different uses of these sources.[14]

We find here a mixture of accurate observation and a tendency to over-problematise. Of course Burns 'drew on what resources he could'. The implication that Scottish cultural history denied him some set of superior source-materials is simply cultural idealism of the kind we have met already in Gregory Smith and Muir. Burns's mixed experiences and materials are read as a handicap when it is arguable that he becomes a better poet as a result of his struggle with diverse cultural materials. In fact, Daiches himself might be seen to implicitly acknowledge Burns's quite normal artistic ambidexterity or adventurousness as he produces poetry first from his 'immediate environment' and moves toward handling more 'synthetic' materials. For Daiches, though, the problem is that Burns inhabits a national environment which precludes the possibility of expressing fully-flexed national sensibility and language.

What Daiches fails to take account of in his judgement is the proto-pluralistic culture of eighteenth-century Scotland. Saying this is not to deny the power relations which exist between the various strands of this culture where some strands are perhaps regrettably devalued, but to recognise the rapid disintegration and redefinition of cultural norms in not only modern Scotland but modern Western Europe as a whole. Within this cultural pattern, for perhaps longer than three hundred years now, artists have made creative capital. Burns's problem is not so much that he fails to find a national poetics within the context of Scottish culture. It is more the case that certain aspects of his poetic performance exemplify the fact that the bounds of narrow national consciousness were crumbling in the eighteenth century under the rapidly growing awareness that society has a complexity which cannot simply be contained within the paradigm of the nation state. Burns's uneven performance in 'The Vision', where he attempts to harmonise various strands of Scottish experience but finds that he cannot, demonstrates not so much a peculiarly Scottish disability but the bankruptcy of older myths of cultural unity within the context of the nation which is applicable across Europe. 'The Vision' is a poem which implicitly identifies imbalances in wealth and political and cultural power as it synthetically tries to ignore these differentials, and this makes for rather uncomfortable writing. Burns never again makes such an attempt at one-dimensional national statement (unless one includes his patriotic songs) and returns to his true strengths as a great poet of social and cultural tension. As he achieves more properly managed tension or dissonance, as I have already tried to indicate in relation to his usage of the materials of folk culture and more formal culture in 'Tam o' Shanter', Burns is in receipt of the Scottish and European Enlightenment's embryonic awareness of cultural relativism. In 'Tam O' Shanter' Burns more fully extends this awareness, showing the poet here, as elsewhere, in the vanguard of the culturally agnostic Romantic consciousness, a placement which is still inadequately acknowledged.

What I have been trying to sketch is the way in which Burns exemplifies a quite normal poetic development (though it is one which is individually brilliant) when set against the cultural pattern in eighteenth-century Europe. Daiches, though, insists on the peculiar problematics of Burns's Scottish location. He concludes:

> Burns's achievements represent a highly precarious balance between a number of conflicting forces; it was a *personal* achievement, and was not available for fruitful imitation. Even if the industrial revolution had not shortly afterwards so changed the face of a large part of south-west Scotland that later generations used Burns to project their own sentimental nostalgia for a lost and hence idealized rustic way of life, it would still be unlikely that Burns's synthesis could have been handed on unspoilt. For the social, cultural, and linguistic situation was changing all the time and Burns's unstable equilibrium soon became an impossibility.[15]

Here again we find accurate observation over-extended. Daiches is acutely sensitive to Burns's variegated poetic blend and he is right to see this to some extent as a virtuoso or 'personal achievement'. His identification of Burns's 'unstable equilibrium', however, points to a peculiar Scottish cultural context which can only allow him fleeting support, negative support which only a genius can extract. What is disturbing, however, is the conclusion, akin to that arrived at by Gregory Smith, that Burns provides nothing for the future of literature in Scotland. This is true in only the narrowest of terms when we consider the slavish, unthinking imitation of Burns in nineteenth-century Scotland. It can be argued (though this has nowhere yet been done) that his larger literary legacy to Scotland is to be found in fiction of the early nineteenth century where we have the likes of Walter Scott, John Galt and James Hogg writing in a fashion which, similarly to Burns, presents and explores the 'unstable equilibrium' of the variegated (often difficult to resolve) cultural strands of modern Scotland.

To sum up, I have been questioning the three most central critics in twentieth-century Scotland who lead the way for so many others as they identify a hopelessly broken culture which cannot sustain a very satisfactory literary tradition. One of the points I have been trying to argue is that literary tradition often develops in relation or reaction to the uncertainties of cultural context and that this is no bad thing. The critics who lament a properly managed literary culture in Scotland which has somehow been lost as a result of the vagaries of history are idealistic or essentialistic, with the result that a writer such as Burns is read as being internally handicapped (the materials he uses are debased in an *a priori* fashion) when his real struggle is with the external situation of wielding his materials in a literary (rather than any kind of idealised national) fashion.

It is the essentialist or generalist critical tradition which to this day prevents more fluid readings of both the achievements of Burns and the wealth and diversity of achievement in the Scottish literary tradition in general.

NOTES

1. G. Gregory Smith, *Scottish Literature: Character and Influence* (London, 1919).
2. For the extended description of this trait, see Gregory Smith, pp. 41–70.
3. Gregory Smith, p. 133.
4. Gregory Smith, p. 134.
5. Edwin Muir, *Scott and Scotland* (1936; reprinted Edinburgh, 1982). p. 3.
6. For Muir's postulation of 'homogenous' literary language, see especially pp. 6–14.
7. Muir, p. 32.
8. Muir, p. 32.
9. Muir, p. 42.
10. Muir, p. 62.
11. Muir, p. 71.
12. Muir, p. 13.
13. David Daiches, *The Paradox of Scottish Culture* (Oxford, 1964).
14. Daiches, p. 87.
15. Daiches, p. 88.

Burns and Gaelic

WHEN Gairm (in 1978) published my *Leth-cheud Bliadhna*, a collection of original Gaelic poems, Derick Thomson suggested that two translations which he had previously seen (namely 'To a Haggis' and 'Tam o' Shanter') should be included. When the collection appeared, some people thought that these two poems by Burns were better than my own! Then followed *Ceud Oran*, 100 songs of Burns in Gaelic translation; and the interest became an obsession; and in five short years, in the new-found freedom of retirement, all 646 pieces had transposed themselves into Gaelic.

At the outset, a disclaimer may be in order. I am not a 'Burns expert' in the sense that many of you are. My only qualification for speaking here is that, in translating all of the poetical works, I have had to study carefully every single line and every single word – and, even more, to try to interpret holistically the meaning and message of each complete piece.

This leads us to consider *Guiding Principles in translation*. It is obvious that different translators adopt varying guiding principles. For example, in the case of Burns's work in Gaelic, it would seem that the only other serious attempt at covering a wide spectrum made in recent times, that produced in 1911 by Charles McPhater, was governed by a desire to give a literal and direct translation into Gaelic, without much reference to rhythm; whereas today's translator places great emphasis on rhythm, rhyme, cadences; that is, in the case of the songs, singability; and in the case of the poems a certain undefinable 'family resemblance'. In other words, what one does is to try to imagine, to visualise, to 'auralise' *what Burns would have written had he been writing in Gaelic instead of Scots*. One tries, of course, to be as faithful to the original as possible, and one has to strike a balance between literalness and essential authenticity as poetry. But when it comes to the impasse where a choice has to be made, literalness has to give way to poetry.

Another question which is frequently raised is *'How much does the original lose in translation?'* R. Peel, writing on 'Burns into Gaelic' in a 1990 edition of The Burns Chronicle, says, 'Poetry in translation is never really satisfying if it can be read in the original' ... 'But', he adds graciously, 'it does have its interest'. If I thought that, I would lay down my pen or try another tack! Without making any claims for my own work, I fully believe that translated poetry *can* be as effective as, and on rare occasion more effective than, the original. To prove my point, I invite bilingual readers to read aloud 'The Witch of Dundrum',[1] in Scots first, then in Gaelic. Of course, this comparison may not be entirely fair, as I am referring to what is undoubtedly Burns's worst poem. Similarly, with 'The Ruined Farmer' – but then again, I refer to what is perhaps his second worst!

Relation of Scots to Gaelic. R. Peel describes the problems of poetry translation as 'enormous' – and this is very often true. But in the case of rendering Burns into Gaelic the problems are not as immense as we might think. There is a certain compatibility between Burns's Scots and present-day Gaelic – more so, I venture to suggest, than is the case with present-day Scots, which has moved further away from its Gaelic associations.

It may sound paradoxical, but the most difficult pieces to translate are those songs which are best known and loved. The reason for this is that we have come to associate tremendous emotions with phrases which are in themselves really meaningless. 'A man's a man for a' that' has come to have a profound, even spiritual, meaning: but on the face of it, apart from its context, these seven words tell us nothing at all – certainly not anything that a child in Primary 1 does not already know! An even better example is 'Scots wha hae'. When we stop to think of it, these three words by themselves are ridiculously meaningless. Yet they are charged with emotion, patriotism, and nation-consciousness. But HOW to translate them into another language, without losing these meanings in their entirety?

Before concentrating on the question of language as such, it may be helpful to sketch in some comparisons between Burns's daily concerns and the equivalent concerns today, especially in the Highlands and Islands.

Firstly, social concerns. A sense of social justice, extending even to the animal world (the humble mouse), if not also the inanimate (the daisy), seems to burn forever in the Bard's heart. This is what makes his poetry required reading in parts of the world where the works of other British writers have hardly penetrated.

If we take one specific and topical social question, it has been claimed that in his own day, by virtue of some of his poems, Burns was '*in the forefront of the feminist movement*'. The poem on which J. A. Mackay bases this statement is 'The Rights of Woman'. But as I study this piece, I find the construction so insecure, and so untypical of the Bard, that I wonder if he was deliberately conveying a view which was at odds with his words; in other words, I have almost a 'tongue-in-cheek' feeling about this poem. And certainly, viewing his works on a broad canvas, we would have to agree that his 'feminism' was not such as would commend itself to the feminists of our day. I will only say that, at the same time, it bears some remarkable resemblances to the contemporary feminism of some parts of the Highlands and Islands.

Perhaps the most telling comparison between Burns and our day in the Islands is the expression of strong, sometimes wild, Celtic independence which, in Burns's case, we find in such songs as 'A Man's a Man', and is also most potently expressed in the Gaelic songs of Lewis. Whether the theme is poaching or weaving, peace or war, there is often a subtle undertone which exults and exalts 'the common man', at the expense of the landlords, the mill-owners, and the captains, who regard themselves as a cut above the rest!

Again 'The Cotter's Saturday Night' may not generally be regarded as among Burns's best work, but it is revered above all others in certain circles in the Islands, because it describes in graphic detail a situation which was fully current only a few years ago – and still is in many families today. And *it is those same 'Psalms of David'* which could be heard issuing strongly, if not always melo-diously, from every house from one end of the village to the other signalling the beginning and ending of the day.

Political comparisons may not be as easy to pinpoint as the social ones, but again, the land raids and Clearances are still fresh in our own folk memory, and one feels that Burns, had he been a Government official present in Tiree or Uist or Lewis or Sutherland at the time of the Clearances, would have been severely torn by a conflict of loyalties. The language of some of the political and election ballads is rather turgid, and the sentiments rather ambivalent. No doubt his verses helped the Whig cause, but sometimes personalities counted for more than political colour. One has only to study the candidates elected to Parliament for the Western Isles in recent years to realise that this tendency is still very much alive.

Perhaps the most interesting and fruitful field of study of comparisons between Burns and the Gaelic world of our day is that of *religious and ecclesias-tical questions* – and it is one where language and dialectic enter strongly. Scotland has been noted and notorious ever since the Reformation (some would say even before) for its ecclesiastical sectarianism; and in this respect, Burns's day, as reflected in his poetry, was no different from our own. But in spite of the Bard's strictures on some of the Kirk's representatives (and in one place he even had something *good* to say of the much maligned Presbytery of Ayr), he was not at all anti-religious. He was in this, as in other respects, a product of his time, in which religion pervaded every aspect of his life to an extent not known in our day, other than in comparatively remote communities. He seems to have accepted Church discipline, and this raises the interesting question whether he was a member in communion with the National Church.

His attitude to the Bible was markedly different from his attitude to the church. Mackenzie's *The Man of Feeling*, we are told, he valued 'next to the Bible'. He has many references to the Old Testament – which, like many Highlanders today, he seems to have preferred to the New – references which would send even well-informed people scurrying for their concordances! In the one poem, he refers to the story of creation ('His prentice hand he tried on man') and to the story of Solomon ('The wisest man the world knew'); while not many outside Divinity Faculty or pulpit would realise that his 'a fountain shut up and a book sealed' is a slight *mis*quotation from the Song of Solomon!

But as the main interest of this session is *language*, the remaining part of this contribution is devoted to this aspect, in relation to the general theme of 'Burns and Gaelic'. Perhaps the obvious and easiest way to proceed is first to consider vocabulary; and for convenience I have again used Dr Mackay's *Complete Works*. I have gone through the glossary and marked those words which seem to me to have a Scots-Gaelic connection. In most cases the Scots is derived from the Gaelic, and in some vice versa; while in some it is difficult, without an exhaustive specialist study, to decide which is which. Altogether, there are 94 such words – too many for detailed consideration within the confines of this paper.

Words of special interest. Some individual words do deserve more consideration, for example: '*Cranreuch*' is a difficult one from the translator's point of view, since, although its derivation is Gaelic, it is not a current Gaelic word as such; and it is only recently that I have come across a form of it in actual use – in a poem by the Rev John MacIntyre which appeared in the Gaidheal in 1877:[2]

'Thigeadh dùdlachd a' gheamhraidh, le *crainndeachd* is fuachd'.

'*Luath*', which does not appear in the glossary (the name of the non-aristocrat of 'The Twa Dogs') is, of course, borrowed from the Fingalian Sagas, but was probably chosen by Burns for its meaning – 'fast' – which would be the first requirement in a working sheepdog. The Bard, however, gives it two syllables while it should be one, balancing it with the definitely two-syllable word, 'comrade'.

'*Cackit*' is not a very 'nice' word. It occurs in 'There was Twa Wives' – in the last line, as a horrible climax to a horrible story. The powerful imagery is unsurpassed. This word, even if not 'nice', is still very interesting. Even the Scots form which the Gaelic word takes is notable. In Gaelic also 'cac' is both a noun and a verb, while with the addition of an 'a', it is also an adjective. It has found a place in English in the word 'cack-handed', even although the Concise Oxford does not get the etymology quite right. Being much more commonly used in Gaelic than in Scots ('Ith mo chac' is a favourite curse of the travelling fraternity – 'Eat my cack'), one assumes that it was adopted by Scots from Gaelic; although, of course, the ultimate derivation is Latin, *cacare*, to defecate. How many politicians when calling their opponents 'cack-handed' realise what they are literally saying?

Individual word problems. All readers and students of Scots will be well aware what a pithy, terse language it is, and how economical it is in the use of words, especially in poetry, and that many of the words are themselves short and even stark. Now Gaelic words tend to be longer, and idiomatic construction, as in French (*est-ce que vous êtes fatigués?*), by comparison, longer still. This creates an obvious problem but, conversely, an advantage. In a given instance, it becomes obvious to the translator that he cannot possibly get all the five adjectives in the original into the one line; so – he can choose which four to pick out of the five, and omit the one for which there is no exact Gaelic equivalent. (Remember the translator is not a mere translator – he is also an interpreter of poetry.)

A good example of this occurs in 'The Rights of Woman', where, in one line, we have no fewer than seven nouns strung together: '*smiles, glances, sighs, tears, fits, flirtations, airs*'. To get seven nouns compressed within ten syllables is a feat in itself, and to get them to fit into a rhythmic pattern, an achievement daunting in the extreme. The best that the Gaelic translator (this one anyway) can make of it is: '*Gaire is sealladh, aogas, osna, deoir*'. As will be seen, the score is 5 out of 7!

Place-names. Fitting the Ayrshire, Dumfries-shire, and Borders placenames into a Gaelic translation constitutes another problem – sometimes, again, an opportunity. And in the Election Ballads, and other works with frequent references to local lairds, the man is often named after the estate. I take four common place-names at random: *Shanter, Mauchline, Kilmarnock*, and *Boghead*. I consult Nicolaisen's 'Scottish Place-Names',[3] and find no reference at all to 3 of them, and only a partial reference in the case of Kilmarnock.

Some names, for which a Gaelic form would be either impossible or ridiculous, have sadly to be absorbed as they stand; but the translator decides that none of these four come into that category. So, in view of the paucity of material easily available, he has to *improvise*, and trust that his informed guess is on or near the mark, and acceptable to his readers.

'*Shanter*', no doubt the name of Tam's farm, is obviously Gaelic. The 'ter' must be 'tir', 'land'. 'Shan' could be 'seann', 'old', which seems unlikely, or 'sian' ('weather or storm'), which seems much more likely, or yet again 'seun' ('has to do with charms and enchantments'), which seems so appropriate to the story that we are tempted to plump for it, probably wrongly! The translator is happy to leave it at 'Sian-tir', or, in the genitive 'Tomas Shian-tir'.

'*Mauchline*' also calls for some choice between competing possibilities. It being obviously Gaelic in origin, the translator is content with 'magh' ('field' or 'plain') + 'lin', genitive of 'lion', 'flax' or 'linen'. So the Gaelic form favoured is Maghlinn.

'*Kilmarnock*' is easier, 'Kil' being the Gaelic 'cille', Latin 'cellum', 'cell' or 'church' + the Saint's name, which in Gaelic would be Màrnag, but in the genitive, as here, Cille-Mhàrnaig.

'*Ceann-Bog*' for '*Boghead*' is a tongue-in-cheek choice (meaning 'Soft Head'), but it does have the virtue of being pure Gaelic, and fitting into the rhythm. After all, even a Gaelic translator must have some fun sometime!

Other place-names which deserve attention are: *Cumnock* (Cam Chnoc) 'squint hill'; *Sannock* (Sannag) 'pertaining to Hallow-tide'; *Garpal* (Garbh Pholl) 'rough peatland'; *Sanquhar* (Seann Chathair) 'old fort'; *Dumfries* (Dun Phreas) 'fort, or mound, of bushes'; *Ecclefechan* (Eaglais Fichein) 'the church of Fichin' (thought to have been an abbot); *Kirkconnel* is a dedication to St Conval.

Constructions

Given that Gaelic was not long dead in Ayrshire when Burns wrote (William Neil[4] has demonstrated that the last native speaker died the year after Burns was born), we might expect some Gaelic idioms to appear in his poetry; it may surprise us to find there are few, if any. What we do find examples of are Gaelic usages and constructions. We may pick out a few examples from Mackay's glossary:

'*Deil a*', '*Deil na*', and '*Deil nor*' constitute a group of three phrases with the same meaning, 'not a' or strong negative. This corresponds very closely with the Gaelic usage, e.g. Chan eil an Diabhal sgillinn agam'. (Literally – 'I have not got the Deil of a penny'.)

'*Feint a*' is also given as a strong negative, 'feint' presumably being another form of 'fiend', for which the Gaelic word is 'deamhain', which is used in exactly the same way.

Some may find it surprising that 'mercies' means 'liquor', but this is also a common Gaelic usage, the exact word being 'tròcairean'. We are reminded of the famous grace after meat ending –

> Let Meg now take away the flesh,
> And Jack bring in the spirit.

This compares with John McCodrum's equally famous grace at Loch Hastin in North Uist when the Loch was being drained, on being given a glass of whisky with the toast 'Uisge Loch Hastainn' (Loch Hastin water):[5]

> 'Gum beannaicheadh Dia uisge Loch Hastainn
> Ma's math ailleadh, 's fhearr a bhlas
> Is ma tha e mar seo gu leir,
> Bu mhor am beud a leigeil as.'

> 'God bless the water of Loch Hastin,
> If its scent is good, its taste is even better
> And if it is all like this,
> It were a great loss to let it go.'

It is, then, the *construction* of Burns's poetry, rather than idiom or usage, which points up the Gaelic connection – and this is a great help to the translator. What it means is that in perhaps 95% of cases, each line translates into the corresponding line in Gaelic. We may illustrate this by reference to the Gaelic translation of verse 2 of 'A Drunk Man looks at the Thistle' –

> Tha 'n uilinn a' dol cugalach tre thim,
> Caol-duirn chan eil cho supailt 's a bha

> An sgornan 'call a mhothachaidh 's gu fior
> Tha meall an sgòrnain fhein gle mhall a' fàs.

To coin a phrase, MacDiarmid's Scots is, I would suggest, much less 'Gaelic-friendly' than Burns's. And, of course, this is also true of Burns's own English poems, which are the least satisfactory in translation; as also, I believe, in the original.

Religious Language. It has often been noted how religious references unexpectedly creep into Burns's poetry, as, for example, in 'Corn Rigs'. But in some, as in 'The Cotter's Saturday Night', he shows a wide-ranging knowledge of the Bible, from Abraham, Moses, Amalek, David (the 'Royal Bard'), Job, Isaiah, and the other holy seers; and about each one named he makes appropriate comment.

One of the charming features of popular Gaelic love-songs is how artlessly the song-writer with gentle irony often brings in a snatch of a 'religious' theme. In one such song, the singer, the girl awaiting her lover's arrival, hints that the best time to sneak into the house is when the family are all kneeling down for the prayer at evening worship – when, presumably, their eyes would be *shut* as well! And how idiomatic! – 'Ged a bhiodh m'athair air an urnaigh, dheid-headh tu ann an cùil am falach'. (Literally, 'Although my father should be *on the prayer*, you would go to hide in a corner'.)

Bawdry. A very different – but equally interesting – aspect of Burns's poetry is the bawdry. In Burns, as in real life, these two aspects set off, each the other. Some of these songs are really hot stuff, and I understand that one of the songs sung by Jean Redpath on the excellent LP series of Burns, in conjunction with the late Serge Hovey, has been 'banned' by a Scottish radio station. Frankly, I am not surprised!

A glance at Mackay's glossary shows how many words are employed by the Bard for 'fornication' or sexual intercourse (at the last count I found over 20!) – and one wonders how many of these associations were invented by himself. There are probably euphemisms for these terms in every language.

'Houghmagandie' is one of Burns's favourite words – and one of the most graphic. I don't suppose he invented it, but it was very useful to have such a word which could mean anything – and yet everyone knew what he meant by it. In Gaelic, the corresponding word is 'horogheallaidh' which also, if you will pardon the expression, covers a multitude of sins! But I have heard a fairly straight-laced minister using it not disapprovingly in the pulpit in the sense of innocent conviviality!

Other well-known phrases are: (my own all-time favourite) 'The Reel o Stumpie', which I think is a marvellously subtle piece, whose subtlety has eluded some of the commentators! – and also 'lawless leg'. Such phrases do present difficulties to the translator, for though we Gaels are reputed to have more words for 'love' than any other language, they are of a more exalted nature than Burns's collection! Even to translate the 'lawless leg' verse from

'Holy Willie's Prayer' presented problems; and it is only since my book was published that I have found a form of words to satisfy myself – which I now give for the record:

> Is aithne dhuit le Meg a raoir –
> Mathanas iarram ort gun fhoill –
> 'S na biodh e na phlaigh, mar thoill,
> 'Toirt dhomh eas-onair!
> Is sliasaid neoghlaine a chaoidh
> Cha tog mi oirre.

Cadences. I have gradually come to the conclusion that cadences are at least as important as any of the other criteria by which poetry translation is to be judged. This is particularly true of the songs, of which I have already said that rhyme and rhythm are both essential for 'singability'. There is nothing more satisfying to the translator – as to any song-writer – than to hear his work sung beautifully by a talented and intelligent singer, with an appreciative audience showing their approval. But in the case of the very best known and loved of the songs, the singer and the audience have to be 'tempted' with cadences as well as rhythm and rhyme. This applies particularly to those lines and phrases which are repeated in refrain, and have acquired a particularly 'hallowed' status – the 'sheet-anchor' of the song, one might almost say.

An obvious example is 'For a' that', translated as 'Air sgàth sin'; in both cases, two short vowels, or syllables, with a long one between, and the long 'aw' of the original matched by the long 'a' of the Gaelic.

The translator wishes he had found as happy a union of cadences in all the songs as he thinks he has found in the last verse of this one:

> 'N sin guidheamaid gun tig an làth,
> Is thig na thràth, air sgath sin,
> San rioghaich anns an talamh làn
> Tuigse is àgh, air sgath sin,
> Air sgàth sin, air sgàth sin;
> A' teachd tha 'n làth, air sgàth sin,
> San còmhlaich fear le fear an gràdh,
> Mar bhraithrean bàigh, air sgàth sin.

NOTES

1. Not in Kinsley but see Mackay, *Collected Works*, 1968, p. 615.
2. Poem on page 44 of bound volume, verse 4.
3. Batsford, 1976.
4. Paper on survival of Gaelic in Galloway and Ayrshire, not yet published.
5. *Uist Bards*, edited by Archibald Macdonald, 1984, p. xxix.

From Mrs Dunlop to the Currie
Edition: the Missing Links

THE FIRST VOLUME of James Currie's edition of *The Works of Robert Burns* begins with a lengthy dedication to Captain Graham Moore of the Royal Navy, one who, Currie says, 'first recommended to my particular notice the poems of the Ayrshire ploughman'. He seems an odd nominee, not a person of rank nor a figure of cultural eminence. Yet Currie paid him an unusually high compliment when he said, 'On the land or on the sea, I know no man more capable of judging of the character or of the writings of this original genius'.[1]

Who was this person, and how particularly did he figure in Currie's involvement with one of Scotland's great poets? His role in this edition is not entirely evident.

Robert Thornton has provided us with an account of how Currie in Liverpool came to put together this significant edition of Burns's poems and letters. The project was conceived originally by friends of Burns in Dumfries as the second of two benefits on behalf of the poet's widow and children. As soon as Currie was informed of their plans, he responded with encouragement and began a charitable drive within his circle in Liverpool. As for the edition he advised Syme that it should include some sort of 'authorized' biography to lay to rest any false or exaggerated conceptions regarding the poet's character (about which he had heard many rumors), and prevent anyone with inadequate knowledge of Burns from rushing into print with a shallow or biased account. In his letter of 15 August 1796, Currie expressed his assumption that the people in Dumfries already had someone in mind, and he offered on behalf of the author William Roscoe and himself any assistance in completing this project. But he added that if there were no one else, he might do this project himself. (One infers that Currie had no burning desire to turn biographer; he just felt strongly that the project needed done.) Syme, we are told, recognized at once that Currie was more qualified for the task than anyone else at hand, and made him the offer. At first Currie declined; in mid-September he accepted.[2] From that point he became fair absorbed in the search for letters, unpublished poems, and other materials. Chief among his pursuits was Dr John Moore in London, who he knew possessed Burns's famous autobiographical letter of 2 August, 1787.

How did he know this? Indeed, one might ask how Currie became so interested in Burns in the first place, long before he became involved in the heavy task of preparing Burns's work for the press? The dedication to Graham Moore should be accepted as part of the entire 'text' of the Currie edition since this essay will serve as an introduction to the dedicatee, but first we need to establish the connection between Mrs. Dunlop and James Currie to explain how Currie became interested in Burns originally, and where Graham Moore fits in.

If a chain of circumstances that led to the edition of 1800 ends with Currie, it begins with Mrs. Dunlop and her husband John Dunlop of Dunlop, especially with the friendship between her husband and family of the above-mentioned John Moore. The beginning of this relationship cannot be precisely dated, but John Dunlop came from one of many families of that name living in Glasgow, making their way as 'merchants' and overseas traders in that city.[3] Dunlop and John Moore were hardly contemporaries; the former was twenty-two years his senior. The older man was born in Glasgow in 1707, the son of Francis Dunlop of Dunlop and his wife Susanna Leckie. The marriage to a Leckie suggests a stronger, longer-standing relationship between the Dunlops and the Moores, since one of the witnesses at the baptism of this infant heir to the Dunlop name and estate in Ayrshire was one of the great Glasgow merchants of the latter half of the seventeenth century, John Anderson the Younger of Dowhill (1636–1710), who was about seventy years old at the time. Anderson was great-grandfather on the maternal side to John Dunlop; he was also John Moore's maternal grandfather. This means that though John Dunlop was a generation older than Moore, he was Moore's first cousin once-removed. Dunlop and Moore's mother were virtually the same age.[4] So there was kinship and friendship between Moore's mother and Dunlop when young John Moore began practice in 1750, and Dunlop had been recently married to a woman twenty-three years younger than he, Frances Anna Wallace. Moore and she ('Mrs. Dunlop') were just five months apart in age.[5] Mrs. Dunlop told Burns that

> The doctor and I ... were friends half a dozen years before you saw the light – I do not mean of the Muses, but of Apollo himself. It was even some years before that period he brought me his bride that I might join their hands before the priest. When they lost their children 'twas me shared and dryed their mutual tears. I esteem her above all the women I ever knew, and like her almost as much as I do her husband. While they were in Scotland we lived in the happiest intercourse. It sweetens the very hope of heaven to think we shall there renew it.[6]

Both Frances Dunlop and Jean Simson produced large families in time. One of Moore's sons, the fourth, was named Francis, and since there is no other of that name in either Moore's family or his wife's, one cannot avoid the conclusion that he was named after his female friend.[7] In 1761 Mrs. Dunlop inherited the estate of Loch Ryan on the western coast in Wigtownshire upon the death of her mother. This became a favorite vacation resort of her family in summer. Moore's wife and daughter were often invited to join them.

The relationship was interrupted to some extent in 1772 when Moore accepted the position as foreign tutor to the Duke of Hamilton; he and his charge were abroad five years. Upon his return in early 1777, Moore made plans to leave off practice for good and move his family to London. Mrs. Dunlop's letters to Burns imply that Moore and she remained fairly regular correspondents after this decisive break. The family connection continued in the sons of both families who made careers together in the military. This is simply to show that while Moore seems to be a sidelight to the relationship between Mrs. Dunlop and Burns, he and his family were very much a part of Mrs. Dunlop's life even though he had moved to London. And she saw him as an equally important part of her relationship with Burns.

It is well-known that after the death of her husband in 1785, Frances Dunlop fell ill and became very depressed. Stationed in the Irish Sea and on the lookout for smugglers, Moore's son Graham took shore leave in July 1786, to seek her out and comfort her. Then late in 1786 some unknown friend placed in her hands a copy of the Kilmarnock edition of Burns's poems, published that summer. Reading over the poems, especially 'The Cotter's Saturday Night,' revived her spirits, and she resolved to obtain more copies of this work and make the acquaintance of its author, especially since he hailed from the same district. (He lived only fifteen miles away.) Once she obtained these extra copies and a written response from Burns, she sent a copy express to Moore in London. Moore was quite excited with what he had, and began to read aloud from the book to his London friends – to Helen Maria Williams, Mrs. Barbauld, to the Locks of Norbury Park, and to the Earl and Countess of Eglinton – glossing the vernacular for those who could not follow. Meanwhile, Mrs. Dunlop replied to Burns, indicating that Moore had just written to her about the volume, and the famous relationship between these two most unlike persons got under way. As part of her many advices to Burns she urged him to write to Moore to explain the subscription of the forthcoming Edinburgh edition and to acknowledge his interest in Burns's work.[8] This supplementary correspondence began with Burns's letter to Moore 17 January and Moore's almost immediate reply, which led to the exchange of letters wherein Moore commented on Burns's work thus far and suggested more attention to poems in English and a different 'voice' and 'identity' as northern poet, a constant concern for Burns.[9]

Moore shared the Kilmarnock edition with his wife and children. To Burns he wrote 28 February, 'You are a very great favorite in my family; and that is a higher compliment than perhaps you are aware of. [My family] includes almost all of the professions, and of course is a proof that your writings are adapted to various tastes and situations.' Moore's youngest son, Charles, a pupil at Winchester, had tried his hand at translating some stanzas of 'Hallowe'en' into Latin.[10] Presumably Graham Moore, on duty in the Irish Sea, had also seen some of the poems.

The Edinburgh edition was published 21 April. Mrs. Dunlop sent £15 for forty-five copies, five of which were designated for the Moores in London and six to Moore's brother-in-law, George Macintosh. One of the London copies was sent to Graham.

Graham, born 1764 in Glasgow, was the third of Moore's sons to reach adulthood. Like his older brother Jack ('Sir John'), Graham achieved distinction in military service, obtaining a commission when he was only thirteen. He was promoted commander in 1791; in 1795 he sailed, in the *Melampus*, in the fleet under the flag of Sir Richard Strahan that participated in the blockade of France from 1795 to 1798. In 1800 he saw action in the West Indies but returned home in the following year so ill and emaciated that he almost preceded his father in death. By this time he had captured so many prize ships that he had become wealthy. In 1803 he sailed under Cornwallis; in 1811 he was promoted to Rear Admiral. In 1815 he was knighted; in 1819 he had command in the Mediterranean. Besides correspondence, the principal record of his life is his unpublished diary of thirty-four volumes, now in the library of Cambridge University.[11]

What was he really like, this early enthusiast of the poetry of Robert Burns?

The more we read of him, the less likely a sailor he seems to be. When he was a lad first off to sea, his father said of him, 'He might have been a Scholar for he was well advanced for his age, but he preferred Salt Pork & Pease Pudding to the Castalian streams'.[12] Indeed there ran in the family a general assumption that of all of Moore's sons Graham was the most likely candidate for a professor's chair because as a child he was such an avid reader. Moreover, there always seemed something self-indulgent about him, from his portrait that highlights his dark hair, his shining white teeth, and his huge, innocent eyes,[13] to the youthful effusions recorded in the journal he kept aboard ship. In his twenties he was still studying the classics of the Glasgow schoolboys, the Latin of Tacitus and the plays of Shakespeare, and writing down the speeches and passages that stirred him most. He copied passages not only from Shakespeare, but from poets like Gray, Collins, MacPherson's Ossian, Beattie, and lesser poets like William Roscoe. His decidedly 'romantic' taste can be further measured by his admiration for the work of the Swiss painter Henry Fuseli (1741–1825), a frequent visitor to his father's house. 'I sat about three hours yesterday with Fuseli the painter,' he noted in 1797; 'I know no man whose conversation is so much to my taste as that of Fuseli; it is full of grandeur and sublimity. With regard to his works, they interest me more than those of any other Painter that ever I have seen ... Not being a judge of the art, but being strongly attracted by the terrible, the sketches of Fuseli please me more than the finished Paintings ...' To Currie he said, 'As Hume said of Montrose, something of the vast and unbounded characterize [Fuseli] ... I ... am afraid to speak my sentiments on his works, but they amuse and interest me like reading Milton and Ossian.'[14]

Sometimes it is difficult to tell whether Graham is romantic and typical of many youthful contemporaries of developed sensibility, or whether he is excessively sentimental and prone to love.[15] Having so much time on his hands at sea, he had ample opportunity to indulge all these ecstasies of mind. For several years he nurtured a secret passion for Amelia Lock (1776–1848), younger daughter of his father's close friend, William Lock of Norbury Park. Whenever he had some time off in London, he accompanied his father to Norbury where he felt warmly welcomed, because he was a good friend of the elder son, William; at the same time the *elder* daughter, Augusta, cherished toward him an undeclared attachment. A published history of this interesting Surrey family expresses some puzzlement that Graham and Augusta never made a match,[16] but Graham's journal reveals the truth – that he had held off any clarifying declaration to the daughter he really loved because he felt he was in no position to marry. The war was on, and he believed he would not be able to support her until he had earned about £10,000 in ship-prize money. In 1799, when it was rumored that she was about to become engaged, he was obliged to declare his feelings. It was too late. Graham was profoundly broken-hearted and bitter, as one can well imagine who has read his journal; he felt 'stupified' by his rejection, 'unworthily used,' adding that he felt he would never get over this as long as he lived. He added, as salve to his injured pride, that he doubted whether she truly loved her fiancé, an heir to immense wealth; at any rate, her marriage 'levels her in my opinion with the common run of women'.[17]

Graham was thirty-four when this occurred; he eventually married, but not until he was forty-eight.

What I have been describing is something of the emotional profile of an enthusiast of the poetry of Robert Burns. Yet his interest in Burns grew out of a soil that was fertile with particularly Scottish enthusiasms. This can be discerned in both his letters to Currie and his journal entries. In great part his family had severed its Scottish roots and made themselves English, a late manifestation of the Scottish brain-drain that coincided with the early stage of the Scottish Enlightenment. I would not qualify the enthusiasm and appreciation Graham Moore and Currie shared for the poetry of Burns, but only observe that both men seem, in their circumstances – both living out of their native land – to be particularly susceptible to what we might call the 'sentiment of the expatriate,' that made them especially responsive to a new poet from their homeland. Whereas his father, on account of his travels, had become more European in his outlook and took an enthusiastic interest in the French Revolution, Graham hated the French, especially after 1789.

No one in the family more then Graham maintained such strongly Scottish prejudices. This can be seen in many instances. Besides his love of the Ossianic material, he told Currie, 'I love the name of Wallace, he was the Hero of my childhood and boyish days ... I need not mention James Graham the gallant Montrose,[18] that eternal stain to our country, which was not worthy of

producing him'.[19] Whenever he heard a piper, he was carried away by national-
istic sentiments.[20] He felt a special bond with the commander of his fleet, Sir
Richard Strahan, because

> he is of Scottish descent and you [know?] that altho I am not illiberal or
> narrow minded[,] that I give willingly into certain original prejudices which
> I think a man the better for—id est, I am a little national—[...] yet as I have
> somewhat of Romance in my taste, if not in my judgement, I set a value on
> the train of ideas which these delusions draw up along with them.[21]

But nowhere does his prejudice show so clearly as in an incident involving
Lady Susan Gordon, the Duchess of Manchester, whom Graham encountered
aboard her husband's yacht in Liverpool in 1796.

> There is a feeling towards Scotland and what is Scotch in me that is productive
> of much pleasure, and of a consequent painful sensation when the persons
> or circumstances which are shared with them either cease to exist or are
> removed from me. The Duchess is not a beauty, but she interested me
> exceedingly by her native pronounciation, her frankness, her open counten-
> ance, and, above all, by her taste for Scotch music, and her universal and
> particular acquaintance with all the genuine songs of that country, numerous
> as they are ... How often have I been the dupe of this heart of mine! There
> is no love in this case, it is only friendship.
> It is a curious thing that I should be deranged at parting with these people
> in the yacht, not one of whom, I believe, cares two pence about me, now
> that I am out of sight. It is a string of ideas with which they form a part
> that endears them to me; partly the family of Lock, my brother Frank, and
> Scotland; my mind finds food and I draw pleasure from the states of Memory
> ... I could walk and talk with that home bred Duchess and lose the reckoning
> of time. She is full of my prejudices, and has all my tastes.[22]

We are not too far from words like these: 'There is scarcely any thing to which
I am so feelingly alive as the honor and welfare of old Scotia; and, as a Poet,
I have no higher enjoyment than singing her Sons and Daughters.' This is Burns
to the Earl of Eglinton.[23] This brings us to Burns and Currie.

Stationed in the Irish Sea, on the lookout for smugglers, Graham got ashore
on many occasions. In 1785 he visited Liverpool frequently and got to know
quite a number of interesting persons, including two young women he took a
liking to.

This is the same time that Graham first met Currie. Noting with satisfaction
that his new friend was a 'countryman of mine', Graham recorded that 'in this
gentleman's society I spent many an agreeable and instructive evening. His wife
is a very pretty and amiable woman. Currie is a man of a delicate constitution,
but a strong and vigorous mind. I used to go there generally on Sunday to
sup'.[24] He was invited back after the Christmas holiday. Later he observed that

Currie 'was a man whose friendship I am proud of, and I think the advice his letters afford me may be beneficial to me'.

In June of the following year, after Moore and his children had become so interested in the Kilmarnock edition, Graham requested that his father send a copy to Currie. The doctor in Liverpool was delighted, especially because the volume had come from Moore. 'Such a present from such a man is doubly valuable', he told Graham. He was very enthusiastic about what he read:

> The poems of Burns have certainly great merit. An original poet, which he may be called, is most highly welcome to every man of taste and feeling, after the disgust which arises from listening to a long succession of copyers of copyers ... This west-country poet (the first, I believe, which that psalm-singing region has produced,) has that admirable simplicity which is the attribute of true genius. His thoughts are natural, and flow easily; and by turns he is humorous, pathetic, and sublime ... I agree with you that Burns ought to keep clear of politics, and we may add religion, which, from its very nature, cannot be made the vehicle of good poetry ...'[25]

Thus began Currie's interest in Robert Burns. I have no doubt that they frequently spoke of Burns when they were together. The two men continued to comment on Burns's poetry in their letters, but not constantly; much of their correspondence in 1788 dealt with the controversy over the slave trade. In 1789, Currie proudly wrote that he had received two poems by Burns in manuscript from a young man just come down from Ayrshire; Graham replied that Burns had sent copies of the same to his father, adding significantly, that Burns and his father maintained a correspondence. This is the first mention, it would seem, of a potential source of primary material for anyone editing a posthumous edition of the poet's work.

Not much further comment passed in correspondence between these two enthusiasts about Burns until after the poet's unfortunate death. Graham happened to read an account of the poet that interested him 'exceedingly,' though it bothered him as well. He complained to Currie about 'the Bodies in Scotland treating Burns as they did – making a Gauger[26] of him, and fostering nothing in him but his faults. I rank him with Collins in the sublime; and I do not know who to compare him with in the comic'.[27] Currie replied at great length (and I will quote only in part):

> I observe what you Say of Burns – He was a genius of the first order, and died under the pressure of his own sensibilities. I have seen his form & countenance[28] which indicated his mind: erect, daring & heroic. He had a cast of wildness in his face, which had a most interesting effect, especially when lighted up by his genius, or softened by his sensibilities. His penetration into character exceeded that of any man of the present day, and so did the strength of his judgment – so also did the strength of his passions – and the strength of his benevolence. He was greater than Fuseli, great as he is; and

his Countenance excelled even the sublimity of Fuseli. What more can be said? [29]

By this time Currie had committed himself to the task of writing the 'authorized' memoir of Burns and editing the posthumous edition of his poems and letters. Taking a cue from what Graham had told him, Currie sent his friend William Roscoe to London later this month to ask Moore what he had of Burns's letters. Moore generously showed Roscoe 'Letters, papers, & poems' that he had in manuscript from Burns; this included the valuable biographical letter of 2 August, 1787. All in all, Moore gave Currie eight letters. Only some of these have survived.

When Graham received Currie's dedication to him, needless to say, he was moved. 'Nothing could be more flattering to my vanity and so soothing to my breast than the most unlooked for compliment you have paid me in this dedication of such a work to your undeserving friend.' For Currie had written, in words that recall Graham's sensitive temperament, his love of his native land, and the valuable friendship that supported him during his depressed spirits after the rejection by the woman he loved:

> The works of Burns will be received favorably by one who stands in the foremost rank of this noble service, and who deserves his station. On the land or on the sea, I know no man more capable of judging of the character or of the writings of this original genius. Homer, and Shakespeare, and Ossian, cannot always occupy your leisure. These volumes may sometimes engage your attention, while the steady breezes of the tropics swell your sails, and in another quarter of the earth charm you with the strains of nature, or awake in your memory the scenes of your early days. Suffer me to hope that they may recall to your mind the friend that addresses you, and who bids you ⇀ most affectionately – adieu! [30]

NOTES

1. *The Works of Robert Burns*, 4 vols, edited by James Currie, 2nd edn (London, 1801), I, v.
2. The foregoing account is taken mostly from Robert Thornton's *James Currie, the Entire Stranger* (Edinburgh, 1963), chapter 12; see also Carol McGuirk, 'The Politics of *The Collected Burns*,' *Gairfish* (1991), pp. 36–50.
3. Besides the Dunlops of that Ilk, there were the Dunlops of Carmyle, of Craigton, of Garnkirk, and of Tollcross – all cadets of the original family.
4. Anderson had female issue by two wives. Dunlop's grandmother, Susanna Anderson, and Moore's mother, Marion Anderson, were half-sisters. See Charles Rogers, *The Book of Robert Burns*, 3 vols (Edinburgh, 1889), I, 187; James Paterson, *History of the Counties of Ayr and Wigton*, 3 vols (Edinburgh, 1863–66), III, 231; and George Macintosh, *A Memoir of Charles Macintosh, F.R.S* (Glasgow, 1847), pp. 172–73.

5. Moore was born 29 November, 1729; Mrs. Dunlop was born 16 April, 1730. See also William Wallace, *Robert Burns and Mrs. Dunlop*, 2 vols (New York, 1898), I, 49.

6. Wallace, *Robert Burns and Mrs. Dunlop*, I, 49–50. The marriage is registered in Glasgow for 16 June, 1754 (Parochial Registers, Co. of Lanark, Glasgow 6441/25), but its actual location is indicated in notes in the Book of Knights, Order of the Bath, V, 75 (College of Heralds, London), which was copied from the Bible Marion Anderson gave her eldest son, Sir John Moore, in 1770 (now in the possession of Anthony Heath, Putney).

7. Francis Moore (1767–1854), another of Moore's sons to distinguish himself, found employment as a clerk in the Foreign Office in 1784 through the patronage of Moore's friend, the Duchess of Devonshire. He participated in negotiations with Paris before war was declared in 1793 and advanced to be Deputy Secretary of War from 1803 to 1809. After the death of his wife, he retired to southern France and died on the island of Ischia (*Gentleman's Magazine*, 1854, ii, 410).

8. Wallace, I, 6 and 9.

9. See Kenneth Simpson, *The Protean Scot: The Crisis of Identity in Eighteenth Century Scottish Literature* (Aberdeen, 1988), the chapter on Burns.

10. Robert Chambers, *The Life and Work of Robert Burns*, rev. William Wallace, 4 vols (Edinburgh, 1896), II, 56.

11. Nearly every volume of this long journal has been mutilated with scissors, especially where he discusses family and very personal concerns, but it is still a helpful account of his states of mind.

12. Moore to Alexander Mure, 25 Dec. 1777 (NLS MSS. 4946, f. 271). Cited with permission.

13. I am referring to the portrait by Sir Thomas Lawrence, painted in 1792, and now hanging in the National Portrait Gallery.

14. Journal, vol. IX (20 Mar. 1797); and GM to Currie, 19 Jan. 1797 (National Library of Ireland MSS. 10975, #13). Both cited with permission.

15. Professor Carol McGuirk has suggested to me that Graham Moore seems a real-life version of Jane Austen's Captain Benwick in *Persuasion*. He certainly has the same taste, and he lived under very similar circumstances.

16. The Duchess of Sermoneta, *The Locks of Norbury Park* (London, 1940), p. 241.

17. Journal, vol. XI (19 July 1799). Her fiancé was John Angerstein (c. 1774–1858), eldest son and heir to the financier John Julius Angerstein. The Locks and Moores had known the Angersteins for more than a decade.

18. After whom he may well have been named.

19. GM to Currie, 27 Sept. 1795 (NLI MSS. 10975, #10).

20. Journal, vol. VIII (16 Nov. 1796).

21. GM to Currie, 19 Jan. 1797.

22. Journal, vol. IX (19 Aug. 1796). Graham added that the Duke of Manchester 'is perhaps the handsomest man in England now that the Duke of Hamilton's day is over. – I think his wife and he are extremely well together, but there seems a want of attention to each other on both sides.' He was prophetic. Manchester had a very successful political career, but after seven children his wife and he were eventually separated.

23. Cited in Simpson, *The Protean Scot*, p. 210.

24. Journal, vol. III (Nov. 1786).
25. Currie to GM, 11 June 1787 (Cowie Collection, Mitchell Public Library; reprinted W. W. Currie (ed.), *Memoir of the Life and Correspondence of James Currie*, 2 vols [London, 1831], II, 99).
26. 'One who is ever looking after his own interests' (*Chambers Scots Dictionary*, p. 205b); 'an exciseman' (*The Concise Scots Dictionary*, p. 227b).
27. GM to Currie, 17 Jan. 1797.
28. Currie visited Burns in Dumfries May, 1792 (Thornton, p. 282).
29. Currie to GM, 2 Feb. 1797 (Cowie Collection). Cited with permission.
30. GM to Currie, 6 Nov. 1800 (Cowie Collection); and *The Works of Robert Burns*, I, v.

Robert Burns, Patriot

IT IS DIFFICULT to speak about patriotism in this cynical age. We all instinct-
ively remember that Samuel Johnson said that it was the last refuge of a
scoundrel. Boswell's explanation when he recorded this is less familiar. Johnson,
he says, 'did not mean a real and generous love of our country, but that
pretended patriotism which so many, in all ages and countries, have made a
cloak for self-interest'.[1] A 'real and generous', and I should add passionate, love
for Scotland is a good description of a feeling and conviction which Burns
clearly and repeatedly revealed in his writing, both in verse and prose.

Burns himself tells us how he thought it began. In his famous autobiographical
letter to Dr. John Moore on 2 August 1787 he said: 'the story of Wallace poured
a Scottish prejudice in my veins which will boil along there till the flood-gates
of life shut in eternal rest'. Thomas Carlyle said that Burns was too modest
when he called his 'deep and generous' patriotism a prejudice. And he added:

> We hope, there is patriotism founded on something better than prejudice;
> that our country may be dear to us, without injury to our philosophy; that
> in loving and justly prizing all other lands, we may prize justly, and yet love
> before all others, our own stern Motherland … Certainly in no heart did
> the love of country ever burn with warmer glow than in that of Burns.[2]

Carlyle was right. In this sense, Burns was a patriot, or, if you prefer, a nation-
alist, especially because he deeply resented Scotland's loss of independence.

Consistently with this, Burns revered Wallace as our great national hero.
One of the reasons why he corresponded so eagerly with Mrs Dunlop was that
she claimed descent from his family. In his first letter to her on 15 November
1786 he referred to Wallace as her 'illustrious Ancestor, the SAVIOUR OF HIS
COUNTRY.' He said that he had walked to the Leglen wood, which was associ-
ated with Wallace, 'with as much devout enthusiasm as ever Pilgrim did to
Lorreto' and that his 'heart glowed with a wish to be able to make a Song
equal to his merits.' He used similar language many times in his letters and
poems, as in the 'Epistle to William Simpson':

> At Wallace' name, what Scottish blood,
> But boils up in a spring-tide flood!
> Oft have our fearless fathers strode
>   By Wallace' side,
> Still pressing onward, red-wat-shod,
>   Or glorious dy'd!

If Burns placed Wallace first, no doubt because of his humbler origin, uncompromising patriotism and dreadful end, he also held Bruce in high regard. He refers to both of them in a letter to Robert Muir on 26 August 1787, where he describes the first day of his tour to the Highlands:

> This morning I kneel'd at the tomb of Sir John the Graham, the gallant friend of the immortal WALLACE; and two hours ago, I said a fervent prayer for Old Caledonia over the whole in a blue whin-stone, where Robert de Bruce fixed his royal Standard on the banks of Bannockburn.

Burns's diaries of his Border and Highland tours consist mostly of very brief notes, but his entry about this event is passionate. He imagines his 'heroic countrymen' approaching 'the oppressive, insulting, blood-thirsty foe,' and 'gloriously triumphant, exulting in their heroic royal leader and rescued liberty and independence.'

These thoughts on the field of Bannockburn immediately suggest the words of 'Scots Wha Hae', although the song was not written until sixteen years later on about 30 August 1793. He describes the circumstances in a letter to George Thomson, where he refers to the old air, 'Hey Tuttie Taitie' and then says:

> There is a tradition, which I have met with in many places of Scotland, that it was Robert Bruce's March at the battle of Bannock-burn. – This thought, in my yesternight's evening walk, warmed me to a pitch of enthusiasm on the theme of Liberty and Independance, which I threw into a kind of Scots Ode, fitted to the Air, that one might suppose to be the gallant ROYAL SCOT's address to his heroic followers on that eventful morning.

At the end of the song he wrote: 'So may God ever defend the cause of Truth and Liberty, as he did that day! Amen!' There is a further postscript to the letter: 'the accidental recollection of that glorious struggle for Freedom, associated with the glowing ideas of some other struggles of the same nature, *not quite so ancient*, roused my rhyming mania.'

What were these other struggles? Burns may have been thinking generally of French revolutionary ideas, but there was another event much nearer home and of a precise coincidence of date. On the same 30 August the trial of Thomas Muir of Huntershill for sedition began in Edinburgh. Muir, who advocated parliamentary reform and Scottish independence, was sentenced to transportation. In 'Scots Wha Hae' therefore, Burns was drawing a parallel between Bruce's struggle for the independence of Scotland and the situation in his own time. Murray Pittock has pointed out that the song also uses Jacobite language. 'For Scotland's King and Law' is a Jacobite phrase, and 'chains and slaverie' could refer to the Jacobite prisoners who had been transported as slaves to the colonies. Pittock says that 'the idea of a heroic, traditional Scotland as having to wage perpetual war against English might and gold in order to secure its very existence was one central to Jacobite images of native heroism.'[3]

Burns himself said in a letter of 15 December 1793 to Mrs Dunlop that he was 'really proud' of 'Scots Wha Hae'. Carlyle, in the essay already quoted, said of it that so long as we have warm blood, 'it will move in fierce thrills under this war-ode; the best ... ever written by any pen.' Tom Crawford described it as 'the noblest of all Burns's national songs' and David Murison as 'a kind of national anthem of a nation that may even yet find the moral courage to sing it'.[4]

It may seem paradoxical that a man of egalitarian spirit like Burns should have looked back nostalgically, not only to Bruce, but to the entire line of the Scottish monarchy. In his 'Address to Edinburgh', for instance:

> Edina! Scotia's darling seat!
> All hail thy palaces and tow'rs,
> Where once beneath a Monarch's feet,
> Sat Legislation's sov'reign pow'rs!

That last line is quite specific. His regret for the loss of the Scottish monarchy is regret for the loss of sovereignty and legislative power. His bitter sense of loss, and his Jacobitism, is even more apparent in the lines 'written on the Window of an Inn in Stirling':

> Here Stewarts once in glory reign'd,
> And laws for Scotland's weal ordain'd;
> ....
> The injur'd Stewart-line are gone,
> A Race outlandish fill their throne:
> An idiot race, to honour lost;
> Who know them best despise them most.

This did not mean that Burns wanted to see a return to arbitrary monarchy. He had a sophisticated sense of historical change. A letter which he sent to the editor of the *Edinburgh Evening Courant* on 8 November 1788 was no doubt written, as David Daiches has said, 'to put himself right with officialdom' and 'free himself to engage with Jacobite song';[5] but it also insisted that past events should not be judged by contemporary standards and that allowances must be made for the circumstances of the time.

Burns had particularly strong feelings about Mary, Queen of Scots, whom he called, in a letter of 25 April 1791 to Lady Winifred Constable, 'our greatly injured, lovely Scottish Queen'. The English Elizabeth, on the other hand, in a letter of 28 February 1791 to John Moore, was 'the infernal Bess Tudor'. Burns's 'Lament of Mary Queen of Scots' is deeply compassionate.

These feelings for the 'injured Stewart line', more, I think, because they were Scottish then because they were royal, were no doubt an element in Burns's Jacobitism; but there were others which were probably even more compelling. George Rosie has drawn attention to a passage in the writings of Hugh Miller where he suggests that Burns was in a state of intellectual confusion in professing both Jacobitism and Jacobinism at the same time.[6] In fact, this combination of ideas was not unusual and was certainly not confined to Burns. There were solid reasons for it. Jacobitism in Scotland was largely a patriotic, nationalist attempt to overthrow the Union. Also, as Murray Pittock has argued, Jacobite and Jacobin shared the view that the Hanoverians had caused 'something rotten in the state of Scotland' and that there was a need to defend traditional values against an oppressor for whom money was all that mattered.[7]

In supporting Jacobitism, Burns knew exactly what he was doing. He did not imagine that a Stewart could be restored to the throne. It was an expression of his detestation of the Union and of the arrogance and corruption of wealth. Walter Scott, who had Jacobite leanings himself, wrote of Burns that 'a youth of his warm imagination and ardent patriotism', brought up at that time could 'hardly escape' Jacobitism.[8] Burns wrote or adapted about 30 Jacobite songs and they include some of his best and most passionate.

Andrew Noble has suggested that Burns's analysis of the Scottish situation is as valid now as it was in his time. In Noble's words, Burns was concerned with 'the corrupting politics and psychology generated by the Union; the degeneration of parliament and other British civic and fiscal institutions, causing increasing disparity between rich and poor'.[9] All of these things are at least as obvious now as they were in the eighteenth century.

There are other ways in which the ideas of Burns are still apposite to our present situation. He wrote in a letter to Mrs Dunlop on 10 April 1790: 'Alas! have I often said to myself, what are all the boasted advantages which my country reaps from a certain Union, that can counterbalance the annihilation of her Independance, and even her very Name!' That is precisely how many of us still feel. The same is true of

> We're bought and sold for English gold,
> Such a parcel of rogues in a nation!

The theme and refrain, Kinsley tells us, were current before Burns made them into a powerful and passionate statement. We find James Boswell, for example, making virtually the same point many years earlier. When he came across a copy of the text of the Declaration of Arbroath in Leipzig in October 1760, he wrote in his Journal:

> I felt true patriot sorrow. O infamous rascals, who sold the honour of your country to a nation against which our ancestors supported themselves with so much glory! ... Alas, poor Scotland.

In the nineteenth century historians, with the honourable exception of Walter Scott, did their best to play down the role of bribery in securing a majority for the Union in the Scottish Parliament. Modern scholarship has proved beyond doubt that Boswell and Burns were right.

Burns's nationalism derived from a deep love of Scotland which he repeatedly expressed. To the Earl of Eglinton, February 1787, for instance: 'There is scarcely anything to which I am so feelingly alive as the honour and welfare of old Scotia.' Mrs Dunlop on 22 March 1787: 'The appelation of, a Scotch Bard, is by far my highest pride; to continue to deserve it is my most exalted ambition. – Scottish scenes, and Scottish story are the themes I could wish to sing.' And in the 'Epistle to the Guidwife of Wauchope-House':

> Ev'n then a wish (I mind its power)
> A wish, that to my latest hour
> Shall strongly heave my breast;
> That I for poor auld Scotland's sake
> Some useful plan, or book could make,
> Or sing a sang at least.

That last statement was not a rhetorical flourish, but a serious declaration of intent. He approached his self-imposed task of collecting, making or amending Scots songs in precisely this spirit. Although pitifully short of money, he refused to take any payment for the work. He wrote to George Thomson, the publisher of the *Select Collection of Scottish Airs* on 16 September 1792:

> As to any remuneration, you may think my Songs either *above*, or *below* price; for they shall absolutely be the one or the other. – In the honest enthusiasm with which I embark in your undertaking, to talk of money, wages, fee, hire &c. would be downright Sodomy of Soul.

He attributed the same patriotic motive to others. When he wrote to Sir John Sinclair in August 1791 about his *Statistical Account*, he called it 'your patriotic publication'. He used the same phrase in a letter to James Johnson on 19 June 1789 about his *Scots Musical Museum*.

In his autobiographical letter to John Moore, Burns said that it was coming across Fergusson's Scotch Poems that he strung his 'wildly-sounding, rustic lyre with emulating vigour'. Both in verse and prose he paid many tributes to Ramsay and Fergusson as his models and inspiration, from the reference to them both in the Preface to the Kilmarnock edition to the inscription which he placed on Fergusson's grave: 'My elder brother in misfortune / By far my elder brother in the muse'. Like Burns, Ramsay and Fergusson wrote in Scots, and, like him again, both were strongly nationalist in feeling and wrote poems against the Union. Does this suggest that writing poetry in Scots was in itself a nationalist act of defiance against the prevailing pressures of Anglicisation?

No doubt Burns wrote in Scots at least partly because it pleased him and came naturally. He wrote to George Thomson on 19 October 1794: 'These English Songs gravel me to death. – I have not that command of the language that I have of my native tongue. – In fact, I think my ideas are more barren in English than in Scotish.' No one can doubt that he was right. On the other hand, he was under pressure from the literary grandees of the time to write in English. Burns often said that Henry Mackenzie was one of his favourite authors and that *The Man of Feeling* was a book which he prized next to the Bible. The same Mackenzie wrote the first review of the Kilmarnock Edition and in it he regretted that Burns wrote in a 'provincial dialect' which was read with difficulty even in Scotland and in England 'cannot be read at all'.[10] Pressure like this could only be resisted by strong conviction.

Burns told George Thomson on 16 September 1792 that he had an 'enthusiastic attachment to the Poetry and Music of old Caledonia'. This was an enthusiasm which he often expressed in his letters and Commonplace Book. He was determined to preserve the melodies of Scottish songs by writing new words where the old ones had been lost, were inadequate, or where only the refrain survived. It was a patriotic labour of love similar in spirit to Walter Scott's collection of the Border Ballads. Burns began to contribute songs to Johnson's *Scots Musical Museum* in November 1787 and to Thomson's *Select Collection of Scottish Airs* in September 1792. He contributed 213 songs to Johnson and 114 to Thomson. With the important exception of 'Tam o' Shanter', this meant that for the last nine years of his life Burns's writing was almost entirely devoted to songs.

There are those who regret this concentration on song and regard it as a degeneration of his powers. In his essay on Burns, Stevenson wrote: 'The man who had written a volume of masterpieces in six months, during the remainder of his life rarely found courage for any more sustained effort than a song.' He went on to speak of a 'loss of moral courage' and said that it was melancholy that 'a hand that seemed capable of moving mountains, should have spent his later years in whittling cherry-stones'. Cedric Thorpe Davie was right, I think, to protest about this attitude.[11] Scottish song is one of our greatest national treasures and it would be immeasurably poorer without Burns's formidable contribution.

Alexander Scott has suggested that there were two reasons for the decline in Burns's satirical writing after the publication of the Kilmarnock edition in 1786, 'rootlessness and respectability'. Burns was rootless because he had left the community which had given him the substance for his attacks on religious orthodoxy and artistocractic privilege, and respectable because he had become an officer in the Excise.[12] That last point is probably the main reason, and in fact the dates neatly coincide. Burns began to collaborate seriously with the *Scots Musical Museum* in November 1787 and in January 1788 he wrote to Robert Graham of Fintry to solicit his patronage for an appointment in the Excise. He began work as an Excise Officer in September 1789, and was therefore a civil servant of a government that was in a state of panic over its fear of revolutionary ideas from France. Muir and the others who were sentenced to transportation in 1793 were no more revolutionary in their ideas than Burns himself and he had even attempted to send guns to France to support the Revolution.

Burns clearly understood his vulnerability. He wrote to Mrs Dunlop on 6 December 1792 about an episode in the theatre in Dumfries when 'God save the King' had been hissed and the French revolutionary song, 'Ça ira' repeatedly called for:

> For me, I am a *Placeman*, you know; a very humble one indeed, Heaven knows, but still so much so as to gag me from joining in the cry. – What my private sentiments are, you will find out without an Interpreter.

His caution was not sufficient to prevent a denunciation of him as a person disaffected to Government, and the Board of Excise ordered an enquiry. He sent two abject and frantic letters to his patron, Robert Graham. Even dismissal from the service, without any more serious penalty, would, he wrote on 31 December 1792, turn his wife and family adrift 'without the necessary support of a miserable existance.' In the second letter of 5 January 1793 he went through the humiliation of obligatory conformity: 'As to Reform Principles, I look upon the British Constitution, as settled at the Revolution, to be the most glorious Constitution on earth, or that perhaps the wit of man can frame.' (The Revolution in this case is, of course, that of 1688–89, in which Scotland was still nominally independent with her own Parliament.) Graham knew Burns well enough to understand how seriously to take these loyal protestations, but they were sufficient to satisfy the inquisition. It was, no doubt, as part of the same insurance policy that Burns joined the Dumfries Volunteers on 31 January 1795 and wrote their anthem, 'Does Haughty Gaul Invasion Threat?', with the lines:

> Be Britain still to Britain true,
> Among ourselves united!

There have been people who have seized on these prudent insincerities to try to represent Burns as a pillar of the establishment. These were the grounds for Hugh MacDiarmid's complaints about the Burns Clubs which he thought had done precisely that. That may have been so in the Thirties when MacDiarmid wrote his celebrated essay on the subject; but I think that there is now a much more realistic appreciation of Burns's egalitarianism and nationalism. Perhaps we are now beginning to respond to the call with which MacDiarmid ended his essay:

> Burns knew what he was doing when he repudiated all the canting Anglicisers and reverted to the Scots tongue and the Scots spirit. The need to follow his lead at long last is today a thousand times great than when he gave it.
>
> We can, if we will. We can still rescue Scotland from the crash of England's collapse and the ruins of an Empire vitiated by England's infernal Ascendancy policy. We can still affirm the fearless radical spirit of the true Scotland. We can even yet throw off the yoke of all the canting humbug in our midst.[13]

REFERENCES

Abbreviations:

Critical Heritage: Robert Burns; The Critical Heritage, edited by Donald A. Low (London, 1974)

Critical Essays: Critical Essays on Robert Burns, edited by Donald A. Low (London, 1975)

NOTES

1. James Boswell, *The Life of Samuel Johnson* (Everyman's Library: London 1935).
2. Thomas Carlyle, essay in the *Edinburgh Review* (December 1828). In *Critical Heritage* p. 372.
3. Murray Pittock, *The Invention of Scotland* (London, 1991) pp. 81, 82, 83.
4. Thomas Crawford, *Burns: A Study of the Poems and Songs* (Edinburgh, 1994), David Murison, *Critical Essays*, p. 68
5. David Daiches, *Critical Essays*, p. 143
6. George Rosie, article in *The Herald* of 22 July 1995 and his *Hugh Millar: Outrage and Order* (Edinburgh, 1981), pp. 154–5.
7. Murray Pittock, *op. cit.*, pp. 79 and 153
8. Sir Walter Scott, unsigned review in the *Quarterly Review* (February, 1809). In *Critical Heritage*, p. 203
9. Andrew Noble in *Burns Now*, edited by Kenneth Simpson (Edinburgh, 1994), p. 188.
10. Henry Mackenzie, unsigned essay in *The Lounger* (9 December 1786). In *Critical Heritage* p. 69
11. R. L. Stevenson, 'Some Aspects of Robert Burns' in *Familiar Studies of Men and Books* (Everyman's edition, London, undated), pp. 168. Cedric Thorpe Davie in *Critical Essays*, p. 157.
12. Alexander Scott in *Critical Essays*, p. 103
13. Hugh MacDiarmid, 'The Burns Cult' in *At the Sign of the Thistle* (1934). In *Hugh MacDiarmid: Selected Prose*, edited by Alan Riach (Manchester, 1992).

Burns and American Liberty

O N 25 JUNE, 1794, Robert Burns, now fully mature in his poetic art and radical politics, wrote the following letter to his beloved aristocratic correspondent, Mrs Dunlop:

> I am just going to trouble your critical patience with the first sketch of a stanza I have been framing as I passed along the road. – The Subject is, LIBERTY: you know, my honored Friend, how dear the theme is to me. – I design it as an irregular Ode for Genl Washington's birth-day. – After having mentioned the degeneracy of other kingdoms I come to Scotland thus –

> Thee, Caledonia, thy wild heaths among,
> Thee, famed for martial deed [and (*deleted*)] & sacred Song,
> To thee I turn with swimming eyes;
> Where is the soul of Freedom fled?
> Immingled with the mighty Dead,
> Beneath the hallowed turf where Wallace lies![1]

In the 'Ode for General Washington's Birthday', the concept of liberty emerges as a powerful symbol that unites America and liberty in the person of Washington:

> No Spartan tube, no Attic shell,
> No lyre Eolian I awake;
> 'Tis Liberty's bold note I swell,
> Thy harp, Columbia, let me take.
> See gathering thousands, while I sing,
> A broken chain, exulting, bring,
> And dash it in a tyrant's face!
> And dare him to his very beard,
> And tell him, he no more is feared,
> No more the Despot of Columbia's race.
> A tyrant's proudest insults braved,
> They shout, a People freed! They hail an Empire saved.

> Where is Man's godlike form?
> Where is that brow erect and bold,
> That eye that can, unmoved, behold
> The wildest rage, the loudest storm,
> That e'er created fury dared to raise!

Avaunt! thou caitiff, servile, base,
That tremblest at a Despot's nod,
    Yet, crouching under th' iron rod,
    Canst laud the arm that struck th' insulting blow!
Art thou of man's imperial line?
Dost boast that countenance divine?
Each sculking feature answers, No!
But come, ye sons of Liberty,
Columbia's offspring, brave as free,
    In danger's hour still flaming in the van:
Ye know, and dare maintain, The Royalty of Man.[2]

As to the possible meaning of Washington's significance as the symbolic embodiment of American liberty for Burns, I shall return at the end of my discussion.

Since Burns wrote only two poems that dealt directly with America, the 1784 'Ballad on the American War' or 'A Fragment' and the 1794 'Ode for General Washington's Birthday', it would appear that the material for my topic is too meagre. But a deeper investigation of Burns's letters, poems and songs reveals his extensive knowledge of America and his powerful admiration for the cause of American liberty. The critical question this essay seeks to answer is how did Burns reach poetic and political maturity in relation to his idea of American liberty by 1794. My answer is that Burns's art and politics developed through three distinct stages relative to this question: 1) his awakening to and ambivalent attitude toward America before 1783; 2) his celebration of the American victory in the War of Independence through his satirization of British military and political leaders, from 1784 to 1788; and 3) his identification of America with liberty, 1793–1794.[3]

Robert Burns lived in a world in which the 'language of liberty', to use Jonathan Clark's apt phrase, dominated discussion in the political culture of the British Empire in the long eighteenth century. Although the idea of liberty was ubiquitous in Enlightenment discourse, no nation embraced it more powerfully than Great Britain in its self-definition. Recently, a number of American and British scholars have sought to redefine the meaning of liberty in Anglo-American political thought in this period.[4]

When Burns began to write poetry in the 1770s, he could and did draw not only upon a general British tradition of liberty, but also upon a long, distinctively Scottish philosophical, poetical and political tradition of liberty. For centuries before the Union of 1707, incessant warfare against the English since earliest times as well as religious differences arising out of John Knox's Calvinist Reformation in Scotland during the sixteenth and seventeenth centuries shaped the Scottish sense of liberty in its nationalistic and patriotic manifestations. Before, during and after the Union, a brilliant line of Scottish philosophers, including Gershom Carmichael, Francis Hutcheson, David Hume, Adam Smith and Thomas Reid, developed variations on the theme of liberty in their works. Although Hutcheson died long before the American Revolution broke out in the early 1760s, his concept of liberty contributed directly to American arguments for freedom from British imperial domination. Hume, Smith and Reid lived through part or all of the Revolution and were sympathetic to the cause of American independence. Hume, especially, and, to a lesser degree, Smith and Reid, contributed substantially to the political ideology of such American founders as John Adams, Alexander Hamilton, Thomas Jefferson and James Madison.[5]

Burns also benefited from a Scots poetical tradition that included a deep sense of liberty running back to the Renaissance. Among his most recent predecessors, however, James Thomson, Allan Ramsay and Robert Fergusson stand out. Although born a Lowland Scot, Thomson left Scotland to seek his fortune south of the border. Best know for *The Seasons*, Thomson also composed an important political poem, *Liberty*, an 'attempt to trace Liberty, from the first ages down to her excellent establishment in Great Britain'.[6] Ramsay, on the other hand, was not only the leader of the eighteenth-century Scottish literary renaissance, but he was also known for his patriotism and nationalism which were largely derived from his hatred of the Union and his rejection of non-Scottish influences, English or otherwise. His *The Ever Green, a Collection of Scots Poems wrote by the Ingenious before 1600* of 1724 stressed cultural freedom in its advocacy of Scots. Robert Fergusson, like Ramsay before him, was a patriot, but he expressed his cultural patriotism even more powerfully than Ramsay, and he did it in the context of Edinburgh as a truly urban poet.[7] In political thought Hutcheson, Hume, Adam Ferguson, Smith and Reid, among others, carried on, in various ways, the tradition of the late seventeenth- and early eighteenth-century patriot, Fletcher of Saltoun.[8]

Robert Burns was, as Thomas Crawford has correctly argued, a political poet *par excellence*, a radical who expressed his political viewpoint continuously against the high and mighty. Crawford has also provided us with the most detailed and most subtle analysis yet published of the many meanings liberty had for Burns – artistic, civil, national, personal, religious, social.[9] Not surprisingly, as a Scot, Burns's satirical targets were often English political leaders. A fine example is his bitter attack on William Pitt the Younger's oppressive rule in 1793: 'In Politics if thou would'st mix/And mean thy fortunes be,/Bear this in mind, be deaf and blind,/Let great folks hear and see'.[10] Furthermore, Burns was a political poet for whom the idea of America and the idea of liberty were synonymous. Throughout his adult life Burns's evolving political views shaped his concept of America, views which espoused a political philosophy based on his fight against privilege and rank. 'What though on hamely fare we dine,/Wear hoddin gray, and a' that./Give fools their silks, and knaves their wine,/A Man's a Man for a' that'. These lines from his 1795 'Song – For a' that and a' that' – represent what Burns called his 'few first principles of politics, which I believe

I would not easily part with – I have all the national prejudice which I believe glows peculiarly strong in the breast of a Scotsman'.[11]

But these sentiments represent the mature Burns writing a year before his death. What of his political ideas, especially his concept of American liberty, before 1783? Burns's response to the American Revolution and War of Independence, while those events were unfolding in Britain and across the Atlantic, was ambivalent and only hinted at in his earliest writings. A clear understanding of his emotional and intellectual reaction to the American struggle for liberty and George III's efforts to suppress that struggle can only be judged from the evolution of his political ideas between 1784 and 1794. Indeed, Burns's last political statement was a declaration of Scottish liberty inspired by America's achievement of independence:

> Liberty to me with my National prejudices, how dear that theme is. Liberty is *invaluable* and never too dearly bought ... An ancient nation [Scotland] that for any ages has gallantly maintained the unequal struggle for Independence with her much more powerful neighbor, at last agrees to a Union which should ever after make them one people. But what are all the boasted advantages which my country reaps from the Union that can counterbalance the annihilation of Independence?[12]

Thomas Crawford has argued plausibly that the context for Burns's knowledge of the American Revolution and War consisted of three elements: 1) from 1775 on he heard of the revolutionary events in America from Scottish seamen; 2) during the same period he read about the War of Independence, which ended in 1781, and the Peace of Paris of 1783; and 3) beginning in 1780 he discussed American affairs with friends at the Tarlbolton Bachelors' Club.[13]

Indeed, Burns's first mention of America occurs in his 21 June 1783 letter to his cousin, James Burness, which is equivocal at best in his attitude toward the War of Independence. He complains about 'the present wretched state of this country', about the economic havoc the War is having on Ayr, about how both trade and farming are 'at a very low ebb with us ... In short, my dr Sir, since the unfortunate beginning of this American war, & its unfortunate conclusion, this country has been, & still is decaying very fast'.[14] Burns's ambiguous view that America's triumph over Great Britain in the War was an 'unfortunate conclusion' is somewhat of an enigma, because just eighteen months later he was satirizing the King's war with the new nation. Before 1784, Burns appears to have had little, if any, inclination toward political issues, especially relative to the American War. His politics in 1783 were moderate in sentiment and supportive of British policies, but he was against the War because of his personal experiences in the context of its harsh economic impact on southwest Scotland. Still, barely a year and one-half later, Burns revealed a strong propensity toward political ideology in his writings in support of American liberty. Why did this transformation in Burns's politics happen?

The causes of the transformation in Burns's political thought, especially his changing attitude toward American liberty in 1784 and after, are part and parcel of his evolution toward maturity as an artist and intellectual. Indeed, his powerful ambition to become a great poet was intimately linked to his developing political ideology. Burns expressed his artistic ambition in terms of literary nationalism in his *Commonplace Book* in August, 1785:

> However, I am pleased with the works of our Scotch poets, particularly the excellent Ramsay, and the still more excellent Fergusson, yet I am hurt to see other places of Scotland ... immortalized in such celebrated performances, whilst my dear native country ... famous both in ancient and modern times for a gallant and warlike race of inhabitants; a country where civil and particularly religious Liberty have ever found their first support, and their last asylum; a country, the birthplace of many famous Philosophers, Soldiers, and Statesmen, and the scene of many important events recorded in Scottish History, particularly a great many of the actions of the Glorious Wallace, the Saviour of his country; yet, we have never had one Scotch Poet of any eminence to make the fertile banks of Irvine, the romantic woodlands and sequestered scenes of Aire, and the healthy mountainous source, and the winding sweep of Doon emulate Tay, Forth, Ettrick, Tweed, etc. This is a complaint I would gladly remedy, but Alas! I am far unequal to the task, both in native genius and education. Obscure I am, and obscure I must be, though no young poet, nor young soldier's heart ever beat more fondly for fame than mine.[15]

During the Mossgiel period (1784–86), Burns's political views also matured in the context of political reform movements in Britain that owed much to the inspiration of the American victory in the War of Independence. Letters advocating Scottish freedom began to appear in the Scottish press in 1782–83. The radical Richard Price, who had sided with the American cause in the recent military struggle, expressed similar reform sentiments in his April, 1784 letter to the *The Scots Magazine*:

> God grant that this spirit may increase till it has abolished all despotic governments, and exterminated that slavery which debases mankind: Their spirit first rose in America – it soon reached Ireland – it has diffused itself into some foreign countries; and your letter informs me, that it is now animating Scotland.[16]

In such a political context, Burns began to define his idea of America through a series of satirical poems aimed at the political trickery, the sham and the folly of Britain's military and political establishment. Additionally, Burns's participation in Freemasonry from 1781 onward shaped his political perspective through its emphasis on the dignity and equality of man, liberty and progress, and brotherhood and philanthropy.[17]

That Burns had moved a long way toward positive recognition of America and its War of Independence from his 1783 reference to the colonists' victory as an 'unfortunate conclusion' to the fighting is illustrated in his 1784 'Epistle to J. R *****, Enclosing some Poems'. Here we begin to detect a powerful theme in his attitude toward America – his exposure of Britain's military and political foolishness through the use of biting satire. After throwing poetic barbs against the 'Auld Licht' clergy in the early stanzas, Burns quickly shifts his attention to the American Revolution. Instead of merriment, the tone is now half-serious:

> Tho' faith, sma' heart hae I to sing!
> My Muse dow scarcely spread her wing:
> I've play'd myself a bonie *spring*,
>   An' *danc'd* my fill!
> I'd better gaen an' sair't the king,
>   At Bunker's hill.[18]

The joke about enlisting in the royal army to fight the Americans exemplifies Burns's maturing disposition toward the Revolution and War. In making fun of the King's rigid attitude toward the colonists, Burns unmasks the folly of George III's decision to make war on the rebels.

Burns's mention of Bunker Hill was not simply an offhand reference to recent history. Rather, it was the beginning of a more profound understanding of history and politics, past and present, in his mind and in his poetry. Recent and contemporary politics, focusing both on event and personalities in Britain and America, now come under the imaginative scrutiny of the satirist. And so, too, did Burns's idea of America emerge initially through these same satires on Britain's conduct of the War. In 1786, for example, Burns satirized William Pitt the Younger and his policies: 'I'm mistrusting *Willie Pitt*,/When taxes he enlarges'.[19] Similarly, he characterized the Irishman Edmund Burke: 'For Paddy *B-rke*, like only Turk,/Nae mercy had at a', man' and Charles James Fox, the gambler: 'Then Clubs an' Hearts were *Charlie*'s cartes' in the poetic fragment of the same year, 'Ballad on the American War'.[20] Nor did the monarch and his family escape Burns's barbs. The playful first line of 'A Dream' ... 'Guid morning to your MAJESTY!' soon gives way to a much more serious attack:

> For me! before a Monarch's face,
> Ev'n *there* I winna flatter;
> For neither Pension, Post, nor Place,
> Am I your humble debtor:

The monarch's son is the 'young Potentate o' W——,' who has been quickly moving 'Down Pleasure's stream, wi' swelling sails'. Indeed, the outcome of George III's misguided handling of the American crisis resulted in the loss of the colonies and the resultant shrinkage of the empire:

Tis very true, my sovereign King,
My skill may weel be doubted;
But *Facts* are chiels that winna ding,
An' downa be disputed:
Your *royal nest*, beneath *Your* wing,
Is e'en right reft an' clouted,
And now the third part o' the string,
An' less, will gang about it
Than did ae day.[21]

Burns's reaction to the American Revolution in this period of his poetic and political maturation is done in his typical satirical fashion. His attacks on the King's ministers focused more on them as individuals and their policies than their political ideas in 1784: 'No Statesman nor Soldier to plot or to fight'.[22]

No poem satirized England's 'great folks' better in relation to America than Burns's 'Ballad on the American War'. Compared to the 'Epistle to J. R*****, Enclosing some Poems' and 'A Dream', the range of his subject is much larger and the historical references much more pointed. Although Burns alluded to Dundas, Fox, Rockingham and Shelburne, the major focus of his satire had shifted to the fighting in the War of Independence. Typically, his virulent attacks fell on Britain's military leaders. Conversely, Burns offered his high regards to Richard Montgomery, the American general, and to the cause of the Second Continental Congress. The American Revolution and War was the focus in the first four stanzas in which Burns outlined its history from 1774 to 1781. But it was not simply a chronological ordering of revolutionary events, for the poem was a selective reading of the recent past in ridiculing such British 'heroes' as North, Carleton, *Tammy G-age, Willie* Howe, Burgoyne, Clinton and Cornwallis. Contrasted with British military and political leaders, American generals and statesmen are Burns's true heroes.[23] Burns's political response to the American Revolution is especially sharp in his satire 'Address of Beelzebub' of 1786 in which he makes the cause of American liberty synonymous with the plight of the poor. His great admiration for winning American military and political leaders such as Franklin, Hancock, Montgomery and Washington is contrasted with his equally great disdain for the losing British political and military leaders, North, Sackville, Clinton and Howe. For Burns, these heroic Americans are representatives as well as representations of freedom over British tyranny.[24]

Hence, Burns's artistic and political maturation corresponded with the origin of his view of America as the land of liberty. News accounts of America were, of course, widely available in Scottish magazines such as *The Scots Magazine* and newspapers such as the *Edinburgh Evening Courant*. And there is ample internal evidence in Burns's writings that he drew freely on those accounts in shaping his understanding of America. Burns was a brilliant student of history, and it is clear that he read and interpreted American politics with the same care and originality he did British politics. Especially notable is the precision of his historical references, past and present, in his correspondence, poems and songs.[25] Furthermore, Burns's genius is abundantly evident in his amusing and clever way of treating historical events. Again, 'The Ballad on the American War' is not only a fine example of Burns's poetic art, it is also a fine example of his deep knowledge of history. Indeed, the correspondence between *The Scots Magazine* in reporting American military and political events and Burns's use of those same events in his poem is striking.[26]

By 27 November, 1786, when Burns went to Edinburgh to celebrate his arrival as a major poet, he was developing a mature political outlook. A fundamental element of his maturing political outlook was his idea of America. He had already powerfully expressed his image of America in 'Ballad on the American War' in his respect for the Second Continental Congress's determination to 'quite refuse our [British] law'.[27] The American victory in the War confirmed his belief that mankind could attain independence from oppression. While Burns satirized Britain's American policies, he simultaneously represented America as the land of civil and political liberty. His idea of America, then, was a wonderful contemporary example of his multi-faceted concept of liberty – civil, personal, religious, social. He understood clearly the meaning of American independence long before the outbreak of the French Revolution in 1789. Kline has observed, 'America became more of a "working" concept in the same sense that his mind constantly reverted to the colonial struggle to buttress his own convictions ... America's revolt against authority was a larger version of his own feelings, and it is no wonder that it was the "revolutionary" aspect of her struggle that appealed to him, what he called the "search for that fantastic thing – Liberty"'.[28] In Burns's mind, America emerged as a society in which oppression had been overthrown and liberty enshrined. Burns's America represented justice, political and social; it was a country in which the people in general made the 'rules and laws they please' and even the 'sons of dirt' had freedoms and rights guaranteed by law.[29]

During the last decade of his life, Robert Burns continued to broaden and deepen his understanding of America as the land of liberty. In his famous letter of 8 November, 1788, Burns argued that the American Revolution of 1776 was as important an event as the English Revolution of 1688:

Man, Mr. Printer, is a strange, weak inconsistent being – Who would believe, Sir, that in this our Augustan age of liberality and refinement, while we seem so justly sensible and jealous of our rights and liberties, and animated with such indignation against the very memory of those who would have subverted them, who would suppose that a certain people, under our national protection, should complain, not against a Monarch and a few favourite advisers, but against our whole legislative body, of the very same imposition and oppression, the Romish religion not excepted and almost in the very same terms as our forefathers did against the family of Stuart! I will not, I cannot, enter into the merits of the cause; but I dare say, the American Congress, in 1776, will be allowed to have been as able and as enlightened, and, a whole empire will say, as honest, as the English Convention in 1688; and that the fourth of July will be as sacred to their posterity as the fifth of November is to us.[30]

Less than a week later in a letter to Mrs Dunlop, Burns reiterated a similar sentiment, but now his allusions to the Hanoverian monarchy were marked by irony:

Is it not remarkable, odiously remarkable, that tho' manners are more civilized, & the rights of mankind better understood, by an Augustan Century's improvement, yet in this very reign of heavenly Hanoverianism, and almost in this very year, an empire beyond the Atlantic has had its Revolution too, & for the very same maladministration & legislative misdemeanours in the illustrious and sapientipotent Family of Hanover as was complained of in the 'tyranical & bloody House of Stuart'.[31]

The people's right to revolt against an oppressive government, as the Americans had done in 1776, was now an essential component of Burns's political thought.

The last seven years of Burns's life coincided with the twin events of the French Revolution and the political reform movement in Britain. These simultaneous events had a special significance for his political ideas, since Burns's idea of American liberty deepened even more as he viewed the American Revolution through the lenses of French and British radicalism. Although Burns did not respond politically to the French Revolution until 1792 in 'Here's A Health To Them That's Awa', he sided with the politics of Charles James Fox and, through Fox, with Thomas Paine's political philosophy in the *Rights of Man* (1791–2):

> Here's a health to them that's awa,
> Here's a health to them that's awa;
> Here's a health to Charlie, the chief o' the clan,
> Altho' that his band be sma'.
> May Liberty meet wi' success!
> May Prudence protect her frae evil!
> May Tyrants and Tyranny tine i' the mist,
> And wander their way to the devil![32]

In 1792 'Citizen' Paine embodied the cause of liberty. The exact impact of Paine's political thought on Burns is difficult to measure. Still, there is some evidence to suggest that Burns studied Paine's writings with great care and approval. Especially telling are clear correspondences between passages in Burns's 'Song – For a' that and a' that' and Paine's *Rights of Man*.[33]

Between his letters to the *Edinburgh Evening Courant* and to Mrs Dunlop in November 1788 and 1793, Burns said nothing on the subject of America in his poetry, prose or song. But the *Rights of Man* and similar works of other British and French radicals revived Burns's interest in America. Indeed, Paine not only dedicated his famous work to George Washington, but he also held up America as the very representation of liberty. As one author has noted, 'A new lyrical note appears in Burns's treatment of America after 1793'.[34] No longer was Burns simply empathizing with the American Revolution, while ridiculing British military and political blunders. Rather, he was now universalizing the War of American Independence by making the outcome a victory for liberty the world over. His mature idea of America still represented freedom fighting oppression. Clearly, Burns was writing in defence of liberty; not in some ideal sense, but rather in relation to the Scots' own struggle for political reform. During the years just before his death in 1796, Burns wrote some of his most powerful political poems in which he intimately linked America with liberty. His letter to George Thomson, about 30 August 1793, was accompanied by the poem he put to song as 'Bruce to His Men at Bannockburn', which was a fine example of that identification and on which Burns noted:

> There is a tradition, which I have met with in many places of Scotland, that it was Robert Bruce's March at the battle of Bannock-burn. – This thought, in my yesternight's evening walk, warmed me to a pitch of enthusiasm on the theme of Liberty & Independance, which I threw into a kind of Scots Ode, fitted to the Air, [which (*deleted*)] that one might suppose to be the gallant ROYAL SCOT's address to his heroic followers on that eventful morning. –

The poems begins with the striking opening line: 'Scots wha hae wi' Wallace bled'. And the final four stanzas are a ringing outcry against universal oppression:

> Lay the proud Usurpers low!
> Tyrants fall in every foe!
> LIBERTY's in every blow! –
> Let us DO – or DIE!!!

Burns follows this stanza with the powerful declaration: 'So may God ever defend the cause of Truth and Liberty, as he did that day! – Amen!'[35]

By the summer of 1793 Burns idealized the American Revolution and War of Independence with 'glowing ideas' and treated his political images accordingly. In 'Scots Wha Hae', he best expressed his idea that American liberty would prove victorious over tyranny. And his 'Song – For a' that and a' that' from the same period is equally, if not more, successful than 'Scots Wha Hae' in capturing Burns's identification of America's cause with the cause of liberty. At the same time Burns may or may not have written 'The Tree of Liberty', a powerful expression of liberty, a universal symbol that was common in Britain throughout the eighteenth century and which was also popular in American during the Revolution and War. Later, it reappears in Scotland and, of course, at the time of the French Revolution.[36]

Lastly, let's return to where this essay began, with the 'Ode for General Washington's Birthday', of 1794. James Mackay has argued,

> Like 'Scots wha hae' … this long poem was not quite what it appeared at first glance. Washington's birthday occurred on 22 February and not in June; perhaps Robert was still smarting at the recollection of the manner in which the Loyal Natives had turned the celebration of the king's birthday three weeks previously into a raucous demonstration of their patriotism. George Washington, who had recently been re-elected for a second term as president of the United States, was merely an excuse for Robert to dwell upon 'the degeneracy of kingdoms'. As in 'Scots Wha hae', he waxed lyrical on the golden age of Scottish history when William Wallace (whom the recipient of this letter like to regard as her ancestor) fought for freedom.[37]

Although Mackay was partly correct in viewing Washington in this light, yet I think there is an additional meaning and significance to Burns's interpretation of Washington. In his essay, 'A Man on Horseback', Richard Brookhiser analyzed the man behind the myth, the human qualities of Washington that constituted the core of his personality – his physical frame, his intellect and, finally, his presence and, especially, his character, a quality Burns admired above all others. Brookhiser concluded,

> His character may be described as a three-story building.
> The top floor was furnished with the political ideas of eighteenth-century America, with which we are quite familiar. But the other two stories were equally important. The second was his morals – and to these we will return. The ground floor consisted of what was given to him by nature and cultivated by the conditions of his life, his physicality and his temperament. His form was imposing, and his temper dangerous. Displaying the one and controlling the other were essential to his success as a leader.[38]

Brookhiser went on to argue, quite convincingly, that few men in history had 'a bearing, an attitude of his body that helped to make his fame. Washington was possessed of a strong and flaring temperament, which lent energy to his purpose but made his anger terrible. And, to contain and channel his high feeling, he had a personal moral code built upon maxims he had studied from youth'.[39]

Like Burns writing poems on horseback, during the War of Independence Washington 'could stay awake on horseback for days' leading his troops. Brookhiser concluded his analysis of Washington's character as follows: 'Character was seen in Washington's time as a role one played until one became it; character also meant how one's role was judged by others. It was both the performance and the review'.[40] In the many roles and voices of Robert Burns, there are striking parallels to the roles and voices of George Washington. Hence, it is not surprising that no other American Founding Father, 'first in war, first in peace, first in the hearts of his countrymen', appealed to Burns more than the great general and president as the true representation both of American liberty and the new American nation as the hope of mankind's future.

During the early seventeen-nineties, Robert Burns, like his fellow–democrat Thomas Paine, whom he admired so much, also emerged as a 'Citizen of the World', the great poet of liberty. And, in the two centuries since his death, Burns has, indeed, become the world's foremost poet of democratic aspirations.

Regarding the United States of America specifically, if the Revolution, the War and Washington provided Burns with enormous inspiration for his ideas of liberty and democracy, Americans gladly returned the favour by adopting Burns as their favourite poet. The first American edition of his Kilmarnock poems appeared in 1788, two years after their publication in Scotland, and numerous editions of his poems and songs soon follows.[41] Early critical reception of Burns in America followed the standard Scottish view of the time that he was Henry Mackenzie's 'Heaven-taught ploughman'. But by the mid-nineteenth century a much more sophisticated view of his art had emerged among American authors. To Ralph Waldo Emerson, the great New England Transcendentalist writing on the occasion of his centenary, Burns was 'an exceptional genius. The people who care nothing for literature and poetry care for Burns ... Yet how great a poet he is! And the poet, too, of poor men ... He has given voice to all the experiences of common life ... His muse and teaching was common sense, joyful, aggressive, irresistible'.[42]

But it was Walt Whitman, America's greatest nineteenth-century poet of democracy, who not only admired and praised Burns, but who also captured best the inextricable linkage of American liberty and the common man in Burns's art and thought. In his Preface to *Leaves of Grass* (1855), Whitman wrote:

> ... the genius of the United States is not best or most in its executives or legislatures, not in its ambassadors or authors or inventions ... but always most in the common people ... In the make of the great masters the idea of political liberty is indispensable. Liberty takes the adherence of heroes wherever men and women exist – but never takes any adherence or welcome from the rest more than from poets. They are the voice and exposition of liberty. They out of ages are worthy of the grand idea, to them it is confined, and they must sustain it. Nothing has precedence of it, and nothing can warp it.[43]

Was Whitman thinking specifically of Burns when he wrote the above lines? There is very good reason to think so, according to Robert Crawford in his discussion of the Burns–Whitman poetic relationship. Crawford argued that Burns 'acted for Whitman as an incitement toward a more democratic poetry' and in Whitman's essay on Burns, 'Robert Burns as Poet and Person', Whitman took Burns as a 'model' for his own poetry[44] Indeed, Whitman's lines certainly 'fit' Burns well. They capture the same artistic, moral and political sentiments that Scotland's national bard had already expressed so beautifully in letters, poems and songs in his identification of America with liberty and democracy in the late eighteenth century. These same sentiments continue to resonate in American culture and society two centuries after his death as does Burns's identification of the common man with liberty and democracy the world over.

NOTES

1. Robert Burns, *The Letters of Robert Burns*, edited by J. De Lancey Ferguson and G. Ross Roy, 2 vols (Oxford, 1985), II, 297–98. Hereafter cited as *Letters*.
2. Robert Burns, *The Poems and Songs of Robert Burns*, edited by James Kinsley, 3 vols (Oxford, 1968), II 732–34. Hereafter cited as *Poems and Songs*.
3. Older works on Burns and the American Revolution include W. P. Ker, 'The Politics Of Burns', in *Collected Essays: W. P. Ker*, edited by Charles Whibley (London, 1925), 128–146, and Gustave Carus, 'Robert Burns And The American Revolution', in *The Open Court*, vol. 46, February, 1932, 129–36. A valuable study is Alfred Allan Kline, 'Burns', in *The English Romantics and the American Republic: An Analysis of the Concept of America in the Work of Blake, Burns, Wordsworth, Coleridge, Byron and Shelly*, Ph.D. Dissertation, Columbia University (New York, 1953), 70–111. More recent studies are R. D. S. Jack, 'Robert Burns: Poet of Freedom', in *Scotia: American–Canadian Journal of Scottish Studies*, vol. VI, 1982, 41–59, and, especially, Thomas Crawford, *Burns: A Study of the Poems and Song* (Edinburgh, 1994), 79–82 94, 147–92 and 237–56 and *Boswell, Burns and The French Revolution* (Edinburgh, 1990), 19–23 and 51–79.
4. J. C. D. Clark, *The Language of Liberty, 1660–1832: Political Discourse and Social Dynamics in the Anglo-American World* (Cambridge, 1994). Among other notable recent works on liberty in Anglo-American culture and thought in the long eighteenth century are Linda Colley, *Britons: Forging the Nation, 1707–1837* (New Haven, 1992); Barry Allan Shain, *The Myth of American Individualism: The Protestant Origins of American Political Thought* (Princeton, 1994); and John Phillip Reid, *The Concept of Liberty in The Age of The American Revolution* (Chicago, 1988).
5. The scholarly literature on the relationship between the Scottish Enlightenment and the American Revolution is large and growing. Among the more important articles and books are the following: Roger J. Fechner, 'The Godly and Virtuous Republic of John Witherspoon', in *Ideas in America's Cultures: From Republic to Mass Society*, edited by Hamilton Cravens (Ames, 1982), 7–25 and 'Adam Smith and American Moral Philosophers in the Age of Enlightenment and Revolution', in *Adam Smith: International Perspectives*, edited by Hiroshi Mizuta and Chuhei Sugiyama (New York, 1993), 181–198; Michael Fry, 'Scotland and the American Revolution', in *Scotland And The Americas, 1600 to 1800*, edited by Michael Fry (Providence, 1995), 89–97; Jack P. Greene, *The Intellectual Heritage of the Constitutional Era: The Delegates' Library* (Philadelphia, 1986), 45–52; Caroline

Robbins, *The Eighteenth-Century Commonwealthman: Studies in the Trans-mission, Development and Circumstance of English Liberal Thought from the Restoration of Charles II until the War with the Thirteen Colonies* (New York, 1968), 177–220; *Scotland, Europe and the American Revolution*, edited by Owen Dudley Edwards & George Shepperson (Edinburgh, 1976); *Scotland and America in the Age of the Enlightenment*, edited by Richard B. Sher and Jeffrey R. Smitten (Edinburgh, 1990); and, especially, Gary Wills, *Inventing America: Jefferson's Declaration of Independence* (New York, 1978) and *Explaining America: The Federalist* (New York, 1981).

6. Hilbert H. Campbell, *James Thomson* (Boston, 1979), 99–109.

7. David Daiches, *The Paradox of Scottish Culture: The Eighteenth-Century Experi-ence* (London, 1964), 23–30 and 89–92.

8. Robbins, 177–220, and John Robertson, *The Scottish Enlightenment and The Militia Issue* (Edinburgh, 1985) and the essays in *A Union for Empire: Political Thought And The British Union of 1707*, edited by John Robertson (Cambridge, 1995).

9. Thomas Crawford, *Burns*, 79–82, 94, 153–4, 161, 238 and 241–56.

10. *Poems and Songs*, II, 822.

11. *Ibid.*, II, 762 and Burns quoted in Keith Henderson, *Burns – By Himself* (London, 1938), 89.

12. Burns in Henderson, 214.

13. Thomas Crawford, *Boswell*, 19.

14. *Letters*, I, 18–20.

15. Robert Burns, *Robert Burns's Common Place Book, 1783–1785*, edited by David Daiches (Carbondale, 1965), 36.

16. Richard Price, 'Letter to the Secretary of the Committee of Citizens of Edinburgh', *The Scots Magazine*, SLVI (April 1784), 179.

17. Dale Bowling, 'Caledonia and Caledonia's Bard: Masonic Ideology in the Thought of Robert Burns', a paper delivered at the International Bicentenary Burns Con-ference, University of Strathclyde, Glasgow, Scotland, 11 January 1996.

18. *Poems and Songs*, I, 61–63.

19. *Ibid.*, 267.

20. *Ibid.*, 49–51.

21. *Ibid.*, 265–9.

22. *Ibid.*, 38.

23. *Ibid.*, 49–51.

24. *Ibid.*, 254–5.

25. See the numerous examples in Kline, 87–99.

26. *Poems and Songs*, I, 49–51.

27. *Ibid.*, 49

28. Kline, 96.

29. *Ibid.*, 99.

30. *Letters*, I, 334–5.

31. *Ibid.*, 337.

32. *Poems and Songs*, II, 663.

33. Kline, 108–10 and 'On Tom Pain's Death', attributed to Burns in *Poems and Songs*, II, 932.

34. Kline, 110.

35. *Letters*, II, 235–6.
36. *Poems and Songs*, II, 762–3, 707–8 and 910–13. On the question of Burns's authorship of 'The Tree of Liberty', see Thomas Crawford, *Boswell*, 63–70.
37. James Mackay, *A Biography of Robert Burns* (Edinburgh, 1992), 569.
38. Richard Brookhiser, 'A Man on Horseback', *The Atlantic Monthly*, vol. 277, No. 1, January, 1996, 50–64. On Burns's appreciation of the critical importance of character see David Daiches's Keynote Address, 'Robert Burns: The Tightrope-Walker', delivered at the International Bicentenary Burns Conference, University of Strathclyde, Glasgow, Scotland, 11 January, 1996.
39. Brookhiser, 56–64.
40. *Ibid.*, 64. An extended argument of Brookhiser's study of Washington's character can be found in his *Founding Father: Rediscovering George Washington* (New York, 1996).
41. Andrew Hook, *Scotland and America: A Study of Cultural Relations, 1750–1835* (Glasgow, 1975), 129–133. An older work on Burns's reception in America in Anna Mercy Painter, *Burns in America Before 1800*, Ph.D. Dissertation, Yale University, 1930.
42. Quoted in *Robert Burns: The Critical Heritage*, edited by Donald A. Low (London, 1974), 435.
43. Walt Whitman, 'Preface to the First Issue of "Leaves of Grass"', edited by John Valentine (New York, 1928), 475–6 and 583.
44. Robert Crawford, *Devolving English Literature* (Oxford, 1992), 88–110.

Sexual Poetics or the Poetry of Desire: Catherine Carswell's Life of Robert Burns

THE YEAR 1996 is not only the bicentenary of Burns's death but also the fiftieth anniversary of the death of Catherine Carswell, whose *The Life of Robert Burns*,[1] published in 1930, catapulted her into the newspapers' headlines and to national notoriety.

James Mackay refers to the storm which greeted Carswell's book as 'an unprecedented campaign of vituperation equalled in modern times only by the reception of Salman Rushdie's *Satanic Verses*';[2] and Claire Harman continued the Rushdie analogy with her comment that Carswell 'became victim of a sort of Caledonian fatwa'[3] when the *Daily Record* serialised excerpts in the autumn of 1930. Many of Carswell's accusers in the ensuing correspondence were women. A 'Jean Armour' of Ayr urged readers to boycott the book, while another correspondent condemned the way she 'has trampled on and degraded the very name of womanhood by her assertions regarding the (to her) not unwilling victims of the poet's lust'. Male correspondents protested at Mrs Carswell being asked to propose the Immortal Memory, especially at Women's Burns Clubs, and at her 'deliberate attempt to prostitute the character of Burns for commercial purposes'. One headline proclaimed 'Such Trash'; another – one of the few to take an opposite view – 'Highland Lady Defends Mrs Carswell's Burns'. This correspondent commented: 'It is so splendidly free from moralising – the vice of nineteenth-century biographers.' And of the Highland Mary episode as depicted by Carswell she said: 'I thought Mrs Carswell's picture very lovely and tender ... To one of your readers at least Burns has emerged from your pages as one of the most lovable and tragic figures in the history of letters'. More typical, however, was the correspondent who complained that in Burns Carswell had found 'a subject that is obviously beyond her' and that she herself was 'an ant endeavouring to consume Vesuvius by nibbling at its base!'[4]

Carswell had her problems also with the *Glasgow Herald*. In correspondence with the American Burns scholar Professor De Lancey Ferguson whose edition of Burns's letters came out almost simultaneously with her *Life*, she tells how Bruce of the *Herald* had done her husband and herself 'particular ill turns and so hates us personally and statedly. He has even given orders on the *Herald* that no broadcasting or other public activities of the Carswells are to be noted in that paper'.[5] Perhaps estimating that the Burns book was too big a catch to be ignored completely, the *Herald*'s reviewer acknowledged it coolly as failing 'to present as full and true a portrait as Lockhart's excellent Life'.[6] The Burns Federation attempted to have the book suppressed by its publishers, Chatto & Windus but, having failed in this, belatedly printed a damning criticism by the Revd. Lauchlan MacLean Watt in January 1932, when it was described as 'an undocumented libel on the dead'.[7] Such hostile responses were countered by a few favourable accounts: by Hugh MacDiarmid's early praise in a letter to the *Daily Record* of 17 October 1930, by Edwin Muir, writing in the *Nation and Athenaeum*, and by William Power in the *Daily Record* itself.[8] Thanking Professor Ferguson for the kind things he has said about her book, Carswell describes herself as having 'had more kicks than halfpence so far' and as about to undertake a speaking tour of Scottish Burns Clubs in January 1931. She comments caustically: 'I am advised that chain mail may be necessary'.[9] That this might have been more than just a witty comment is suggested by the fact that she did receive a letter signed by a pseudonymous 'Holy Willie' containing a bullet and the instruction to use it 'in a quiet corner' and so 'leave the world a better and cleaner place'.[10]

What kind of work, then, was this controversial biography of Scotland's national poet that it should have attracted such hostility? Carswell's *Life* is certainly not a *feminist* account of Burns. As in her two novels, and especially in *Open the Door!*, Carswell follows D. H. Lawrence in her foregrounding of sexuality, both male and female, and it may be, as the *Daily Record* correspondence suggests, that it was the freedom with which she depicted the sexuality of Burns's women which aroused, even unconsciously, much of the angry comment. There is in her account little if any condemnation of Burns in matters sexual, although it is different when she turns to matters political in his Dumfries period. Burns is portrayed with understanding and sympathy and her fictional account of the responses of his female partners, where given, characterises them not as his victims, but as adoring and willing accomplices. Thus, in relation to the young Burns in the period before his father's death, her omniscient narrator tells us: 'it began to be whispered that an hour with him in the dark was worth a daytime with any other lad' (103). Later, Lizzie Paton, in Carswell's account, admits that 'she had not been taken advantage of or misled by promises; she had merely been heartily, perhaps hopefully in love' (119). Jean Armour is portrayed as being the one to initiate a relationship with the poet and as willing to give herself to him again and again, despite his fickle treatment of her. We are told: 'She wanted him even more than she wanted marriage, which was very loveable of her' (163). There is little advocacy of the rights of woman here, not even rights of the protective and decorously cautious kind put forward by Burns in his ironic Popean address of that title in 1792. It would be fair to say that here and in some of the other descriptive passages dealing with Burns's principal love conquests, one can find an over-inventiveness on Carswell's part which justifies James Mackay's caustic dismissal of parts of the narrative as 'fanciful', 'nonsense' and even 'a Mills and Boon heroine'.[11] I find it surprising also that Carswell should characterise the warm, intimate and joyful tone of celebration in Burns's welcome to Lizzie Paton's daughter: 'Welcome! my bonie, sweet, wee dochter ...' as 'jovial and graceless' (119), and yet quote without comment the truly disgraceful letter to Ainslie of March 1788 about his physical relationship with the pregnant Jean while playing verbal games with Clarinda (267). Despite her acquired reputation for openness in relation to Burns's life and her own claim to have been 'more honest and painstaking than most of my predecessors',[12] Carswell, like these predecessors and no doubt her successors also, can be subjectively selective in her presentation and comment. In addition, her dismissal of 'A Poet's Welcome to his Love-begotten Daughter' points to what is for me one of the disappointments of this biography: the paucity of comment on the poetry and its qualities and thus a degree of failure to give one a sense of Burns the poet as opposed to Burns the man and lover.

On the other hand, subjectivity does contribute to the strength of Carswell's account. There is greater recognition nowadays of the significant fictional element present in both autobiography and biography, not necessarily deliberately or consciously present, but present nevertheless in the author's reconstruction and ordering of a life, whether his or her own or another's. Catherine Carswell's biography is very much a *novelist's* biography. She does not reproduce and weigh up facts and arguments, present and analyse sources as one might find in a more conventional biographical account. Instead she offers the reader a novelistic pattern of a life, what Thomas Crawford calls in his Introduction to the Canongate reprint of her book 'the shape of a tragedy'.[13] Her narrative voice is that of the omniscient narrator of fiction as opposed to the objective and scholarly researcher, and the narrator's perspectives are frequently amplified by a modernistic free indirect style which brings the thoughts and feelings of the principal characters closer to us. In this way, Carswell succeeds in bringing Burns the man alive for us, giving us the sense of his strong ancestry, the creativity within it, of human beings with an independent set of mind. Burns himself is never the 'Heaven-taught Ploughman' in Carswell's narrative, but a young man of inherited intelligence and creativity, ambitious but inevitably constrained by the social hierarchies of his time and by the religious belief in predestination which underpinned them, whatever his intelligence, aspirations and poetic achievement; and a man worn out in the end, like his father, by the exigencies of a farming life without sufficient capital to take advantage of the new improving agriculture. It is this novelistic approach also which leads us to understand the sexual mores of rural Ayrshire in the mid- to late-eighteenth century and so evaluate Burns's sexual behaviour against that of his peers and the conditions of his time, as opposed to the values of a twentieth-century often saved from travail in sexual matters by the knowledge of contraception. It *is* difficult for us with our contemporary emphasis on the need for sexual equality *not* to be judgemental about Burns's relations with Jean Armour and Mary Campbell in particular, and about the casual way in which he loved and left other young women such as Lizzie Paton, Jenny Clow and Anna Park. Yet, if we leave the almost inevitable outcome of pregnancy aside for a moment, Carswell's depiction of willing and joyful relationships between Burns and his country girls leads us at least to consider that such sexual uninhibitedness was less hypocritical and life-denying than the sterile life-styles he was to encounter later in Edinburgh. And one notices that in each case Burns took responsibility, either financially or by taking the child into his own household, for the infants which he fathered.

There is, however, one of Burns's love relationships which has never been satisfactorily explained and one which was raised to new heights of controversy by the publication of Carswell's biography. This is Burns's relationship with Mary Campbell, the 'Highland Mary' of the poetry. Carswell's *Life* was the first account to give the information that the skeleton of an infant had been found in the coffin of the girl when it was exhumed in the nineteen-twenties and the way in which she filled out the story of Burns and Mary caused at least some of the outraged responses to her book. Carswell's letters to Professor Ferguson show how carefully she considered the available information relating to Mary Campbell. She tells him in a letter of 21st January 1930 that she had been given the information about the bones of the baby in Mary's grave by 'the late Philip Sulley, who was present at the private opening of the grave', while in a letter of 19th August 1930 she comments that a Dr Hunter had told her that 'all the inner circles of Burnsians are quite aware that Mary Campbell was having a baby to Burns'.[14]

James Mackay's 1992 biography returns to the vexed question of Mary and the Carswell revelations and through careful analysis of existing information and reasonably substantiable propositions he demonstrates how little is actually known about this affair and how difficult it is to form any safe conclusions about it. Burns himself has been of little help. He gave much less information about this love matter than was his usual practice, a situation which led Carswell to conclude that he had indeed some need to conceal the true facts of the relationship. As she puts it in her letter of 21st January to Professor Ferguson, 'if there had been no baby, why the unforgiving fury of Mary's father and the peculiar stricken and uncommon grief of Robert?' Carswell would appear to have differed from Professor Ferguson in her fitting together and interpretation of the available information, returning to the problem more than once in her correspondence with him. In a handwritten footnote to her letter of 24th April 1930, which deals principally with matters relating to May Cameron and Jenny Clow, she adds:

No. I can't quite share your view of the Mary Campbell business. The making of a Mason mark in the Bible, the solemnity of the texts chosen and the violent subsequent repudiation of 'conjugal acknowledgement' of Jean, all seem to point to serious intentions with regard to Mary, *even if*, when she had gone & Jean was back, he was again overtaken by his fondness for Jean. Mary cannot well have died of puerperal fever which follows a normal birth. It is more likely by the dates & any accounts handed down that she caught typhus or typhoid from her brother & this induced a premature delivery (a shock to her parents from whom till then she had concealed her condition). I have it on the best medical authority that a woman 7 months gone, if she contracted either typhus, typhoid or smallpox, would almost certainly miscarry or give birth to a premature child. The baby would then be buried before. Or, of course, if it happened to be alive, it might survive her by a short time.[15]

It is interesting that one of the more positive letters in the *Daily Record* correspondence of late September 1930 gives the Mary Campbell affair as the reason for her support of Carswell. This correspondent signs herself 'Truth's Best' and comments that she is indebted to Carswell for 'publishing what I myself felt was [sic] the real facts'.[16]

The impression that comes over from this correspondence of Carswell to Professor Ferguson is of the intensive study and thought which went into her preparation of her *Life*. Although she presented the results of her investigations to a large extent in the manner of the novelist rather than the scholar, she did explore her evidence until the jigsaw of the life took on a shape which seemed to her convincing in the face of human life generally and what we know of the facts of Burns's life in particular. One is reminded of her comment that

> for a woman or any being whose nature it is to live through the emotions, clarity of mind can only be got by taking the natural order. And I do think many of us thinking and educated women of this age go against our natures by striving to *force* ourselves to deal first through the intellect, living too much with ideas and not sufficiently trusting ourselves to the truths that would come to us through the deeper sensual and emotional channels ... To *think* for me is entirely different from to 'intellectualise'. One can and should *think* with all one's being – *thought* to be real must be linked up with the stream of the blood. The intellectualising business uses *other people's* and borrowed stuff and is a sort of cutting off and cowardice.[17]

Carswell is talking about novel writing, but one senses that this is the way she went about her biography of Burns also; the letter occurs during the period when she was researching it.

One of her more controversial interpretations is her argument to Professor Ferguson in April 1933 that the love affair between Burns and Clarinda was only

Platonic (technically) until Burns's last visit to Edinburgh when Clarinda
not only forgave him but believed herself to be rejoining her husband and
leaving the country never to return. The difference between the late letters,
the way he drops playfulness, calls her his Nancy (for the first time), the
fact that she destroyed several letters – he also – the fact that they felt a later
friendship to be impossible when she returned, the characters of the two
people & the whole situation – these seem to me to make a pretty strong
case. The date of 'Ae Fond Kiss' & its quality – I don't see Burns writing
that in his earlier period with the lady – and his misleading note about the
impassioned letter being the rhodomontade of youth are all in favour of such
a supposition.[18]

Whatever the truth about all these enigmatic and provocative love relation-
ships, Carswell does make out a convincing case for her interpretations. As a
result of her characterisation of Burns, who 'went about his field work with
one of the world's worst novels in his pocket ... ardently believing it to be the
world's best' – as she ironically comments in regard to *The Man of Feeling*
(78) – one can share in his impetuosity, his astonishment at his dismissal by
the Armours, naive perhaps but understandable in a narcissistic young man;
his inclusion of Jean in his anger when he believes her parents' tale that she is
considering the more reliable offer of another suitor and his eventual consoling
himself with Mary Campbell. Carswell's approach makes us aware too of
distance and the difficulty in keeping in touch in an age without easy transport
or telephone communication. Mary, returned to her parents' home in Campbel-
town in Kintyre, was almost as distant in bridgeable time and space as was the
Jamaica Burns had signed himself up for, but continually succeeded in avoiding.
Carswell paints a convincing picture of genuine distress and disorientation in
Burns at this time, caught between his honour and obligation to Mary and his
strong physical attraction and love for Jean; between his published declaration
for Jamaica and his personal fearful elation at the prospect of the publication
of his poems and what this might bring in terms of staying in Scotland and
escaping from farming. In later episodes such as her lively, if sceptical, account
of late-Enlightenment Edinburgh, she shows Burns at a loss with the higher-
class Edinburgh women who are delighted to flirt with him but who quickly
put him in his place when he attempts a more intimate relationship. And her
account of his pastoral dalliance with Clarinda is convincing too, although one
could have wished for a firmer narratorial irony or even outright condemnation
of his role-playing with Mrs McLehose while Jean was bearing his illegitimate
children in Ayrshire, and May Cameron and Jenny Clow likewise in Edinburgh.

While her open presentation of male and female sexuality in her *Life* was
largely responsible for the controversy it aroused, Carswell's focus on Burns's
love relationships suggests how closely his sexuality was related to his creativity
as poet. The interdependence of male sexual desire and artistic creation, the
artist's passion for his 'Muse' – whether real woman or transcendent female

symbol – has become almost a cliché. We have only to visit the Picasso Museum in Paris to feel the force of this truism as it is documented visually in the way each regenerative phase of the painter's artistic development is ushered in by a new female model and mistress. (What happens to the female Muse in an age of equality or the female artist who also has need of a Muse is a question for another paper!) Burns himself early recognised 'the connection between Love and Music and Poetry'. He entered his first poem written to a 'Muse' – although he did not know then to call her that – in his Commonplace Book in 1783 and commented: 'For my own part I never had the least thought or inclination of turning Poet till I got once heartily in Love, and the Rhyme and Song were, in a manner, the spontaneous language of my heart'.[19] He also described the harvest ritual which first threw him together with a young woman and the thrilling of his heartstrings like an Eolian harp – heard but not understood – as he removed the nettle stings and thistles from her fingers. It was at this time too that he heard about a laird's son who had composed a song for the girl he loved, so that the emulative streak in his own personality was encouraged: 'Thus with me began Love and Poesy; which at times have been my only, and till within this last twelve month, have been my highest enjoyment.'[20]

Burns's love songs are among the best-known and best-loved of his works, and as with Picasso's paintings many of these songs are linked in our minds with a particular woman loved by Burns. Here the life and work appear in a symbiotic relationship. To view Burns's song-writing exclusively in this way, however, is to undervalue the artist and craftsman. It disregards Burns's contribution to a long tradition of love poetry of different kinds, including courtly love poems, Elizabethan sonnets and pastorals, Romantic and post-Romantic love lyrics, where the theme of love can be both mundane and transcendent; actual or symbolically and artistically enabling. Thomas Crawford makes a distinction between what he calls the 'personal' songs and the 'impersonal', finding the latter group on the whole the more artistically satisfying.[21] It is this *impersonality*, the separation between – to adapt a phrase of Eliot – the man who loves and the mind which creates the finished art work, which marks Burns out as a master song writer one would not hesitate to place alongside lieder composers such as Schubert, although, unlike the usual lieder method of composition, Burns wrote his love poetry to an existing tune as opposed to the composer who sets existing words to music. In both approaches, however, there is in the successful work an unbreakable marriage between words and melody, mood and musical mode and cadence, which is the hallmark of the creative artist as opposed to the talented amateur. And this is what we find in Burns's love songs, which are fictional works of art, even while they call upon folk song for influence.

Many commentators have pointed to the motif of protectiveness in Burns's songs. There is, however, another motif which occurs consistently in the love songs. This is the motif of absence, of loss or yearning, occurring at times even when the surface lyric appears positive in its mood or meaning. And indeed this note of yearning is often conveyed not through the words but through the mode and cadences of the melodic line. Although 'Ca' the Yowes' speaks of love, of trysting, of the young man's vowed inability to part from his lover, the melody is situated in the minor mode which, when combined with the slow dotted rhythm and its evocative structure of leaps and steps, subverts the positive communication of the words and creates a sense of longing or potential absence which points beyond the present moment to that 'I can dee but canna pairt', which then takes on a resonance beyond its surface affirmation of undying love. Much of the poem is written in the future tense. Its haunting refrain is tender with that note of protectiveness already mentioned, but as a whole the song seems to evince a yearning for the unrealisable ideal. Similarly, in one of Burns's last songs, 'O wert thou in the cauld blast', by tradition written during his final illness for Jessy Lewars who had come to the house to help Jean, the dominant note is again one of stretching out to the ideal relationship, with the longing balanced against the repeated recognition of the succour needed in a harsh sublunary world: O wert thou in the cauld blast, I'd shelter thee, I'd shelter thee'. One notices the conditional tense here and remembers that in real life at this time Burns himself was the one in need of protection.

Rilke gives this definition of *Sehnsucht*: 'Das ist die Sehnsucht: wohnen im Gewoge/Und keine Heimat haben in der Zeit' – 'That is what longing is: to dwell in a state of flux/And to have no homeland in the world of Time.'[22] Clearly Burns did in one sense have a homeland in this world of time as can be seen by the rootedness in Ayrshire and Scotland which comes over in the imagery and scenarios of his poetry. In another sense, however, Burns was in a state of flux and without a true home. As an artist he was caught between worlds – and it is interesting that one of Carswell's supporters in the *Daily Record* correspondence, refuting charges by earlier correspondents of Burns's 'abnormal psychology', made the point that 'the only sign of abnormal psychology in Burns was his ability to make immortal songs'.[23] Burns's outstanding creative talent did make him 'abnormal', an outsider in the society of his time which could not accommodate a crosser of boundaries such as he aspired to be, and as Carswell makes plain in her Edinburgh scenes, there was nowhere he could go to find a place where he could function and people would accept him as the professional artist he was, as opposed to the freakish, if engaging, ploughman they wanted him to be. Caught by his own at-one-ness with his rural environment and the life of his own people, yet frustrated at his inability to find the necessary stimulus and creative interaction with his own intelligence and aspirations there; tempted by the attractions of urban life and minds which matched his own, yet disgusted by the city's trivial pursuits and its frivolous disregard of what he considered dear; caught between his despair at the thought of returning to farming, as was constantly being urged upon him by so-called benefactors, and his pessimism about finding an alternative way to fulfil his creative aspirations without poverty, Burns understandably struck so often the note of *Sehnsucht* in his songs, openly or implicitly. Burns in so many ways was a man with no homeland in the world of Time. It is this motif of longing, of desire for the unattainable which links Burns with the Romantics, with the songs of Schubert, with Goethe's Mignon and her longing for her lost land. As Donald Low points out in his Introduction to *Critical Essays on Robert Burns*, Burns differs in several ways from the English Romantic poets of the late-eighteenth and early nineteenth-centuries. Nature does not have the mystical significance for him that it has for Wordsworth and the scepticism and irony of his satires and epistles belong to the earlier age of Enlightenment. Yet as Low comments, Burns, with Blake, was the earliest poet of his century 'to stress as dynamic values freedom, both personal and national, simplicity and joy'.[24] I would suggest that he is at one with the Romantics also in his expression, through the erotic love metaphors of his poetry, of a desire for what D. H. Lawrence in *The Rainbow* called 'the beyond', for the ideal, the unattainable vision which is yet somehow at the heart of our spiritual life and our sense of humanity.

Explanations have been offered over and over again for the consistent popularity of Burns, both in Scotland and abroad, but no explanation is satisfactory which does not take into account this desire for the ideal, the yearning for what is beyond us, for what is beyond Time. And though they may not be able to articulate this desire, I believe it is the recognition of it, even unconsciously, in the poetry of Burns which draws readers of all qualities and cultures to it. It is one of the strengths of Catherine Carswell's biography that its focus on sexuality points us towards this poetry of desire.

NOTES

1. Catherine Carswell, *The Life of Robert Burns* (1930; reprinted Edinburgh: Canongate Publishing, 1990, with introduction by Tom Crawford). Quotations from the Canongate edition will be referenced by page numbers in parenthesis in the text.
2. James Mackay, *Burns: A Biography of Robert Burns* (Edinburgh: Mainstream Publishing Company, 1992), p. 197.
3. Claire Harman, 'Myth of a Ploughboy' (Review of *Dirt and Deity: A Life of Robert Burns* by Ian McIntyre), *Independent on Sunday*, 10 December 1995, pp. 34–5.
4. Excerpts from Carswell's *Life* were serialised in the *Daily Record* in September 1930. Quotations from the ensuing correspondence are from the issues of 26, 27 and 29 September 1930.
5. Letter from Catherine Carswell to Professor De Lancey Ferguson 19 August 1930, Ms 53/5, p. 2, Mitchell Library Glasgow.
6. *Glasgow Herald* 16 October 1930, quoted by Tom Crawford in Introduction to Canongate Classics edn, p. viii.
7. *Burns Chronicle* January 1932, Canongate Classics edn, p. x. Also referred to by Carswell in letter to Professor Ferguson of 2 February 1932, MS 53/9, p. 1.

8. Edwin Muir, 'A New Interpretation of Burns', *Nation and Athenaeum*, 8 November 1930, p. 212; William Power, *Daily Record*, 7 October 1930.

9. Carswell to Professor Ferguson, 11 November 1930, Ms 53/6, p. 3.

10. Introduction, Canongate Classics edn, p. ix.

11. Mackay, *A Biography of Robert Burns*, pp. 24, 133, 155.

12. Carswell to Professor Ferguson, 5 December 1929, Ms 53/1, p. 1.

13. Tom Crawford, Introduction to Canongate Classics edn, p. xii.

14. Ms 53/2, p. 4; Ms 53/5, p. 3.

15. Ms 53/3, p. 2.

16. *Daily Record*, 26 September 1930, p. 11.

17. Carswell to F. Marian McNeill, 30 April 1928, *Lying Awake: An Unfinished Autobiography and Other Posthumous Papers*, edited with an introduction by John Carswell (London: Secker & Warburg, 1950), pp. 187–8.

18. Letter of 20 April 1933, Ms 53/12, pp. 1–2.

19. Quoted by David Daiches in *Robert Burns* (1950), Spurbooks reprint (Edinburgh, 1981), pp. 51–2.

20. *Ibid.*, pp. 50–1.

21. Thomas Crawford, *Burns: A Study of the Poems and Songs* (Stanford: Stanford University Press, 1960), p. 268.

22. Rainer Maria Rilke, 'Das ist die Sehnsucht', *The Harrap Anthology of German Poetry*, edited by August Closs and T. Pugh Williams (London: Harrap, 1957), p. 498.

23. Correspondent 'A Highland Woman', *Daily Record* 26 September 1930, p. 11.

24. Donald Low, *Critical Essays on Robert Burns* (London: Routledge & Kegan Paul, 1975), pp. 4–6.

Burns and the Folksinger

B EFORE I EMBARK on this subject I had better arrive at some kind of
definition of a folksinger, as there are so many different connotations of it
in people's minds. Obviously it is someone who sings folk songs, but some
sing for love and some sing for money. This isn't really satisfactory as a
distinction because there are so many cross-overs from one to the other. Many
full-time professionals have a passionate love of their songs, while many who
sing for pleasure will seldom refuse payment if it's offered. I like to divide
folksingers into those who say, 'Listen to this wonderful song' and those who
say, 'Listen to *me* singing this wonderful song'. There has existed in the Sixties
and Seventies a dividing line between the traditional singers who inherited their
songs from their family or community background and those who were drawn
into the Revival and learned their songs from it. That dividing line has largely
disappeared now. You would listen in vain in folk clubs in the nineteen-sixties
for Burns songs, but now they are in most folksingers' repertoires.

To find out what the picture was before that, I will cite the first comment
on the relationship between Burns and the folksinger that I recall seeing. It was
made by the Aberdeenshire song collector, Gavin Greig, in his retiring Presiden-
tial Address to the Buchan Field Club in December 1905. Greig was descended
from a branch of the same family as Burns, his great-great-great-grandfather
and Burns's grandfather being brothers. Greig said:

> 'Folksong by a kind of social gravitation always seeks the lowest level and
> keeps it. It is necessarily of the people and for the people, and all attempts
> to raise it are soon met with an invincible inertia, for it cannot transcend the
> average lyric sense and sanction of the plebs. Every attempt to give folk song
> literary form and distinction fails beyond a certain point. Songs written for
> the people from the outside – from the outside laterally or vertically, are
> pretty certain to fail. The new claimants to popular favour and acceptance
> simply do not 'catch on'. There is no critical storm raised over the issue –
> no literary squabbles – for the folk-songist has no such word as literature
> in his vocabulary. He knows what he wants to sing; and there is an end of
> it ... He has his own anthology and he wants no exotics. His flowers must
> suit the climate and do without attention ... Yes, your folk-songist knows
> what is what – knows his own mind; and if he wants the daisy, the broom,
> or the heather, you cannot get him to take the rose or the lily. Absolute,
> instinctive, unreasoning confidence may be decried, but it is usually the final
> note of relative truth. And the folk-songist is right. His daisy, broom and

heather are the best for *him*; and if he cared to think of it, he could set his
superior critics a fairly hard task to show that his wildings were not *per se*
as perfect as the rose and the lily. If Scottish folk song could have been raised
Burns was the man to do it; but not even *he* succeeded. He has not given
the people a new and higher type of folk song, he has only reinforced and
enriched in meaureless degree a kind of song that, however it may have hung
on the horizon, has never quite been folk song. The rustic knows his Burns
and likes on occasion to hear his songs rendered by those who *can* sing them.
But they are hardly for *him*. He will sing *about* Burns, but it must be in
lays that have got the folk song hall-mark, in ditties that have little literary
kinship with the poet's own songs. Though he does not offer to sing

> Ye banks and braes and streams around
> The castle o' Montgomery

he will throw all his heart into 'Burns and his Highland Mary'. And although
'There was a lad was born in Kyle' is not exactly in his line, he will declaim
with infinite zest 'The Cottage where Robbie was Born'.

The most significant fact about this extract is not that it reveals that Greig
was a thundering snob, with his talk of plebs and rustics – he seems to have
forgotten that Burns himself was a man of the people – but that this speech
was delivered in 1905. That was before he and James Duncan had embarked
on their song-collecting project for the Spalding Club which was to have such
startling results. His views reflected received opinion on folk song and folk
singers, strongly influenced by the mores of his time and by the English Folk
Song Society's formation which he refers to in this same speech, and of which
he was a member. Much of what he says does apply to folk song in many
European traditions but it doesn't apply to Scotland, as he was to discover. He
was regarded as something of an authority on Scottish song tradition even
before he embarked on the collecting project, and gave frequent lectures on it,
illustrated by singers who were no doubt of the drawing-room variety. What
he talked about were the songs of Burns, Hogg and Lady Nairne, which had
found their way into print and were sung in concerts and recitals, by trained
singers, hi-jacked as it were by the art-song world. Many of them had not been
collected or written as art songs, but had come from the spring well of the oral
tradition, which has different criteria altogether from the more literary art-song
tradition. Nearly all our early song collectors were literary men who misunder-
stood and misjudged the material they collected, constantly apologising for its
crude and primitive nature and in some cases 'improving' or 'refining' to its
detriment as oral literature and an authentic legacy of the past.

Greig also didn't seem to know about the oral tradition that was all around
him and which he was amazed to discover when he and James Duncan began
collecting songs locally and found that after a short time they had heard on
the lips of living singers hundreds of songs, many in multiple versions, which

he had not known existed. This undoubtedly opened Greig's eyes to the fact that there was more to Scots folk song and folk singing than he had supposed; that the folk who sang were not just representative of the humblest sections of society but were drawn from every walk of life; that their songs were not just so much doggerel; and that their art was not something to belittle or patronise. Like generations of Scots before him and since, he had missed something which Burns felt in the very core of his bones and which he expressed in many of his songs and poems and writings, most neatly encapsulated perhaps in 'A Man's a Man for a' That' which owes its popularity to the fact that it strikes a universal chord in the human heart, particularly the hearts of Scots. In Scotland when we talk of the people, we mean all the people, from king to beggar, from scholar to farm worker. This is something particularly hard to get over to people in the Glasgow area, I have found. But it does not need to be argued about; history proves it. Even today, if you go to any folk festival you will find every sort of person there: high and low, young and old, rich and poor, educated and uneducated.

The idea that a song tradition which included the big ballads and a whole variety of lyrical and narrative song had any need of being 'raised', as Greig called it, is absurd. He made the same mistake that almost all our song collectors have made of judging the songs of oral tradition by literary standards that do not apply to them. The work of twentieth-century folklorists such as Albert Lord and our own late lamented David Buchan has helped to establish the idea that oral culture has its own canons and standards that differ considerably from those of the literary world. Even in the age of computers, 'word of mouth' has a quality that cannot be superseded. With hindsight Greig did revise many of his opinions and thought it worthwhile to make his collaboration with James Duncan the most important part of his life's work.

When he ran his column in the *Buchan Observer* for several years, Greig had song versions sent in to him from all kinds of people, from farm servants to ministers. Indeed, the family of the Rev. James B. Duncan were a rich source of songs for the collection. This highlights a misunderstanding that exists even today, and certainly existed in Greig's time and in the time of Burns, as regards the nature of Scottish society. It has never been the case that people of humble origins cannot become literate and well-read, or even highly educated or go to University and enter the professions. Class distinction has crept in upon us along with all the other anglicisation we have suffered, but historically and instinctively, Scots have a more democratic outlook – which Burns gave expression to *in excelsis* – and our education system has never in the past been the preserve of the elite and the rich, but rather has the connotation of the poor scholar with the poke of meal and a passion for learning. Glasgow University, when I as a working-man's daughter attended as a student in the early 1950s, had an annual holiday called Meal Monday, dating from the days when students were allowed time to *walk* back home to bring a new supply of meal to sustain them for another term. Burns's father couldn't afford to send him to University but, as many Scots have done, he did make sure his children were well schooled; and there was a respect and admiration for learning that is still ingrained in the Scots psyche at all social levels.

Every time I hear the phrase Ploughman Poet, I think of letters sent to the late Arthur Argo, Greig's great-grandson, by a man called John Reid. They are written in the most elegant literary style, that made me think he must be a minister or a dominie. He was a ploughman; but also, in his own words, a book-lorist, a lover of poetry, and he became a successful writer himself under the pen-name of David Toulmin. Like John Reid, Burns was no unlettered rustic, and neither were many of Greig's informants. In fact, as Dr Ian Olson has observed, Aberdeenshire in Greig's day contained fewer illiterate peasants per square mile than anywhere else in Europe. This could very well apply to the whole of Scotland.

Certainly, in Burns's day and in Greig's most of Scotland was mostly rural but nowadays the great population centres are cities and towns. People go where the work is. Nowadays there is not so much work particularly in heavy industry, so perhaps the population distribution will change again. But when the Folk Song Revival took place in the 1960s, folk clubs sprang up mostly in urban areas, and the revival singers were largely town-based. Even with the founding of the Traditional Music and Song Association, to make sure the urban revivalists were brought into touch with the largely rural based tradition-bearers, the folk clubs continued in an urban setting. The beginnings of the Folk Song Revival – and in those days the emphasis was on song – were from across the Atlantic, in the American skiffle craze, the political protest movement and the songs of Dylan and Baez, and artistes like The Weavers, Pete Seeger and Peter, Paul and Mary. But in Scotland, people like Hamish Henderson, the late Arthur Argo, the late Norman Buchan, Drew Moyes and others steered the movement towards the native tradition and made wonderful discoveries like Jeannie Robertson, the Stewarts of Blair and Willie Scott. Did Burns have anything at all to do with all this?

At first it would seem that I would have to agree with Gavin Greig's words in 1905 and say folksingers like Burns songs but don't sing them. Belle Stewart sings 'Burns and Highland Mary' but no Burns songs as such. On the other hand, traditional singer Bobby Robb of Girvan told me that when he looked for Ayrshire songs in his own locality all he could find were Burns songs. Like most Scots, he'd been put off Burns by having him pushed down his throat at school, so he didn't want to sing them in folk clubs. At the same time, there is another Ayrshire singer, Joe Rae, of Beith, who inherited his songs and stories from his grandfather who was a herd in Galloway and whose repertoire includes versions of songs collected by Burns, such as 'Coming Thro the Craigs o' Kyle' and 'Under Her Apron'.

In school, I can say from experience, Burns is presented as the only Scots poet and only as a poet : his song collecting and song writing are never dealt with. Children are given Burns's songs to *recite* in the English class, with his Scots being regarded as a problem, as if it were a foreign language. Or they are taught them in classical style in the music class. Thus in the Folk Revival, which was in essence a rebellion, singers didn't asociate Burns with 'folk'. Another reason the Revival singers did not sing Burns songs was that they were associated with the stuffed shirt Burns Supper scene and the clasped hands delivery that was exactly what the Revival was aiming to get away from. I must say I have always detested the rendering of Burns's songs with what I call the 'simmer and mither' syndrome; this arises when trained singers stick faithfully to Burns's Scots words but enunciate them in an anglicised way. I also shudder at the semi-operatic treatment of Burns that completely falsifies the beauty of the songs, like hanging rhinestones on the branches of a bonnie birken tree. I recently heard Rod Paterson, one of our best folksingers, say on the radio that it took the singers of the folk revival to show people how to sing Burns's songs as they should be sung, and I must say I agree with that. Those who disagree, must disagree – I have no problem with that; it's a free country after all, but I wonder how many of our folksingers such people have actually listened to.

Something that is never considered by almost anyone is that Burns himself must have been a singer, or he could never have written such songs. It should be pretty clear to anyone that songs are not written by non-singers. When I say he was a singer I don't mean that he was a Singer with a capital S, as on the concert platform or the variety stage. It's hard to imagine Burns singing with piano accompaniment or in art song style like an eighteenth-century Kenneth McKellar. But he lived in an age when people provided their own entertainment and most people 'didnae need muckle priggin tae sing' as one present-day singer has put it to me. Singing was looked on as a natural human activity. In his social life, Burns obviously sang in his family circle, and with his friends in inns and taverns, and at social gatherings. He heard songs and stories all round him in his daily life and was a part of that tradition. He had a most acute ear for the rhythms and nuances of language, as well as the subtleties of music and was able to match the two so well that neither needed to be wrenched to make them fit in with each other. That is one of the secrets of good song-writing.

It's interesting to read in his correspondence with George Thomson how the two men frequently disagreed about matters of taste and style. 'What pleases me as simple and naive disgusts you as ludicrous and low', Burns wrote. He felt less at home with English than with Scots when it came to writing songs and on one occasion in an outburst of candour complained, 'These English songs gravel me to death'. Thomson preferred English words, which he thought more refined, but which Burns was well aware did not always sit easily with the tunes or with the Scottish ear.

In describing how he went about writing a song, he described how he first made himself complete master of the tune, in his own singing. Then he considered the feelings that the tune evoked and chose a theme that suited that. Then he would compose his first verse, which he said was generally 'the most difficult part of the business', after which he would walk out and look about him for suitable imagery to harmonise with his thoughts and feelings, all the time humming over the tune to the verses he had composed. This seems an excellent and very practical plan of action to be recommended to budding songwriters of whatever musical persuasion.

He would learn songs and write songs, and often made his own versions of songs, adding verses or changing existing ones or writing whole new songs for the collections of Johnson and Thomson. You would think from the way this is talked about in literary circles that this was something new and unique. But he was only doing what folksingers all over the world have done since the beginning of time, and are still doing today. Folksingers constantly recreate and remould songs, put new words to old tunes, or old words to new tunes. They tell the story as they feel they want to tell it, create the mood the song evokes in them, whittle down or add to, as they feel appropriate. Continuing to sing the old songs need not be as some suggest boring and repetitive because of the very nature of folk-singing itself. No two singers sing the same song in the same way. This is one of the beauties of folk singing, which is a creative art – or perhaps, more correctly, a recreative art.

One reason why I still go to a folk club every week, when possible, is to hear this multiplicity of versions that is the sign of a living tradition. And believe me, it can still be heard, even including the present-day songs, that are treated in the same way. For example, at my local folk club we recently had a Singers' Night, and I heard several old songs, including two versions of 'The Shepherd Lad', 'The Pace-Egging Song', 'Whistle and I'll Come tae ye my Lad', 'McPherson's Rant', 'I Aince Loed a Lass', 'The Lea Rig', 'By Yon Castle Waa', 'New York Girls', a setting of William Soutar's ballad 'Surely Ye Hae Seen My Love', as well as a sprinkling of modern songs, one written by a club member about his father's sea-going life. Four Burns songs, three sung unaccompanied and one, with guitar, suggests that Burns is now very much a part of the folksinger's repertoire.

So instead of agreeing with Greig that Burns has little to do with folk song tradition, I believe he is at the heart of it. Greig did alter his ideas once he had had his Road to Damascus experience while engaged in his collecting project. I also think Scottish folk singers changed their attitude to Burns when they began to realise that many of his songs are indistinguishable from other songs that have come down to us in tradition, and in some cases they are his versions of some of these songs. For example, just about every folk-song tradition has a song that corresponds to 'My Love is Like a Red Red Rose' whose imagery is in fact archetypal. 'Ye Banks and Braes' is a similar case. Songs like 'Ae Fond Kiss', 'A Man's a Man for a' That' and 'Sic a Parcel o Rogues' have all come to be heard in folk clubs, sung by our best-known singers including Archie Fisher, Tich Frier and Dick Gaughan, whose version of 'Westlin Winds and Slaughtering Guns' is beautiful, moving and direct, in spite of the flowery poetic diction it contains. One of the singers who has done more than almost anyone to popularise Burns on the folk scene is Jean Redpath, although she hasn't been heard in a folk club or at a folk festival for a long time. I could also add many other names, like Dougie McLean and the McCalmans. I must also mention a superb version of 'Wha'll Mowe me Noo' by Glasgow's Gordeanna McCulloch, who makes so much more of it than just a bawdy song; and an equally poignant 'By Yon Castle Waa', by Kilmarnock's Heather Heywood. There are also many singers whose names are quite unknown, but who are nonetheless to be numbered as folksingers, whose repertoires include Burns songs and who take pleasure in singing them. These nameless singers are just as important as the famous ones, because a tradition is not carried on by a handful of star performers.

But there is another aspect to the singing of Burns's songs by present-day folksingers. A new confidence in and understanding of the song tradition has led some singers to do more than that. Burns collected a song composed by Isobel Pagan, the proprietress of a local howff, and made it into 'Caa the Yowes tae the Knowes'. Nowadays the original version can be heard sung. Another singer, Tommy Blackhall, took 'The Tarbolton Lasses' and set it to the tune of 'The Earl of Errol', with a chorus from 'The Brewer Lad'. 'There Was a Lad was Born in Kyle' is more often heard sung to the tune it was set to, that of 'Dainty Davie', which suits it infinitely better than the rather warbly one that becomes almost operatic on the lips of bel canto singers. A present day songwriter, Ian Walker, has taken the words of the Selkirk Grace and used them as an ironic chorus in a song that protests about the state of affairs in a world where one part of the human race is surfeited with 'food for breakfasts, dinners, teas and in between meals feeding' while the rest 'spend their living, dying'.

The singer-songwriter has been one of the main features of the Folk Song Revival and after. This is a mixed blessing of course, as not all our singer-songwriters have had Burns's talent. Song writing is a much under-rated art and also a very difficult one. If it is done well, in addition to being entertainment, it can also give expression to cultural identity. You can tell a lot about a person from the songs he or she likes, even if they don't sing them. That man ahead of his time, Andrew Fletcher of Saltoun, around the time of the Treaty of Union in 1707, agreed with whoever said that if he was permitted to write a country's songs, he need not care who made its laws.

It is because folksingers recognised, perhaps unconsciously, in Burns's songs an expression of their own Scottishness and their democratic values, that they now sing Burns songs. There may also be other reasons for this. Perhaps I could outline my own, which are not necessarily typical. With family roots in Ayrshire, I grew up knowing that when I visited my grandparents in Dalry, I was very likely walking on ground that Burns had trod, and was looking out at the kind of landscape that would have been familiar to him. The Ayrshire doric of my relations and their friends and neighbours filled my ears and became ingrained in my consciousness. For that reason, the language of Burns's songs and poetry strike a chord within me. I know Burns's poetic genius gives it a heightened quality, but it still to me has the authentic ring of Ayrshire about it. I was even told a legend about the ford near my grandfather's door being the very one where Jenny 'draigled all her petticoatie comin thro the Rye' carrying travellers across – the Rye being the river Rye, a tributary of the Garnock.

I never had any aversion to things I was taught in school, however badly – except perhaps mathematics – so I retained a love of Burns songs and Scots songs generally, all through my childhood, along with classical and pop songs, music hall ditties and hymns. Among my party pieces as a child were 'Duncan Gray', 'Comin Thro the Rye', 'The Wee Cooper o Fife' and 'Will Ye No Come Back Again?' As I grew up I came to appreciate the bawdy song tradition, in which Burns – if I may put it without intending a double entendre – looms very large, and my repertoire has for long included for example the earthier version of 'John Anderson my Jo', 'To the Weavers Gin Ye Go', 'We're Geyly Yet', 'Laddie Lie Near Me', and 'Hey for Houghmagandie'. Of course I also love 'The Lea-Rig', 'Mary Morison' and many other of the love songs.

That is just my personal account: there are many singers both well known and unknown, who sing Burns songs now. To me the term folk singer applies to anyone who sings folk songs as folk songs; that is, with respect for the song. For a good number of years, the word conjured up a picture in most people's minds of someone thrashing a guitar and singing through their teeth. Fortunately the Traditional Music and Song Association by promoting good unaccompanied singing provided a corrective to this. But just as it's now possible to hear folk music on the radio in amongst other kinds of music, it is possible to hear folksingers singing outside the folk ghetto which the folk clubs tended to create. I think it has become better understood that many of Burns's songs can be regarded as traditional in the sense that they have been widely sung and passed on through generations.

Those people who try to make strictures about songs not being regarded as traditional because they have appeared in print fail to take into account the bookish nature of the Scots tradition, in which songs have gone in and out of print and yet still get passed on orally. In most countries of course literary tradition and folk tradition are at opposite ends of the spectrum; in Scotland they constantly meet and mingle. It is also inappropriate to regard them as belonging to the lowest social class, since our muse is a democratic one, as Ailie Munro has highlighted in the title of her up-dated version of her book on the Folk Music Revival in Scotland, soon to be published by the Scottish Cultural Press. I was told in the nineteen-sixties by a typical Glasgow revivalist – lapsed Catholic turned Communist, of course – that I had no right to consider myself a folk singer because I was a school teacher. Would the same person have tried to tell Burns he couldn't be a poet because he was a ploughman?

Three years ago I presented a paper at the International Ballad Conference in Los Angeles, on one of the themes of the conference, Ballads and Boundaries. In preparing that paper I became even more aware of the unique nature of Scots ballad and song tradition, which does not so much cross all boundaries of class, language, time and place, as behave as if they didn't exist. I believe that this is also the characteristic of Burns that has made him such an important international figure and endeared him to people the world over from a wide variety of cultures. It is also what the folksinger has recognised in him, once all the cumbersome paraphernalia of tartanry and kitsch had been cleared away. MacDiarmid made a very good job of this in 'A Drunk Man Looks at the Thistle', when he said:

> Mair nonsense has been uttered in his name
> Than in ony's barrin liberty and Christ.

and the acute observation of how mediocre nobodies being invited to propose the Immortal Memory make this 'an excuse for faitherin Genius wi *their* thochts'. He asks, 'What unco fate maks *him* the dumpin-grun/For aa the sloppy rubbish they jaw oot?' What the folksinger recognises in Burns is someone who is a part of the song tradition, who devoted much of his life to sustaining it and who wrote songs we can sing, songs that express what we believe in. If you have never heard some of our folk singers singing Burns's songs, let me recommend to you that you listen.

Another point I must make is that folksingers have drawn attention to the fact which many Scots don't bother to consider: that *all* Scots songs were not written by Burns, which would have pleased Burns himself very much. His efforts in collecting and writing songs were very much the result of his own awareness of the existence of an on-going tradition, and it was the failure of those who made a cult figure out of him to take account of this that nearly killed the tradition. He, on the other hand, was always ready to honour another poet or songwriter, whose work he admired; for example, Robert Fergusson, whom he thought so much of that he erected a stone to his memory in Canongate Kirkyard. Fergusson was renowned as a singer and songwriter in the Edinburgh of his time and, like Burns, loved the convivial life as a break from the drudgery of a dreary job. But it was not just people like Fergusson that he respected. Burns collected the original version of 'Ca the Yowes' from Isobel Pagan, and 'Comin Thro the Craigs o Kyle' from Jean Glover, who gave up respectability to become a wandering entertainer. These two songs are attributed to Burns often without any mention of their origins, although he faithfully acknowledged his sources. The fact that it is often not easy to find the dividing line between what Burns collected and what he composed to me is proof, if proof were needed, that he is integral to the song tradition.

Burns and the Jacobite Song

D ISCUSSION of Burns's relationship to Jacobitism and the Jacobite song has, in the last twenty-five years especially, tended to fluctuate between two polarities, each in its way an extreme statement of the case. The first states that Burns was a Jacobite, writing in a living anti-Union tradition: as William Donaldson writes, 'Burns's Jacobitism was perfectly genuine, as genuine as his patriotism, and intimately connected with it.' The second, usually though not universally by contrast, emphasizes the factitious nature of the Jacobite song, and stresses Burns's role as the creator of a sentimental, rather than the preserver of a patriotic tradition. It has proved possible for some writers to adopt both positions simultaneously: no doubt in its way a tribute to the MacDiarmid-like quality of Burnsian Jacobitism, to 'Aye be whaur/Extremes meet'. The present essay does not seek to explore the question of Burns's personal views further than this, save by the implicit route of diagnosing the nature of the thematic alterations Burns made to the tradition he inherited: for my argument will assume that he wrote in a living subgenre, largely contemporaneous with the events it described. As has become clear in recent work towards an edition of James Hogg's *Jacobite Relics*, a very significant part of the Jacobite song tradition can be found circulating in some form before the Romantic period (for example, my forthcoming article in *Studies in Hogg and His World* demonstrates that over 80% of songs in the First Series of the *Relics* have some affiliation to lyrics or airs of the Jacobite era). In this essay, I examine Burns's relationship to the Jacobite song from three perspectives: first, derivation of air or set; secondly, Burnsian reinterpretations of the role and character of the singer; and thirdly, more general thematic alterations, with particular concentration on the Jacobite/Jacobin nexus. In doing this, my aim is to set up a series of positions which can form the basis of more specalist interpretation.[1]

Burnsian indebtedness to the Jacobite tradition is apparent throughout his songwriting. He is especially fond of the 'Highland Laddie' cycle, the songs which, emerging out of a tradition of gipsy or Highander as erotic raider, became (roughly contemporary with Ramsay's no doubt deliberately polite codification of the theme) an expression of Jacobite patriotism with uncannily close echoes of the Gaelic *aisling* tradition, found both in Ireland and Scotland. In this genre, the nation is portrayed as a woman, abandoned, neglected and wrong, whom the poet envisions, and whom he (for *aislings* are normally gender-specific in these terms) hears will be redeemed by the messianic return of the delivering hero, usually in the eighteenth century the Stuart monarch.

In the 'Highland Laddie' cycle, the mediating poet's role in this encounter is diminished, and quite often the woman herself is the speaker. Burns takes this approach in 'A Highland lad my Love was born', where the hero's military dress echoes the mutual imagery of sexual fulfilment and political liberation used in Jacobite 'Highland Laddie' songs of the 1720–50 period: 'With his ... guid Claymore down by his side,/The ladies' hearts he did trepan' is Burns's rendering of a number of similar collocations, such as 'He wears the Pistol by his Side/That'll gar me laugh for a that' in a *c.* 1747 set of 'Tho Georthie reigns in Jamie's stead'. In 'A Highland lad' however, the female speaker is an ageing widow, and her Highlander has been hanged: a considerable dramatic shift from the cycle of fifty years earlier, and a topic to which I shall return in discussion of Burns's alteration of the age and character of the Jacobite singer.[2]

'The White Cockade' (Kinsley no. 306) uses a more traditionally young singer in its revisitation of the 'Highland Laddie' topos of abandoning material possessions (the fruits, on one level, of the Union's false comforts) for the purity of Highland (though note that 'my love was born in Aberdeen', so is only a thematic Highlander, i.e. a patriot) militarism. Again, as in the original cycle, erotic self-abandonment is linked to the horrific risks of loss of life and fortune taken by the 30,000 Scots who rose in arms for the Stuarts in the sixty years after 1688:

> I'll sell my rock, my reel, my tow
> My gude gray mare and hawkit cow;
> To buy mysel a tartan plaid,
> To follow the boy wi' the White Cockade.

Economic suffering and a totalizing love are the signs of political purity, but behind them lurks the suffering of the poverty they imply.

'Bonie laddie, Highland laddie' (Kinsley no. 353) is more or less a direct lift from the subgenre, brought forward in time to be a song of hate directed against Cumberland, who died in 1765. 'As I cam o'er the Cairney mount' (Chorus: 'O my bonie Highland lad', Kinsley no. 577) in its turn draws directly on one of the better-known 'Highland Laddie' sets with a female speaker ('For on the *Cairnamount* I spy'd/ In careless Dress a Highland Laddie'), which itself may be dated back to the sixteen-nineties through its anti-Williamite satire on '*Butter-Boxes*' (Dutchmen). Similarly 'Highland Laddie' (Kinsley no. 578) appears to be a thinly-revised version of an explicitly Jacobite dialogue between a Highlander and his 'Bonie lassie, Lawland lassie' found in National Library of Scotland Acc 9202. 'There grows a bonie brier-bush' (Kinsley no. 587) uses similar imagery ('He's coming frae the North that's to fancy me') as does 'Leezie Lindsay' (Kinsley no. 565), though here it is apparently free of Jacobitism, while 'Frae the friends and Land I love' (Kinsley no. 341) adopts the identification of woman and nation which lies at the heart of the 'Highland Laddie' cycle. Its 'Banished' who will be brought home again is also closely related to the Jacobite rhetoric on which it draws: 'An ilk loyal, bonie lad/ Cross the seas and win his ain', as Burns says in the inherited voice of Jacobite exile.[3]

Exile of course is also clearly if briefly apparent in 'Auld lang syne' (Kinsley no. 240) in the line 'But seas between us braid hae roar'd'. If this song, lamenting a vanished and beloved past reclaimable only though sentiment, is not itself originally Jacobite (and it may be), a number of its earliest sets certainly are, including one of 1717 which laments the broken 'Union ... thou [Scotland] had of late with France' (under Queen Mary). Burns adopts the theme of exile in certain other songs, including 'It was a' for our rightfu' king' (Kinsley no. 589), while 'The bonie lad that's far awa' (Kinsley no. 348) echoes 'O'er the hills and far away', a set found frequently in Jacobite propaganda from at least 1710 onwards (John Gay uses it in *The Beggar's Opera*), and which became emplaced in 'Tho Georthie reigns in Jamie's stead' ('He's far ayont the hills the night/ Whom I loe well, for a' that'). This song in its turn won its lasting fame through Burns's use of its air and some aspects of its set in 'Is there, for honest Poverty' (Kinsley no. 482): on one level, his transmutation of the patriotic theme of the song into universal terms.[4]

'To daunton me' (Kinsley no. 209) has a very clear Jacobite ancestor from the 1740s of the same name, while 'Greensleeves and tartan ties' (Kinsley no. 280) seems to be related to the jacobitical 'Greensleeves and pudding pies', which was supposed to be the favourite song of Allan MacDonald of Kingsburgh. 'Jamie come try me' (Kinsley no. 295) has a long history before Burns, possibly dating back to the Reformation, some of it perhaps as an erotic Jacobite song, while the Jacobite 'Awa whigs awa' (Kinsley no. 303) is found in David Herd's MSS. 'McPherson's Farewell' (Kinsley no. 196) is Burns's adaptation of a 'social bandit' song dating back almost a century: such songs were usually associated with a rhetoric of dissent of a radical-reactionary kind, theoretically outlined in E. J. Hobsbawm's study *Bandits* (1969) and found in popular Jacobite culture.[5]

Burns also uses the air of 'Push about the jorum' (a seventeenth-century Royalist song) in 'The Dumfries Volunteers' (Kinsley no. 484) and the air and some of the set of 'O'er the Water to Charlie' (Kinsley, no. 211), which had appeared in Ramsay as 'O'er the Moor to Maggy'. 'The Campbells are comin' (Kinsley no. 314) is known in an early eighteenth-century Jacobite version 'The Clans are Coming', while 'The Election: A New Song' (Kinsley no. 492) uses as its air that of the nationalist/Jacobite anti-Union song', 'Fy, let us a' to the Bridal'. 'This is no my ain lassie' (Kinsley no. 507) uses the air of 'This is no my ain house', one of the best of Jacobite songs, known by Charles Edward himself. 'You're welcome, Willie Stewart' (Kinsley no. 538) and 'Lovely Polly Stewart' (Kinsley no. 579) alike use one of the better-known airs of 1745, 'You're welcome, Charlie Stuart', while 'Charlie he's my darling' (Kinsley no. 562) is a slight adaptation of a Jacobite song already in circulation by the mid-1770s, and quite possibly considerably earlier. 'The German lairdie' (Kinsley no. 605) adapts 'What merriment has taen the whigs' from 'a murrain has taen the whigs', while Burns's adaptations and resettings of 'Killiecrankie' (Kinsley no. 610) are in tune with both Jacobite and non-Jacobite eighteenth-century practice, erotic as well as military. Likewise the songs on Sherriffmuir ('Up and Warn a' Willie' (Kinsley no. 212) and Burns's version of 'The Battle of Sherra-moor' (Kinsley no. 308)) are structurally dependent on the view of the battle taken in the earlier broadside 'A Race at Sherriff-Muir'. If Burns honours tradition in his use of 'Killiecrankie's' air, he does so equally in his relation with 'Sherriff-Muir's' set.[6]

If Burns is deeply indebted to this tradition, he is also one of its key reinterpreters. In particular, Burns has a tendency to present the singers of his jacobitical sets as ageing, disappointed or bereaved, thus conferring an implicitly elegiac quality on songs which, where they are found earlier in the tradition, can rather be suggestive of hope and deliverance. The mourning widow of 'A Highland lad my Love was born' (Kinsley no. 84) possesses a status as a singer which undermines the traditional promise of the land's renewal, as indeed does the hanging of the virile Highlander himself. A similar situation is visible in 'The Highland widow's lament' (Kinsley no. 590), where the speaker is deprived, mournful and past the best of her life. The singer's transmutation from lover to widow in such songs, on one level a reflection of the aftermath of Culloden, is on another a development of sentiment which is placing unbreakable barriers of nostalgia and foreordained defeat between itself and the past it mourns, thus depoliticizing it or rendering its politics irrelevant. Sometimes, as in 'Strathallan's Lament' (Kinsley no. 168), the dispossessed Jacobite singer appears to have been someone actually killed at Culloden: Viscount Strathallan, who is famously supposed to have received the Last Sacrament under the species of oatmeal and whisky. Such a lament is an ultimate demonstration of loss: that of oneself. In 'Ye Jacobites by Name' (Kinsley no. 371), the singer is 'a Man undone'; in 'There'll never be peace till Jamie comes hame' (Kinsley no. 326), the listener hears the song from a man who sings 'tho' his head it was grey' to mourn his 'seven braw sons' who 'for Jamie drew sword', whose death is a kind of requital for Jamie's own great loss of his throne. Both losses are, however, seen as no prelude to restoration, but are rather part of the ageing process: 'Now life is a burden that bows me down/ Sin I tint my barns, and he tint his crown'. Similar sentiments can be found in the conflation of domestic and national loss in 'Derwentwater's Farewell', versions of which are found in oral tradition from Scotland to Shropshire:

> So fare thee well, George Collingwood
> Since fate has put us down;
> If thou and I have lost our lives
> Our king has lost his crown ...

Here, the urgency of the matter of the lost crown and the contemporaneity of the dialogue arguably foreground the cause more clearly than the distancing elegy of 'Till Jamie comes hame'.[7]

The greatest tragic loss of opportunity, the Union, is regarded in the same kind of way in Burns's famous version of an earlier song, 'Such a parcel of rogues in a nation' (Kinsley no. 375):

> O would, or I had seen the day
>   That treason thus could sell us
> My auld grey head had lain in clay,
>   Wi' BRUCE and loyal WALLACE!

Here the theme of the singer is, as 'Till Jamie comes hame' implicitly suggests, a valediction. Three times 'fareweel' leads off the first three lines, while the 'ancient glory' of Scotland is remembered now only in the ageing speaker, loyal 'till my last hour', a date the poem suggests cannot be far removed.

It was not, thankfully, Burns's sole or even main task to cloak the Jacobite song in the garb of Ossian, though his use of ageing singers as personae suggests something of that effect. He also appears to have bonded the specific patriotic language of Scots nationalist Jacobitism with the universalist pretensions of Jacobin ideals. The inherited idea of Scotland's history as a struggle for liberty becomes in 'Robert Bruce's march to Bannockburn' (Kinsley no. 425) possibly, and in 'Is there, for honest Poverty' (Kinsley no. 482) more certainly, a particularist expression of a general aim of freedom from tyranny (Joseph Ritson, in fact, at much the same time, suggested that Jacobitism could be understood in terms of opposition to tyranny – news to the Whig apologists of 1688). In 'Bruce's March to Bannockburn', which, as Burns confessed to George Thomson in 1793, concerned more recent struggles for liberty than that of Bannockburn, history is collapsed into a perpetual contemporaneity which semantically joins French Liberté with Barbourian 'Fredome' by way of Jacobitism: for the emphasis on Edward II as 'a cruel but able Usurper' (he was none of these things) hardly matches Plantagenet aims or achievements. The first three Edwards may have sought the realm of Scotland, but they did not usurp its crown as did the Hanoverians (for the Scottish Parliament had never passed the Act of Settlement, but had merely been forced to consent to it through incorporation: not the least of the reasons why the Stuarts stood pledged to repeal the Union). Burns's emphasis on usurping and usurpation in connexion with 'Bruce's march', both in the song and his letters, suggests a tripartite historical periodicity (1314, 1746, 1789) collapsed into the perpetual contemporaneity of the need for liberty/freedom, whether under the cloak of 'Scotland's King and Law' or in another guise.[8]

'Is there, for honest Poverty' takes this process a stage further, towards the universal in space, as well as time. Although its air may well have had other applications, 'the earliest verses ... marked for the tune *'For a' that'* are in the

scarce collection of *Loyal Songs*, 1750', though their companion song, 'Tho'
Georthie reigns in Jamie's stead' is probably earlier, as stated above. In Burns's
fresh set promising universal brotherhood, Jacobite ideas of the corrupting
power of English court gold, the aristocratic betrayal of the honest ordinary
patriot (cf. *Braveheart* for this construction set at an earlier date) and the
language of resistance to the metropolis are recast. The invitation to the 'man
of independant mind' to resist the beguiling bribes of power transmutes the
'honest Poverty' of the sometime Jacobite patriot ('honest man' was a Jacobite
code, and the 'Independent Electors of Westminster' largely a Jacobite front)
into a type of perpetually contemporary integrity; while the 'fools' who have
'silks' and the 'knaves' who have 'wine' are implicitly English or Anglicized.
Their 'rank is but the guinea's stamp', and the guinea, bearing the head of
George III (and thus a symbol of Hanoverian power: the 'stamp' carries
overtones of imposed (excise) duties and general oppression, as in O'Brien's
vision of the future in *Nineteen Eighty-Four*, a boot stamping on a human face
forever), was a coin which had no equivalent in the Scottish currency before
1707: indeed, its valuation was strongly tied to the sterling exchange rate and
through it to the National Debt. In addition, the terms of abuse levelled at the
aristocratic parasites, 'yon birkie ca'd, a lord ... He's but a coof' are strongly
Scottish ones, sturdy appraisals of value from a people who developed the very
philosophy of 'the pith o' Sense'. The 'He's comin yet for a' that' of 'Tho'
Georthie reigns in Jamie's stead' becomes here an 'It's', promising universal
brotherhood rather than the restoration of kingly justice: but its genesis is
recognizably the same. Jacobite language is made a contemporary vehicle for
radical value, and as a byblow, Burns crystallizes the Jacobite critique in an
egalitarian, proletarian vision of the Scottish identity's gift to universal value,
a vision of the 'pride o' worth' on which we arguably still culturally de-
pend.[9]

Burns's treatment of the Jacobite song thus reveals a degree of indebtedness
to an established tradition, and the remaking of that tradition in both sentimen-
tal-elegiac and radically transformed ways. Small wonder that there are polarities
in the discussion of Burns's Jacobitism, for the poet occupies both of them.

NOTES

1. William Donaldson, *The Jacobite Song* (Aberdeen, 1988), 76; Murray G. H. Pittock,
   'Text and Context: Editing the *Jacobite Relics*', *Studies in Hogg and his World*,
   forthcoming (1997).
2. *The Poems and Songs of Robert Burns*, edited by James Kinsley, 3 vols (Oxford,
   1968), vol. II. All references in the text are to this edition. Cf. Murray G. H. Pittock,
   Poetry and Jacobite Politics in Eighteenth-Century Britain and Ireland (Cambridge,
   1994), chs 2, 4 and 5; 'Tho Georthie Reign' found in Aberdeen University Library
   MS 2222, published as 'New Jacobite Songs of the 'Forty-five' by Murray G. H.

Pittock, *Studies in Voltaire and the Eighteenth Century* 267 (1989), 1–75. For 'Highland Laddie' cycle, cf. also Donaldson (1988), 49 ff.

3. Donaldson (1988), 56; also Donaldson, 'Highland Laddie: The Making of a Myth', *Scottish Literary Journal* 3:2 (1976), 30–50; James Dick, *Notes on Scottish Song by Robert Burns* (Edinburgh, 1908), 8.

4. Pittock (1994), chs 2 and 4.

5. For the radical-reactionary side of Jacobite culture, see Paul Monod, *Jacobitism and the English People* (Cambridge, 1989) and Frank McLynn, *Crime and Punishment in Eighteenth-Century England* (London, 1989); Dick (1908), 35–36, 97n.

6. Pittock (1989)/ AUL MS. 2222 for 'The Clans are Coming'; Murray G. H. Pittock, *The Invention of Scotland: the Stuart Myth and the Scottish Identity 1638 to the Present* (London and New York, 1991), ch. 2; Donaldson (1988), 27 for facsimile of 'A Race at Sherriff-Muir'; T. F. Henderson, '"Charlie he's My Darling" and other Burns' Originals', *Scottish Historical Review* 3 (1906), 171–78; Dick (1908), 101n for pre-1745 existence of 'This is no my ain house'.

7. The story of Viscount Strathallan is alluded to in Bruce Lenman, 'The Scottish Episcopal Clergy and the Ideology of Jacobitism', in Eveline Cruickshanks (ed.), *Ideology and Conspiracy: Aspects of Jacobitism 1689–1759* (Edinburgh, 1982), 36–48 (47); cf. Donaldson (1988), 85–86; Pittock (1994), ch. 2.

8. Pittock (1994), ch. 5; *The Letters of Robert Burns*, ed. J. De Lancey Ferguson and G. Ross Roy, 2nd edn, Volume II (1790–96) (Oxford, 1985), nos. 582–84; 612 to the Earl of Buchan; Donaldson (1988), 86–87.

9. Dick (1908), 107n; cf. William Bernard McCarthy, *The Ballad Matrix* (Bloomington and Indianapolis, 1990), 16 ff. for radical use of the ballads by the singer Agnes Lyle.

Loose Canons: Milton and Burns, Artsong and Folksong

> If I may venture to give my own definition of a folk song I should call it 'an individual flowering on a common stem.'
>
> Ralph Vaughan Williams, 'National Music'

ECHOES OF Milton's 'L'Allegro' and 'Il Penseroso' are so frequent in eighteenth-century poetry that I will begin by just mentioning Burns's habitual introduction of Miltonic flora (such as the hawthorn and the laurel) and fauna such as buzzing nocturnal beetles (Burns's 'bumclocks') and flitting bats ('bauckie-birds'). Burns, like Milton, often celebrates pastoral groves and the crystal streams by which pensive speakers devise their daily quota of verses – though Milton's favour octosyllabics and Burns's a variety of quatrain and octave settings. In Burns, too, by contrast to Milton, the speaker may be in a penseroso state of mind only because, as in 'Afton Water', his mistress will not wake up and keep him company. It is difficult to say in cases of pastoral nature imagery whether Burns's primary source is Milton himself or such eighteenth-century Milton-impersonators as Edward Young, Thomas Gray, or James Thomson. Burns could even be echoing his Scots predecessor Robert Fergusson, whose little-studied but very funny burlesques in neoclassical English send up Miltonic diction.[1]

Burns's appropriations of Milton are undoubtedly primary in his prose letters. 'No!' Burns writes in 1795, the year before his death, 'if I must write, let it be Sedition, or Blasphemy, or something else that begins with a B, so that I may grin with the grin of iniquity, & rejoice with the rejoicing of an apostate Angel. 'All good to me is lost;/Evil, be thou my good!'[2] In that letter, by 'something else that begins with a B,' the context makes it clear that Burns means bawdry: Milton's Satan is invoked (as he so often is by Blake) to characterize the trangressive spirit of poetry itself. References to Milton in Burns's letters also express Burns's admiration for Milton's dramatic charac- terizations: 'I have bought a pocket Milton which I carry perpetually about with me, in order to study the sentiments – the dauntless magnanimity; the intrepid unyielding independance; the desperate daring, and noble defiance of hardship, in that great Personage, Satan' (1, 123). Elsewhere Burns admires Milton's portrait of Satan as 'the wild broken fragments of a noble, exalted mind in ruins' (1, 198).

In one vernacular poem ('Address of Beelzebub') and one letter (written after a violent quarrel with the Riddell family), Burns gives his return address as 'Hell.' *Non serviam*: Burns identifies with the refusal of Milton's Satan to bow in submission to authority: 'I would face the Arch-fiend, in Miltonic pomp, at the head of all his legions; and hear that infernal shout which blind John says: "Tore hell's concave," rather than crawl in, a dust-licking Petitioner, before the lofty presence of a Mighty Man, & bear ... the swelling consequence of his d-mned State, & the cold monosyllables of his hollow heart!' (2, 52). That letter of 1790, written to protest an investigation into Burns's alleged political disaffection being conducted by the Board of Excise, suggested to me that Burns is not only alluding to but 'de-canonizing' Milton. Familiarly addressed as 'Blind John,' the most high-minded of poets becomes merely a kind of English country cousin to Blind Harry, the Scottish metrical historian – another chronicler of ancient doings.

In irreverent allusions to Milton's Satan, Burns seeks to use for his own purposes what might be termed Satan's elastic properties. The archfiend is central to many discourses, official and unofficial, from Scripture itself – the original canon – 'down' the hierarchy of literary genres to Miltonic epic, fire-and-brimstone Calvinist sermons (immortalized in Burns's under-rated satire 'The Holy Fair'), and finally the orally-transmitted superstitions prevalent among rustics in the Scottish countryside (as in Burns's now-neglected *tour de force* 'Address to the Deil'). Satan in Burns's mind is not only Milton's un-repentant rebel but also an umbrella signifier for multiple realms of discourse, from the so-called 'high' (the Bible, or the stories God has told us about Satan) to the so-called 'low' (folklore, or the stories our grannies may have told us about Satan). As Ihab Hassam defines it, '[Decanonization] applies to all ... conventions of authority ... a massive delegitimization of master-codes, a desuetude of the master-narratives ... Derision and revision are versions of subversion.'[3] Burns subverts not so much scripture itself as the canonized status of Milton's writings; and he does so by placing Milton's fallen angel in such close proximity to the less exalted Satans of folk-lore and country sermonizing.

The poem by Andrew Marvell that prefaces Milton's epic discusses exactly this matter of Milton's own potential decanonization of scripture in selecting a sacred subject for *Paradise Lost*. Marvell admits fearing that his friend, by the very act of dramatizing (which is to say fictionalizing) the holy text, would 'ruin' it by contamination with folk narratives (what Marvell calls 'fable and old Song'):

> the Argument
> Held me a while misdoubting his Intent,
> That he would ruin (for I saw him strong)
> The sacred Truths to fable and old Song.[4]

Marvell concludes that his initial fears were groundless: 'All that was improper dost omit.' For Burns, however, unlike Milton or Marvell, bringing 'high' and 'low' literary realms into so-called improper contact is evidently his intention in sitting down to write.

Burns is drawn to Milton's Satan because Satan—like William Blake's true poet – goes wherever he likes. In Book 4 of *Paradise Lost*, a gated high wall secures the perimeters of Paradise: Satan 'in contempt' flies over it – even though the gate stands open: 'When the arch-felon saw/Due entrance he disdain'd, and in contempt,/At one slight bound high overleap'd all bound/Of hill or highest Wall, and sheer within/Lights on his feet' (179–183). Burns, more out of exuberance than 'disdain', has an equal disregard for proper boundaries, especially the neoclassical generic prescriptions that during the eighteenth century required a decorous separation of 'high' and 'low' diction and subject-matter. In Burns's frequent invasion of the sacred ground of Miltonic characterization and diction, the poet – like Milton's Satan – impenitently raids.

Paradise Lost, because of its inimitable characterization of Satan and no doubt also because of its prestige, is the work by Milton most often raided by Burns, and not only in Burns's later songs but also in his early vernacular poems. In 'Address to the Deil', for instance, Burns offers a cheeky précis of *Paradise Lost* that shrinks Milton's twelve-book epic down to just twelve lines, two Standard Habbie stanzas:

> Lang syne in *Eden*'s bonie yard,
> When youthfu' lovers first were pair'd,
> An' all the Soul of Love they shar'd,
>   The raptur'd hour,
> Sweet on the fragrant, flow'ry swaird,
>   In shady bow'r.
>
> Then you, ye auld, snick-drawing dog!
> Ye cam to Paradise incog,
> An' play'd on man a cursed brogue,
>   (Black be your fa'!)
> An' gied the infant warld a shog,
>   'Maist ruin'd a'.[5]

Among other Milton poems that Burns revisits and revises is the pastoral elegy 'Lycidas', a text central to one of Burns's best vernacular epistles. The epistle 'To James Smith', like Milton's 'Lycidas', addresses issues of friendship and bereavement, fame and obscurity, poetic immortality and premature death. Burns's speaker, like Milton's in 'Lycidas', mixes professions of ideal friendship with harsher satire: Milton lashes hireling priests; Burns attacks the unco' guid, who cut themselves off from other people – and from their own humanity – with their self-righteous smugness:

> Nae hare-brain'd, sentimental traces,
> In your unletter'd, nameless faces!

> In *arioso* trills and graces
>   Ye never stray,
> But *gravissimo*, solemn basses
>   Ye hum away.
>
> Ye are sae *grave*, nae doubt ye're *wise*;
> Nae ferly tho' ye do despise
> The hairum-scairum, ram-stam boys,
>   The rattling squad:
> I see ye upward cast your eyes –
>   – Ye ken the road –
>   (Kinsley 1, 183)[6]

The ship carrying Milton's Cambridge classmate Edward King, a poet and minister, to his parish in Ireland sank suddenly in a calm sea on a sunny day, so that there is an emphasis in Milton's elegy (an emphasis Burns echoes) on the caprices of Fate. 'Lycidas' expresses a mixture of emotions: grief for Milton's drowned former classmate but also anger at the incapacity of those who survive and who will make far poorer pastoral shepherds, and anxiety on the part of the speaker over his own possibly futile personal hope for immortality through achieving fame and glory as a poet. Burns echoes but reaccentuates these Miltonic motifs in his epistle to Smith.

For references to drowning and tragic voyaging, to sudden and 'inglorious' death, equally suffuse Burns's poem; the verse-letter (in which appears Burns's first reference to his intention to seek fame by publishing in 'guid black prent') is just as obsessed as Milton's elegy with the hazards of a poetic vocation.[7] In an especially sardonic stanza, Burns replaces Milton's visualization of dolphins 'wafting' the sea-changed body of Edward King with curiously intense images of the dead and decomposing books of learned writers:

> 'There's ither Poets, much your betters,
> Far seen in *Greek*, deep men o' *letters*,
> Hae thought they had ensur'd their debtors,
>   A' future ages,
> Now moths deform in shapeless tatters,
>   Their unknown pages.' (Kinsley 1, 179)

In Milton's text, Fate has intervened to prevent King from playing the exemplary poetic and pastoral role for which both he and the shepherd-speaker have been educated:

> Fame is the spur that the clear spirit doth raise
> (That last infirmity of noble mind)
> To scorn delights, and live laborious dayes,
> But the fair Guerdon when we hope to find,
> And think to burst out into sudden blaze,

> Comes the blind *Fury* with th' abhorred shears,
> And slits the thin-spun life.   (II, 70–76)

In Burns's epistle, the fatal sister Atropos – here a homely Scots spinster – likewise snaps the 'brittle thread' of life:

> I'll wander on with tentless heed,
> How never-halting moments speed,
> Till fate shall snap the brittle thread;
>   Then, all unknown,
> I'll lay me with th' *inglorious dead,*
>   Forgot and gone!   (Kinsley, 1, 180)

The epistle to Smith, while echoing Miltonic themes, reveals a contrary definition of poetic vocation that evidently constitutes Burns's rejoinder to Milton. In 'Lycidas', the young speaker declares that the man of noble mind scorns delights and lives 'laborious days' in his quest for poetic fame. Burns refuses that extreme high seriousness, embracing instead a L'Allegro-like ideal of social glee and pleasure:

> This life, sae far's I understand,
> Is a' enchanted fairy-land,
> Where Pleasure is the Magic-wand,
>   That, wielded right,
> Maks Hours like Minutes, hand in hand,
>   Dance by fu' light.   (Kinsley 1, 180)

James Smith was eighteen – Burns's junior by six years – when the poet addressed him. Evidently the two friends had been discussing emigration, which forms one context for the nautical imagery in the poem. Burns had booked his passage to Jamaica in January 1786 – about a month before he wrote to Smith – though the wild success of his first volume of poems in midsummer 1786 led him first to postpone and then to cancel the booking. James Smith himself did sail to the West Indies in 1788 and, according to Robert Cromek in 1808, died soon after arriving. At the time of writing, Burns feared – as it happened, correctly – that he and Smith both were fated to die young, like Edward King. The very epigraph of this high-spirited yet deeply anxious epistle is taken from Robert Blair's *The Grave*, a gloomy, obsessive meditation on death that makes sober Milton's 'Lycidas' seem giddy by comparison.

In his prose letters and such vernacular poems as the verse-epistle to James Smith, Milton is a key figure for Burns. Yet, as seen above, Burns's transpositions of Milton from epic to discursive contexts usually have a parodic or de-canonizing inflection: these are not subservient echoes but rejoinders; the epistle to Smith addresses not only Jamie Smith but also 'blind John' Milton. Burns's songs, by contrast, exhibit more reverent (and more problematic) examples of Burns's use of Milton. In the lyrics of his later songs especially,

Burns continues to separate Miltonic images from their parent-form, shrinking epic allusions down to size. But the outright parody of 'Address to the Deil' or pastiche of the epistle to Smith are usually suppressed. Milton's epic style is still miniaturized in Burns's songs, but not to burlesque or satiric effect. Instead, Milton's massive epic characterizations are pressed into the service of fragmentary but poignant anecdote.

In 'Strathallan's Lament', for instance, the speaker is James Drummond, a defeated Jacobite. The son of William, fourth Viscount Strathallan, Drummond is imagined in the song as soliloquizing (rather turgidly in the first eight lines) in the cave where the historical Strathallan took refuge after the battle of Culloden:

> Thickest night, surround my dwelling!
>   Howling tempests, o'er me rave!
> Turbid torrents, wintry swelling,
>   Roaring by my lonely cave.
> Chrystal streamlets gently flowing,
>   Busy haunts of base mankind,
> Western breezes softly blowing,
>   Suit not my distracted mind.
>
>   (Kinsley 1, 350)[8]

Hiding from the victorious British troops, Strathallan grieves for his father, who has just been killed in the battle. The historical James Drummond forfeited his estates under the Act of Attainder and died in France in 1765. Burns visited these former estates of Strathallan on 28 August 1787, during one of his Highland tours, and evidently wrote 'Strathallan's Lament' immediately upon his return to Edinburgh.

In his lovely final stanza, Burns positions his speaker as another Adam, yet refuses Milton's emphasis in *Paradise Lost* on providential outcome:

> In the cause of Right engaged,
>   Wrongs injurious to redress,
> Honor's war we strongly waged,
>   But the heavens deny'd success:
> Ruin's wheel has driven o'er us,
>   Not a hope that dare attend,
> The wide world is all before us –
>   But a world without a friend!

Unlike Adam and Eve in the concluding lines of *Paradise Lost*, the speaker of 'Strathallan's Lament' is a defeated survivor, not a heroic founder: having just lost his father in battle, James Drummond (who himself fathered no child) stands as the last, not the first, of his kind. Burns's less compelling first stanza opens with an evident echo of *King Lear* ('Blow, winds, and crack your cheeks');

his strong concluding stanza alludes to the third and fourth last lines of *Paradise Lost*: 'The World was all before them, where to choose/Thir place of rest, and Providence thir guide.' Yet unlike Milton's epic couple, Strathallan is quite alone, 'without a friend' or guide. The forlorn hero of Burns's stanzas speaks at and for the end, not the beginning, of historical process. Burns's revision of Milton here is poignant rather than parodic.

When Burns adapts Milton in his songs, he is prone (as in 'Strathallan's Lament') to the use of English rather than Scottish diction and to the rhetorical scheme anastrophe (inverted rather than ordinary word order, as in the phrase 'honor's war we strongly waged'). Burns may insert pastoral lists ('chrystal streams', etc.) rather than more realistic description. Pastoral or classical allusion (as in the reference to the western breeze zephyr in stanza one) colonizes the language in such songs, tending to predominate over indigenous (strongly and identifiably national) Scottish imagery. Consensus has long condemned this so-called 'artificial' diction in Burns's songs. In 1949, Hilton Brown lamented the 'endless wearisome catalogues of [Burns's songs] ... lambs and laverocks, primrose and hawthorn, violet and woodbine, Cynthias and zephyrs, all wimpling and warbling and languishing and anguishing to despair.'[9] The heavily inverted English of such songs as 'Strathallan's Lament' – 'turbid torrents, wintry swelling' – is a particular grievance to such critics, being seen as wholly 'alien' to Burns's presumably more spontaneous and 'natural' Scottish folk models. I think that too often such verdicts have been pronounced without taking into account the effectiveness of this stylizing Miltonic diction when Burns's songs are sung: I believe that in many (not all, but many) cases the heroic language sheds its nimbus round the speaker, the awkward displacements of diction in 'Strathallan's Lament' serving as a token in language of the displaced, distrained speaker himself. At the very least, the haunting recording by Jean Redpath of 'Strathallan's Lament' as arranged by the late Serge Hovey should be heard before any judgment is reached on this neglected song.[10]

'Strathallan's Lament' is, like so many of Burns's lyrics, a hybrid. Partaking of the Scottish folk tradition in its use of a historical speaker and its imaginative reconstruction of national historical experience, the song partakes also of art-song precisely in its artfulness, its evident premeditation. Burns's note to this song asserts that both tune and text were preconceived as Jacobite: 'The air is the composition of one of the worthiest and best-hearted men living – Allan Masterton ... As he and I were both sprouts of Jacobitism, we agreed to dedicate the words and air to that cause' (quoted in Kinsley, 3, 1243). Masterton himself mixed folksong with art-song merely by sitting down deliberately to write a Jacobite air, a composed folksong being something of an oxymoron.

To the English composer and folk-song collector Cecil Sharp (1859–1924), the level of self-conscious intentionality is precisely what separates folk from art music:

Art music is the work of the individual, it is composed in, comparatively speaking, a short period of time, and being committed to paper it is forever fixed in one inalterable form. Folk music is the product of a race and reflects feelings and tastes that are communal rather than personal; it is always in solution; its creation is never completed, while at every moment in its history it exists not in one form but many.[11]

Folksong resists canonization, in short, in the most basic sense of resisting being fixed in a unified, authorized, and 'inalterable' form. Thus, if Burns de-canonizes Milton by switching modes, shrinking Milton's massive epic characterizations into the reduced if gemlike lyric voicings of such songs as 'Strathallan's Lament', Burns also canonizes the folk tradition—by the very act of systematically revising and publishing folk songs. From Joseph Ritson to Hugh MacDiarmid, commentators intent on emphasizing the collectivity of 'authentic' folk tradition have been rather dismissive of Burns's songs – even though (speaking of canons) according to the *Grove Dictionary of Music*, the lyrics of 'a significant percentage of the published repertory of Scottish National Song' – in fact, about 35% of all Scots folksongs published before 1800 – were actually written by Robert Burns (492).

Bertrand Bronson argued in 1959 that the 'relatively impassive outlines of a folk-tune suggest no latent shades of verbal meaning. Psychological implication, innuendo, irony, cannot be heard ... and this is, of course, a source of strength as well as a limitation ... [T]heatrical hints of a sub-surface understanding shared by singer and hearer are an offense to the ... powerful impersonality [of folk song].'[11] Robert Burns in such lyrics as 'Strathallan's Lament' clearly commits this offence of 'psychological implication, innuendo, irony' – this affront to the communitarian collectivity of folk tradition. Burns is as aggressive, wilful and insubordinate in his appropriations of folk-collected stanzas as in his burlesques and revisions of Milton. Indeed, with his co-editor James Johnson, Burns not only intentionally set out to provide a canon of Scottish national song – and to impress upon the folk-collected scraps the stamp of his own experience and literary genius – he even agreed to the title *The Scots Musical Museum*. The contemporary novelist Ishmael Reed calls museums 'Centers for Art Detention,' museums being in postmodern eyes only marginally less canonizing and codifying than encyclopedias.

I will conclude with an examination of Burns's use of an implicitly Miltonic (in this case, Satanic) speaker in one of his songs to Highland Mary. The popular title of this song is 'To Mary in Heaven', though both extant manuscripts are titled only 'A Song–' and that phrase occurs nowhere in the stanzas. This title actually contradicts the predominant emotion of the stanzas, which derive their hysterical intensity precisely by the speaker's bewildered and disoriented questions:

> Thou lingering Star with lessening ray
> That lovest to greet the early morn,

> Again thou usherest in the day
>> My Mary from my Soul was torn –
> O Mary! dear, departed Shade!
>> Where is thy place of blissful rest?
> Seest thy Lover lowly laid?
>> Hearest thou the groans that rend his breast?
>>> (Kinsley, 1, 492)

In the first line, memories of a brief affair (and a sadly abbreviated life) are hailed as light from the morning star as it lingers in the brightening sky on the anniversary of Mary's death. (Burns had courted Margaret Campbell during his estrangement from Jean Armour in Spring 1786; the girl he called 'Highland Mary' had left Ayrshire for Greenock in May – possibly to prepare for marriage to Burns, but possibly to recover from their broken engagement. He had received news of her death, possibly from postpartum fever, that autumn, and 'Thou lingering star' was written three years later, in November 1789).

There is a covert dialogue with Milton in this song, for the image of the morning star carries for Burns, with his long immersion in Milton, a strong association with Satan as Lucifer, once the morning star but fallen from heaven. That the song is initially addressed to the morning star unites the speaker not directly with Mary herself (as the lines emphasize, the speaker is not sure where Mary is) but rather with a prelapsarian Lucifer; the affair itself becomes another paradise lost, perhaps through the seduction and betrayal of another Eve.[13] The flowering and wooded landscape of all the songs to Highland Mary – in 'Thou Lingering Star' the poet emphasizes the sylvan setting of their final tryst – strongly recalls the 'hallowed' and 'sacred' groves of Milton's Eden:

> That sacred hour can I forget,
>> Can I forget the hallowed grove,
> Where by the winding Ayr we met,
>> To live one day of Parting Love?
> Eternity can not efface
>> Those records dear of transports past;
> Thy image at our last embrace,
>> Ah, little thought we 'twas our last!
>>> (Kinsley, 1, 493)

The imagery in these stanzas is ambiguous. The lines derive their neurotic power from an implied struggle with guilt as well as grief. In the final analysis, Burns's songs for Margaret Campbell contain more (in Bronson's phrase) of 'innuendo' and 'irony' than folkish impersonality: the songs to Mary are – more clearly even than 'Strathallan's Lament' – art-songs. For one thing, unlike 'Strathallan's Lament', they allude to personal, not to national, history.

In the final analysis, assessment of Burns's stanzas for songs should probably allow them their ambition, their multiplicity of reference, rather than imposing procrustean standards of 'simplicity' or 'impersonality' on often intensely wrought and deeply felt dramatic lyrics. If Burns is unique in literary history, it is in his ambidextrous capacity to give equal weight to the so-called high and so-called low – to folk-collected bawdry and to English epic. In the epigraph, Ralph Vaughan Williams offered a genial definition of folksong, calling it an 'individual flowering on a common stem.'[14] Only using that broad a formula could Burns be considered mainly a writer of folk-song – though, as this essay has discussed, Burns sees no reason not to consider John Milton's writings as another branch leading to his own creative flowering.

NOTES

1. Burns does not mention Milton when he discusses his education and early reading in his autobiographical letter to Dr. John Moore, though he does quote Milton habitually (if mockingly) in other letters, early and late: e.g., '... whatever Milton had, I have no idea of a Cherub six feet high' (*Letters* 1, 322). John Murdoch, the tutor who instructed Robert and Gilbert Burns during the mid-1760s, is in his own letters a great quoter of Milton, suggesting that Burns was acquainted with the English poet from early schooling. Writing after the poet's death, Murdoch uses a phrase from 'L'Allegro' to describe the poet's younger brother, Murdoch's favorite among the Burnes children: 'Gilbert's face said, "Mirth with thee I mean to live"; and certainly if any person who knew the two boys had been asked which one of them was most likely to court the Muses, he would surely never have guessed that Robert had a propensity of that kind.' Maurice Lindsay, comp., *The Burns Encyclopedia* (New York: St. Martin's, 1980), p. 250.
2. *Paradise Lost*, Book 4 (109–110) as quoted by Burns. In J. De Lancey Ferguson and G. Ross Roy (eds), *Letters of Robert Burns* (Oxford: Clarendon, 1985), 2, 382. Subsequent quotations are from this edition.
3. Ihab Hassam, paraphrasing Jean-François Lyotard on 'delegitimization' in 'Pluralism in Postmodern Perspective.' From *Exploring Postmodernism*, Matei Calinescu and Douwe Fokkema (eds) (Amsterdam/Philadelphia: John Benjamin, 1987), pp. 32–3.
4. Merritt Hughes (ed.), *John Milton. Complete Poems and Major Prose* (New York: Odyssey, 1957), p. 209. Subsequent quotations are from this edition.
5. James Kinsley (ed.), *Poems and Songs of Robert Burns* (Oxford: Clarendon, 1968), 1, 171. Subsequent quotations are from this edition.
6. The musical terms 'arioso' and 'gravissimo' are not Miltonic but Shandean: cf. *Tristram Shandy*.
7. That even later in his life Burns associated Milton's writings with his own poetic ambitions is suggested by the seriocomic coat of arms he devised for himself in 1794: 'I am a bit of a Herald; & shall give you, Secundum artem, my ARMS. – On a field, azure, a holly-bush, seeded, proper, in base; a Shepherd's pipe & crook, Saltier-wise, also proper, in chief. – On a wreath of the colors, a woodlark perching on a sprig of bay-tree, proper, for Crest. – Two Mottoes: Round the top of the crest – 'Wood-notes wild' – At the bottom of the Shield, in the usual place –

'Better a wee bush than nae bield.' – (*Letters*, 2, 285).

Burns not only borrows 'wood notes wild' from 'L'Allegro,' where it expresses Milton's praise of Shakespeare, but also places the Miltonic motto 'above' the vernacular motto. The poet's coat of arms, in fact, represents rather vividly the delight in juxtaposing contrasts (the classical bay tree; the folkish holly) that characterizes Burns throughout his poetic career.

8. For an explicit association of Milton's rebel angels with Jacobites, see *Letters*, 1, 93: 'I was nearly as much struck ... as the brave but unfortunate Jacobite Clans who, as John Milton tells us, after their unhappy Culloden in Heaven, lay "nine times the space that measures day & night," [*PL* 1, 50] in oblivious astonishment, prone-weltering on the fiery Surge.' Here Burns adopts Miltonic diction as well as Miltonic allusion.

9. Hilton Brown, *There Was a Lad: An Essay on Robert Burns*, quoted in *Literature Criticism from 1400 to 1800*, James E. Person, Jnr (ed.) (Detroit: Gale, 1986), p. 85.

10. In Volume Six of *Songs of Robert Burns* (Philo–1114, 1987).

11. Cecil Sharp, quoted in *The Music Lover's Handbook*, edited by Elie Siegmeister (New York: William Morrow, 1943), pp. 36–37.

12. Bertrand Bronson, *Traditional Tunes of the Child Ballads* (Princeton: Princeton University Press), 1, pp. x–xi.

13. That Burns particularly admired Milton's portrayal of Eve is suggested by references in his letters. Of Eliza Burnett, Lord Monboddo's youngest daughter, for instance, Burns wrote: 'There has not been anything nearly like her, in all the combinations of Beauty, Grace and Goodness the great Creator has formed, since Milton's Eve on the first day of her existence' (*Letters* 1, 76).

14. Ralph Vaughan Williams, 'National Music' in *National Music and Other Essays* (London: Oxford University Press, 1963), pp. 32–33.

'The Wee Apollo': Burns and Oswald

A pigmy scraper wi' his Fiddle,
Wha us'd to trysts an' fairs to driddle,
Her strappan limb an' gausy middle,
    (He reach'd nae higher)
Had hol'd his heartie like a riddle,
    An' blawn't on fire.

Wi' hand on hainch, and upward e'e,
He croon'd his gamut, one, two, three,
Then, in a Arioso key,
    The wee Apollo
Set off wi' allegretto glee,
    His giga solo.

THE WEE APOLLO. The fun of the thing lies in the sportiveness of the contrast of register. The wee Apollo. Allegretto glee. But behind it all is a deeply serious intention, one which explains many of the dichotomies in Burns and which demonstrates in him a profound artistic ambition which, I am going to suggest, was partly inspired by a fellow-Scot and musician, James Oswald.

Oswald was born in 1710 of a musical family from Crail. He became a dancing-master in Dunfermline, then Edinburgh, and finally London. There he eloped with Mary Anne Melville. He played the violin and cello, and taught those instruments but was until recently best known as a music publisher. Now I am happy to say he is best known as a composer. He was chamber composer to George III. He died in 1769 a wealthy man in his own right, having married the widow of his friend, Robinson Lytton. He was a Freemason and composed at least two masonic anthems. He founded a society called The Temple Of Apollo, which put on concerts and published music. The English music historian, Burney (in fact of Scottish blood and originally MacBurney) tried to claim that this society consisted solely of himself. This was not true. There is clear documentary evidence of the Society's existence and activities which have little to do with Burney, if anything. Oswald was its moving spirit, Robinson Lytton's household was used for its concerts.

So what?

Well, first of all, Burns himself regarded Oswald highly. When writing in praise of 'Bess The Gawkie' he declared, 'This song shows that the Scottish Muses did not all leave us when we lost Ramsay and Oswald.' Considering the reputation and influence of Ramsay, this puts Oswald very high in Burns's estimation.

He possessed a copy of Oswald's *Caledonian Pocket Companion* – a twelve-volume collection of tunes, mostly Scottish and many by Oswald himself, and published in the 1750s. Apparently Burns heavily annotated his copy of the *Caledonian Pocket Companion* and gave it to Nathaniel Gow. I wish I knew where it was now. Oswald was Burns's great predecessor as a collector, and Burns used several of Oswald's tunes for his massive input into Johnson's *The Scots Musical Museum.*

The title, *Caledonian Pocket Companion*, chosen by Oswald, tells us much about his intentions. He had already published in Edinburgh in 1740 a substantial number of melodies which were later to appear in the *Caledonian Pocket Companion*, but the Edinburgh publication (*A Curious Colllection...*) has bass lines, several of them figured, whereas the Pocket Companion has none, though some of the tunes clearly require them as they are printed with rests. The point of this publication was that it was a pocket one. Whether professional or amateur, you could carry it about with you – it would be possible to carry the entire publication in its two-volume format in two pockets of a greatcoat. You could play from it on your flute (there were walking-stick flutes) or your fiddle (readily portable) in the middle of a field or an assembly.

Pocket editions were not new, but Oswald's is noteworthy for its somewhat Spartan appearance. There are no vignettes, the tunes are crowded onto the pages, the titles and indications of tempo or mood are squeezed in between the staves, the margins are very small, and there are no words. It is designed to get as much as possible onto a minimum amount of paper and therefore to sell at a cheap price; to be available to the average punter rather than the gentleman amateur. It was, if you like, an excercise in musical democracy – and it was Caledonian. This does not mean that every tune in it was claimed to be Scottish. Not at all. All it means is that it reflects Scottish musical taste at the time and naturally there is a preponderance of Scottish tunes.

What about the great scheme to which Burns contributed – *The Scots Musical Museum*? The word 'Museum' meant then 'a temple for the muses'. The muses are ultimately instructed by Apollo. We have the same assertion as was inherent in Oswald's career as composer, publisher, promoter and creator of The Society Of the Temple of Apollo – namely that Scottish music and song belonged in the Temple of Apollo, not of Pan who, if I am not mistaken, gets little mention in Burns.

This association of the rustic (as native airs would generally have been regarded) with the higher gods, and with art, takes its cue from Horace.

Oswald quoted a Horace Ode on the cover of his *Airs For The Seasons*, many of which are Scottish in character – 'Now Venus leads the dance' – and the handsome illustration shows her with Cupid above and the three Graces and two Nymphs dancing with a chain of flowers. Enfolding them all in his cloak is a man quaintly adorned with ruffed collar and broad-brimmed hat, perhaps representing Horace, or Oswald himself in old-fashioned rustic garb. Whether or no, the quotation is an explicit claim for the Scottish dancing-master to make, placing himself directly in that classical tradition which, in Horace, exemplified the marriage of nature and art, but evoking the Goddess of Love as the source of his inspiration.

Oswald's *The Narcissus* is a perfect example of this approach.

There are just two movements for the brief dancing life of *The Narcissus*. The first one is in the style of a Scottish air, but with reflections and echoes added because Narcissus fell in love with his own reflection and was beloved of Echo. This is a perfect example of the native and the classical in each other's arms. The second movement reflects the fact that the Narcissus was a dancer's plant. The medicine from it was good for strained sinews and stiff joints; and the Narcissus bending in the breeze leads the first dance of spring – and this dance is a Scottish jig full of the cheerfulness of the season. It comes from the first set for Spring.

In asserting an exemplary purpose, often of considerable subtlety, for Oswald's *Airs for the Seasons* we must not lose sight of their unpretentious directness. That directness is in fact part of their purpose. They are miniatures; a posy of flowers, laid metaphorically perhaps on the altar of the Temple of Apollo; but they are not an attempt to build that temple, as the Adam family might have done. There are no Corinthian columns or grand porticos in Oswald's design, only a natural and unaffected beauty, wit and candour that form one of the most remarkable musical compendiums ever assembled.

However, the Horace Ode which he quotes ends with the death of Lycidas (the ideal of the shepherd with his pipe), and the Oswald carries Winter in the implication of Spring (it was Winter which first inspired Thomson and Armstrong) – but whether this has any particular meaning for the music is not clear, though it is not unlikely that the potential death of the rustic ideal of native music under Italian influence was already in Oswald's mind. He had satirised that influence in two popular mini-cantatas – entractes – while at the same time composing in a style which owes much to the Italians – *The Sonata On Scots Tunes* being an obvious example, using Scottish melodies as the basis for an Italianate Sonata da Camera.

That fear for the artistic rights of the vernacular (which were upheld so magnificently by Burns) was not uncommon, at least among the Scots, who largely turned their backs on the new musical architecture of Haydn, Mozart and Beethoven and on anything that seemed to be leading towards it, in order to defend a musical environment which they believed was too beautiful and too vulnerable to risk. All the stranger, then, that Burns got drawn into Thomson's up-market publications in which Haydn, Beethoven and others were involved. In my opinion they underline the dichotomy that faces any so-called vernacular culture under pressure from a culture which has assumed the mastery

– for 'vernacular' is derived from the word for 'slave', and slavery was that
from which men like Oswald and Burns were struggling to escape, while wishing
to assert the validity of their own cultural roots. One of Burns's heroes, Robert
Fergusson, could scarcely have put it more clearly, describing the Italian ver-
nacular which had assumed the mastery as 'a bastard breed':

> On Scotia's plains, in days of yore,
> When lads and lasses tartan wore,
> Saft Music rang on ilka shore,
>   In hamely weid;
> But harmony is now no more,
>   And music dead ...
>
> Now foreign sonnets bear the gree
> And crabbit queer variety
> Of sound fresh sprung frae Italy,
>   A bastard breed!
> Unlike that saft-tongu'd melody
>   Which now lies dead ...
>
> MacGibbon's gane: Ah! waes my heart!
> The man in music maist expert,
> Wha cou'd sweet melody impart,
>   And tune the reed
> Wi' sic a slee and pawky art;
>   But now he's dead.

Fergusson's lines from his 'Elegy On The Death Of Scots Music' reflect this
awkward cultural situation. Writing in the 1770s, why should he have felt
Scottish music was so threatened? The man whose death he laments (McGibbon)
could be as Italianate as the next man. Among a few immigrant continental
musicians Domenico Corri, whose technique did not stretch to any great
complications of style, was ready enough to publish Scottish airs and Fergusson
was himself an opera-goer, a good singer, and very young for such doomsday
views – he died at the age of twenty-four. So do we take this poem as anything
more than a *jeu d'esprit*? The answer has to be 'yes'. He was far from being
alone in his views. *An Essay Towards The Improvement Of The Musical Art*,
published in Glasgow in 1798, shows Alexander Mollison introducing a serious
analysis of musical structures and their moral virtues (which harks back to
Plato, the most restrictive of the Greeks) as justification for a similar aesthetic:

> The writer of the following essay had, from early youth, felt the delightful
> effects of simple and pathetic melody. He frequently noticed, what many
> others no doubt have experienced, that different strains made different im-
> pressions on his mind – that some highly exhilarated the spirits, while some
> gently soothed the mind, inclining it to tenderness and pleasing melancholy;

and others inspired it with a kind of mental courage and elevation, easier to be felt than expressed. He eagerly sought the enjoyment of those pleasant sensations: and, in the Scottish airs, he frequently found that simple and pathetic expression which suited his taste. After having long admired and enjoyed these, he bestowed some attention on that refined harmonic music which is in such general use at present. In this 'mingled world of sounds', however, he found his expectations disappointed, and his feelings not a little tantalized. The intricate modulations of the melody, and the perplexing combinations of the harmony, seemed, with regard to expression, to be a mere chaos; ill suited to gratify the mind which had felt the strong influence of the music that moves the passions.

Robert Burns defended his own tastes in similar fashion:

I am sensible that my taste in Music must be inelegant and vulgar, because people of undisputed and cultivated taste can find no merit in many of my favorite tunes. – Still, because I am cheaply pleased, is that any reason why I should deny myself that pleasure? – Many of our Strathspeys, ancient and modern, give me most exquisite enjoyment, where you and other judges would probably be shewing signs of disgust. – For instance, I am just now making verses for Rothemurche's Rant, an air which puts me in raptures: and in fact, unless I be pleased with the tune, I never can make verses to it' (Burns to George Thomson, September 1794).

Burns may have had his tongue in his cheek, but it still reads defensively. He wrote to Thomson in April 1793 saying 'Whatever Mr Pleyel does, let him not alter one iota of the original Scots Air; I mean, in the Song department ... but, let our National Music preserve its native features. They are, I own, frequently wild, and unreducable to the more modern rules; but on that very eccentricity, perhaps, depends a great part of their effect.' Which quotation goes to show just how sensitive a musician Burns was himself. Other collectors like him were like minded.

The first part of Patrick MacDonald's *A Collection Of Highland Vocal Airs* was gathered by his brother Joseph, who wrote home from India in 1760 with all the nostalgia of the Scot abroad:

What would I give now, far from the theatre of those delightful scenes, for one night of my old beloved society, to sing those favourite, simple, primitive airs along with me? It would bring me back to the golden age anew.

Similarly from the frontispiece and Introduction of Fraser's *Airs And Melodies Peculiar To the Highlands Of Scotland*, first published in 1816, it is clear that the ideals of the Temple of Apollo were still very much alive. Niel Gow on the left and a member of the extinct bardic class complete with harp on the right are crowned with laurels by a muse. It is quite likely that the harpist is intended to represent Rory Dall Morrison. In the background the rural idyll continues untouched by famine and emigration, and the obedient natives are pictured on the right rowing the tourists of Europe to Fingal's Cave.

The Golden Age. The Musical Museum. The Temple Of Apollo. Set alongside 'wild and unreducable' 'simple and pathetic' 'simple and primitive'. Never a word of Pan. What these collectors achieved, from Ramsay, the earlier Thomson, and Oswald, through Burns, the MacDonalds, Fraser and others, was and remains an artistic triumph, particularly for Robert Burns who has achieved international status primarily on the basis of his vernacular work; but also, at long last for James Oswald – also, by the by, for Scott's music tutor, Alexander Campbell, who is entitled more nearly to an Oscar for the music for the film *The Piano*, than anyone else, the main tune being substantially his own, though better known with Tannahill's great lyric, *Gloomy Winter's Noo Awa*. Perhaps the Oscar Awards are not quite the Temple Of Apollo, but I suppose they'll do!

No more compelling example could be given of this complex cultural crosscurrent than the origins in Oswald's work for one of Burns's very greatest lyric achievements – 'Ae Fond Kiss'. It is not insignificant in this context that this superb lyric was addressed by a Sylvander to a Clarinda. Sylvander intended that Clarinda should hear it with figured bass realised on harpsichord or fortepiano and sung by someone probably schooled in the style of Tenducci or Corri. So what is so culturally complex about it? The answer lies in its origins.

First, Burns's choice of 'Rory Dall's Port'. We do not know which of the two most likely candidates for Rory Dall composed this music, quite possibly neither of them. David Johnson has suggested (*Scottish Fiddle Music* p. 74) it was very probably composed by Oswald himself, who (despite Burns's own remarks on 'Roslin Castle') undoubtedly composed a number of tunes which he did not publicly claim. Such music as survives of the earlier Irish Rory Dall O'Cahan, who was frequently in Scotland, has little in common with the style of this brief but lovely piece. As for Rory Dall Morrison, the other and more likely candidate (being a Scottish harper born circa 1656) there is no certainty that he composed anything at all, but the pieces most likely to have been by him are again quite distinct in character, being much less regular than the tune published by Oswald.

My personal opinion is that David Johnson is right to suggest that the piece is by Oswald himself, ascribing it to a famous harper to give it an added cachet. Whether or no, it is truly lovely, perfectly shaped and balanced by a varied symmetry. How mid-eighteenth-century one sounds in describing its beauties!

Now for the words. These were, by general agreement, inspired by a poem of Robert Dodsley's – 'The Parting Kiss'. Dodsley, like Oswald, like Burns, was a man of humble origins who had made it in the aristocratic world of art, music and letters. It is entirely possible that Burns got to know this poem through Oswald's setting of it, but he could hardly have used Oswald's tune again for his own version. That would have been a straight and obvious theft. But perhaps he felt an obligation to Oswald none the less, and therefore chose a tune that would fit from one of Oswald's collections. Whether he guessed that 'Rory Dall's Port' was most likely by Oswald himself, I cannot say.

'Ae Fond Kiss' considered as a poem is something of a mixed bag. 'Warring sighs and groans', 'Peace Enjoyment Love and Pleasure' are not the stuff of personal feeling. They are standard guff of the sort that would not disgrace a cheap valentine and they have their source in the kind of stuff Dodsley was writing. Of course the rest of 'Ae Fond Kiss' is mostly very much better, famously so: but once you sing it, it all coheres, the good and the mediocre. The music carries it, just as Schubert's music carries Muller's supreme lyrics and as Irish traditional music carries Tommy Moore's supreme lyrics. Burns, Muller and Moore: all three of them knew very well what they were doing. In their lyrics they were writing for singing, and in Moore's and Burns's cases they were musical and chose the music themselves. It was Schubert's miracle to reverse the process, finding the music for the lyrics.

What then of poor old Dodsley and Oswald? Well, if you listen to their song, I think you will hear that the pair of them were pretty good too. Oswald's *Colin's Kisses* song cycle has a good claim to be the first true song cycle ever; but it is several decades earlier than the romantic effusions of Muller, Burns and Moore, dating as it does from 1742. It is a sophisticated little comedy of manners, gently, affectionately satirical. 'The Parting Kiss' has to be understood in that light. Sentimental? Yes. Beautiful? That too.

Back in 1992, I was invited by Bryan MacMaster to programme five concerts of Scottish classical music for the EIF. Nothing like it had been attempted at an Edinburgh Festival and it was a great success for audiences. However, it was rather less of a success with the Scottish music critics. One said of Oswald that he 'was not really a composer at all' – a simple lie in terms both of his substantial output and his official position as Chamber Composer to George III; but much more seriously, a slur on the quality of Oswald's work which is now being greedily exposed in concerts, on Radio 3 and on CD. I am not trying to make out that Oswald is the neglected Purcell of Scotland. But his music is beautiful and also significant and I believe that it was setting out on an aesthetic mission much more daring than the performance of a Scottish-style sonata in the Temple of Apollo rather than that of Pan.

Apollo is the sun God. All the way back to Egypt and right through to Freemasonry, where the eye of God is shown in the sun. But it was more significant than mere schoolboy learning.

The Temple of Apollo. Of Zoroaster. Of Sarastro in Mozart's Magic Flute, where the sound of a simple solo instrument, the flute, derived not from Apollo, but from Pan, is the provider of the magical music which protects from fear and permits entry into Apollo's Temple where the traditional instrument is the lyre or, once the Picts had invented it, the triangular framed harp. Interesting that Mozart avoids the harp. Had he been a Scot it would have been the perfect instrument, having been part of what was an aristocratic tradition reduced to the status of that very vernacular which Mozart's opera substantially extols and which was part of masonic musical culture.

Put it all together. Oswald and Burns are not only great folk-music collectors and disseminators. They are conscious pursuers of an aesthetic ideal which ultimately links music to the whole of creation. To the sun as centre of the universe and centre of life, light and, specifically, music. Apollo plays a lyre. With seven strings. The Pictish stones show David with his harp with seven strings. All of these connections were widely known and widely studied and imitated, from Pythagoras to Plato to Vincenzo Galileo to Kepler to Newton. They were particularly studied by the Freemasons. Of the two pillars in the Temple of Solomon, which is a basic model for Freemasonic ideals, one was inscribed with astronomical revelations, the other with the secrets of music. The musical pillar was executed by Jubal, the biblical first musician. You can see the fifteenth-century equivalents of those pillars in Rosslyn Chapel near Edinburgh.

Burns and Oswald knew Roslin of course. They were also both Freemasons – as were many musicians, who were usually granted free entry to lodges, because music was so highly valued. But that is another story with political overtones for which there is no time.

> Wi' hand on hainch, and upward e'e,
> He croon'd his gamut, one, two, three,
> Then, in a Arioso key,
>   The wee Apollo
> Set off, wi' allegretto glee,
>   His giga solo.

The wee Apollo. So Burns, like Oswald, saw Scottish music as worthy of Apollonian status, though what he describes is decidedly Dionysiac. The dichotomy remains unresolved to this day. We are the richer for it. For here in Scotland with our musical traditions alive and our classical music at last finding the attention and respect it was always due, we may join hands and dance merrily from the Temple Of Apollo to The Temple Of Pan, and not give a damn which one is which, though without any intention of dismantling either of them. Amongst many others, Burns and Oswald are two who particularly deserve our undying gratitude for preserving for us that wonderful aesthetic freedom.

'Thus with me began Love and Poesy': Burns's first song and 'I am a man unmarried'

BURNS'S SONG, 'O once I lov'd a bonnie lass' or 'Handsome Nell', had a special interest for him since it marked his entry into his vocation as poet. It is quite short, and the words run in their entirety:

> O once I lov'd a bonnie lass,
>   An' aye I love her still
> An' whilst that virtue warms my breast
>   I'll love my handsome Nell.
>   Fal lal de dal &c.
>
> As bonnie lasses I hae seen,
>   And mony full as braw,
> But for a modest gracefu' mein
>   The like I never saw.
>
> A bonny lass I will confess,
>   Is pleasant to the e'e,
> But without some better qualities
>   She's no a lass for me.
>
> But Nelly's looks are blythe and sweet,
>   And what is best of a',
> Her reputation is compleat,
>   And fair without a flaw;
>
> She dresses ay sae clean and neat,
>   Both decent and genteel;
> And then there's something in her gait
>   Gars ony dress look weel.
>
> A gaudy dress and gentle air
>   May slightly touch the heart,
> But it's innocence and modesty
>   That polishes the dart.
>
> 'Tis this in Nelly pleases me,
>   'Tis this enchants my soul;

> For absolutely in my breast
> She reigns without controul.[1]

The possibility of matching these words with the music Burns had in mind arises since Burns noted in his commonplace book that the tune was 'I am a man unmarried'.[2] The song of this name was untraced for over a century but eventually surfaced in a letter sent by George St. J. Bremner from San Francisco to the *Weekly Scotsman* and published on 14 March 1925. Bremner included the tune (see Figure 1)[3] and wrote as follows about the song and the context it had for him:

> In your issue of the 24th of January, 'A. E.' writes an interesting article on 'Burns's Songs, Tunes, Unknown, Lost, or Lacking.' I can put 'A. E.' on the track of at least one tune, 'I Am a Man Unmarried.' to which Burns wrote the song, 'O Once I Loved a Bonnie Lass.' Across the waste of nearly sixty years I can remember my grandfather singing it. I enclose the notes, as well as I can remember; you will see that it is on the pentatonic scale, the 4th and 7th being omitted, and is one of those tunes that can be played on the black keys of the piano. When played in reel time, it makes a capital dance tune.
>
> The words, which were really clever, though indecorous, were as follows:–

> I am a man unmarried,
>   And hae been a' my life,
> But now I am resolved
>   To gang and seek a wife,
>   Singing fal, lal, &c.

> And if I marry a puir ane,
>   A puir man I will be.
> And if I marry a rich ane
>   She'll cast it up to me,
>   Singing fal, lal, &c.

> And if I marry a bonnie ane,
>   A cuckold I will be.
> And if I marry an ugly ane,
>   The rest will laugh at me.

> The other verses showed that he went to a market and there he saw a lady who seemed to hit his fancy, but after a rather spirited conversation, he wisely concluded that it was better to bear the ills he had than fly to others which he knew not of – but surmised.[4]

This folksong actually has quite a wide currency, though not in the precise form with the opening line, 'I am a man unmarried', by which Burns identified it. It occurs in Scottish chapbooks as 'The Roving Bachelor' beginning 'I am a roving bachelor', and versions with tunes have been collected in England and Ireland.[5] However, the only other known version that has the opening line quoted by Bremner was noted down in 1827 by Andrew Crawfurd from a tailor called John Smith living in Lochwinnoch, Renfrewshire.[6] Smith's date of birth is not known but his marriage took place in 1783 and, if he married at the age of twenty, he would have been about four years older than Burns. His boyhood was spent in Stranraer. All Smith's songs were apparently learnt in south-west Scotland, and those few for which particulars are available were acquired in his youth. Since Smith's version of the song, which he called 'The Old Bachelor', is localised in Burns's home area and quite possibly stems from the period when Burns was growing up, it comes as close as we are likely to get to the song text as Burns knew it. It runs:

> I am a man unmarried
>   And has been all my life
> Now I am resolved
>   For to go seek a wife
>
> Such a wife I must have
>   Is scarce for to be found
> And such a wife I must have
>   Scarce walks upon the ground
>
> A bonnie a braw wife
>   A wife with meikle gear
> If I dinna get a bonnie wife
>   I'll want another year
>
> A bonnie wife if she be na gude
>   She is gude companie
> And if she be gude
>   Sho is pleasant to the ee
>
> If I marry a tall one
>   I am sure she'll crack my crown
> And little women is peevish
>   They'll pull a strong man doun
>
> If I marry a black one
>   The lads will laugh at me
> And if I marry a fair one
>   A cuckle I am sure to be
>
> If I marry a young one
>   She'll ruin me with pride
> And if I marry an old one
>   They'll say she has been tryde

> But as I was musing
>   Mark what came to pass
> In my sight appeared
>   A handsome tall young lass
>
> The first question that I speired at her
>   What was her name
> The answer she gave to me
>   Was modesty and fame
>
> The next question that I asked her
>   If she was a maid
> And the answer that she gave to me
>   I was once what you said
>
> The next question that I asked her
>   If she was one just now
> And the answer she gave to me
>   And I may be one for you
>
> The next question that I asked her
>   If she wad take a man
> The answer she gave to me
>   A little now and then
>
> The next question that I asked her
>   If she wad marry me
> And the answer that she gave to me
>   It's no be what may be
>
> The green it is a bonny thing
>   Till ance it gets a dip
> And he that courts a bonnie lass
>   Is sure to get the slip

Although Burns gives a much more ideal picture than the cynical folksong, something has been carried over into his composition in the idea of defining the qualities desirable in a young woman, especially in Burns's third verse:

> A bonny lass I will confess,
>   Is pleasant to the e'e,
> But without some better qualities
>   She's no a lass for me.

There is even a verbal correspondence, 'pleasant to the e'e', occurring in this verse by Burns and in Smith's fourth verse, which seems to indicate that the song as Burns heard it had this wording and that Burns is echoing his source.

Even more important than the words, however, is the tune, and here it seems that we cannot do better than turn to Bremner. We naturally cannot say that the tune was precisely as Bremner gives it but his tune is the only Scottish one at present known for this song and Burns's words fit it well. The presence of a 'Fal lal' refrain also provides a useful link. 'O once I lov'd a bonnie lass' as written in Burns's own hand in his commonplace book has the refrain indication, 'Fal lal de dal &c.', and the refrain of Bremner's version of 'I am a man unmarried', as given in full with the music, runs:

> Singing Fal lal de low ral laddie
> Fal de row ow ral laddie
> Fal lal de low ral laddie
> Fa ral oo ral lee

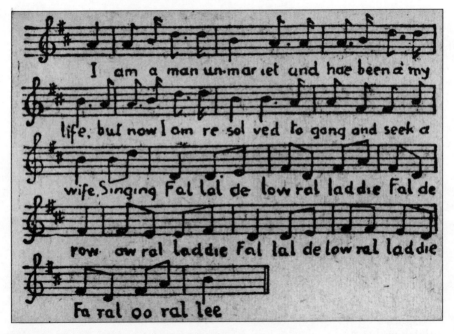

Figure 1. By permission of the British Library.

'I am a man unmarried' is a cheeky, jaunty song with a catchy air, and it was, Burns tells us, a favourite with the 'Nell' or 'Nelly' (Nelly Blair or Nelly Kilpatrick) to whom his own song was addressed.[7] She was his partner in harvest work when he was fifteen or sixteen years old and she a year younger. Burns describes her and his experience of falling in love and becoming a poet in the following words:

She was a bonie, sweet, sonsie lass. – In short, she altogether unwittingly to herself, initiated me in a certain delicious Passion, which in spite of acid

Disappointment, gin-horse Prudence and bookworm Philosophy, I hold to be the first of human joys, our dearest pleasure here below. – How she caught the contagion I can't say; ... but I never expressly told her that I loved her. – Indeed I did not well know myself, why I liked so much to loiter behind with her, when returning in the evening from our labors; why the tones of her voice made my heartstrings thrill like an Eolian harp; and particularly, why my pulse beat such a furious ratann when I looked and fingered over her hand, to pick out the nettle-stings and thistles. – Among her other love-inspiring qualifications, she sung sweetly; and 'twas her favourite reel to which I attempted giving an embodied vehicle in rhyme. – I was not so presumtive as to imagine that I could make verses like printed ones, composed by men who had Greek and Latin; but my girl sung a song which was said to be composed by a small country laird's son, on one of his father's maids, with whom he was in love; and I saw no reason why I might not rhyme as well as he, for excepting smearing sheep and casting peats, his father living in the moors, he had no more Scholarcraft than I had. –

Thus with me began Love and Poesy; ...[8]

We find, then, that, at this turning-point in his life, Burns was empowered by the existence and currency of a love-song said to have been composed by the son of a country laird which provided him with a not-unrealisable model; that he was inspired by his love for Nelly conjoined with his aesthetic response to her singing; and that the tune of 'I am a man unmarried' as sung by Nelly served as the vehicle for his words. We are provided here with a wonderfully detailed representation of the release of a major creative talent which is of great interest for the understanding of inspiration in general as well as for Burns scholarship in particular. When Burns later gave a verse account of his experience he described first the building up of a directionless force and an inarticulate striving and then the beginning of the ordered shaping that was to initiate his career as poet which came to him with Nelly's singing in the harvest field:

> But still the elements o' sang
> In formless jumble, right an' wrang,
>   Wild floated in my brain;
> Till on that hairst I said before,
> My partner in the merry core,
>   She rous'd the forming strain.[9]

NOTES

1. The main text is from *The Scots Musical Museum*, edited by James Johnson (Edinburgh, 1787–1803; reissued 1853), No. 551 (revising 1.3 'an'' and 6.3 'its') and the refrain is from Burns's commonplace book (see below).

2. *Robert Burns's Commonplace Book, 1783–1785*, edited by James Cameron Ewing and Davidson Cook. Revised edn (Centaur Press: London, 1965), p. 3.

3. The tune is published here in enlarged facsimile. A dot has evidently been accidentally omitted after the second note.

4. A.E.'s article headed 'Burns's Songs. Tunes Unknown, Lost, or Lacking.' is in the *Weekly Scotsman*, 24–1–1925, p. 3, col. 1, and Bremner's letter is in the *Weekly Scotsman*, 14–3–1925, p. 7, col. 1. The tune was published with 'Handsome Nell' in *Robert Burns: Selected Poetry and Prose*, edited by Robert Thornton (Houghton Mifflin: Boston, 1966), pp. 97 and 258, but Thornton gave a mistaken date for the *Weekly Scotsman* letter. We are both much indebted to Thomas Crawford who located the newspaper reference originally and also when it was again sought for. In spite of Thornton's publication of 'I am a man unmarried', the tune was still treated as unidentified in the major recent works on Burns's songs, *The Poems and Songs of Robert Burns*, edited by James Kinsley (Clarendon Press, Oxford, 1968), III, 1003, and *The Songs of Robert Burns*, edited by Donald A. Low (Routledge, London, 1993), p. 42.

5. See, e.g., National Library of Scotland, L. C. 2864:20 *Kattie's Answer to Wabster Jock, Together with, Jock's Reply, with, The Roving Batchelor, and Roger of Coverly* (Stirling, Printed for the Booksellers, 180[?]), pp. 4–6 'The Roving Bachelor', *The Wanton Seed*, edited by Frank Purslow (E.F.D.S. Publications: London, 1969), p. 100, and *Sam Henry's Songs of the People*, edited by Gale Huntington and revised by Lani Herrmann (University of Georgia Press: Athens, Georgia, and London, 1990), pp. 263–4.

6. *Andrew Crawfurd's Collection of Ballads and Songs*, edited by E. B. Lyle (Scottish Text Society: Edinburgh, 1975–96), I, lii, 175–6.

7. Her identity is discussed in James Mackay, *R.B.: A Biography of Robert Burns* (Mainstream: Edinburgh, 1992), pp. 50–2.

8. *The Letters of Robert Burns*, edited by J. De Lancey Ferguson and G. Ross Roy (Clarendon Press: Oxford, 1985), I, 137–8, Letter 125, to John Moore, 2 August 1787.

9. Kinsley, No. 147B 'The Answer to the Guidwife of Wauchope-House', I, 326.

Burns, Genius and Major Poetry

THIS PAPER is in part a response to a review of the 1994 reprints of David Daiches' and my own books on Burns.[1] Daiches' book was first published in 1950; mine ten years later. The reviewer was Hamish Mathison and the periodical *Eighteenth-century Scottish Studies* 9 (Spring 1995). In that review Mr. Mathison maintained that in the last resort both Daiches and I have no other explanation for Burns's achievement than his individual genius, and that this is A BAD THING.

I want to do two things this afternoon which are closely connected:

(1) address some of the issues raised by Mr. Mathison's remarks about genius, and (2) talk about the nature of Burns's achievement, which I shall phrase in the form of a question – was Burns a major poet?

I'll begin by quoting from Mr. Mathison: 'The conditions which made the phenomenon of Burns a possibility will remain obscured so long as we allow the identity of Burns to go unchallenged'. I am reminded here of a platitude of Mao-Tse-Tung's, once thought to be profound: 'Why is a stone a stone, and not some other thing? Because of the conditions'. – Why was Burns the Burns we know, or at least the Burns we have a body of evidence about, and not some other Burns: why was Burns Burns, and not David Sillar or James Lapraik? – Because of the conditions.

When Mr. Mathison speaks about the phenomenon of Burns, I presume the term covers both the real live man the biographers have researched and the type and quality of the works he produced. But as for 'identity' – that rather stumps me: 'so long as we allow the *identity* of Burns to go unchallenged'. Has Mr. Mathison crossed over into the debateable land of Doppelgängers and doubles, and by the 'identity' of Burns does he mean 'the degree of continuity of his personality' – a special case of the primary dictionary definition of 'identity', which is 'the quality or condition of being the same – absolute or essential sameness; oneness'?

Now 'Genius', the word and concept 'genius', and the various changes they were undergoing in the eighteenth century, were surely part of those conditions which, in Mr. Mathison's terms, made possible the phenomenon of Burns. Let me mention my King Charles's head, that other Ayrshire notable, James Boswell. Why does Boswell's second separate publication, issued anonymously in 1760 when he was only twenty years old, have the following on its title page:

Observations GOOD OR BAD, STUPID OR CLEVER, SERIOUS OR JOCULAR, on Squire Foote's Dramatic Entertainment, intituled, *The Minor*, By a GENIUS.

(The person whom Boswell calls 'Squire Foote' was Samuel Foote, a well-known actor and dramatist, and *The Minor* was a piece ridiculing the Methodists.)

Boswell put 'By a Genius' on the title-page not because he was claiming to be one of those great geniuses, 'the prodigies of mankind', as Addison had called them way back in 1711, 'who by the mere strength of natural parts, and without any assistance of art or learning, have produced works that were the delight of their own times and the wonder of posterity ... these great natural geniuses that were never disciplined and broken by rules of art' (*Spectator 160*).[2] When Addison wrote this, what he had in mind were of course the Ancients, especially Homer; but Boswell was thinking of a contemporary specialization or divagation of that sense, namely someone who could make a splash in any art or science without application and with the minimum of acquired knowledge; a sense that wouldn't apply to Homer or Aeschylus, but would hold good of people like Stephen Duck, the Wiltshire agricultural labourer whose poems created a sensation in 1736. Boswell was using the word lightly and humorously, with some, perhaps all, of the connotations that Fielding had attached to it at the beginning of Book XIV of *Tom Jones*:

> As several gentlemen in these Times, by the wonderful force of Genius only, without the least Assistance of Learning, perhaps, without being well able to read, have made a considerable Figure in the Republic of Letters; the modern Critics, I am told, have lately begun to assert, that all kind of Learning is entirely useless to a Writer; and, indeed, no other than a kind of Fetters on the nátural Spriteliness and Activity of the Imagination, which is thus weighed down, and prevented from soaring to those high Flights which otherwise it would be able to reach.[3]

It's not until Samuel Johnson's *Lives of the Poets* (1781–83), only three years before the Kilmarnock edition, that we find, in the *Life of Cowley*, a definition of genius that has a scientific as well as an authoritative ring. 'The true genius', Johnson wrote there, is 'a mind of large general powers accidentally determined to some particular direction'.[4] Johnson, it seems, was very much of the opinion that, although some minds have larger powers than others, yet all minds are basically of the same sort. Reporting a conversation of 16 March 1776, Boswell says:

> He allowed very great influence to education. 'I do not deny, Sir, but there is some original difference in minds; but it is nothing in comparison of what is formed by education. We may instance the science of numbers [i.e. mathematics], which all minds are equally capable of maintaining.'[5]

(A piece of Johnsonian pontification which must surely go against the experience of many in this room!)

What have the psychologists to say about genius? Well, in the early twentieth century the American psychologist L. M. Terman applied the term 'near genius' or 'genius' to those with IQs of over 140, without any mention of special abilities, which would seem to place Terman in the same camp as Dr. Johnson. In contrast the British psychologist R. H. Thouless (again, early twentieth-century) insisted that genius 'is best described as the combination of high IQ with some high specific capacity'.[6]

I propose, for the purposes of this paper, to accept the existence of inborn special abilities, and to regard them as proven, to the eye of ordinary common sense, by the existence of musical morons and calculating prodigies of low intelligence. I'm using exactly the same technique as Johnson himself, when he refuted Berkeley's philosophical idealism by 'striking his foot with mighty force against a large stone, till he rebounded from it': the appeal to everyday experience.[7]

Let us now make a great leap forward to Henry Mackenzie's review in *The Lounger* of 9 December 1786, with its famous description of Burns as the 'Heaven-taught ploughman' and its title: '*Surprising effects of Original Genius, exemplified in the Poetical Productions* of Robert Burns, an *Ayrshire Plough-man.*'

Mackenzie's notion of genius is nothing like Boswell's dilettanteish and exhibitionist posturings of 1760. He defines genius as a 'reach of mind' – 'that supereminent reach of mind by which some men are distinguished'. Although Mackenzie is careful to say that he is 'very far from meaning to compare our rustic bard to Shakespeare', yet it seems to him that what characterises Burns above all is the same sort of 'intuitive' ability to 'discern the characters of men' and catch 'the many changeing hues of life' that Shakespeare had: and it is in the context of Burns's handling of character and everyday life that Mackenzie uses the expression 'heaven-taught': the 'uncommon penetration and sagacity' with which 'this Heaven-taught ploughman ... has looked upon men and manners'.[8]

Burns's own role in creating an image which would appeal to contemporaries still influenced by Rousseauistic primitivism has often been discussed, and must have surfaced more than once at this conference. For example, there is the passage in the preface to the Kilmarnock Edition where he quotes William Shenstone: 'Humility has depressed many a genius to a hermit, but never raised one to fame'.[9] And again, after his lionisation in Edinburgh, and after the 'heaven-taught ploughman' review, there's the following passage in the Preface to the Edinburgh edition of 1787:

> The Poetic Genius of my Country found me as the prophetic bard Elijah did Elisha – at the *plough*; and threw her inspiring *mantle* over me. She bade me sing the loves, the joys, the rural scenes and rural pleasures of my natal Soil, in my native tongue: I tuned my wild, artless notes, as she inspired.[10]

In the Kilmarnock preface, 'genius' has a personal application; it is a term for a single outstanding *individual*. In the Edinburgh preface the word has moved to another sense quite common in Burns's time, 'the controlling spirit of a nation'. Notice that this 1787 Genius of Scotland is feminine, and is a development of the 1786 Muse-figure of Coila in *The Vision*, who takes her name from Kyle, Burns's native district of Ayrshire. In that poem, Coila is merely one of a whole squadron of helpers, some of whom – like Coila herself – are assigned to particular geographical regions. Over them all is 'the great Genius of this land', that is, the Genius of all Scotland, and that Genius, in *The Vision*, is male. Coila tells Burns that someone with his measure of talent cannot possibly be a literary giant like Thomson, or Shenstone, or Gray. No – he is not like the great tree that is the monarch of the forest; he is much more like the hawthorn growing 'adown the glade' (11.257–8). Not a great genius then, merely a considerable local talent: that seems to be what Coila is telling her favourite protégé.[11]

However, there are indications that, fairly early on, Burns had intimations that he was something more than that. In an entry in his first Commonplace Book dating from 1783, when he would be twenty-four, Burns wrote that there was a class of young men 'whose heads are capable of all the towering of genius, and whose hearts are warmed with the delicacy of Feeling'.[12] It is difficult not to suspect that as early as this Burns knew that he belonged to this last class, knew that his was an intellect that was capable of towering and his a heart already warmed with the delicacy of feeling.

Three years after the Commonplace Book entry, in the aftermath of the Kilmarnock edition, first of all in Ayrshire and then in Edinburgh, Burns's intellect was deployed in keeping his end up with the genteel and the literati. One of the earliest of these was John Mackenzie, the Mauchline physician who was later to become the Provost of Irvine. Dr. Mackenzie first met Burns when he attended the poet's father at Lochlie in 1783, and later compiled this record of his early impressions:

> (Burns at Lochlie) 'seemed distant, suspicious, and without any wish to interest or please. He kept himself very silent in a dark corner of the room ... When the conversation ... had taken the turn he wished, he began to engage in it, displaying a dexterity of reasoning, an ingenuity of reflection, and a familiarity with topics apparently beyond his reach by which his visitor was no less gratified than astonished' (CW i. 59).

It was Dr. Mackenzie who introduced Burns to Dugald Stewart, on 23 Oct. 1786, and it was Stewart who left us one of the most impressive accounts of Burns as genius:

> The idea which his conversation conveyed of the powers of his mind, exceeded, if possible that which is suggested by his writings ... All the faculties of Burns' mind were, as far as I could judge, equally vigorous; and his predilection for poetry, was rather the result of his own enthusiastic and

impassioned temper, than of a genius exclusively adapted to that species of composition (Kinsley, iii. 1534).

Dugald.Stewart's account, of course, agrees perfectly with the Johnsonian definition of a 'Genius': 'a mind of large general powers accidentally determined to some particular direction'. Maria Riddell, who knew Burns really well, had some of the same impressions as Stewart: 'I hesitate not to affirm ... that Poetry was actually not his *forte*'. What she admired most in Burns was his intellect, his ability to argue and to debate, and his mastery of expository speech. 'None certainly outshone Burns', she wrote, 'in the charms – the sorcery, I would almost call it – of fascinating conversation; the spontaneous eloquence of social argument, or the unstudied poignancy of brilliant repartee (Kinsley, iii. 1545).

We can obtain a faint idea of Burns's general intellectual power from his quite dazzling autobiographical letter to Dr. Moore, and from the magnificent letter he wrote for the *Edinburgh Evening Courant* under the nom-de-plume of 'A Briton', setting out his political position in the year before the outbreak of the French Revolution (published 22 Nov. 1788).[13] However, as soon as we read at all widely in Burns's poems, or hear a fair number of his songs, it becomes impossible to deny his special ability in the business of writing poetry and setting fit words to tunes.

In fact, Burns's ability in the mechanical and technical side of poetry may even be measurable through, say, comparison of his rhymes and metrics with those of Ramsay and Fergusson in poems of the same sort. One proof of his special poetic ability is the remarkable turn he had for spontaneous composition – for example in the 'Extempore Verses on Dining with Lord Daer', written just after he had met Lord Daer at Catrine in the house of Dugald Stewart, the poem containing the famous lines:

> The fient a pride, nae pride had he,
> Nor sauce, nor state, that I could see,
> Mair than an honest Ploughman. (ll. 40–1)

A truly delightful extempore is the poem entitled *The Calf*, which rings the changes on the various words for male cattle (some Scots, some Scots-English). The poem was written, as Burns reveals in a letter to Robert Muir, 'on a wager with Mr. (Gavin) Hamilton that I would not produce a poem on the subject in a given time'.[14] It's addressed to the Rev. Mr ——, on his text, Malachi, ch. iv. vers. 2. 'And they shall go forth, and grow up, like Calves of the stall'. Mr. ——- was in fact James Steven, and 'steven' in eighteenth-century Scots meant 'voice', indeed a loud voice, which adds to the joke. Here it is:

> RIGHT, Sir! your text I'll prove it true,
> Tho' Heretics may laugh;
> For instance, there's yoursel just now,
> God knows, an unco *Calf*!

And should some Patron be so kind,
 As bless you wi' a kirk,
I doubt na, Sir, but then we'll find,
 Ye're still as great a *Stirk*.

But, if the Lover's raptur'd hour,
 Shall ever be your lot,
Forbid it, ev'ry heavenly Power,
 You e'er should be a *Stot*!

Tho', when some kind, connubial Dear
 Your But-and-ben adorns,
The like has been that you may wear
 A noble head of *horns*.

And, in your lug, most reverend J(ames),
 To hear you roar and rowte,
Few men o' sense will doubt your claims
 To rank among the *Nowte*.

And when ye're numbered wi' the dead,
Below a grassy hillock,
Wi' justice they may mark your head –
 'Here lies a famous *Bullock*!'

That spontaneity, so evident in the Extempores, was dependent on certain of the 'conditions' which made Burns possible – above all, on these two:

(1) The linguistic complexity of lowland Scotland, which Burns himself was well aware of, according to Robert Anderson: he even admitted to Anderson 'the advantages he enjoyed in poetical composition from the *copia verborum*, the command of phraseology, which the knowledge and use of the English and Scottish dialects afforded him' (Anderson to James Currie, 28 Sept, 1799).[15]

(2) The existence of congenial British stanzas and metres (some Scottish, some not).

Both factors – linguistic complexity and congenial stanzas and metres – combined in Burns to create a poetry of even more artful spontaneity than that seen in the extempores. Burns's most impressive achievements in the 'spontaneity line' are to be found in the 'Standard Habbie' stanza, whose use, first by small lairds and their families; then by poets like Ramsay, Fergusson and Burns, aspiring to professional or bardic status; then by their imitators, ordinary folk in towns and villages, particularly in the nineteenth century, is a fact of Scotland's literary history.

Here is Burns's spontaneity almost flaunting itself in Standard Habbie (from the Second Epistle to John Lapraik):

> Sae I gat paper in a blink,
> An' down gaed *stumpie* in the ink:
> Quoth I, 'Before I sleep a wink,
>> I vow I'll close it;
> An' if ye winna mak it clink,
>> By Jove, I'll prose it!'

This is extraordinary. Two things we associate with flowing, colloquial verse are absent – enjambment (rapid run-on from one line to another), and near rhyme rather than true rhyme: all the rhymes here are true rhymes. Only the short lines end with a weak syllable – 'close it', 'prose it'. And yet the verse positively skips along! Another device that makes for the colloquial is a varied caesura (i.e. a pause or pauses within the line); here there is an absolutely delightful compromise between regularity and variation. In three of the long lines (eight-syllabled lines) the caesursa comes after the fifth syllable; in the third, after the second – 'Quoth I'. In the two short, five-syllabled lines, the caesura comes after the second syllable ('I vow', 'By Jove'), which is as close to regularity as you can get. One feature of the grammar which seems daringly colloquial at first sight is 'prose' as a transitive verb – we're more used to 'prose' as intransitive, without an object. However, Burns was not really an innovator here: the OED's first example of 'prose' as a transitive verb comes from Chaucer, though not in a vivid passage.

Incidentally, while we are still fairly close to my first mention of the caesura, I'd like to draw attention to my favourite example of Burns's manipulation of pauses, the first line of 'To a Mouse', where on my reading there's a distinct pause after every word, reflecting the poet's slow and concentrated contemplation of the successive qualities of the mouse in the act of perceiving her:

> Wee, sleeket, cowran, tim'rous *beastie*.

Let's now pass on to the next stanza in the Second Epistle to Lapraik, the one after the 'stumpie' stanza:

> Sae I've begun to scrawl, but whether
> In rhyme, or prose, or baith thegither,
> Or some hotch-potch that's rightly neither,
>> Let time make proof;
> But I shall scribble down some blether
>> Just clean aff-loof.

There is quite a contrast in style with the previous stanza. There *is* enjambment – between the first line and the second ('but whether/In rhyme or prose'), and there's more variation of the caesura than in the 'stumpie' stanza. All the rhyming words in the long lines are dissyllables, the last syllables being weak. Further, there's a marvellous flitting between near rhyme and true rhyme in the long lines. If you pronounce 'whether' as 'whether', then there's a true rhyme with 'blether' in the fifth line, but near rhyme with 'thegither'. If you pronounce it as 'whither', as it was in my family in my childhood, there is a true rhyme with 'thegither' but near rhyme with 'blether'. And whether you pronounce the other end-word in the long lines as 'neither' or 'naither' it can only be in near rhyme with the other words. Burns is in this stanza taking advantage of the phonetic complexity he was heir to, and making use of a whole spectrum of diphthongs and vowels, which is another of those linguistic conditions that underpin his achievement. A further characteristic of colloquial verse is to bring in as rhyme as many minor parts of speech as possible – adjectives, adverbs, pronouns, conjunctions – which is well illustrated in this stanza. Of the long-line rhymes, only 'blether' is major – a noun.

Steven McKenna, if I read him correctly, plays down the role of any spontaneity intrinsic to the language and the verse form in this and other epistles. To him, Burns has a 'spontaneity formula' to 'give the illusion that the epistle is an effortless and unpremeditated outpouring of thought and feeling neatly arranged in the intricacies of the Habbie Stanza form'.[16] I agree that openly drawing attention to his spontaneity is a rhetorical device with structural force enabling Burns to move from the particulars of his own situation and of his relationship to the person he is addressing, on to 'poetic universals' and statements of principle. I would agree too that the spontaneity formula is a matter or art – but perhaps no more a matter of art than the 'unaccustomed as I am' formula of so many public speakers, and as much a matter of art as the structural formula of the prayer which carries forward 'Holy Willie's Prayer': Invocation (Ist St. – 'O thou that in the heavens does dwell'); Praise (Stzs ii–v) – 'I bless and praise thy matchless might'; Confession and Penitence – 'But yet, O Lord, confess I must'; and Intercession — 'Lord, Bless thy Chosen in this place'.[17]

If I may quote Steven McKenna once more: 'Burns no doubt worked for hours over these seemingly spontaneous stanzas'.[18] It's true that McKenna isn't referring to the 'stumpie' passage, but to comparable lines in the 'Epistle to James Smith'; and I am assuming Mr. McKenna would maintain that the 'stumpie' passage, too, might have taken hours to write. Quite frankly, I don't believe it of either Epistle, though of course I have no evidence, just a gut feeling. I believe that the process of writing the 'stumpie' passage was likely to have been the same as the process by which, Cromek tells us, these lines from 'Tam o'Shanter' came to Burns:

> Now, *Tam, O Tam*! had they been queans,
> A' plump and strapping in their teens,
> Their sarks, instead o' creeshie flannen,
> Been snaw-white seventeen hunder linnen!
> Thir breeks o' mine, my only pair,
> That ance were plush, o' gude blue hair,
> I wad hae gi'en them off my hurdies,
> For ae blink o' the bonie burdies!   (ll. 151–158)

Cromek reported Mrs Burns as telling him that the poem, or a good part of it, was composed by Burns on the banks of the Nith. He had been all morning by the river, and was joined by Jean and the children in the afternoon. Seeing that Burns was 'crooning to himsel', she 'loitered behind with her little ones':

> Her attention was presently attracted by the strange and wild gesticulations of the bard, who now, at some distance, was agonized with an ungovernable access of joy. He was reciting very loud, and with the tears rolling down his cheeks.

What Burns was reciting was the 'Now Tam, O Tam, had they been queans' passage.[19] Lockhart concluded from Cromek's account that the whole poem was written in a day, though legend has it that Burns got stuck at the part I've quoted, and didn't finish the poem for another month or six weeks.[20] Be that as it may, I would maintain that on either hypothesis, Burns showed a high degree of special poetic ability when writing the 'Stumpie' passage and 'Tam o' Shanter', whether these were the fruits of genuine spontaneity, or the laboured illusion of spontaneity, or a blend of the two. A high degree of special ability is required for either process.

Surely, then, we cannot reasonably doubt Burns's high general ability in the Johnsonian sense, or his high special abilities in Thouless's sense. The talent, the genius, the genotype he had were sufficient for him to take advantage of the conditions, social and cultural, which he found himself in, in order to become the phenomenon of the Robert Burns we know, or think we know. But – was the Burns we know really a major poet? That's a question we can't answer until we've decided what we mean by a 'major poet'. There have been many poets with IQs of 140 and over and great technical expertise whom many readers would hesitate to term 'major' in the sense in which Homer or Virgil or Dante or Shakespeare or Goethe are considered major. Some of the great Victorian sages, even those who praised Burns highly, denied him that accolade – the title of 'major poet' – because they thought his poetry lacked 'high seriousness' (Matthew Arnold's great touchstone); because the ideas behind it were second-rate, those of the 'Sentimental Era'; because he never achieved either of the highest forms, tragedy or epic; because in the latter part of his life he degenerated into a mere song-writer – 'whittling cherry-stones', as Stevenson put it.

There have been twentieth-century critics, too, who have queried Burns's major status – like the American editors of a paperback anthology, *English Minor Poets of the eighteenth Century*, in the once popular Laurel books of poetry (1978), who obviously thought highly of him but classified him as minor simply by including him in their collection; or like the great American critic Cleanth Brooks, who evidently saw Burns as minor compared to Blake, praising Blake for 'restoring liberty to the imagination', whereas Burns was good mainly at satire and light verse – inferior genres for Brooks, as they had been for

Matthew Arnold.[21] In Scotland, those determined to deny his major status often concentrated on his faults, like Edwin Muir with his 'Burns and Scott, sham bards of a sham nation';[22] like Hugh MacDiarmid, who claimed that Burns 'betrayed the movement Ramsay and Fergusson began ... betrayed his keenest realisations of the kind of poetry he should write, lapsing back on to too easy models and compromising too much with English standards';[23] or like Norman MacCaig, who declared in the year of the bicentenary of Burns's birth: 'Burns's scope is narrow, his vision small ... I don't think he was a great craftsman'.[24]

I do not have a single definition of 'major poet', but here are four criteria which I think such a poet must satisfy:

1. A major poet must have a total output of a certain length and a certain weight or solidity.

2. His work must be in some way central to his nation and/or his culture.

3. His work must express the universal through the particular.

4. His work must please us because of its technique.

I shall dismiss the last of these, technique, arguing that I have already said enough about it in discussing those two stanzas of the Second Epistle to Lapraik, and I deny absolutely MacCaig's rejection of his craftsmanship. I shall take (2) and (3) together: 'central to his nation or his culture' and 'expressing the universal through the particular'.

Right: centrality to nation and culture; expressing the universal through the particular. – Burns's development was from poet of the parish to poet of Scotland to poet of the World, and indeed all three aspects are shown in that comparatively early poem 'Holy Willie's Prayer'. Who could be more of a parochial figure than William Fisher, the village hypocrite; and who could have more in common with hundreds of thousands of hypocrites in our own century, in every country of the world, the self-deluded slaves of doctrines that destroy the humanity of those who believe in them?

Willie is both amusing and terrible because he is the man who thinks he is God, acting in a merely human way. Yet even so he becomes a thing in the very moment of making himself the equal of Supreme Power. When Willie likens himself to an object as hard as a rock, as unyielding as a pillar or a metal shield, we realise that you cannot aspire to become more than human without at the same time running the risk of turning yourself into stone – or, for that matter, into steel; and we remember, perhaps, a certain Joseph Djugashvili, a man of many aliases, the last being Stalin – man of Steel.

In considering Holy Willie, we have moved directly from the parish to the World. But what about the middle term? What about Scotland? Well, it is there in the peculiarly Scottish features of the all-European doctrine that justifies Willie's self-reification, if I may use a jargon term for turning one's self into a thing. And it's there in the biographical fact that, in the beginning, one of Burns's motives for writing was to serve Scotland. In his autobiographical letter to Dr. Moore Burns presented the Kilmarnock volume as, in the words of Professor Daiches, 'his legacy to his native country before he left it for Jamaica, something by which Scotland might remember her lost poet'.[25] Thus his relation to Scotland was in his mind from at least 1786, and probably from earlier, from the very moment he decided to emulate Ramsay and Fergusson. As he wrote to Mrs. Dunlop on 22 March 1787: 'The appelation of, a Scotch Bard, is by far my highest pride; to continue to deserve it is my most exalted ambition'.[26] And during his last period, when his main creative work was the writing, editing, and adaptation, of songs, his motives were equally patriotic: so much so, that he refused to take payment: as he wrote to Thomson, 'to talk of money, wages, fee, hire, &c. would be downright Sodomy of Soul'.[27]

But – is a writer's nation really of importance in assessing whether he is major or minor? Carol McGuirk quotes Vladimir Nabokov:

> the nationality of a worthwhile writer (should be) of secondary importance ... The writer's art is his real passport. His identity should be immediately recognized by a special pattern or unique coloration. His habitat may confirm the correctness of the determination but should not lead to it.[28]

(By 'determination' Nabokov means something like 'judgement'). This is an extraordinary statement for Nabokov to have made when one considers the greatest writers of Nabokov's ancestral language. Even Turgenev, the most westernizing of the nineteenth-century giants, cannot be appreciated apart from his Russianness, let alone Tolstoy. And Dostoevsky, the least westernized and most Russian, is for some readers the most all-encompassing of the three; yet his universality seems absolutely inseparable from his national qualities. Raskolnikov's universality is as thirled to his Russianness as Holy Willie's is to his Scottishness.

I have left the first of my criteria to the end: is Burns's output large enough, solid enough, weighty enough for him to be classed as a major poet? This criterion overlaps with the second, national and cultural centrality, which in Burns's case provides the link between the local and the universal. The matter has never been better put than by W. B. Yeats, in the passage I used for an epigraph to *Burns: a Study*:

> To the greater poets everything they see has its relation to the national life, and through that to the universal and divine life ... to this universalism, this seeing of unity everywhere, you can only attain through what is near you, your nation, or, if you be no traveller, your village and the cobwebs on your walls ... One can only reach out to the universe with a gloved hand – that glove is one's nation, the only thing one knows even a little of.
>
> (2 Sept. 1888)

In the last analysis, whether Burns's output was large enough for him to be termed a major poet depends on how you rate the songs he wrote and collected.

If with Scott you 'deeply regret that so much of his time and talents should have been frittered away in compiling and composing for large musical collections'; if you think with him that this activity 'degenerated into a slavish labour which no talents could support';[29] and if you agree with Stevenson that 'it is not the less typical of his loss of moral courage that he should have given up all larger ventures, nor the less melancholy, that a man who first attacked literature with a hand that seemed capable of moving mountains, should have spent his later years in whittling cherry-stones',[30] then for you his claim to be a major poet depends on the Poems in the Kilmarnock Edition, plus 'Love and Liberty', plus 'Tam o' Shanter', plus 'Holy Willie's Prayer' and a few others. That may well be enough: after all, T. S. Eliot was disposed to class Samuel Johnson as a major poet on a verse output considerably less bulky than that! But if, like Francis Jeffrey, you give Burns's song collecting and writing what I believe is their proper due; or if, like J. De Lancey Ferguson, you go even further and contend that Burns's true bent was in song-writing, and that even the great satirical and comic poems were in a sense a deviation from his real mission in life, then there can be no doubt about it.[31] Burns was both a genius – a man of exceptional general ability and exceptional special abilities – and a major poet.

NOTES

1. David Daiches, *Burns – the Poet* (Edinburgh: EUP, 1994); Thomas Crawford, *Burns: a Study of the Poems and Songs* (Edinburgh: Canongate Academic [now Tuckwell Press], 1994).
2. *Critical Essays from the Spectator by Joseph Addison, with four essays by Richard Steele*, edited by Donald F. Bond (Oxford: Clarendon Press, 1970), p. 250.
3. *The History of Tom Jones*, edited by M. C. Battestin amd F. Bowers (Oxford: Clarendon Press, 1974), ii, 739.
4. *Lives of the Poets* (London: Dent, 1954), ii. 2.
5. James Boswell, *Life of Samuel Johnson, LL.D*, edited by G. B. Hill and L. F. Powell (Oxford: Clarendon Press, 6 vols, 1934–50), henceforth cited as *Life*, ii. 436.
6. For Terman and Thouless, see R. H. Thouless, *General and Social Psychology* (London: University Tutorial Press, 1937), p. 423 and n.
7. *Life*, i. 471.
8. Reprint of Mackenzie's *Lounger* review in *Robert Burns: the Critical Heritage*, edited by Donald A. Low (London: Routledge, 1974), pp. 67–71.
9. *The Songs and Poems of Robert Burns*, edited by James A. Kinsley (Oxford: Clarendon Press, 3 vols, 1978), henceforth cited as Kinsley, iii. 971.
10. Kinsley, iii. 977–8.
11. Kinsley, No. 62 (i. 103–113).
12. *The Life and Works of Robert Burns*, edited by Robert Chambers, revised William Wallace (London and Edinburgh: W. & R. Chambers, 4 vols, n.d.), henceforth cited as CW, i. 107.

13. *The Letters of Robert Burns*, edited by G. Ross Roy (Oxford: Clarendon, 2 vols, 1985), henceforth cited as *Letters*, i. 133–46, 332–5.

14. *Letters*, i. 52.

15. Kinsley, iii. 1537–8.

16. Steven R. McKenna, 'Spontaneity and the Strategy of Transcendence in Burns's Kilmarnock Verse-Epistles', *Studies in Scottish Literature*, xxii (1987), 78–90 (79).

17. For the prayer formula, see Kinsley, iii. 1048–9.

18. McKenna, *loc. cit.*

19. Cromek MS in J. G. Lockhart, *Life of Robert Burns*, cited Kinsley iii. 1348.

20. Kinsley, *loc. cit.*

21. Cleanth Brooks, *Modern Poetry and the Tradition*, cited in Hugh MacDiarmid, *Burns Today and Tomorrow* (Edinburgh: Castle Wynd Printers, 1959), pp. 3–4.

22. 'Scotland 1941', line 30.

23. MacDiarmid, *op. cit.*, pp. 25–6.

24. Quoted MacDiarmid, *op. cit.*, p. 19.

25. David Daiches, *Robert Burns* (London: Bell, 1952), p. 105.

26. *Letters*, i. 101.

27. *Letters*, ii. 149.

28. Carol McGuirk, *Robert Burns and the Sentimental Era* (Athens: University of Georgia Press, 1985), p. xiv.

29. (Scott), review of R. H. Cromek, *Reliques of Robert Burns*, *Quarterly Review*, i. (1809). 30–2.

30. R. L. Stevenson, 'Some Aspects of Robert Burns', *Familiar Studies of Men and Books* (London: Chatto & Windus, 1920), p. 52.

31. J. De Lancey Ferguson, *Pride and Passion* (New York: Russell and Russell, 1939), pp. 247–8.

Index

[For subject-headings see also under 'Burns's Life, Career and Legacy'; for individuals see also under 'Burns, Letters']

A WARM Greeting TO GOOD EATING

Traditional Scottish Cuisine

South West Scotland gives you the true flavour of Burns Country, with our wealth of scenery, quality of natural produce and our internationally renowned, Warm Scottish Welcome.

We offer you, A WARM GREETING TO GOOD EATING!

Thousands of tourists are attracted to the South West of Scotland for its great history and heritage but there are many more secrets we shall unveil to our visitors.

Our Taste of Burns Country Members offer quality catering using the best local produce, thus ensuring your visit to our region will be a truly memorable one.

A TASTE OF · BURNS COUNTRY ·

ENTERPRISE AYRSHIRE

Dumfries and Galloway Enterprise